Information Literacy and Information Skills Instruction

INFORMATION LITERACY AND INFORMATION SKILLS INSTRUCTION

New Directions for School Libraries

FOURTH EDITION

Nancy Pickering Thomas, Sherry R. Crow,
Judy A. Henning, and Jean Donham

 LIBRARIES
UNLIMITED®

An Imprint of ABC-CLIO, LLC

Santa Barbara, California • Denver, Colorado

Library of Congress Cataloging-in-Publication Data

Names: Thomas, Nancy Pickering, author. | Crow, Sherry R., author. | Henning, Judy A., author. | Donham, Jean, author.
Title: Information literacy and information skills instruction : new directions for school libraries / Nancy Pickering Thomas, Sherry R. Crow, Judy A. Henning, and Jean Donham.
Description: Fourth edition. | Santa Barbara, California : Libraries Unlimited, 2020. | Includes bibliographical references and index.
Identifiers: LCCN 2019055201 (print) | LCCN 2019055202 (ebook) | ISBN 9781440844515 (paperback) | ISBN 9781440844522 (ebook)
Subjects: LCSH: Library orientation for school children—United States. | Library orientation for high school students—United States. | School libraries—Activity programs—United States. | Information literacy—Study and teaching (Elementary)—United States. | Information literacy—Study and teaching (Secondary)—United States.
Classification: LCC Z711.25.S36 T48 2020 (print) | LCC Z711.25.S36 (ebook) | DDC 027.62/5—dc23
LC record available at https://lccn.loc.gov/2019055201
LC ebook record available at https://lccn.loc.gov/2019055202

ISBN: 978-1-4408-4451-5 (paperback)
    978-1-4408-4452-2 (ebook)

24 23 22 21   2 3 4 5

This book is also available as an eBook.

Libraries Unlimited
An Imprint of ABC-CLIO, LLC

ABC-CLIO, LLC
147 Castilian Drive
Santa Barbara, California 93117
www.abc-clio.com

This book is printed on acid-free paper ∞

Manufactured in the United States of America

Contents

Preface to Fourth Edition

Previous editions of *Information Literacy and Information Skills Instruction*, published in 1999, 2004, and 2011 respectively, called attention to the importance of information literacy competence and relevant research literature as a guide to school librarians in teaching within the context of emerging and evolving technological changes. As we enter the third decade of the 21st century, the challenges librarians face persist and are more critical than ever due to the nearly universal access by our students to social media and the immediacy of smartphone and Internet access anytime, anywhere. While this access provides an exceedingly rich environment for student learning, it is neither always value-free nor benevolent. On the contrary, it can expose students to unethical behavior, racism, bigotry, inequities, and iniquity. Our belief is that information literacy, which involves critical thinking and the search for truth online, and emphasizes ethics, fairness, inclusivity, and equality for all, is the best and most effective protection for students and adults online today.

As in earlier editions of this book, we argue for the need to revisit the roots of library instruction, even as we add research into contemporary problems and issues to topics previously considered but still relevant. In addition, we continue to emphasize evidence-based practice (Todd 2009) in education and school librarianship and to draw attention to new professional publications, including the *National School Library Standards for Learners, School Librarians, and School Libraries* introduced in 2018 by the American Association of School Librarians.

The new and updated text continues to benefit from insights and perspectives of the book's coauthors, all of whom have extensive practical and professional knowledge that comes from combining personal experience as school librarians with academic credentialing as active researchers. Our editorial process began with a careful and independent review of the content of the third edition, followed by collaborative brainstorming sessions framed to consider issues of content and arrangement. A new outline was created to tighten the organization and presentation of ideas and reduce redundancies. Conventional databases were searched in the areas of responsibility by each coauthor, and the new studies were reviewed. Individual chapters were then revised, rewritten, or rearranged to reflect insights from library research studies published since the publication of the third edition in 2011.

This new edition of a classic work aims to be informative and suggestive, rather than prescriptive. As such, it is meant to inspire scholars to broaden and deepen their research efforts, and library educators to use effective theories and methods as the basis of an information literacy curriculum. Both activities are of critical importance if school librarians are to ensure that all students develop critical thinking and information competencies so vital to their success as responsible citizens of the world.

Introduction

Emerging social issues, particularly the presence and influence of online news media, make research into best practices for teaching information literacy, data literacy, and the critical examination/curation of online sources pressing and crucial concerns.

—Johnston & Green (2018)

For at least the past 50 years, library professionals have embraced the "brave new world" of an interconnected informational universe in their continued acceptance of a "fundamental responsibility" for providing "the largest possible number of individuals access to and delivery of the largest possible amount of information" (Ghikas 1989, 124). It is this dedication to the twin goals of ensuring information access and teaching information literacy skills that drives research on information seeking and use. Indeed, it is our belief that efforts to create relevant, inclusive, and technologically savvy user-education initiatives at all library levels will continue to be the hallmarks of instructional stewardship and define learner-centered library services well into the future. By the same token, the political realities of life in a globally networked world and a volatile economic context create challenges that will undoubtedly continue to affect library practice for decades to come.

For those with a concern for educating the nation's young people, information literacy programs undertaken in public, school, and academic libraries represent an instructional continuum that, ideally, is initiated before children enter school and reinforced during all the years of their formal education. It is, as Liesener (1985) suggests, the "cumulative effect" of instruction in critical thinking and problem solving "throughout the learner's school experience" that "leads to the development of a self-directed learner able and motivated for lifelong learning" (13).

INFORMATION LITERACY: A MOVING TARGET AND AN EVOLVING CONSTRUCT

In the literature of librarianship and education, the term "information literacy" has evolved alongside the changing meanings of "information" itself. Writing in the 1970s, for example, Zurkowski (1974), defined information literacy as "the ability to use techniques and skills 'for the wide range of information tools as well as primary sources in molding information-solutions to . . . problems'" (quoted in Eisenberg & Spitzer 1991, 264). A decade later, the National Commission on Excellence in Education explained information literacy as "the skills required for new careers and citizenship" and "life-long learning" (Baumbach 1986, 279). By the mid-1990s, the American Library Association's Presidential Committee on Information Literacy was describing an information literate person as one who "recognize[s] when information is needed," has "the ability to locate, evaluate, and use [it] effectively" (264), and has "learned how to learn" (Breivik & Senn 1994, 4).

Drawing on a model created by Christina Doyle (1994), the California Media and Library Educator's Association went on to characterize information literacy as "the ability to access, evaluate, and use information from a variety of sources" (2), while Breivik and Senn (1994) discussed information literacy as the "ability to acquire and evaluate whatever information is needed at any given moment" (4). In their definition, Kirk, Poston-Anderson, and Yerbury (1990, as cited in Todd 1995) attempted to indicate the complexities involved by conceptualizing information literacy in terms of seven skill areas: (1) "defining the tasks for which information is needed," (2) "locating appropriate sources of information to meet needs," (3) "selecting and recording relevant information from sources," (4) "understanding and appreciating information from several sources," (5) combining and organizing the information "effectively for best application," (6) "presenting the information learned in an appropriate way," and (7) "evaluating the outcomes in terms of task requirements and increases in knowledge" (133).

Whereas most of these information literacy definitions apply to users generally, Loertscher (1996) framed literacy specifically in terms of the information needs of youngsters. Information-literate students are, Loertscher said, avid readers, critical thinkers, creative thinkers, interested learners, organized investigators, effective communicators, responsible information users, and skilled users of technological tools. A year later, Montgomery (1997) expanded on this theme, acknowledging that information literacy has become an umbrella term encompassing electronic searching and information retrieval skills, library skills, media skills, research skills, reference skills, learning skills, and study skills.

EVOLUTION OF A DEFINITION FOR A NEW CENTURY

Whereas the 19th-century appreciation for basic skills as life skills were reframed by the end of the 20th century to include recognition of the information explosion and the demands of digital age economics and technologies, the beginning of the new millennium saw a continuing professional focus on information and media literacy within the varied contexts of education, business, and government. New and compelling are arguments that posit various literacy skills as fundamental for success in an increasingly global economy. For example, the North Central Regional Educational Laboratory lists scientific literacy, technological literacy, visual literacy, cultural literacy, and global awareness along with basic reading and information skills as essential frameworks for a new generation of children. At the same time, the goal of educating citizens to act responsibly in a democratic society expanded to include both an understanding of the relationships that exist between and among nations and an appreciation of and respect for diversity in thinking and living in a world made smaller through advances in transportation and communication. Furthermore, attention that was once focused on ensuring electronic access has shifted to an emphasis on the critical appraisal of information and information sources—skills that are sometimes referred to as "media literacy."

In 2016, the ACRL (Association of College and Research Libraries, a division of the American Library Association), adopted a new *Framework for Information Literacy in Higher Education*. In the introduction, the authors suggest that our information ecosystem is constantly in flux, so that information literacy instruction should be "focused on foundational ideas about that ecosystem" (7). They go on to outline the evolving roles and responsibilities for students, teachers, and librarians in this ever-changing information environment:

> Students have a greater role and responsibility in creating new knowledge, in understanding the contours and the changing dynamics of the world of information, and in using information, data, and scholarship ethically. Teaching faculty have a greater responsibility in designing curricula and assignments that foster enhanced engagement with the core ideas about information and scholarship within their disciplines. Librarians have a greater responsibility in identifying core ideas within their own knowledge domain that can extend learning for students, in creating a new cohesive curriculum for information literacy, and in collaborating more extensively with faculty. (7)

Helping children and young adults make sense of information and information seeking has long been the special task and achievement of school librarians. Reformulating curricular goals, refining techniques for database as well as Internet searching, capitalizing on student interest in Web 2.0 technologies to both motivate and build technological competencies, and fostering student awareness of intellectual property, research ethics (Dow 2008), and online safety (Moran 2010) are some of the ways school librarians responsibly deal with evolving information contexts. Added to these educational goals are new responsibilities brought about by our increased capabilities to manipulate information; for example, how to ensure understanding of and adherence to copyright laws in an age of information mashups and remixes (Menell 2016).

Assuming responsibility for student learning—which includes the planning, conducting, and assessment of curricular activities—continues to mark these dedicated professionals as equal and equally accountable partners with class-room teachers. In addition, a common belief held by librarians that "age should not be a barrier to the ability to access, receive, and utilize information" (Hooten 1989, 268) has placed them in the vanguard of championing the rights of our youth to unfettered access to and use of the most advanced technologies and virtual resources. While this continues to be an important concern and a focus in schools still struggling to provide resources of all kinds for increasingly diverse school populations, where barriers to physical access are fading (Carvin 2000a, 2000b; Wilhelm, Carment, & Reynolds 2002), the critical issue has become one of intellectual access, translated as the ability to think critically and evaluate information and information sources selectively (McDonald 1988). The increasing sophistication and complexity of online research environments argue persuasively for a continuing and vital role for school librarians in preparing students capable of fulfilling the learning goals central to a digital age literacy agenda.

APPLYING RESEARCH TO PRACTICE: VALUE AND BENEFITS

Writing in 2009, Todd created a model for understanding the mandate of evidence-based practice, which classifies school library research studies in terms of three relevancies: "evidence *for* practice," that is, "the essential building blocks" that can serve as the basis of instruction; "evidence *in* practice," the "integration of research into instruction" and "evidence *of* practice," which considers outcomes for students as a result of information literacy instruction. By combining a review of the theoretical basis for instructional decision making with insights from published library research to inform curriculum planning, the "evidence" reviewed in this edition falls within the definitions of the first two of Todd's categories. It is hoped that this review will help school librarians better understand the complexities in teaching and learning information literacy skills as well as anticipate potential behaviors and concerns exhibited by youngsters undertaking research tasks and school-based inquiry assignments.

As with earlier editions, this book brings together the research literature on information skills instruction with emphasis on models related to information seeking and the information search process explored in the research of Kuhlthau (1988a, 1988b, 1993b, 2004) and conceptualized by research scholars in library and information studies (LIS). Our goal in providing this updated version of relevant research insights is to provide a cumulative record of research in order to inform both practitioners' and future researchers' endeavors.

Studies reviewed for this book include doctoral dissertations, research reports, academic and professional journal articles in LIS and related fields, and the writings of scholars and practitioners relevant to an information literacy curriculum. For "preservice" graduate students seeking certification or licensure, the book provides an introduction to school librarianship as an area of specialization and an overview of its historical development, an introduction to the major models and approaches that currently guide instructional best practices, and an understanding of the social aspects of teaching, learning, and service in school settings. Students and practitioners interested in bibliographic instruction in academic libraries will also find useful the overview of the development of bibliographic instruction provided in the first chapter, particularly the lessons learned with regard to the creation and implementation of the bibliographic instruction curriculum. For practicing school librarians, this text will help clarify issues and identify challenges encountered by others in the field and suggest research-based solutions. For many principals and teachers, this work will serve as an introduction to the contemporary practice of school librarianship and to the instructional activities that are part of the "package" offered by dynamic school librarians.

LIS educators and PhD students will find useful a literature review that not only confirms the contributions of many LIS researchers but also brings together the growing body of scholarly work as groundings for further research on information literacy instruction. Taking stock of what we know will, we hope, serve as a springboard to new thinking and reveal new directions for research related to information-seeking activities and practices of children and youth. Then, too, Todd (2009) recognizes the potential value that librarians' knowledge of research evidence offers to their school communities while also demonstrating "that they are part of a sustained research culture" (92).

CHAPTER OVERVIEWS

Chapter 1, "Reference Traditions: From 'Personal Assistance' to Instructional Intervention," provides an overview and a history of reference services as they developed in academic and public libraries and includes new strategies and techniques for bibliographic instruction. Information literacy on the international front is also a new addition.

Chapter 2, "The School Library Idea: From Dream to Reality," explores the evolution of school libraries as centralized facilities with instructional responsibilities anchored in professionally created guidelines and standards. This edition includes an overview of the *National School Library Standards* (2018), the Common Core Standards, and the Standards from the International Society for Technology in Education (2016, 2017), important standards for today's students, teachers, and librarians.

Chapter 3, "The Information Search Process: Kuhlthau's Legacy," summarizes traditional and alternative approaches to information skills instruction and traces the development of process models as created by Callison (1986), Sheingold (1986), and Kuhlthau (1988a, 1988b). Special attention is given to Kuhlthau's (1993b) research on the information search process and process intervention and the research stream that continues to explore the usefulness of the information search process and its theory base across contexts. A deeper dive into the emphasis of the *National School Library Standards* (2018) on inquiry is provided, as well as an overview of the Stripling Model of Inquiry (Small, Arnone, Stripling, & Berger 2012).

Chapter 4, "Cognitive and Social Frameworks for Teaching and Learning," reviews constructivism as a theoretical grounding for both LIS research and instructional design and considers current "best practices" in terms of instructional contextualization, effective lesson planning, and student motivation (including a new section on the effects of culture on student motivation). Lee and Hannafin's (2016) "Own It, Learn It, Share It" design framework is a new section in this edition.

Chapter 5, "Diagnosing Informational and Instructional Needs," presents Grover's model along with discussion of Taylor's levels, Belkin's information problems, Dervin's information seeking as sense making, and Maslow's hierarchy of needs. Theories of cognitive development and complexity and an overview of theories and update of research in the area of learning styles and learning modes are also included. This chapter now features a section on services to children with disabilities.

Chapter 6, "Building Information Competence: Designing Instruction for Today's Learners," considers the information-seeking behavior of Generations X, Y, and Z, the realities of the "digital divide" as it is now variously defined, and the challenges these pose for school librarians and administrators. A new section on understanding Gen Z youngsters has been added.

Chapter 7, "Creating Effective Inquiry-Based Educational Tasks," seeks to improve the depth of student learning though the creation of information-based tasks that not only engage learners' interests but also involve them in thinking critically and searching effectively. This edition has an expanded discussion on inquiry-based learning and includes a new section, "Cognitive Barriers to Inquiry."

Chapter 8, "Evaluating Students, Librarians, and Libraries," reviews school reform issues related to assessment options and to contemporary approaches to school library evaluation. A new section on the school librarian's use of formative assessment has been added.

Chapter 9, "Attending to the Social Needs of Today's Learners," considers interpersonal communication within the context of the school library and explores the social nature of information seeking and virtual digital reference services. Also included is an updated discussion on the state of virtual reference services.

Professionalism, service, advocacy, and leadership for school librarians are addressed in the Epilogue.

CONCLUSION

As much as we might sometimes wish it were so, there is no single instructional formula for raising student achievement and skill levels that will be effective and engaging for all students, at all grade levels, under all conditions, and in all situations. Such formulaic pronouncements, when they are presented, essentially ignore the value of differentiated instructional practices in meeting the many and diverse instructional needs observed in today's students. It is hoped that by careful consideration of research related to information skills instruction, reflective practitioners will be able to create a "best-fit" guide based on their knowledge of evidence-based instructional approaches and professional assessment of the unique needs of the students they serve. Such a review will also succeed in bringing into sharper focus the educational complexity that developing literacy and technical competence poses for students and the many challenges they face in making sense of information—not in the sort of "predigested, carefully selected, or logically organized" libraries and textbooks of their parents' youth but rather within a "vast network of resources" now ubiquitously available to most users (Kuhlthau 2001).

Even though information seeking for lifelong learning ultimately requires that the "seekers" create their own best ways to find, use, and evaluate information for effective problem resolution and decision making, the research literature reviewed here provides ample evidence that learning the skills on which information literacy depends cannot be left to chance. These skills must be taught, and students must receive support and guidance from knowledgeable instructors as the skills are practiced and ultimately personalized within relevant, interesting, and meaningful curricular tasks. It is up to instructional teams made up of teachers, school librarians, and other professional educators to ensure that today's youngsters can survive and thrive in the "knowledge society."

1

Reference Traditions

From "Personal Assistance" to Instructional Intervention

> A librarian should be more than a keeper of books; he [sic] should be an educator. . . . No such librarian is fit for his place unless he holds himself responsible for the library education of his students.
> —Otis Robinson (as quoted in Tuckett & Stoffle 1984)

While programs of instruction are most often considered the special province of academic and school libraries, the realization that public libraries could and should contribute to the creation of an informed citizenry emerged in American public libraries as early as the 1820s. Indeed, the practice of educating the library user to locate and use appropriate library resources can best be understood as an outgrowth of traditional forms of reference services in public libraries that date back almost two centuries. As chronicled by Rothstein (1955, 1994), Lubans (1974), Hardesty, Schmitt, and Tucker (1986), and others, the first efforts in this direction, which actually predated the adoption of formal reference services by many decades, included provision of all the information requested by library patrons as well as "guidance and direction in" its pursuit (Schiller 1986, 191). This direction established the practice of courteous "personal assistance," which eventually evolved into the public service orientation that still guides contemporary approaches to reference and instruction.

"PERSONAL ASSISTANCE" IN PUBLIC LIBRARIES

Slightly more aggressive patterns of reference service than the sporadic offerings of the personal assistance characteristic of the early years first appeared

1

at the Boston Public Library in the 1850s, where "a naive faith in the efficacy of 'good' reading in the preservation of virtue" (Rothstein 1955, 16) prompted the institution to commit itself to popular education. Although entirely consistent with the values of the times, the Boston Public Library's vision of itself as "a new tool for scholarship" did not immediately usher in a golden age of library service nor inspire the creation of similar projects in other institutions. On the contrary, limited collections and low levels of funding combined to slow the adoption of a reference service ethic by most public libraries until after the Civil War. Nonetheless, it was during this period that libraries first became concerned with demonstrating their value as community resources; and it was not long before they seized on reference services as a vehicle for expanding their usefulness, their horizons, and their visibility.

The next real milestone in the development of "reference" as an important aspect of library activity was a program for reading assistance devised for library users at the Worcester (Massachusetts) Free Public Library, under the guidance of Samuel Swett Green (1837–1913). Green's public advocacy of a more formal approach to reference services came in 1876 in a paper delivered at the first conference of the American Library Association (ALA). Because, Green reasoned, the people who come into a library frequently lack knowledge of library books and the background and skills needed to use its catalogs, it is the obligation of the library staff to lend them a hand. To this end, Green trained his staff to assist library patrons, stressing the importance of accessibility to materials and "cordiality" in addressing users' questions. Rothstein (1955) opined that Green hoped to do "well," by currying public favor, and to gain public funding by appearing to do "good."

Although Green's ideas for a "new method" (Rothstein 1955, 22) were greeted by some of his colleagues as forward looking, others were less sanguine. One librarian, for example, rejected the idea, claiming that the questions of ordinary library users were bound to be largely "frivolous" and a waste of the librarian's energy and time and that in most cases library staff lacked the expertise necessary to assist scholars in any meaningful way. Even so, Green's somewhat tentative move in the direction of instructional services eventually gained support and with it a realization that libraries should employ every means at their disposal to make their resources useful to the publics that funded their activities. Early efforts at library advocacy thus began.

By the late 1880s, the proliferation of Green's approaches to public service was evidenced in Frederick Morgan Crunden's (1847–1911) study of public libraries. One of the founders of the ALA and an early ALA president, Crunden found "a growing sentiment in favor of the provision of personal assistance by the librarian as the most effective form of aid to the reader" (Rothstein 1955, 26). Within the next 10 years, what often began as "casual, intermittent help" came increasingly to be "replaced by specific administrative organization" (28) of such services. Indeed, by 1891, the new service even had a formal name— "reference work"—which replaced the earlier and decidedly more ambiguous "aids to readers" and "access to librarians" (Rothstein 1994, 542).

Another early proponent of user education in libraries was Charles Ami Cutter (1837–1903), who proposed teaching library patrons to use catalogs and book lists so that they would be able to find their own information and answer their own reference questions. While Cutter's plan served the rather pragmatic end of keeping library visitors from troubling the library staff, Melvil Dewey's "concern over the library's role as an educational institution" was considerably more benevolent and proactive. For Dewey, instruction was seen as a core rather than a "peripheral" activity (Rothstein 1955, 31). Because of his commitment to improving services in both college and public library sectors, Dewey's work created a bridge between the two that facilitated the spread of his "modern library idea" (quoted in Rothstein 1955, 27) in academic as well as public library circles.

By the 1920s, most public librarians had adopted a dual service model, although reference service most frequently consisted of librarians providing answers and information directly to library users rather than giving instruction—unless they specifically requested it. As libraries grew in popularity, demands for services also increased. The strain that this new "traffic" placed on reference departments and concerns to maintain both quality and service led librarians to create a number of innovative approaches to reference service. In cities that supported multiple library buildings within a single system, some directors farmed out readers' advisory services to the library's branches while retaining responsibility for more "serious" research at the central facility. Others found a solution in the creation of a separate information desk, which could handle directional inquiries expeditiously while channeling more "important" information questions to experts in the reference department. Where funding and staffing were available, reference departments were themselves divided into specialty areas (e.g., science and technology, business, history, and genealogy) similar to existing patterns in the disciplinary specialties (e.g., science, history, social science, and humanities) increasingly prevalent in academic libraries so that librarians could provide even higher levels of service.

An interesting innovation and one that suggested a degree of engagement seldom encountered in other settings at the time was the creation of positions at the Library of Congress known as "interpretive chairs." Conceived by Herbert Putnam (1861–1955) during the 1920s, interpretive chairs were reference librarians trained to provide "active aid and counsel" to researchers working in the library. The "extra measure of assistance" available through these individuals included advice on relevant sources and special reference materials, suggestions on procedural and stylistic matters related to the creation of the user's manuscript, and "constructive criticism" (Roberts, quoted in Rothstein 1955, 92) of the final product.

During the course of the past half century, reference services in public libraries have developed further to include ready-reference or fact-finding functions undertaken by a centralized reference unit with specialized assistance programs, such as genealogy and local history, often made available in separate units or departments. However, "the public library has lagged far behind in pursuing a pedagogically progressive version of information literacy as a central part of its mission" (Elmborg 2016, 548). Elmborg goes on to suggest that the influence of boards of trustees, often composed of "economic elites," contributes to the reluctance of public libraries to advance an information literacy agenda; such boards, he opines, may see this initiative as "political activism" and therefore inappropriate for a publicly funded entity. Elmborg's perspective may suggest that Green's concern for currying public favor lives on. While public libraries continue to shy away from information literacy as a concept or a program, initiatives for teaching digital literacy are common as evidenced in the Public Library Association "Digital Learn" project that provides digital technology tutorials for public libraries (Public Library Association 2013). Such programs address the technical aspects of information work, but do not address the critical thinking and evaluative processes inherent in information literacy. Finally, in libraries where homework assistance has become an important aspect of youth services, a specialized form of reference assistance to youngsters combines information services and instruction (Mediavilla 2018).

SERVICE TRADITIONS IN ACADEMIC LIBRARIES

The status of the library as a cultural institution par excellence has seldom been questioned. Rather grandly, Francis Lieber (1882, quoted in Rothstein 1955) described libraries as "the bridges over which Civilization travels from generation to generation and from country to country" (11). In higher education, the affinity between the library as cultural artifact and the library as educational workplace seems to have been appreciated even in the earliest days of the Republic. Rothstein noted, for example, that although academic libraries at the beginning of the 19th century were "indifferent" to most activities other than those involved in acquiring materials, "teaching the use of books and libraries did arouse some considerable interest" (14). In 1816, George Ticknor (1791–1871) described the library as "the light and spirit" of the university and its "first convenience" (10–11). "Give me a library," wrote Benjamin Ide Wheeler at the end of the 19th century, "and I'll build a university about it" (quoted in Rothstein 1955, 11).

Writing about the same time, Frederick A. P. Barnard (1883, quoted in Rothstein 1955), the president of Columbia University, expressed his enthusiastic support for "instruction and aid to undergraduates as shall enable them in all their after lives to do their individual work more readily and more successfully" (14), while the American historian Herbert Baxter Adams (1887, quoted in Rothstein 1955) found highly commendable a course in "bibliographical information" taught to students "by the librarian of their college or university" (14). Finally, the words of Otis Robinson (quoted in Tuckett & Stoffle 1984) reflect the sentiments of more visionary 19th-century library educators:

> A librarian should be more than a keeper of books; he should be an educator. . . . No such librarian is fit for his place unless he holds himself responsible for the library education of his students. . . . All that is taught in college amounts to very little; but if we can send students out self-reliant in their investigations, we will have accomplished much. (58)

In a very real sense, the transformation of the librarian from archivist to educator facilitated and was facilitated by the transformation of the university library from literary "sanctum" to intellectual "workshop."

The Move to Instruct Users: Justin Winsor's Legacy

Near the end of the 19th century, the development of an instructional model for reference service was advanced at Harvard University, where the "professor of books," librarian Justin Winsor (1831–1897), actively encouraged both library staff and ordinary library users to provide research assistance. According to a procedure created by Winsor, information seekers could post "notes and queries" (Rothstein 1955, 24) on a spindle in the reference room; anyone interested in finding the answer to someone's question could post it for others to read. Winsor also advocated the preparation of book lists "in anticipation of students' essays." "If our colleges would pay more attention to the methods by which a subject is deftly attacked, and would teach the true use of encyclopedic and bibliographic helps," Winsor wrote, "they would do much to make the library more serviceable" (24).

Winsor (1986) also proposed opening the university collections to individual students and faculty and providing instruction in the "use of books and libraries." Although his somewhat modest model for instruction limited library lessons to locating and accessing library materials, Winsor's vision of the library as "the grand rendezvous of the college for teacher and pupil" (7) placed him well ahead of his time; many contemporary college and university librarians of his time were not nearly so accommodating. Indeed, it was not until universities began to adopt the German model of lectures and seminars as vehicles for instruction that textbooks came to be replaced by materials that were housed in campus libraries. Interestingly, if perhaps not surprisingly, state universities initially welcomed the establishment of personally assisted reference services with more enthusiasm than did librarians at older and perhaps more conservative private universities.

Another 19th-century librarian who championed accessibility to collections and the amplification of services was William Frederick Poole (1821–1894). While to contemporary ears his announcement that his "office door [was] always open" to anyone seeking assistance may sound at best reactive, at the time it must have seemed positively magnanimous. Poole also favored the creation of a university course in the "scientific methods of using books" and sought faculty status for professor-librarians to whom would fall the responsibility for providing this instruction. Following Poole's leadership, Raymond C. Davis (1836–1919) created a course on bibliography and reference tools at the University of Michigan as early as 1881.

Columbia College's Melvil Dewey

As innovative as these instructional courses were, it was Melvil Dewey (1851–1931) who, at the turn of the 20th century, finally regularized reference and established "organized personal assistance" as an integral instrument of the Columbia College library's educational purpose. Writing as early as 1884, Dewey set forth his expectations: in addition to organizing and cataloging library materials and providing reference resources, librarians were to furnish advice and instruction so that students would gain knowledge of the best library resources and be competent "to use them intelligently" and in the proper order. For Dewey, the "first and paramount duty of the Reference Librarian" was to set an example, counsel students, and train library users in the delights of the library and the "habit of hunting" information (Rothstein 1955, 28). The importance that Dewey's imprimatur gave to establishing the legitimacy of library instruction cannot be overstated.

Princeton's William Warner Bishop

It was left to William Warner Bishop (1871–1955), a classical scholar who served as a librarian at Princeton and at the University of Michigan, as well as at the Library of Congress, to articulate a comprehensive framework for instruction that has an amazingly contemporary ring. Noting the "deluge" of new material published each year, Bishop in 1912 recommended that students be educated in acquiring a scholar's "attitude toward the printed page" (Bishop 1986, 83) through a sequential program of instruction that should begin in elementary school and continue until a student graduated from college.

Vassar's Lucy Maynard Salmon

Another visionary who explored the idea of instructional integration was Lucy Maynard Salmon (1853–1927), a history professor at Vassar, who, at the ALA conference in 1913, argued persuasively for the incorporation of instruction in books and libraries as part of regular college courses. Salmon believed that because the professors knew individual students and their particular research needs, they were in the best position to provide library instruction relevant to ongoing course assignments and requirements. Not only did it made good sense to "incorporate knowledge of how to use a library with the subject matter included in a particular course" (Salmon 1986, 88), she opined, but it would also save everyone's time. Further, the "knowledge acquired" in the course of instruction would fall "naturally into its place in connection within definite, concrete work" (88) and be more easily assimilated by college students.

In order to put her ideas on library instruction into play, Salmon (1986) created a course for new students that included a library tour and designed "bibliographical work" within a "definitely planned . . . systematically carried out" progression of courses directly related to the specific and individual work of every student. From time to time conferences [were] held by members of the library staff and the instructors in history, and these conferences enable[d] each department to supplement and complement the work of the other and thus avoid repetition and duplication" (93). Salmon characterized the roles of the librarian as friend, counselor, guide, and, ultimately, teacher:

> It is often his duty not to give, but temporarily to withhold information; not to answer but to ask questions; to answer one question by asking another; to help a student answer his [sic] own question for himself, work out his own problems,

and find a way out of his difficulties; to show him how to seek and find for himself the material desired; to give training rather than specific information; to be himself a teacher and to co-operate with other instructors in training the students who seek his help. (94)

TAXONOMY OF REFERENCE SERVICE LEVELS

As noted above, the earliest models for reference services developed within individual academic and public libraries and thus differed widely, depending on whatever patterns of assistance were in vogue at those specific institutions (Schiller 1986). J. I. Wyer (1869–1955) described these differences in terms of a taxonomy of service levels: conservative, moderate, and liberal (Wyer 1930). At the conservative level, the librarian was characterized as an "intelligent guidepost," with the "self-development" of the library user as the ultimate goal of any services extended. In practice, librarians espousing a conservative view considered the act of offering more than directional assistance or the "means of gathering information" a disservice in that it "deprive[d] patrons of the invaluable benefits derived from the experience of personal investigation" (Spofford 1990, quoted in Rothstein 1955, 42). According to Rothstein, this service approach was based on an "a priori assumption that the library [as] an educational institution" had a responsibility to provide formal instruction in the use of its resources but that the "truly deserving university student or public library patron" would desire no more assistance than that. As Rothstein (1955) noted, "Presumably readers more egregious in their demands were to be rejected out of hand, or to be brought to realize that less aid really did them more good than more aid" (44). Rothstein himself found this claim "dubious," an example of inverted logic, and contrary to popular wisdom; surely, he thought, increasing services would ultimately mean an increase in the library's popularity and community support.

The conservative model of service was reflected in the public library arena in the work of such early library notables as John Cotton Dana (1856–1929) and Charles Ami Cutter (1837–1903), both of whom judged library users fully capable of finding the answers to their own inquiries. Although it may be hard to imagine in light of today's professional concern for bibliographic instruction (BI), at the time few disputed the inherent contradictions in these "less-is-more" policies, possibly because, as Rothstein (1955) suggested, as a rationale it tended to fit contemporary practice. Indeed, according to Rothstein, "the 'conservative theory' never ceased to find adherents" (75), particularly in academic library settings. Perhaps for this reason, the real focus of instructional attention prior to World War I was the "inexperienced library user" (45), with guided tours and formalized library courses outside the context of students' course work as the most commonly used instructional methods. Other, less intrusive and less interactive methods of instruction, namely, the creation of subject bibliographies and finding lists, were also standard practices.

Interestingly, where a conservative or limited service model characterized reference practice, it was usually invoked for faculty as well as for students. "Just what educational purposes were being served by denying to faculty more than minimal assistance," Rothstein (1955) suggested, were at best "seldom made clear. Tacitly, however, the policy was undoubtedly based on the old assumption that the mature scholar did not need help—or at any rate ought not to need it" (75) and that students did not deserve it (Schiller 1986). In point of fact, the assumption that "the value of a study [ought to be] measured by the personal labor of its author" (Rothstein 1955, 87) was entirely consistent with the social values inherent in a Puritan/Protestant work ethic (Sillars 1991) and an American preoccupation with the self-reliance characteristic of the period. According to Rothstein (1955), direct services in the form of information provision were often saved for those he characterized as the truly "helpless," that is, "foreigners" and the "timid" (75–76).

There were, however, other voices in academic librarianship arguing for reference librarians to assume a more active role in assisting library users with their information tasks. For example, J. Christian Bay (1871–1962), writing in 1924, opined that librarians should "illumine" (quoted in Rothstein 1955, 76) as well as recommend specific sources, an approach that Wyer (1930) would later describe as typical of a moderate level of service. The interpretation of information and its utilization, however, continued to be regarded as the responsibility of the library user.

At a third, or liberal, level of Wyer's (1930) service taxonomy, the librarian was obliged to use her or his expertise to find the information sought by patrons and to provide direct assistance in establishing the relevance, authority, and authenticity of particular titles. An articulate and enthusiastic proponent for this enhanced service model in this era was William Elmer Henry (1857–1936), a librarian at the University of Washington and founder of the library school there in 1911, who offered as a rationale for his understanding that the essential task of scholarship was the creation of a thesis rather than the mechanics of identifying, searching out, and obtaining particular sources. The most immediate consequence of Wyer's "liberal service" idea was the development of academic subject specialties by reference staff so that they could provide a more scholarly level of assistance than had previously been available or expected.

As seen above, academic libraries have, over time, provided varying levels of reference support. Although most did not adopt one mode or level of service over another in a formal statement of library policy, they tended to operate at a moderate level of service, established not by design but by default, often in response to traffic flow. However, the development of subject specialties by librarians with degrees or advanced levels of knowledge in academic domains, which became a part of the organizational pattern in many academic and public libraries during this period, held out at least the possibility that higher levels of service and increased levels of expertise could be made available to library users, at least for faculty. However, as Farber (1995) notes, overall academic librarians tended to expend most of their efforts in acquiring resources and organizing materials to support faculty research. In many institutions, this led to a sort of double standard: personal assistance for teaching and research faculty was modeled on a liberal approach to reference services, while undergraduate students were on the receiving end of minimalist or conservative service levels (Rothstein 1994).

In a departure from the trend of the academic reference librarian's role as "specialist," generalists were hired at Cornell University in the 1930s to assist faculty members in identifying resources outside the scholar's area of specialization and to procure materials from other libraries when necessary. This departure from the specialist model of academic reference work made use of the librarian as a consultant, considered by some to be a step closer to information provider or instructor.

DISSENTING VIEWS AND CRITIQUES OF REFERENCE SERVICES

It is perhaps not surprising to note that the conservative and liberal approaches to reference service were seldom embraced with equal enthusiasm within the same institution. Indeed, across the profession, there has never been anything akin to total agreement as to what constitutes "best practice" in the delivery of user services (Schiller 1986). Over time, the liberal "direct-provision" camp of librarians has promoted its view with eloquence and humor, often dismissing as "ludicrous" the very notion that the library should be in the business of educating users. Jesse Shera (1903–1982), for example, called on librarians to "forget this silly pretense of playing teacher" (1954, quoted in Hardesty et al. 1986, 189), while Rothstein (1964, quoted in Schiller 1986) argued that, although instruction might be defensible for children and youth, adults had "no more reason to be guided in the techniques of finding out than they have in being shown how to fix a defective carburetor" (193).

For his part, Stoan (1984) warned academic librarians against presenting "information skills" as "research skills," which, as he asserted, were not equivalent "nor bear any organic relationship to each other" (105). According to Stoan, activities that academic librarians frequently referred to as "research" are more properly information seeking and "library use," while "research," within the parlance of academic scholars, is a "quest for knowledge" (105) entailing the systematic collection of original "uninterpreted" (100) data, conducted according to methodologies consistent with particular academic disciplines. The appropriate use of library resources within the context of a scholarly research agenda, Stoan suggested, consists of footnote and citation chasing in the secondary literature to find relevant readings. Since it is through footnotes that "scholars communicate with each other," they are more useful as keys to the utility of an article in relationship to a particular topic than are access "tools," such as subject headings and descriptors, which represent a "layer" of interpretation created by "a third party" (103).

Stoan (1984) has also argued against trying to teach students a single, generic research strategy because scholarly approaches to information seeking are personal, domain specific, subjective, and intuitive. In his view, such approaches constitute an amalgam of insights, experience, and luck sparked by engagement with resources encountered (sometimes serendipitously) along the way. Furthermore, Kaplan (quoted in Stoan 1984) argued that researchers are often unable to describe their own methods of information seeking and frequently employ "logic-in-use" (102) strategies rather than using the indexing and abstracting resources and reference "tools that librarians deem so central to the research process" (101).

20TH-CENTURY INSTRUCTIONAL INITIATIVES IN ACADEMIC LIBRARIES

The most common approaches to library instruction during the early years were library lectures, which were usually followed by some sort of assignment that required students to use the library and its array of bibliographic tools and resources. It became evident over time that the stronger programs were those in which the librarian worked closely with the college professors. In fact, the importance of professor-librarian partnerships was a central finding of research conducted within the context of liberal arts colleges by Harvie Branscomb and published in 1940 as *Teaching with Books: A Study of College Libraries* (Hardesty et al. 1986).

Peabody College's Louis Shores

Louis Shores (1904–1981), librarian at Peabody College for Teachers (Nashville, Tennessee) in the 1930s and early 1940s, launched an ambitious program based on his idea that the library is the college—and the college, the library (Shores 1986). What Shores envisioned was a library college, in which all the teachers would be library trained and in charge of supervising and tutoring individual students in independently conducted reading and research projects. Among Shores's notable contributions to the discourse of academic librarianship were the ideas that learning should be student-centered and interdisciplinary and that creating independent learners was the appropriate goal of education. At the time, Shores's program had little immediate impact on the practice of his contemporaries. However, his understanding that library instruction could make a valuable contribution to the achievement of the broader educational goals of the institution aided in the development of a vision for instructional programming in academic and school libraries that was implemented later in the century.

The Mid-Century Information Explosion

Although the explosion of scientific knowledge immediately evident in the years following World War II raised concerns of many mid-century librarians about the problems that this "Niagara" of information might pose for the general public as well as for students, little progress in user instruction in the academic library was made during the next two decades (Rothstein 1955). In fact, in spite of a burgeoning undergraduate population and expanding collections, the lack of library staff, lack of "a viable conceptual framework" (Hardesty et al. 1986, 148), lack of enthusiasm, and/or lack of instructional finesse (Kirk 1977, cited in Hardesty et al. 1986) together led most academic librarians to limit their instructional efforts to orientation sessions and library tours.

TABLE 1.1 A Summary of Themes and Insights in Early Efforts at Library Use Instruction

- Roles for librarians as teachers, advisers, consultants, and information providers
- Pedagogical training as a prerequisite for "teaching" librarians
- Importance of faculty and librarian collaboration in planning
- Importance of teaching library use skills in context of a research task
- Value of "information use" skills over "location and access" skills
- The librarian as an identifier of relevant resources
- The librarian as assistant with research products and their evaluation

When they were available, library education courses were typically taught in stand-alone sessions, with content decisions most frequently based on the expertise and interests of the librarians rather than the information needs of the students themselves. As a result, instructional programs in many universities languished. Even so, insights gained through the implementation of the innovative programs championed by Dewey, Shores, Salmon, and others created frameworks for the development of instructional programs to come. (A summary of new roles and activities is provided in Table 1.1.) Especially compelling in this regard were prototypes for librarians that featured active participation in the process of student learning.

KNAPP'S EXPERIMENT

The program that rekindled the flame of interest in bibliographic instruction (BI) among academic and school librarians was created by Patricia Bryan Knapp (1914–1972) at Wayne State University (Detroit, Michigan) in the early 1960s. Convinced that "competence in library use" constituted "one of the liberal arts" (Knapp 1986, 156), and recognizing the key role that college faculty played in student use of library resources, Knapp (1966) launched an initiative to "instruct the instructors" in the use of the library, its resources, and its educational value by integrating library instruction into a wide variety of courses in order to demonstrate the applicability of library skills across the curriculum. In addition, Knapp devised a plan to implement these skills through a series of instructional experiences carried out over time, which she hoped would lead students to develop positive attitudes toward the library and an appreciation for its utility.

Featured prominently in Knapp's (1966) approach were assignments based on problem-solving activities rather than paper-and-pencil tests or "makework" practice assignments loosely linked to course content. In this way, she hoped to emphasize the "intellectual processes involved in retrieval of information and ideas from the complex system our society uses to organize its stored record" (81). And although Knapp's program was essentially librarian initiated, the delivery of BI was truly a cooperative effort between university librarians and the teaching faculty. The program itself called for the articulation of specific objectives, including the organizational schemes used to structure library collections, the identification of essential reference books, and

TABLE 1.2   A Summary of Insights from the Knapp (1966, 1986) Project

- Library use as a multidimensional activity involving knowledge, skills, and attitudes
- The value of teaching library use skills in context
- The value of integrating library use skills within and across subject domains
- The importance of systematic planning for instruction
- The importance of cooperation and coordination between librarians and teachers
- The importance of practicing library use skills within "authentic" tasks
- The importance of evaluation in the use of information resources

the creation of criteria that could be used to interpret and evaluate the information obtained.

It must be admitted that Knapp's (1966) dynamic instructional program was not greeted with unbridled enthusiasm by Wayne State students and faculty. However, her insights made a major contribution to the field of library and information studies in general and to school librarianship in particular. Especially influential have been Knapp's understandings that library use is a multidimensional activity involving "knowledge, skills, and attitudes" (Farber 1995, 24) and that library use skills are best learned over time and when presented within the context of ongoing classroom assignments. In fact, the systematicity of her instructional program, her emphasis on "process" over "content," and her understanding of the key roles played by course instructors are now regarded as foundational for the successful implementation of instructional programming in school libraries. Table 1.2 lists important insights anchored in Knapp's research.

THE VALUE OF TEACHING LIBRARY USE SKILLS IN CONTEXT: THE EARLHAM COLLEGE EXPERIENCE

Another major contribution to the development of BI models was the exemplary program of library instruction created at Earlham College (Richmond, Indiana) in the mid-1960s and implemented by librarians Evan Ira Farber, Thomas B. Kirk, and James R. Kennedy. Founded on the bedrock of active cooperation between departmental scholars and college librarians, Earlham's approach to instruction featured three central principles: integration, demonstration, and gradation (Kennedy 1986, 233). Integration was achieved by embedding all library instruction within courses that most often required students to use library resources. Demonstration was chosen as the central instructional strategy and included an introduction to the search process as well as to specific types of library resources. Annotated bibliographies of course-relevant materials were also created and distributed as part of the instructional program. Gradation was achieved through the implementation of a planned sequence of instructional sessions, which were conducted over the four years of a student's college career. Elements that librarians viewed as key to the successful implementation of the program included rapport and synergy

TABLE 1.3 Key Elements of the BI Program at Earlham College

- An academic culture that "demands" library use
- Commitment of librarians and teaching faculty to the goals of the program
- Active rapport and collaboration between librarians and the teaching faculty
- Selection of appropriate courses for library skills instruction
- Highly motivated and interested students
- High teacher expectations for student performance
- Small class size
- "Just-in-time" delivery of instructional intervention
- Instructional quality and creativity

between the librarians and the teaching faculty, the selection of appropriate courses for library skills integration and appropriate projects within the courses, small class size, and a "just-in-time" approach that based decisions related to course scheduling directly on the needs of students. Kennedy (1986) identified the following strategies as contributing substantially to the overall success of Earlham's innovative program: a college culture that "demands library use," the commitment of librarians, the motivation of students, high teacher expectations, and quality and creativity in instructional techniques (see Table 1.3).

Although in many respects Earlham's experience and success reflected the unique qualities of that institution and its librarians, the program created at Earlham resulted in a veritable explosion of interest among academic librarians in the 1970s and continues today. The first tangible evidence of this interest was the creation of an Ad Hoc Committee on Bibliographic Instruction within the Association of College and Research Libraries and the subsequent establishment of the Bibliographic Instruction Section of that organization in 1977. The founding of the Library Instruction Round Table by the ALA in 1977 and a series of conferences, newsletters, and clearinghouses for information on bibliographic instruction followed, some of which included elementary and secondary librarians (e.g., the Library Orientation Exchange).

BI IN THE 21ST CENTURY: STRATEGIES AND TECHNIQUES

The vestiges of BI history are evident in many of the trends in instruction evident in 21st-century academic libraries. The intent to reach students has led to a variety of strategies, some of which have proven to be more efficacious than others. However, effective approaches to information literacy instruction require support and adoption by teaching faculty. A key to that "buy-in" is communicating clearly to faculty, using concepts and vocabulary that are both meaningful and familiar within their respective disciplinary cultures. Farrell and Badke (2015) assert that because each academic discipline may handle information and engage in research differently, it is to the librarians' (and ultimately to the students') advantage to align information literacy instruction within the frameworks of disciplinary goals and the specialized character of information seeking and use within a content area. Of course, it is also the case where practical considerations interfere with the successful implementation of disciplinary strategies, and some compromises will have to be made.

For this reason, a range of strategies for instruction in academic libraries continues to be the overall trend.

One-Shot Instruction

A growing body of research evidence (see Bowles-Terry & Donovan 2016; Epps & Nelson 2013; Mery et al. 2012; Walker & Pearce 2014) suggests that stand-alone instructional sessions are not sufficient to meet the information literacy needs of most students. However, because instruction based on this model is often the only way librarians can garner access to students and instructional time, the use of one-shot sessions persists and is often applied to first-year student library orientation. For this reason, academic librarians continue to seek ways to make the best of this instructional delivery form. For example, Walker and Pearce (2014) attempted to increase student engagement in one-shot sessions by using personal response systems such as clickers and Web-polling applications. Results of their comparison study revealed no significant differences in outcomes between students whose class used the response systems and those with traditional instruction. Meanwhile, academic librarians are making efforts to move beyond library orientation to creating instructional experiences for students with specific assignments. For example, in a comparison study, Bash (2015) found that students who received individualized instruction were more successful on an assignment in a psychology class than those who experienced a "one-shot" group instruction. Presenting these kinds of research results is one way academic librarians can make a case to faculty for more targeted instruction with students over time.

Information Literacy Credit-Bearing Courses

Following the 1881 model of Raymond C. Davis at the University of Michigan referenced earlier, a more intensive way in which librarians seek opportunities to provide the instruction they believe students need is by offering for-credit courses in information literacy, both in face-to-face and virtual modes. While credit-bearing courses are often aimed at first-year students, at the University of Wyoming, librarians offer upper division for-credit courses with a disciplinary focus (Mayer & Bowles-Terry 2013). These courses feature active learning and include both disciplinary learning activities and lifetime learning experiences (e.g., political fact-checking). In addition, with an emphasis on metacognition, students in these courses engage in reflective writing about their research processes. This disciplinary course approach represents a step toward an integrated information literacy instruction.

Unfortunately, Cohen et al.'s (2016) national survey of academic libraries found that only 19 percent of the 691 responding libraries offered credit-bearing information literacy courses, with most of these using a face-to-face instructional model. In addition, more respondents reported plans to discontinue credit-bearing courses than those that planned to add or increase them, while a full 41 percent of respondents reported plans to move from face-to-face to online delivery.

Making Connections for Integrated Instruction

Prevalent today are efforts to invoke the Earlham College library program, namely to reach out to faculty and to integrate instruction into disciplinary courses in a just-in-time mode to connect instruction to student needs. Concomitant with this trend is a move away from librarians staffing the library reference desk. In fact, Coleman, Mallon, and Lo (2016) conducted a national survey and found a 41.2 percent decline in professional staffing at the reference desks, based on 420 respondents. For example, at the University of Minnesota Bio-Medical Library, professional reference librarians now work in liaison roles and devote their time and efforts to collaborating with faculty and providing appointment-based consultation to students (Aho, Beschnett, & Reimer 2011). Reflecting current academic library trends, specialized desks for circulation, reference, and other services are being combined into one point-of-contact student service desk. Similarly, at Oberlin College, "[t]he typical number of hours that reference and instruction librarians work at the desk has dropped by more than 50% in the last decade, reflecting a belief that our time is better spent teaching and working with students in research appointments" (Mitchell et al. 2011, 363).

Indeed, it is increasingly common to see academic librarians working from their offices as consultants, often as disciplinary specialists. At Cornell College (Iowa), for example, librarians are called "consulting librarians" and serve specific academic domains, that is, for fine arts, natural sciences, humanities, or social sciences (Donham & Green 2004). Working closely with faculty, these librarians also serve as consultants to students, teaching course-based, just-in-time classes followed by individual consultations with students.

Online assistance is another way for librarians to connect with students who are working on specific projects. In a recent study, five virtual reference services—instant messenger chat, e-mail, telephone, text messaging, and Skype videoconferencing—were preferred for the delivery of library services (Chow & Croxton 2014). Its immediacy and the familiarity of the interface may contribute to its appeal to students. A 2015 study of virtual reference services in academic libraries revealed that of the 362 libraries surveyed, approximately 74 percent used at least one of these technologies for virtual reference: e-mail, phone, chat, IM, text, and video chat (Yang & Dalal 2015). The most popular mode of connecting to the library was text messaging in a study by Tewell et al. (2017).

Another effort to expand availability of reference expertise at point of need is a collaborative approach to reference service. The best known such effort is the OCLC/Library of Congress initiative called *QuestionPoint*, which promised collaborative reference on a global scale. Detractors have seen this as a solution in search of a problem; Coffman (2002) asserted that the demand for such service in academic libraries is overshadowed by a tendency to teach students *how to search* for their own answers rather than actually finding the answers; for this reason, they concluded that such services are of minimal value in those settings. However, in best-case settings, librarians are collaborating with faculty to work with students on specific assignments and then making themselves available for follow-up by providing "virtual" assistance through online technologies and service venues such as Google's Hangout Chat or Hangout Meet.

Embedded Librarians

In another approach to collaboration and course-centered assistance, the embedded librarian model has emerged as a strategy for connecting instructional librarians with specific courses. Of importance to the embedded librarian model is the partnership the librarian must develop with the teaching faculty. Schulte (2012) explains the history of the term *embedded librarianship,* referring to the practice of embedded journalism, where a journalist becomes a participant with a fighting unit in order to cover a war as a participant. This partnership brings together the librarian and the course instructor to co-design assignments and then arranges opportunities for the librarian to deliver both class instruction, focused on the information literacy needs for successful completion of the assignment and individual librarian-student consultation based on the specific needs of particular students (Abrizah, Inuwa, & Afiqah-Izzati 2016). Embedded librarians work both face-to-face and virtually. In face-to-face situations, the librarian is likely to be identified on the course syllabus, to attend class sessions, and team-teach with the disciplinary faculty to address immediate information literacy needs of students just-in-time. For example, Donham, Heinrich, and Bostwick (2009) describe this form of collaboration in an undergraduate education seminar, where the librarian participated in designing the major course assignment, taught whole class sessions to guide students in developing an authentic research question, then followed up with one-on-one consultations with each student in the class to structure a literature search, and finally cotaught a writers' workshop focused on the integration of found information as a cohesive final paper.

While Donham et al.'s (2009) example represents the embedded librarian working face-to-face, virtually embedded librarians are also meeting the information literacy needs of students studying at a distance (Abrizah, Inuwa, & Afiqah-Izatti 2016). These librarians employ a variety of methods to teach information literacy, including embedding content into course management systems, using online chat or tools like *LibGuides*™—an online platform that enables development of a website to support instruction and includes online tutorials and links to information resources designed for a particular assignment, course, or department. According to Mokia and Rolen (2012), "*LibGuides* can be ideal for the development of information literacy pages that have real meaning to the students due to the collaboration of the library, students, and faculty to connect with course content." German (2017) also discusses the use of *LibGuides*™, applauding their inclusion of instructional design principles in creating an e-learning experience for students. While this tool is highly relevant for distant learners, it is also an effective tool to support instruction for on-campus students, providing 24/7 access to virtual assistance and resources.

The Commons

Expanding the notion of integration is the development of the *Commons* in academic libraries. Karasic (2016) suggests a variety of ways such spaces can provide a student-centered approach to learning. Commons often include incorporation of writing, technology, and other learning centers into the physical library and attendant collaboration between librarians, faculty, and learning specialists. At Oberlin College in Ohio, for example, an Academic Commons includes a library services desk, a computer lab with printers, a multimedia production area, an electronic classroom, a collaborative seating area, group study rooms, scattered lounge seating, an information-technology help desk, and the writing center. A wireless network provides connectivity throughout the Commons, which is accessed extensively by students using their own laptops (Mitchell et al. 2011).

Ferer (2012) describes numerous examples of collaboration between writing centers and libraries to promote each other's programs among faculty and students and to coteach, whether they are colocated or not. She points out that the two programs have many goals in common, all aimed at helping students succeed in writing effective research papers. Her examples include both large universities and small colleges (see also Napier et al. 2018). Donham and Steele (2008) describe an instruction program that brings together a librarian, a writing consultant, a technology consultant, and a quantitative reasoning consultant to collaborate with teaching faculty in providing coordinated lessons for the various stages of the student's research process.

The Challenge of the First-Year Student

Despite Jesse Shera's mid-century admonition that library instruction is appropriate only for children and youth, academic librarians have turned considerable attention to the information literacy needs of first-year college students. Research on the challenges of the transition from high school to college underscores the importance of instruction at this level. Indeed, Hinchliffe, Rand, and Collier (2018) conducted a study in which they identified nine misconceptions held by first-year students and nine correlated learning outcomes that can be targeted in first-year college instruction. For example, first-year college students commonly believe:

- the library is only a place to get books or to study;
- research is a linear, unidirectional process;
- freely available Internet resources are sufficient for academic work;
- Google is a sufficient search tool;
- accessibility is an indicator of quality;

- they are information literate;
- all library sources and discovery tools are credible; and
- every question has a single answer.

By considering these misconceptions, librarians can design lessons and experiences to counter them.

Regarding specific aspects of information literacy competency, Smith et al. (2013) administered a standardized test to students in three high schools in Edmonton, Alberta, Canada. They found that students scored poorly on categories of questions, including "articulation of the nature and extent of information needed," efficient information access, evaluation of information, integrating found information into a knowledge base, and ethical and legal use of information (91). Other studies (e.g., Dubicki 2013; Fabbi 2015; Head 2013; Saunders et al. 2017) confirm the need for instruction at the postsecondary level. Indeed, in a study of information literacy competency of college students, Lanning and Mallek (2017) concluded that regardless of demographic factors or year in school, "no group is doing well" (448).

A variety of responses to the information literacy deficiencies of first-year college students have been documented. For example, many colleges and universities have created positions for first-year-experience (FYE) librarians (Angell 2018). For these librarians, the most commonly reported responsibility is to teach information literacy sessions for students enrolled in first-year academic courses. Angell reported that most of these librarians work in close collaboration with staff or faculty in first-year experience programs. She found that many of these librarians reported a particular concern about library anxiety among first-year students. However, even in colleges that do not offer a designated FYE librarian, academic librarians are reaching out to first-year course instructors to integrate information literacy into assignments and to include information literacy concepts and skills into grading criteria (see, e.g., Dauterive, Bourgeois, & Simms 2017). All of these findings offer valuable insights for school librarians as they develop their information literacy curricula to prepare students for the college transition.

WHAT TO TEACH: A FRAMEWORK

Deciding what to teach in instructional programs for college students is a primary concern for academic librarians. While ACRL had identified the competencies demonstrated by information literate students, the *ACRL Framework for Information Literacy in Higher Education* (Association of College and Research Libraries 2015) redirected instructional attention to a framework of "big ideas," organized as six core concepts regarding information literacy. This focus is consistent with the work of Grant Wiggins and Jay McTighe (2005), who called for all educators to think about learning as enduring understandings and not just as discrete skills and facts. This approach to information literacy acknowledges its complexity. Each conceptual frame in this model offers a set of related knowledge practices and dispositions. Briefly stated, the threshold concepts are (1) scholarship is a conversation, (2) research as inquiry, (3) authority is

TABLE 1.4 A Summary of Trends in 21st-Century Academic Library Information Literacy

- Library orientation sessions are useful only if followed by in-context instruction.
- Collaboration with faculty affords opportunities to teach information literacy at the point of need.
- Librarians connected to specific academic domains, departments, or specific courses are able to serve students' information literacy needs.
- Online resources, like *LibGuides,* enable 24/7 assistance with online tutorials and resources identified for specific departments, courses, or assignments.
- Collocation and collaboration with other academic support programs like writing centers or technology centers affords the opportunity for integrated instruction and one-stop assistance.
- Emphasis on first-year college students is important as assessments continue to document that incoming students are often not prepared to meet academic expectations in terms of research.
- A conceptual understanding of aspects of information literacy takes students beyond skill learning toward enduring understanding of information work.

contextual and constructed, (4) information creation as a process, (5) searching as strategic exploration, and (6) information has value (ACRL 2015). While the *Framework* has met some resistance—largely because of its complexity—its defenders suggest that it suits the academic environment well in that it shifts the librarians' concern for teaching specific databases to "the larger concern of professors [that] their students embrace and reflect the scholarship of their disciplines" (Badke 2016). Clearly, the concepts expressed in the framework align well with that goal. Table 1.4 provides a summary of trends in academic library information literacy.

INFORMATION LITERACY INTERNATIONAL

Meanwhile on the international front, the International Federation of Library Associations (IFLA) has published its own set of information literacy expectations (Lau 2006). The IFLA was founded in 1927 and now has members in 140 countries. The organization also has had a working group focusing on information literacy since 2003. The current guidelines for information literacy, published in 2006, are structured around a three-stage process—access, evaluate, and use information. The guidelines call for institutional commitment to adoption of an information literacy program as well as a commitment to a student-centered rather than resource-centered approach to teaching and learning. Finally, the guidelines lay out a process for developing an action plan for international implementation.

The truth is that many countries outside the United States have impressive records of attention to information literacy. In Sweden, for example, the Chalmers Institute of Technology is perhaps its most prestigious higher education institution focusing on engineering and technology; at Chalmers, information literacy has been integrated into courses for decades. As described in 1983 by librarians Nancy Fjällbrant and Brita Sjöstrand, "instruction is based, whenever possible, on searching for information in connection with projects" (109). Today, interest in effective information literacy teaching continues to be strong in Scandinavia, where recent work focuses on engaging students in authentic inquiry (e.g., Francke et al. 2011; Limberg et al. 2008). Similarly, Australia, New Zealand, and the United Kingdom represent other major English-speaking countries with significant interest in information literacy and an ongoing commitment to research and praxis (Folk 2016). African nations too are focusing attention on information literacy (Baro & Keboh 2012). In short, information literacy is a global issue.

CONCLUSION

It is apparent from this historical review that the lessons learned in public and academic library settings have contributed significantly to the development of theory and practice in school librarianship. Indeed, although the schools have made instruction a central feature of their mission, they owe "innovations in most phases of library instruction, including those of conceptualization, design, experimentation, implementation and evaluation" (Tucker 1994, 364), to the efforts of visionaries in academic and public institutions. An appreciation of these contributions, as well as the insightful programs and theoretical frameworks from which they arose, provide useful points of departure for school librarians engaged in designing their own instructional programs for elementary and high school students. Especially significant are the characterizations of libraries as intellectual centers and learning laboratories; the recommendation that students examine the authority of information sources; advocacy for increasing the accessibility of library resources; models for individualized guidance; the view of information literacy through a conceptual lens; perceptions of students as independent searchers and lifelong learners; and the importance of contextualizing library instruction around students' content-area expectations.

Current thinking suggests that an important aspect of information literacy is recognizing and making use of the expertise available in the person of a professional librarian. In that effort, approachability deserves attention. Some librarians are employing social media in an effort to entice students to reach out for assistance (Stone 2014). It seems clear that in school libraries as well as in their academic and public counterparts, the extent to which library users feel free to seek assistance from library professionals may well depend on the climate of accessibility and acceptance that the librarians themselves manage to create (Radford 1996; Radford & Connaway 2007).

2

The School Library Idea

From Dream to Reality

An effective school library plays an important role in preparing learners for life in an information rich society.
—American Association of School Librarians (2018)

The concept of a school library has evolved over the years from early ideas of a centralized collection of books through expanded collections that include resources in a variety of formats. And, since the turn of the century, the focus has shifted from what the library "has" to what the librarian "does." In fact, once seen as a curator of collections, today's librarian fulfills a number of important roles, including school leader, instructional partner, information specialist, library teacher, and program administrator (American Association of School Librarians 2018). These changes have resulted in an increasing emphasis on the learner and the library as a learning space, and a concomitant shift toward student-centered learning, where youngsters are empowered to formulate questions and launch information-seeking projects based on their own curiosities and interests.

SCHOOL LIBRARY BEGINNINGS: OPENING THE DOOR

History students may remember DeWitt Clinton (1769–1828) as an early governor of New York State and as the father of the Erie Canal, but he should be doubly honored by school librarians for his vision in recommending, in 1827, the creation of libraries in the public schools. Nearly 100 years earlier, Benjamin Franklin's educational vision of "student academies" had called for establishing the library as a central feature (Gillespie & Spirt 1973). Thanks to Clinton and the innovations promoted by the 19th-century educational reformer

Horace Mann (1796–1859), Franklin's earlier dream was realized in state legislation that enabled school districts to purchase library books. In the years that followed, the idea of the library as a key educational resource caught the imagination of many and spread quickly, so that by 1840 libraries had been established to supplement instruction and promote reading in public schools in New York (1835), Massachusetts (1837), Michigan (1837), Connecticut (1839), and Rhode Island (1840).

Unfortunately, this early enthusiasm was short lived. In New York, the decline of school libraries was directly related to the fact that school administrators (when given the option in 1843) used library funds to pay teachers' salaries. In the other states, the fledgling school libraries were in some sense undermined by the success of public libraries, which were then enjoying a period of rapid growth (Cecil & Heaps 1940). Moreover, initial efforts to launch school libraries and sustain the momentum necessary for their continued support were seriously compromised by a lack of identifiable standards, adequate supervision, and trained personnel. Even so, by 1876, 21 states had funding legislation in place to support school libraries as part of public education (Bowie 1986).

As the 19th century drew to a close, interest in establishing school libraries was sustained by concurrent efforts to improve the quality of public education. Among the most influential of the reformers was the German philosopher Johann F. Herbart (1776–1841), who realized, contrary to the conventional pedagogical wisdom of the day, that ideas and intellectual development were ultimately more valuable than the mastery of a specific body of knowledge (Cecil & Heaps 1940). According to Cecil and Heaps (1940), "The Herbartian movement in reading which swept this country, particularly from 1889–1897, was a large factor in the awakening of educators to the potentialities of the library in the school" (50).

COMBINING SCHOOL AND PUBLIC LIBRARIES

During this same period, there was also a good deal of public support for the idea, first advanced by Charles Francis Adams Jr. (1835–1915), that public and school libraries should be combined. Proponents argued that joining the two entities made sense in terms of "economy, convenience, and efficiency" (Carpenter 1905, quoted in Cecil & Heaps 1940, 58). Melvil Dewey enthusiastically embraced this idea, which was also shared by Samuel Swett Green (1837–1918), one of the founders of the American library movement. While Green stopped short of combining public and school libraries in his hometown of Worcester, Massachusetts, he made overtures to the schools by loaning to students and faculty materials from his public library and by encouraging classes to visit.

In the meantime, many other communities experimented with various forms of interlibrary cooperation or amalgamation. For example, the staffs of some public libraries joined with principals in planning school libraries that the principals themselves then ran. In other instances, public libraries maintained branch facilities within public schools, tailoring collections to meet the needs of adults as well as youngsters. In areas without access to public libraries, it was not uncommon for state library agencies to provide "package" libraries of preselected materials to schools (Carroll 1981). During this period, museums in many communities also partnered with school libraries to make their collections available to local school districts (Coleman 1989).

The collaborative spirit representative of this kind of interagency cooperation continues even today brought on largely by economic pressures for both public and school library support (Kluever & Finley 2012). In fact, joint-use libraries where facilities, resources, and staff are shared between school and public library programs are particularly prevalent in rural areas. In Texas, for example, Casstevens (2017) found shared facilities were serving communities ranging in size from 300 to 43,000 people. Case examples of other joint-use libraries in the literature largely feature small communities and county-level libraries such as Pungo, Virginia (Lighthart & Spreder 2014) and Stillman Valley, Illinois (Kluever & Finley 2012). The need for cooperation between publicly funded libraries is likely to continue as long as public revenue for library services remains tight and as populations in rural areas continue to decline.

While standards exist for public libraries and school libraries, no such guidance has been developed for joint-use libraries. As a remedy, Casstevens (2017) used a Delphi research method to create a consensus for a proposed set of standards for joint-use libraries in Texas. Likewise, the State Library of Iowa has seen increased interest in school–public library combinations and has developed a guide to assist in decision making where moves to implement joint-use libraries in Iowa communities are under consideration (State Library of Iowa 2006). Some of the issues regarded as crucial to the success of such cooperative arrangements include setting a mission that suits both entities; adherence to the expectations of two decision-making authorities (Board of Trustees/School Board); determining how financing of staff, resources, and services will be shared; how facility access will be managed; what licensure and certifications will be required of staff; how collection development and maintenance will be shared; and how technology access will be handled. Finally, the literature on public and school library sharing on a more limited scale is replete with examples of joint programming, especially cooperative summer reading programs for children and youth (see, e.g., Bogel 2012, or Maughan 2016).

ESTABLISHING SCHOOL LIBRARY SERVICES

While the tendency of individual teachers to prefer to rely on classroom book collections persists to an amazing degree, the potential of a centralized library to enhance the educational environment of the school though reading promotion and direct programs of instruction was realized quite early among leaders of the educational establishment. In fact, the National Education Association (NEA) and the National Council of Teachers of English, in addition to the American Library Association (ALA), helped institutionalize the idea of school libraries through the creation of special school library departments within their organizations. Indeed, it appears that "these professional bodies had a clear vision of what school library service could become long before school libraries were a widespread reality" (Dike 1993, 744). For example, advocacy for school libraries was clearly stated in the NEA's conference proceedings in 1912, which asserted that "the school library will be the proof of the educational value of the new curriculum" (Dike 1993, 744). The rationale for such a move was that the curriculum of contemporary high schools was now so broad that textbooks could not provide what could be offered in the "laboratory" of the library (Hall 1912, 1274, quoted in Cecil & Heaps 1940, 62). Perhaps inevitably, the NEA also supported the creation of classroom collections of age-appropriate books as "the most satisfactory means of forming a taste for good literature" (Coleman 1989, 46) among elementary school students. Although this model sounds unremarkable to contemporary ears, it must have seemed positively revolutionary in schools where teachers relied exclusively on textbooks and grade-level readers as the primary media of instruction. For many years thereafter, a common practice was to house works of literature in the classroom and nonfiction collections in the school library.

20TH-CENTURY EDUCATIONAL DEVELOPMENTS

The first four decades of the 20th century saw a definite educational turning away from more repressive programs anchored in education as discipline, training theory, and rote learning toward a child-centered theory of education based on the principles of active learning. Some educational initiatives founded on these principles included the Gary Plan (derived from the experiential learning ideas of William Albert Wirt [1874–1938] and John Dewey [1859–1952]), the Winnetka Plan, which featured individualized curriculum, and the Dalton Laboratory Plan (created by Helen Parkhurst [1887–1973]), which emphasized the value of individual study. In one way or another, each of these innovative programs placed the school library at the center of the curriculum (Cecil & Heaps 1940).

However, the Certain Report, *Standard Library Organization and Equipment for Secondary Schools of Different Sizes* (NEA & North Central Association of Colleges and Secondary Schools 1920), published by the ALA, enumerated a spate of problems. Specifically, the report noted the lack of resources and a lack of space for collections, staff, and students. Interestingly, the ALA noted the proliferation of managerial and clerical tasks—what Butler (1933) called the "bittiness" of library practice—that often constrained school librarians trying to provide instructional assistance and library services. In response to these shortcomings, the report recommended the establishment of centralized facilities to manage the schools' burgeoning collections of audio/visual equipment and media as well as print materials, run by "professionally trained librarians" charged with the responsibility for organizing and maintaining the whole. Somewhat prophetically, as it turned out, the report stated, in no uncertain terms, that to require librarians to assume clerical tasks was "wasteful of educational resources and money" (Davies 1979, 398). Clearly, the school library's door to instructional opportunity was now open even if its future was not yet assured.

INEQUITIES IN LIBRARY SERVICES

While interest in public education and public libraries early in the 19th century held out the promise of improving the quality of life for many Americans, a significant proportion of the population was being systematically denied access to these public services. Although public education for African Americans was never supported in the South to any great degree, the institutionalization of segregation by the U.S. Supreme Court in *Plessy v. Ferguson* in 1896 ushered in an era of inequality not seen since the days of slavery before the Civil War. In that decision, the Supreme Court established the doctrine of "separate but equal," virtually guaranteeing to black children a substandard education in the same way that literacy requirements and Jim Crow laws passed during Reconstruction had disenfranchised their parents. Thus, while it is safe to say that although many white children in the public schools of the North during this period lacked easy access to books and resources promised by a centralized school library, the obstacles to such access for black children in segregated schools of the South and West were often insurmountable. Where they existed at all, school library collections maintained for black children most often consisted of donated books and frequently the outdated and worn-out castoffs from "white" schools.

After a setback during the Great Depression years, interest in school libraries re-emerged. Private foundations offered some support for school libraries during this period. Notable among these was the Julius Rosenwald Fund, which provided a measure of library funding for black schools in the South through grants to county libraries that could demonstrate equal service for library users of both races (Cecil & Heaps 1940). According to Hanchett (1988), the Fund also provided directly to black schools money to build library collections. Hanchett (1988) writes, "Rosenwald and his fellow philanthropists succeeded magnificently in raising the level of black education in the South. But they failed in their larger goal of promoting equality. Despite the marked improvements in conditions, in 1930 black students were even further behind whites by almost every important measure than they had been in 1915. Though black schools had improved, white boards were improving white facilities much faster" (4). The same was true for school library collections. Hanchett reports that the total expenditure for library books to white schools in South Carolina during the 1925–1926 school year was $26,982.89. Library budgets for black schools during this same year totaled $205.32. Of the 2,330 black elementary schools operating in South Carolina in 1933, fewer than 10 percent had any library books at all; during the same year, more than 60 percent of white elementary schools had a school library. These gifts did little to close the enormous quality gap in public education funding between white and black schools in the South.

Sadly, the disparities across socioeconomic levels and racial lines persist. A 2016 NEA study revealed that substantially fewer schools with the highest level of student poverty (e.g., 75 percent or more students) have school libraries compared to schools with students from middle- and higher-income families (Tuck & Holmes 2016). In the same study, data highlight the racial divide: "Regardless of their poverty level, schools in low ethnic minority status districts have 3.5 to 5 times more librarians per student than do schools in high ethnic minority status districts" (5). To further emphasize this disparity, the study concludes:

> While the study findings show that the poorest students have the least access to certain resources and particularly to librarians, it is clear that ethnic minority status has an even stronger association with student access to library resources than does poverty level (12).

Of further concern are the differences found in information technologies across the socioeconomic and racial divide. Dolan (2016) analyzed the scholarly literature related to technology access and use and found disturbingly persistent differences. While the gap has narrowed regarding school ownership of technology, the ways in which students use that technology reflect important and significant differences that relate to the instruction that might, could, or should occur in schools with strong technology-savvy library programs. Dolan summarizes the findings of several studies when she states:

> A common finding in the research is that students in low-SES schools appear to use computers more, but in ways that are focused on drill and practice (memorization of content) rather than on higher order thinking strategies or production of materials, such as creating websites, research presentations, or spreadsheets. (26)

Clearly, these studies reveal that there is still much work to be done to overcome the disparities evident in American public education today.

LIBRARY STANDARDS FOR PUBLIC SCHOOLS

The effort to create elementary school libraries was advanced with the publication of the *Elementary School Library Standards*, distributed by the ALA in 1925. However, the primary focus was not on instruction but on creating "a new department" that could "assemble and distribute the materials of instruction'" (NEA & ALA, quoted in Gillespie & Spirt 1973, 9). Yet, these standards also stated that "under no circumstances shall the librarian be expected to do clerical work"; rather, he or she is expected to "work in close cooperation with teachers of the school," introducing "children to many kinds of books on many subjects" (Davies 1979, 403–404). In light of these early reports, a number of regional organizations around the nation made school librarianship the focus of their research. For example, school libraries were the subject of an entire yearbook by the NEA's Department of Elementary School Principals in 1933.

PROGRESS TOWARD CENTRALIZATION OF SCHOOL COLLECTIONS

In many locations across the nation, the 1940s and 1950s saw continuous movement in many school districts toward the development of school libraries as separate, centralized facilities, sometimes to augment and sometimes to replace classroom book collections. Furthermore, *School Libraries for Today and Tomorrow*, published by the ALA in 1945, "defined the educational purposes of the library" to "participate effectively in the school program" and called on school librarians to provide instruction in the use of the library and library materials in addition to offering reading guidance. Through these activities, the report suggested, students would "become skillful and discriminating users of libraries and of printed and audio-visual materials" (Davies 1979, 38). Nonetheless, studies during this period continued to show that half the nation's children did not have access to a library in their schools. An even smaller percentage had access to the services of a trained librarian.

Perhaps not surprisingly, much of the research in school libraries undertaken during this time considered book collections, library facilities, and professional staffing as measures of quality. The launching of *Sputnik* by the Russians in the fall of 1957 proved to be a watershed moment in the history of American public education when, for the first time, the national spotlight was trained on the quality of its schools. The thought of having lost the educational edge to a totalitarian regime was especially galling to Americans proud of the country's educated workforce and its informed citizenry. The initial congressional response was the National Defense Education Act in 1958, which offered matching funds to school districts for professional development of staff and the purchase of instructional resources to support curriculum in math, science, languages, and counseling.

In the National Defense Education Act, many saw an opportunity to improve the quantity and quality of school libraries. A policy statement created jointly by the AASL, the Association of College and Research Libraries, and the Department of Audio-Visual Instruction of the NEA, for example, spelled out the prerequisites for school librarians: teaching experience; a multidimensional knowledge base related to learning, curriculum, and guidance; "educational administration and supervision"; "mass communications"; and specialized knowledge related to the evaluation and use of media resources. As Davies (1979) asserts, "This policy statement serve[d] as the 'declaration of independence' for school librarians" in its unequivocal acknowledgment that school librarians must be directly "involved in the teaching and learning process" (368).

THE STANDARDS FOR SCHOOL LIBRARY MEDIA PROGRAMS: A TURNING POINT

In 1960, AASL's *Standards for School Library Media Programs* (AASL 1960) was issued, constituting what Davies (1979) described as the "single most important document in the history of school library development" (38). If the policy statement in 1958 amounted to a "declaration of independence" for school librarians, then the *Standards* constituted an educational "bill of rights" for students. In fact, the *Standards* explicitly recognized the importance of library resources as "the basic tools needed for the purpose of effective teaching and learning" (Davies 1979, 39). The Elementary and Secondary Education Act (Title II) followed in 1965, providing additional funding for materials and facilities. Ironically and shortsightedly, the act lacked a provision for hiring qualified librarians to superintend the selection, acquisition, and organization of library purchases. Nevertheless, government funding for books and equipment throughout the 1960s, together with powerful statements of policy and direction provided by professional organizations, ultimately made it possible for school librarians to reinvent their libraries.

THE KNAPP SCHOOL LIBRARIES PROJECT

Another major event in the 1960s and one that contributed to the proliferation of centralized school libraries was the Knapp School Libraries Project (1963–1968), which created demonstration libraries at 10 selected elementary and high schools. While Knapp's work was aimed primarily at the improvement of bibliographic instruction in academic settings, her insights with regard to integrating library instruction into ongoing course work, planning experiences for learning, and providing practice and problem-solving activities directly related to classroom requirements eventually found their way into elementary and secondary library media programs nationwide (see Chapter 1). To support the rejuvenation of school libraries and to aid in disseminating Knapp's vision for their instructional programs, the Knapp initiative provided funding to reimburse the travel expenses of school teams so that they could attend demonstration sessions. Eventually, this project spawned hundreds of imitators and with it the demand for certified librarians to re-create the project's programs around the country (Gillespie & Spirt 1973).

NEW STANDARDS IN 1969

The move to institutionalize a centralized library facility within the school received another boost in 1969 with the publication of the *Standards for School Media Programs*, which called for the unification of all library and audiovisual services under one administrative unit (Gillespie & Spirt 1973)—a move suggested almost 50 years earlier in the Certain Report, *Standard Library Organization and Equipment for Secondary Schools of Different Sizes* (NEA & North Central Association of Colleges and Secondary Schools [1920]). By 1974, studies reported that 84 percent of the public schools in the country now had centralized library facilities (Carroll 1981). Unfortunately for school libraries, economic conditions during the 1970s created an increasing concern for bottom-line issues and focused the public's attention on all types of public expenditures, educational and otherwise. Turner (1990) maintains that budgetary downsizing during this period not only put pressure on librarians to justify the value of their programs but also quixotically persuaded school districts to promote librarians as regular members of the teaching staff in order to allow them to cover for teachers in the classroom during teacher planning periods. Ironically, these changes paved the way for the introduction of formal programs of library instruction and the creation of library skills curricula.

DEVELOPING INSTRUCTIONAL PROGRAMS

Since the major preoccupation of the early years of the 20th century was the establishment of centralized library collections, it is probably not surprising that widespread acceptance of a teaching role for the school librarian came about slowly. Interestingly, the first paper that dealt specifically with the instruction of schoolchildren in the use of library resources came from outside the field in a speech delivered by T. J. Morgan, the principal of a State Normal School at a meeting of the NEA in Chicago in 1887 (Cecil & Heaps 1940). Even during those early years, a desire was seen to prepare students to be active, engaged members in a democratic society: "preparing the future citizens for successful participation in the social order" (Wilson 1933, 739).

The fact remains, however, that until the 1960s, the delivery of library skills instruction at the high school level was most frequently managed through English classes. Indeed, English textbooks usually devoted a separate chapter to study skills and the use of library resources. In cases where English teachers felt that their lack of expertise in this area made them unequal to the task, school librarians were often recruited for the purpose of explaining the vagaries of library organization and demonstrating the use of available reference books (Carroll 1981). For the most part, these early library lessons tended to make little use of learning theory, and they relied almost exclusively on lectures that "all too often" seemed aimed at making "miniature librarians of the students" (114).

In the aftermath of the civil rights movement and the Vietnam War, the 1960s ushered in a new perspective on the role of the school and its place in the social order, as educators began thinking about learning in new ways. "School," an institution that had for generations been viewed as "a transmitter of the culture," came increasingly to be considered an "agent of change" (Organisation for Economic Co-operation and Development, quoted in Carroll 1981, 23). As reported by the Organisation for Economic Co-operation and Development, an educational shift was occurring, centered on learning how to learn, learning for a lifetime, and making the school "an extension of the community" (23). Within this context, the acquisition of discrete facts was increasingly thought to be a less important learning task than understanding the principles of knowledge or developing attitudes and skills to support independent inquiry. At the same time, schools gradually came under more pressure to make educational practices more equitable and relevant to the culture of the day (Dike 1993). Increasingly, the school library "was seen as offering the variety of materials required to meet individual needs" (Dike 1993, 744).

SCHOOL LIBRARIES AND SCHOOL REFORM

During this same period, a number of educational innovations were being introduced that would have a profound influence on the development of library skills instruction during the next four decades. These included small- and large-group instruction, the introduction of ungraded schools and open classrooms, the concept of team teaching, the idea of continuous progress evaluation, and an expanded use of media in the delivery of instruction (Carroll 1981). Moves to replace the single-teacher, lecture-textbook format with instructional designs that required students to use a variety of resources and pressures to create instructional units that offered an interdisciplinary approach to curricular topics created both opportunities and challenges for school librarians. Collection development, which had been predicated on the public library model of creating a balanced collection, became increasingly a matter of acquiring resources that directly supported school curricula.

At the same time, renewed emphasis on the instructional role of the school librarian was advanced in the AASL's (1975) *Media Programs: District and School*, which described the "media program and personnel [as including] active, direct involvement in the school's instructional program" (Coleman 1989, 48). It was also during this period that administrators began to "demand more objective data to demonstrate the worth of the school library program" (Aaron 1982, 231), and the concern for educational outcomes of instruction began to surface (Gillespie & Spirt 1973). These changes also put pressure on school libraries to systematize instruction by articulating specific educational objectives for their programs.

TEACHING LIBRARY LESSONS

In general, the overall goals of library skills instruction in the 1970s and early 1980s reflected reform initiatives related to making students self-sufficient users of libraries and information sources (Liesener 1985). The format for the delivery of skills instruction in the library took the form, in the elementary grades, of prearranged library sessions. At the junior high and high school levels, however, the subject of library skills was still most frequently taught as a part of English and language arts courses. Of course, informal instruction was also provided as needed to those individual students who came to the library by themselves. At the same time, independent use of the school library was often strictly monitored, with activities limited to research for school reports and book selection for leisure reading.

It must be acknowledged that the model of instruction implemented during this period reflected a much narrower vision of the library's function within the school than is the case today. Typically, library instruction involved a series of sequentially conducted lessons, which were repeated with increasing degrees of complexity at each level from kindergarten through grade 12. Students introduced to skills and resources in the elementary grades were expected to achieve mastery or competence of these skills as they progressed through their school years. Not surprisingly, results of a survey by Hyland (1978) indicated that these skills involved knowledge of the physical facilities, selection of appropriate materials, use of particular types of materials, strategies to improve reading comprehension, and report preparation. Baumbach's (1986) study revealed that, by 1985, 64 percent of state and territorial respondents reported that some sort of "organized curriculum in information skills" (280) was in place. Of these, the overwhelming majority included research skills, resource tool skills, location skills, and literature appreciation.

NEW FOCUS ON STUDENT LEARNING

Important changes in the school libraries' instructional landscape were on the horizon. Thanks in large part to fallout from the "knowledge explosion" (Dike 1993, 744) of the postwar era, a number of practitioners and scholars developed an interest in the concept of information handling and began to explore the relationship between information and learning. For example, teachers in a study by Irving (1978, cited in Carroll 1981) identified learning from library materials or information use as an essential educational outcome for their students. In addition, Irving's research drew attention to task definition as one of the most important information skills that youngsters needed to learn. This emphasis on the student's ability to recognize the need for particular information and its use in the context of specific tasks seemed to echo Willson's (1965) assertion that using information for decision making was a more educationally appropriate goal for instructional intervention than simply teaching the skills necessary to locate and access that information. These ideas and goals have received timely and contemporary support in AASL's 2018 *National School Library Standards for Learners, School Librarians, and School Libraries,* which identifies the role of the school library in "preparing learners for life in an information rich society" (54).

A number of articles published in the late 1970s and early 1980s continued to focus on the need to reform the library curriculum. New approaches in education and library instruction called attention to the importance of considering both the information "user" and the "cognitive environment" of his or her information tasks (Irving 1983, 4). Irving (1980, cited in Carroll 1981) recognized before many in the field that "the development of abilities and skills in thinking" (121) was the ultimate and most valuable outcome of information skills instruction, and Irving recommended placing these information and study skills within a larger framework of information-seeking tasks to make them both relevant and applicable to real-world tasks. Too often, Irving argued, the student's role in learning and information seeking had been overlooked. This approach represented a shift in paradigmatic focus that had also been realized in other areas of library and information science, where scholars were struggling to make theoretical sense of information behavior in general and information seeking in new media (e.g., electronic resources, databases, and networks) in particular.

The idea that librarians needed to help students learn rather than help them find resources to learn—and to focus on the use of library resources to meet educational goals rather than to achieve library goals—represented a significant shift in direction (Carroll 1981). This shift also made inevitable the preeminence of the school librarian's role as teacher and the information skills curriculum as the centerpiece of school librarianship (Turner 1990).

Although Irving's was one of the earliest voices proclaiming the need for a fresh approach to library skills instruction, hers was not the only one. During the same period, Mancall, Aaron, and Walker (1986) urged that thinking skills replace resource-based curriculum as a focus for library skills instruction. In addition, on the basis of her study of cognitive science and developmental psychology, Kulleseid (1986) argued for the inclusion of both affective/emotional and cognitive/rational domains in aspects of the library media program. Inherent in these initiatives was the realization that learning was not a task confined to formal schooling and that teaching required a commitment to students' intellectual growth as well as to skill acquisition. These were new goals, and they called for the development of new strategies and new outcomes (Turner 1990).

THREE NEW ROLES: *INFORMATION POWER*

The roles for school librarians that *Information Power* (1988) unambiguously described were information specialist, teacher, and instructional consultant, conceived as a type of powerful, interacting, and evolving triad. The unique responsibility that librarians were to assume was clearly and succinctly stated as well: "to ensure that students and staff are effective users of ideas and information" (AASL & AECT 1988, 1998). As best practice, *Information Power* called on school librarians to replace fixed-schedule, stand-alone lessons delivered in a predetermined sequence with fully integrated information skills instruction, planned in cooperation with classroom teachers and conducted as needed. Perhaps for the first time, school librarians possessed the power to define themselves and their activities and to develop the vocabulary needed to express clearly the relationship between library instruction and student learning. Indeed, in describing school librarians as dynamic instructional leaders, *Information Power* created a new face for school librarianship, with the goal of helping practitioners (as well as teachers and administrators) put aside old-fashioned and frequently negative stereotypes, thereby gaining a new understanding and appreciation for the educational potential represented by proactive library programming.

Information Power was also a timely reminder that the earlier goals of creating centralized collections, of selecting multimedia resources, and of hiring professional staff had been reached and that it was time for the field to develop a new vision. Inherent, too, was the realization that providing physical access to what Pierce Butler (1933) described as the "communal store" of our culture was a necessary but not sufficient precondition for supporting the personal, social, and intellectual development of the nation's children (Heeks 1997).

PROVING THE VALUE OF LIBRARY SKILLS INSTRUCTION

Many in the profession entertained high hopes that the use of *Information Power* (AASL & AECT 1988) as the first formal manual, primer, and guide for school librarianship—along with the new roles it identified for school librarians—would result in achievement benefits for students. Unfortunately, research studies conducted during the 1980s failed to prove definitively that library skills instruction results in enhanced student competencies and higher grades. Professional disappointment at this turn of events and anxiety created by shrinking budgets and increasing demands for educational accountability initiated a sort of crisis mentality, which has in some ways characterized the school library profession ever since.

Librarians' consternation over the lack of studies that might justify continuing support for their programs had been exacerbated by research that directly challenged the educational efficacy of library skills lessons (Kuhlthau 1987). Anecdotal evidence from the field, which indicated that skills initially taught in elementary school had been insufficiently learned to allow their application to reference tasks in junior and senior high school (Shapiro 1976, cited in Carroll 1981), was substantiated in library and information science research in a variety of contexts. For example, Biggs reported that college freshmen "lack[ed] all but the most rudimentary library skills" (quoted in Kuhlthau 1985, 35), while Dickinson (1981) found that undergraduates lacked sophistication in their understandings of what doing research entailed and "failed to use logical progression and systematic approaches to checking sources of information" (853). Later in the decade, Goodin (1987, 1991) reported that student learning of library skills neither transferred into new settings nor was being applied to the research tasks that these students encountered as college students.

These same conclusions were advanced by Kester (1994), whose study of 300 college freshmen revealed that, although 85 percent of them "had received library instruction in high school" (15), the "instruction appear[ed] to have little carry over or effect" (17). Specifically, Kester's research revealed that students lacked technical skills related to online catalog use and online searching. Perhaps even more compelling were the results of Kuhlthau's (1993b) initial study, which indicated that, in spite of the sincerest efforts of librarians to teach the skills necessary for students to conduct their own research projects, the students themselves approached their research tasks with feelings of dread and frequently did not know how to begin working on their assignments. Additionally, Julien's (1999) study of Canadian adolescents identified several barriers to information seeking that impede high school students' progress, finding that 40 percent of her study participants were unsure where to go to locate information for investigating career paths.

RENEWED FOCUS ON TEACHING AND LEARNING

Although exceedingly disappointing, this research provided evidence for what many librarians had suspected all along: that a scope-and-sequence skills curriculum presented in stand-alone lessons does not translate into information skills children can apply in completing research tasks even when taught every year. But if, as was now evident, the traditional approach was ineffective, what should be introduced in its place? Young and Brennan (1978, cited in Carroll 1981) identified the following as problems that should be addressed: the lack of cooperation between teachers and librarians, poor teaching materials, stand-alone lessons and artificial assignments, failure to provide instruction to meet student needs, and lack of research on strategies to improve practice. Davies (1974) listed as significant barriers to effective student outcomes in information skills programs: the lack of library skills integration, limited time for planning, failure to contribute to curriculum planning or curriculum guides, and teachers' reliance on textbooks.

A NEW VISION FOR A NEW MILLENNIUM

The immediate response of AASL was the creation of an enriched agenda that allows school librarians to set their sights once again on fresh horizons. *Standards for the 21st-Century Learner* (AASL 2007) outlined a set of learner competencies classified as skills, disposition, responsibilities, and self-assessment strategies. The accompanying document, *Empowering Learners*, deepened and extended perceptions of the roles school librarians carry out. Important in this edition was the intent to focus on student learning, delineate the school library program's role in learning, and provide direction and foundation for school librarians.

Acknowledging the challenges imposed on school libraries by the spate of emerging technological innovations common to all information agencies, in 2007 AASL offered a new set of standards and program guidelines. To a certain extent, these represented an effort to look holistically at learners and learning as well as at the competencies that will engage today's young people in the increasingly global information contexts in which they will be living and working. AASL's *Standards for the 21st-Century Learner* (2007) were built on a foundation of common beliefs, learning standards, and strands of learning. They included recommendations for helping students develop "essential skills, dispositions, responsibilities, and self-assessment strategies" within an overall framework of critical and creative thinking, communication, and collaborative problem solving.

Taken together, these standards outlined nine common beliefs about the learning environment:

1. Reading is a window to the world.
2. Inquiry provides a framework for learning.
3. Ethical behavior in the use of information must be taught.
4. Technology skills are crucial for future employment needs.
5. Equitable access is a key component for education.
6. The definition of information literacy has become more complex as resources and technologies have changed.
7. The continuing expansion of information demands that all individuals acquire the thinking skills that will enable them to work on their own.
8. Learning has a social context.
9. School libraries are essential to the development of learning skills. (AASL 2009, 12–13)

Four strands of learning were embedded in the standards: skills, dispositions, responsibilities, and self-assessment. Skills refer to knowledge of process and content that helps learners grow and develop; dispositions are habits of the mind or attitudes that "transform a learner from one who is able to learn to one who actually does learn" (AASL 2007, 15); responsibilities require students to assume ownership of their own learning and adopt an ethical approach to their use of information; and self-assessment requires learners to employ evaluation skills in judging their own work and that of others.

Empowering Learners: Guidelines for School Library Programs

Empowering Learners built on the vision delineated in both editions of *Information Power* (AASL & AECT 1988, 1998). An editing task force was charged with developing guidelines for a 21st-century school media library program (AASL 2009). In light of an increasingly global information context, the task force decided that a reformulation of the AASL's mission was due. The result was a statement that more clearly articulated instructional outcomes:

> The mission of the school library program is to ensure that students and staff are effective users of ideas and information. The school librarian empowers students to be critical thinkers, enthusiastic readers, skillful researchers, and ethical users of information. (AASL 2009, 8)

In addition, school librarians were charged with the following roles:

- Instructional partner who collaborates with educators and students to design and teach engaging learning experiences that meet individual needs;
- Teacher who instructs students to become critical thinkers and skillful researchers using, evaluating, and producing information and ideas through active use of a broad range of appropriate tools, resources, and information technologies;
- Information specialist who provides access to materials in all formats and uses technology tools for finding, assessing, and using information;
- Program administator who provides students and staff with resources that reflect current information needs and that anticipate changes in technology and education;
- Leader who leads the way in bulding 21st-century skills in the total education program and advocates for strong school library programs as essential to meeting local, state, and national educational goals. (AASL 2009)

In a profession intent on remaining relevant and current, AASL began in 2015 to reconsider its standards with an eye to the next edition. Focus groups and member surveys were used to gather input on what the new standards should be. The call came for simplifying and clarifying the standards documentation. Perhaps most significantly, the next version would eliminate the word *guidelines* and instead use the more widely recognized and respected term *standards*.

National School Library Standards for Learners, School Librarians, and School Libraries

The 2018 rewrite of the AASL Standards aimed for a future-oriented emphasis on the iterative nature of inquiry and innovation, the power of collaboration in an increasingly complex information environment, the value of diverse viewpoints, and the importance of creativity in problem solving. In her assessment of the new standards, Gerrity (2018) opines, "What sets these new standards apart is the application towards future learning environments, an increased focus on diversity and inclusion, and the introduction of growth mindset and iterative design" (456). The standards are grounded in six common beliefs that differ somewhat from the beliefs of the previous edition (American Association of School Librarians 2018, 11):

- The school library is a unique and essential part of a learning community;
- Qualified school librarians lead effective school libraries;
- Learners should be prepared for college, career, and life;
- Reading is the core of personal and academic competency;
- Intellectual freedom is every learner's right;
- Information technologies must be appropriately integrated and equitably available.

Consistent with *Empowering Learners,* the 2018 *National Library Standards* retained five roles for teacher librarians as leader, instructional partner, information specialist, teacher, and program administrator. The organizational framework of the 2018 standards, however, differs markedly from previous editions. For example, the standards are structured around six overarching shared foundations, representing core values synthesized into six verbs: inquire, include, collaborate, curate, explore, and engage. Each of these is defined with a statement of commitment that describes its essence. For example, for the shared foundation *inquire,* the key commitment states: "[b]uilds new knowledge by inquiring, thinking critically, identifying problems, and developing strategies for solving problems" (AASL 2018, 68). These statements taken together provide an overarching schema for designing a library curriculum. Learners build competency by progressing through four domains: think, create, share, and grow, which mirror the inquiry process.

In an effort to integrate all perspectives, the standards for learners, standards for librarians, and standards for library programs are all organized around the same framework of shared foundations, key commitments, and domains and competencies. The learner dispositions characterized in the previous edition are embedded within the description of learner competencies; for example, the disposition stated in the earlier edition, "4.2 Display curiosity by pursuing interests through multiple resources" (AASL 2007, 7) becomes "V. C. 1. Expressing curiosity about a topic of personal interest or curricular relevance" (AASL 2018, 38), where it is classified as a competency rather than a disposition. Likewise, the skills, responsibilities, and self-assessment strategies outlined in the 2007 edition tend to be rephrased and embedded within the domains and competencies described in the 2018 edition.

With each succeeding edition, the American Association of School Librarians strives to define expectations within the context of contemporary educational practices. The complexity of the information universe, the value placed on collaboration, the need to express competencies in language consistent with standards across academic disciplines, the iterative nature of research and discovery, and the importance of creativity in problem solving are examples of the contextual realities surrounding the development of the 2018 *National Library Standards*.

STANDARDS FROM THE INTERNATIONAL SOCIETY FOR TECHNOLOGY IN EDUCATION

The history of national standards for school library programs was characterized by collaboration with other educational organizations. For example, the 1969 *Standards for School Libraries* were a collaborative publication with the National Education Association. In 1975, the creation of *Media Programs: District and School* was a joint effort of AASL and the Association for Educational Communication and Technology (AECT), as were both the 1988 and 1998 editions of *Information Power*. In 2007, AASL diverged from this joint effort to publish *Standards for the 21st-Century Learner* and the accompanying *Empowering Learners* independently. As these recent standards have been developed, a parallel process has been under way with the International Society of Technology in Education (ISTE):

> The ISTE Standards are a framework for students, educators, administrators, coaches and computer science educators to rethink education and create innovative learning environments. The standards are helping educators and education leaders worldwide re-engineer schools and classrooms for digital age learning, no matter where they are on the journey to effective edtech integration. (ISTE 2017)

ISTE offers standards for students, educators, instructional coaches, educational leaders, and computer science educators. Clearly, educational technology is the lens through which these standards have been developed. Yet, the student standards reflect many of the same issues evident in the *AASL Standards for Learners* (2018). In the *ISTE Standards for Students* (2016), student outcome indicators are identified for seven dimensions of information technology use: empowered learner, digital citizen, knowledge constructor, innovative designer, computational thinker, creative communicator, and global collaborator. Many of the specific indicators align with AASL's intentions for learners. For example, as knowledge constructors, "[s]tudents critically curate a variety of resources using digital tools to construct knowledge, produce creative artifacts and make meaningful learning experiences for themselves and others" (ISTE 2016). While the emphasis on technology is clear, this is not markedly different from the key commitment defined under the shared foundation *curate* in the AASL standard, expecting learners to "make meaning for oneself and others by collection, organizing, and sharing resources of personal relevance" (AASL 2018, 37).

It is important to note that ISTE's technology focus raises awareness of the need for the library program to address important issues related to technology. Of particular note in the *ISTE Standards for Students* (2016) are digital citizenship, which admonishes students to act safely and responsibly in their digital environment; global collaboration, wherein students use technology to work collaboratively not only locally but also globally; creative communication, using appropriate digital platforms, tools, styles, and formats; and computational thinking, to solve problems in ways that leverage the power of technological methods to develop and test solutions. School librarians will want to make explicit their commitment to these important 21st-century technology-related competencies.

While the expectations for educators are consistent with many of the expectations delineated in the *AASL Standards for School Librarians*, the *ISTE Standards for Educators* (2017) speak in generic terms about educators and do not identify specifically the unique roles of school librarians in developing learners' information literacy competence. It should be noted, however, that ISTE has a librarians' network aimed at promoting librarians as "leaders and champions of educational technology and digital literacy" (ISTE 2017). Perhaps of greatest importance is the fact that two national educational associations have found information literacy of such importance that they have developed independent sets of standards to attend to this knowledge base in preparing students for life in complex information environments.

THE *COMMON CORE STATE STANDARDS*

Educational reforms and movements have always influenced the school library program. In the 1980s and 1990s, the whole language movement called on teachers to engage students in reading "real literature" rather than focusing solely on textbook selections. This direction was a boon for school librarians whose collections were suddenly center stage in reading and language arts programs and whose expertise in the literature for children and youth was highly valued (Naylor, Emdad, & Ward 1994). Emphasis on literature in the library curriculum accompanied this trend, along with the use of informational trade books and investigative skills to access and use information from various sources rather than a single textbook. However, in 2001, the No Child Left Behind (NCLB) legislation rekindled textbook-based instruction, and the centrality of library resources for reading instruction lessened.

Most recently, the publication of the *Common Core State Standards* (2012) has influenced library program development in many school districts. These standards, released in 2010, responded to an ongoing concern that students needed to be college- and career-ready upon graduation from high school and an assumption that this expectation was not being met in all schools. This initiative was headed by the National Governors Association Center for Best Practices and the Council of Chief State School Officers, and 45 states have adopted all or some of the *Common Core State Standards* (Dickinson, Kimmel, & Doll 2015). While the *Core* does not include a set of standards for information literacy per se, the English and Language Arts Standards in the *Core* includes in the Writing Strand proficiencies to research to build knowledge (Common Core State Standards 2012). These proficiencies, while embedded in the Reading and Language Arts Core Curriculum, fit clearly within the definition of information literacy. For example, within the sixth-grade competencies, under *Researching to Build and Present Knowledge,* is the following statement: "Gather relevant information from multiple print and digital sources; assess the credibility of each source; and quote or paraphrase the data and conclusions of others while avoiding plagiarism and providing basic bibliographic information for sources" (CCSS.ELA-LITERACY.W.6.8). In a similar example, the Reading Informational Text strand for eighth grade includes the competency, "Evaluate the advantages and disadvantages of using different mediums (e.g., print or digital text, video, multimedia) to present a particular topic or idea" (CCSS.ELA-LITERACY.RI.8.7).

As with past educational reform movements, it behooves school librarians to embrace the opportunity for enhancing information literacy instruction by integrating the *Common Core* (if adopted by their school districts) into the overall library program, especially in relation to inquiry-based research, reading, and text complexity (Levitov 2014). In this instance, the *Core* and the library instruction program proposed by school library standards align readily to make such integration logical.

FLEXIBLE SCHEDULING

The 2018 *AASL National Library Standards* express support for a flexible, integrated approach to scheduling instruction in the library (AASL 2018, 59). As early as 1965, the library literature contained reports of efforts to end or modify fixed or rigidly scheduled library class sessions and to implement flexible scheduling (e.g., Wert & Pell 1965). While secondary schools have more typically had flexible scheduling and flexible access wherein classes and students visit the library at the point of need, elementary school librarians have typically met regularly with classes of students as one of a variety of "special" classes, which usually includes physical education, music, and art (Moreillon 2014b). One of the earliest studies to gauge the impact of flexible scheduling in elementary schools concluded that, for flexible scheduling to be effective as a model for teaching a library curriculum, it is best implemented in a setting where the librarian and teachers plan collaboratively and where principals hold expectations for implementation of a library curriculum coordinated with the classroom curriculum (van Deusen & Tallman 1994). The study results also supported the idea of creating a mixed or hybrid schedule, wherein school librarians met with some classes, often at primary grade levels, on a regular basis and other classes flexibly at point of need. Indeed, it has become increasingly apparent that the potential benefits inherent in team teaching and collaborative planning cannot be fully realized without some sort of flexible access policy in place to structure library use (Ray 1994). Moreover, the persistence of rigid scheduling in the library is now considered a barrier to student access to information and to point-of-need instruction.

A study focused on principals lends further credence to the importance of their role for effective implementation of flexible scheduling (McGregor 2002). In this study, findings clearly indicated the importance of the principals' understandings with regard to the potential benefits to students when this model is used. In recent years, the effect of the negotiated teacher agreement has made implementation of full flexible scheduling increasingly difficult, as school librarians have been relied upon to provide contracted release time for classroom teachers and thereby have been assigned regular library classes along with other special teachers. Principals in the McGregor study acknowledged the need to address contracted release time for teachers and were creative in ways to identify alternatives to fixed library classes. However, this barrier to flexible scheduling persists in many elementary school settings and continues to require strong administrative support and teacher buy-in to solve it.

DEMONSTRATING OUR VALUE: AN ENDURING DILEMMA

It has always been difficult to estimate the contribution that library skills instruction makes to student learning. A great many variables contribute to student achievement; for this reason, crediting library skills instruction for variance accounted for as measured on standardized achievement tests has proven to be a formidable task. Over the years a number of estimable attempts have been made to provide the sort of statistical evidence that administrators appreciate. Most influential to date among American studies has been the research initiated by Keith Lance and his colleagues, who have completed 10 state studies examining the relationship between school library programs and student achievement (Lance & Kachel 2018). Additional state-level studies by other researchers have added to Lance's extensive work to bring the total number of state studies to 25 and one province (*School Libraries Work!* 2016). These research studies have demonstrated a clear consensus: school libraries are a powerful force in the education of America's children. In fact, the school library is one of the few school entities whose contribution to academic achievement has been documented empirically, and it is a contribution that cannot be explained away by other powerful influences on student performance, such as socioeconomic status, school funding levels, teacher-pupil ratios, or teacher qualifications (Lance & Kachel 2018).

While the research literature on the impact of school libraries on student achievement is large and varied, a few examples included here are instructive. In a Colorado study, Lance and Hofschire (2012) found that schools where licensed school librarian positions were maintained or increased, students performed at an advanced level in reading assessments, and conversely, in schools where positions declined or did not exist, students did not perform as well in reading assessment. In a meta-analysis of state studies on the impact of school libraries (Lance & Kachel 2018), findings revealed a relationship between full-time librarian staffing and student test scores in reading. Researchers have also explored the relationship between high school information literacy instruction and college readiness to meet writing and research expectations. For example, Smalley (2004) undertook a small-scale investigation to study whether students from high schools in a school district that had high school librarians do better in the Information Research course when compared to students from the high schools that do not have librarians. She found that students from schools with librarians performed substantially better in the college course and achieved significantly higher assessment scores.

More studies will, of course, be needed to establish and understand links between instructional models, academic achievement, and lifelong learning. In 2014, a summit funded by the Institute for Museum and Library Studies convened to study the question of causality between student achievement and school library programs. Entitled "Causality: School Libraries and Student Success," the gathering brought together researchers and experts from across the nation to discuss research methodology that might yield significant findings relating student achievement and school library programs (American Association of School Librarians 2014). The outcome of the summit was a three-phase research agenda featuring initial research and theory development, best practices research, and impact research. A challenge for contemporary scholars will be to demonstrate causal relationships between library programs and student success using this agenda as a guide to future research activity.

CONCLUSION

The continuous development and refinement of standards and student learning outcomes stand as evidence that within the library profession, there is a clear vision of the role for libraries in education. However, challenges persist in asserting this agenda across curricula and establishing the importance of information literacy skills and dispositions among educators more generally. While technology provides rapid and broad access to information, it is the intellectual processing of that information that is crucial. The expertise of librarians as information professionals who understand the navigation of today's information environment is often underrated if considered at all. There appears to be a persistent perception on the part of some educators as well as the general public that providing electronic access to information alone creates equity and parity of educational opportunity for all students. It seems quite likely that this misconception will continue until policymakers come to understand and appreciate the cognitive challenges that exist for students operating online, and the complexities involved in information seeking and learning in dynamic information environments. Recent and persistent charges of "fake news" leveled at the media brings into immediate and sharp focus the need for critical reading and listening as everyday news cycle activities may actually help to counter the argument that access to "information" alone is adequate for informed citizenship (Ireland 2018). Indeed, today's unfettered information world underscores the need for a strong information literacy instructional program.

3

The Information Search Process

Kuhlthau's Legacy

The objective of library and information services and systems is to provide access to sources, information, and ideas.

—Kuhlthau (2005)

I continue to believe that there will come a time when educating for information literacy will be integrated firmly into every syllabus, and classroom instruction in the cultures and process of research will be the norm.

—Badke (2019)

In a review of specific approaches to the teaching of library and information skills, Carol C. Kuhlthau (1987) identified three major models in use for instruction in school library settings in the 1970s and 1980s: (1) the source or library tool approach, (2) the pathfinder or search strategy approach, and (3) the process approach. Whereas the source and pathfinder models involved teaching techniques and tools necessary for the completion of research tasks, process models contextualized library skills and reframed them as strategies for critical thinking and problem solving.

MODES OF INSTRUCTION: THE SOURCE APPROACH

The source approach to library and information skills features lessons related to the organization of library materials in a particular setting and the location and use of specific reference books, indexes, and other resources that are available there. This "how-to" approach dates from the earliest days of school libraries and is emphasized in the "scope-and-sequence" types of library skills lessons. Because lessons built on this model are generally site specific and carefully tailored to local sources and local situations, library sessions are relatively easy to plan and conduct. However, this approach has serious limitations. For one thing, it is often difficult to tailor lessons delivered in a pre-planned sequence to the instructional needs of specific individuals or the exigencies of a specific situation. For another, such lessons are conducted in the library outside the flow of ongoing classroom activities in which students are otherwise involved; for this reason, students often fail to see the relevance of what the librarian is trying to teach them. In addition, the practice sessions that ordinarily follow the demonstration of a particular reference resource and its use are basically artificial or "inauthentic" in that they are made up expressly for the purposes of the lesson and taught out of context. Finally, the source model assumes access to a static library collection of preselected print resources; the introduction of research tools in this way does little to prepare students for information seeking outside the context of the specific library or, indeed, in the absence of the specific resources on which the lessons are based.

MODES OF INSTRUCTION: THE PATHFINDER APPROACH

The pathfinder model is a search strategy that requires students to move from an overview or background source, such as an encyclopedia, through a sequence of progressively more specific sources, leading finally to an examination of the most—and presumably the most pertinent—resources. This approach is particularly useful for students who lack content knowledge of a topic because it forces them to investigate the topic holistically before creating a specific focus or thesis statement. It is also useful conceptually, as it serves to introduce students to different types and levels of resources that may be immediately useful to them in completing their projects. However, as Kuhlthau (1987) notes, it is a rather rigid approach and may have limited utility outside academic tasks and school assignments. Nor does the pathfinder approach allow teachers to take account of the cognitive abilities, information needs, learning styles, and information-seeking preferences of individual students. In short, it is a "one-size-fits-all" instructional strategy.

MODES OF INSTRUCTION: THE PROCESS MODELS APPROACH

The source and the pathfinder approaches represent examples of a resource-centered view of library service in that their primary focus is on texts and documents within a specific collection. Process models, on the other hand, consider information skills as pieces of the information-seeking "puzzle" and can be both better understood and more fully applied if they are practiced within a larger framework. The focus thus moves from direct instruction of specific resources to a holistic awareness of processes involved as the seeker progresses toward a curricular goal. Such approaches are specifically user-centered in that they begin with a statement of the information need as articulated by the student. A number of process models for library skills instruction were developed during the 1980s; the best-known models were created by Sheingold (1986),

Callison (1986), and Kuhlthau (1987, 1988a, 1988b). Many of these models rely on inquiry learning, sometimes referred to as discovery learning rather than direct instruction ("receptive learning") (Gordon 2000), and focus the learner's attention as much on the information-seeking "means" as it does on the end product. A major benefit and outcome of teaching this approach is the student's ability to apply understandings of the process across situations, problems, and projects.

Sheingold's Inquiry Model

Sheingold's (1986) approach is an inquiry model based on educational principles derived from cognitive psychology. As such, it places the learner at the center of instructional interest and makes thinking the central outcome. More specifically, Sheingold asserts that a "child's mind is [not] an empty vase into which information is 'poured,'" nor is the library a place where children go to "get" information. Rather, the library is viewed as an "apprentice's workshop for thinking—a place where" children actively construct their own understandings through interactions with "human, physical," and "symbolic worlds" (80). Within the inquiry process, students come to create meaning by relating what they read to what they already know. Sheingold also suggests that, to be meaningful, the questions that drive the inquiry process should address real-world problems (see Table 3.1).

Callison's Free-Inquiry Model

The "free-inquiry" model advanced by Callison (1986) features a library skills instruction plan that is fully integrated into the curriculum, with the teacher

TABLE 3.1   Sheingold's (1986) Elements of a Quality Inquiry Environment

- Inquiry is a complex process that includes:
  1. Formulating a problem or question;
  2. Searching through and/or collecting information to address the problem or question;
  3. Making sense of the information;
  4. Developing an understanding of, point of view about, or "answer" to the question.

- In an effective inquiry environment, students:
  1. Build on their existing knowledge and skills;
  2. Select topics of interest;
  3. Explore a variety of resources (i.e., books, maps, primary source documents, websites, videos, audios, photographs);
  4. Select the best way to communicate their findings;
  5. Share learning with real-world audiences;
  6. Are evaluated on both process and product;
  7. Evaluate themselves, their peers, their resources, and their teachers.

Source: Adapted from http://eduscapes.com/instruction/inquiry/inquiry7.htm.

TABLE 3.2   Elements of Callison's (1986) Free-Inquiry Model

1. Lessons are planned and taught by librarians and teachers acting together.
2. Lesson objectives are evolutionary and negotiated by student and teacher.
3. Students document the processes of learning and share them with others.
4. Content is driven by questions that students raise and answer by exploring resources in the library and beyond.
5. Teachers provide direction for learning, but students are encouraged to take initiatives and work independently.
6. Time for the learning activity is flexible.
7. Peer tutoring is encouraged.
8. Peer interaction and teaming are supported.
9. Projects are shared with peers and parents.
10. Students may choose to extend their learning.

and librarian acting as an instructional team. For this reason, the lessons based on this model require advanced planning and coordination. However, lesson objectives are not prepared in advance; rather, they are created on an individual basis by students and teachers acting together. Evaluation of student performance is also a responsibility shared by instructors and pupils. Based on the work of Victor (1974, cited in Callison, 1986), the elements of the "inquiry approach to teaching and learning" (21) are summarized in Table 3.2.

Essentially, Callison's (1986) inquiry model attempts to move beyond instructional tasks that require the use of library resources to the process of engaging students scientifically through activities that afford them experience in posing their own questions, finding their own answers, and sharing the results with peers, parents, and community members. Information seeking itself is initiated in response to questions that students devise, and answers are sought from human as well as text-based sources. Traditionally, students create logs to document their activities and their reflections on the processes as they unfold. Evaluation of sources—whether located inside or outside the immediate library environment—is stressed. The model specifically emphasizes the interaction between students and librarians, students and teachers, and students and their peers. Finally, the model explicitly encourages students to develop the skills to act independently in finding solutions to the problems posed.

KUHLTHAU'S INFORMATION SEARCH PROCESS MODEL

The most significant contribution to the development of the process approach to teaching and learning in school libraries has been Carol Collier Kuhlthau's (1988a, 1988b, 1993b, 2004) research. As it is the only theoretical model that has been empirically tested, Kuhlthau's information search process (ISP) model represents a watershed in the development of new strategies for library skills instruction. Over the course of 30 years, the model has continued to demonstrate its value "as a theoretical construct for examining information behavior [and] . . . serves as a diagnostic tool for intervention in different information seeking contexts" (Kuhlthau, Maniotes, & Caspari 2007). For this reason, it deserves special attention.

In brief, Kuhlthau's (1991, 1993a, 1993b, 1997) studies track the creation and testing of a model for inquiry-based information seeking. Particularly noteworthy is Kuhlthau's concern for understanding the experience of information seeking from the point of view of student learners and for sharing her findings with professional as well as academic audiences. Her purpose throughout has been to find effective ways to assist students in the information search process—the process of learning from information. For this reason, Kuhlthau's ISP model has found applications in a variety of informational contexts within and beyond the school library.

Kuhlthau's (1991, 1993b, 2004) ISP model was created on the basis of a series of studies conducted over a 10-year period, designed to consider the experience of information seeking from the point of view of the library user. The initial study involved observation of high school students researching topics assigned for a term paper; in subsequent studies, Kuhlthau broadened her sample to include information seeking by informants engaged in a variety of information tasks in school, academic, public, and corporate libraries. In collecting data, Kuhlthau relied on a number of methods, including observation, case studies, individual and focus group interviews, surveys, journals, and student-produced research papers.

Theoretical Underpinnings

In creating a model to fit her observations, Kuhlthau (1993b) drew from theoretical frameworks in psychology, education, information science, and communication. In particular, her research builds on the personal construct theory of George Kelly (1963), the learning theory of John Dewey (1916, 1933), the cognitive theory of Jerome Bruner (1980), information needs theories in the writings of Robert Taylor (1968) and Nicholas Belkin (1980), and the sense-making model created by Brenda Dervin (1983). (The conceptualizations of information needs in the work of Taylor, Belkin, and Dervin are reviewed in Chapter 5.)

Based on her research, Kuhlthau (1991) posited that, in searching for relevant information, seekers pass through six cognitive stages: initiation, selection, exploration, formulation, collection, and presentation. In creating an instructional model, Kuhlthau (1994, 2001) added a seventh stage, assessment; at this step, students are asked to reflect on what they have learned about the research topic as well as about the ISP as a whole (see Figure 3.1). Although the model appears linear as drawn, Kuhlthau argues that, in practice, students engage the stages recursively, moving back and forth between them as the process unfolds. Thus, students may have to repeat activities typical of the earlier steps if, for example, they find that they have insufficiently narrowed the topic or failed to locate information sufficient to solve the research problem, and so forth.

Following Kelly (1963), Kuhlthau (2001) was also interested in tracking students' affective or "feelings" processes as well as their cognitive or "thinking" processes. In so doing, she observed that the feelings of information seekers varied across the course of the ISP, changing from anxiety to optimism, from confusion to clarity, from uncertainty to confidence, and from apprehension

Model of the Information Search Process (ISP)						
	Initiation	Selection	Exploration	Formulation	Collection	Presentation	Assessment
Feelings (Affective)	Uncertainty	Optimism	Confusion Frustration	Clarity	Sense of direction/ confidence	Satisfaction or disappointment	Sense of accomplishment
Thoughts (Cognitive)	Vague ⟶			Focused			Increased self-awareness
					Increased interest		
Actions (Physical)	Seeking relevant information				Seeking pertinent information		
		Exploring			Documenting		

FIGURE 3.1   Kuhlthau's Model of the Information Search Process (from http://wp.comminfo.rutgers.edu/ckuhlthau/information -search-process)

to satisfaction or disappointment. The complexity of information seeking and the difficulties that students encounter in their research investigations, together with the affective discomforts that such activities often create in novice information seekers, convinced Kuhlthau of the need for instructional intervention by school librarians that would provide "guidance in learning from the information they have located" and support for students far "beyond merely leading students to sources."

Verification of Kuhlthau's ISP

Between 2003 and 2005, Kuhlthau was joined by colleagues Todd and Heinström in reviewing ISP-related research as it has been undertaken over time and across contexts; they have considered its continued usefulness as a "pedagogical framework" for understanding information seeking "in new technologically rich information environments" (Kuhlthau, Heinström, & Todd 2008). They also tested the model in a study that tracked the ISP for more than 500 students in grades 6 to 12. Specifically, the researchers sought to observe changes at each stage of the ISP, any interactions between feelings and knowledge construction within "the context of a collaborative inquiry project," and difficulties in searching. The charting of "information-to-knowledge development" was also a research goal. In the study, students reported feelings of "confidence, disappointment, relief, frustration, confusion, optimism, uncertainly, satisfaction and anxiety." Although there were some variations observed, the study verified feelings reported in earlier studies. For students who failed to find a focus, depth of knowledge remained at a specific fact or superficial level; these students also reported negative feelings of "disappointment, frustration, confusion, and uncertainty" during the ISP. "They were relieved at the end but this relief seemed more related to the project completion rather than a sense of accomplishment." In fact, "not all students progressed through the construction process . . . [but] those who did tended to learn the most." Moreover, "students working in digital environments appear to go through the stages to build knowledge of their topics, but the easy availability of information encourages them to skip stages and thus end up with superficial conceptions of their topics." Overall, the authors conclude, "the model continues to be a useful theoretical and explanatory framework for user studies in librarianship and information science." They also found that the most challenging stages in terms of students in the study were those involving prefocus exploration and focus formulation and concluded that intervention would have been most useful and beneficial to students struggling with these activities.

A CLOSER LOOK AT KUHLTHAU'S ISP

Kuhlthau (1993b, 1999, 2004) characterized the first step or stage in the ISP process as task initiation. For students, this stage generally begins with the assignment of a research task or question. Kuhlthau's informants indicated that many students experience this particular phase as a time of uncertainty and/or anxiety, particularly when they lack knowledge of the subject and/or an understanding of how to proceed.

The selection stage of the model is that point in the process when the students identify a question to explore or a topic in which they have an interest. Students generally experience feelings of optimism during this stage. However, Kuhlthau also found these feelings to be short lived, fading at the exploration stage, especially when students begin seeking information on a topic about which they know little. Feelings of confusion are typical because part of the challenge in the exploration stage is to make sense of new information, some of which may conflict with students' prior understandings or preconceived ideas. "As students encounter inconsistent incompatible information that does not match their expectations," Kuhlthau (1997) writes, "they commonly begin to doubt the appropriateness of the topic, the adequacy of the information sources, and their own ability to accomplish the assignment" (713). Kuhlthau has characterized this drop in confidence as "the dip."

The ability to use information obtained in the exploration stage to draw some preliminary conclusions and create personal understandings enables students to create thesis statements and a personal point of view about the topic at focus formulation.[1] Quite logically, Kuhlthau (1997) considers focus formulation the most important task in the ISP, as it is the focus that guides students in determining the pertinence of information later on. Kuhlthau notes as well that students with a clear idea of where they were headed at this stage in the search process displayed an increased interest in both the topic and the project.[2] During the collection stage, the students Kuhlthau studied went confidently about the task of gathering information pertinent to their research topics and centered on their research focus; at the final or presentation stage, as students prepared to organize their information, to make connections among ideas, and to present their work in their chosen formats, they felt relieved that the search was over and either satisfied or disappointed with the search results. Kuhlthau maintained that students' feelings at the end of the process were often directly related to their ability to formulate a personal focus for their projects.

Interestingly, Kuhlthau (1993b, 1997, 2004) found that exploration was a difficult stage for many students. Indeed, impatience with having to do the reading necessary to obtain an overall understanding of the topic sometimes caused students to jump over both exploration and formulation stages entirely and immediately to begin collecting information. Taking time to reflect on information obtained through exploring a topic thoroughly prepares students to create a focus. Unfortunately, as Kuhlthau notes, most information-seeking sessions are not structured to include time for processing information in this way. As noted above, many students confuse exploration (when any topic-related information may seem relevant) with collection (where students should concentrate on making use of information pertinent to their foci). When this happens, students can end up with too much information of a general nature, experience difficulty in deciding what information to use, and consequently have trouble organizing the information in coherent ways. Providing guidance at this stage is extremely helpful to students, especially those in middle school and junior high for whom research as a process may be an entirely novel concept. Kuhlthau suggests two strategies that may help students work through this stage: (1) reading and reflecting and (2) preparing a list of topic-related ideas that are of interest and relevance to the information seeker. Building time for reflecting and formulating while students are exploring and collecting ensures that they will not miss "the critical stages of learning" (Kuhlthau et al. 2008). Indeed, Kuhlthau asserts that when students do not take the time to reflect, their understandings remain at a descriptive level, and they simply do not learn as much.

Kuhlthau's (1997) and Kuhlthau et al.'s (2008) research indicates that individuals experience the ISP variously, moving through the stages of the ISP iteratively and at different rates. Indeed, some fail to complete all the described stages. Studies subsequent to the first one also indicated that the confidence levels experienced by some groups were found to deviate from the model as initially proposed. For example, searchers in public library settings expressed more confidence in the initial stage of the search than those in academic and school settings. By the same token, college searchers expressed more confidence in the outcomes of these projects than did students in the high school studies. This finding suggests that the feelings experienced during the ISP may be a function of both the nature of the task and the experience of the searcher. Furthermore, the seeker's failure to formulate a personal perspective might be the result of the assigned nature of the task or students' assumptions that it is the views of the "authorities" consulted and not their own that should be expressed in presenting the finished project. Finally, Kuhlthau (1997) reports findings that suggest "that younger children experience the search process in similar holistic ways," although those "under the ages of eleven or twelve" tend to be more involved in building a knowledge base than in creating "a personal perspective" and "experience formulation less intentionally than teenagers," perhaps because they lack the developmental structures to engage in abstract thinking (713).

Kuhlthau's (1991) efforts to track four of her original high school informants in a longitudinal study revealed that, as more experienced information users, these students noted "that interest in a topic increases as a search progresses;

that a topic changes as information is gathered; [and] that a central theme evolves as information is gathered" (368). It was also evident that these students felt more in control of the search process and of their projects and developed a kind of personal "sense of ownership" in the process itself as a "way to learn," above and beyond the more pragmatic goals of fulfilling a school assignment. In a very real sense, the search process became a metacognitive device, wherein the student was made aware not only of stages in the ISP but also of the evolution in his or her own thinking about the topic and in the problem-solving process itself.

Kuhlthau's Research "Moods"

Unique to Kuhlthau's (1991, 1993b) work is her consideration of two attitudes or "moods" exhibited by students in her studies, which she labeled "invitational" and "indicative." When information seekers are in an invitational mood, they are open to exploring their topics, and they eagerly seek and consider new ideas, new information, and new information sources. When students decide that they have enough information to meet their research needs, they move into an indicative mood, which allows them to end the search and proceed with the presentation and assessment phases of the process. As Kuhlthau notes, an invitational mood is especially important at the initiation and exploration stages, when students are trying to understand their topics. An indicative mood, which marks the formulation and collection stages, helps students conclude their searches and is especially important when decisions must be made regarding the creation of a thesis. In Kuhlthau's (1997) view, it is essential that school librarians learn to recognize student moods so that they can intercede if students sustain an invitational mood so long that they are unable to decide on a topic or end a search so early that they select a focus without the necessary reflection. An emphasis on location and access skills in information skills instruction may also serve to encourage students to close down prematurely their information-seeking activities before exploring all their options.

Research Based on Kuhlthau's ISP Model

An impressive number of research studies have drawn on Kuhlthau's (1993b, 1997) pioneering study, and the research stream anchored by Kuhlthau's ISP is unprecedented in the school library literature. When considered together, the insights embedded in study findings have not only extended our understandings of the ISP as Kuhlthau originally described it but can also be used by librarians "in the field" to improve and extend both instruction and service.

In an early study, Kuhlthau's (1993b) model served as a guide to the research process for students in a high school science course team taught by a library media specialist and their science teacher (McNally & Kuhlthau 1994). Science topics served as the focus of student research conducted by junior and senior high students in an action research study[3] conducted by Loerke (1994) and a case study by Watson (2003). McGregor's (1994b) research, as well as Pitts's (1995) dissertation, considered mental models, while Swain's (1996) research focused on the searching behaviors of college freshman. Burdick's (1996) study is notable in that it looked at gender issues in information seeking. Six additional studies of information seeking and children that used Kuhlthau's ISP were conducted by Gordon (2000), Broch (2000), Harada (2002), Holliday and Li (2004), Heinström (2006b), and Hyldegård (2009).

In McNally and Kuhlthau (1994), Kuhlthau's ISP was presented to students as an instructional model and guide to information-seeking activities. Students were required to keep a log of their activities and their reactions to their readings, and instructors also used individual conferences to monitor student progress. Instructors found that student journals were especially helpful to students as they attempted to find an individual focus at the formulation stage. In implementing the ISP, the teaching team actively encouraged students to be "invitational" in their approach to the research assignment and "to be open to ideas" (57). At the selection stage, when students were expected to find a topic for their projects, the instructors encouraged students to browse current periodicals and newspapers to gain background information. Researchers found that students experienced confusion as their exploration activities led them to identify scientists, gather factual information, and encounter the vocabulary that would assist them in online searching. Providing an opportunity for students to share their searches with one another also helped students build their confidence and "clarify the direction of their work." Strategies that students found particularly useful involved "expressing their thoughts aloud" (58) as well as hearing that others in the class were experiencing similar difficulties. The collection phase of the ISP provided an opportunity for the librarian and the teacher to "suggest, introduce, and explain sources as needed" (58–59) in the library and beyond; in the presentation stage, the teacher facilitated the process by helping "students organize their notes" in anticipation of creating a final project. Reflection on the process followed, with students being asked to consider their own study skills and thinking as well as their use of time.

In her study, Loerke (1994) applied Kuhlthau's theoretical frameworks and methods in an "action" study of 120 junior high school students involved in a research project that required the use of library resources. Of particular interest to Loerke were the steps taken by student information seekers, their feelings, and the processes they used to focus their topics. Loerke was also interested in identifying or creating intervention strategies that would help students engaged in the process of focusing. In general, Loerke found that, from the beginning, students experienced feelings that mirrored those of the high school students in studies conducted by Kuhlthau (1993b) and McNally and Kuhlthau (1994); initial uncertainty, which gave way to optimism at the point of topic selection, was followed by a period of confusion during prefocus exploration. Confidence increased as the creation of a focus proceeded and students had a "greater sense of where they were going . . . and felt more confident about what they were doing" (24–25).

Watson (2003) also chose a science topic—the typical science fair project—as the focus of her study of stakeholders' perceptions of such assignments. She interviewed three middle school students, their parents, their teachers, the library media specialist at the school, and the local public reference librarian about their perceptions of the same middle school science fair and found that all parties agreed that the purpose of the fair was to teach process rather than content, though some thought the assignment emphasized the organizational process and others the scientific process. The author posits that by devising and employing a "step-by-step" approach in researching, "the assignment does not represent the kind of inquiry that real researchers do in making meaning of the problematic as defined by Kuhlthau" (1997) since this kind of planning limits "the ambiguous nature of constructing meaning and gaining understanding." She recommends that teachers and school librarians design projects that allow "students to pursue ideas that intrigue them enough to investigate" in more personal and individualistic ways, thus allowing for mistakes and wrong turns that "may offer as much information as successful efforts" (10).

Pitts's (1995) dissertation research used a grounded theory approach to investigate the ISPs of grade 10 students whom she considered novice researchers. Students in this study had been assigned a video production project on a science topic of their own choosing. Pitts determined that difficulties students encountered in completing this essentially unstructured research task were related not only to their lack of background knowledge of the subject but also to their lack of mental models to guide their own information seeking and project completion. Their experiential deficits with research projects of this kind led them to rely on familiar topics and prior interests and the convenience and availability of relevant resources. Another reason for project failure was the fact that students did not automatically consider research projects as vehicles for learning course content.

In another study of students' use of mental models, McGregor (1994a, 1994b) looked at the information-seeking behavior of high school students while finding information for school research assignments in the school library, the public library, and home settings. Her conclusions led her to develop a "model of thinking" that confirmed Kuhlthau's assertion of the "non-linear nature of the process" (McGregor 1994b, 72). In addition, her findings indicated that students followed an intuitive path without being aware of the processes they use, that their purposes for thinking could be either external or internal to the information, and that Bloom's (1956) taxonomy accurately described their thinking processes throughout the different stages of research. She also found that the nature of the research question affected the complexity of students' thinking during the information-seeking process.

Swain's (1996) study of college freshmen enrolled in an English class also sheds some light on information seeking and the information search processes of student researchers. Swain tracked students to compare their information-seeking processes with Kuhlthau's (1993b) ISP. Although students' activities in Swain's research mirrored those that Kuhlthau described, there were some interesting variations. For example, Swain's informants were observed to move through the ISP stages of the ISP recursively and frequently in a different order. In addition, they often combined steps.

Burdick's (1996) study involved youth in grades 10 through 12 who were engaged in research activities in their English courses. Citing a report published in 1992 that raised concerns that models generally used to guide research projects and assignments "might favor males" (19), Burdick elected to test this theory through Kuhlthau's (1993b) ISP. Kuhlthau's model essentially assumes a "generic" information searcher. Using an approach to data collection that Kuhlthau designed when investigating the ISP, Burdick explored gender issues particularly as they related to cognitive and affective information-seeking behaviors and to focus formulation, and Burdick found that students demonstrated gender-related differences in their selection of topics, in their searching behaviors, and in the feelings they reported experiencing. (A summary of Burdick's findings related to gender and information seeking appear in Table 3.3.) For example, the girls Burdick observed were "more likely to work together" and were more reflective than were the boys, while the boys were more active in their approaches to research tasks and "less likely" to seek assistance. While Burdick did not include the subject area of the topic as a research variable in the study, the tendency on the part of some girls to prefer affective approaches and some boys' preference for logic suggests that "there might be gender associations with either the information seeking or the subject domain of the class in which the process takes place"

TABLE 3.3   Research-Based Recommendations for Implementing the ISP Model

- Exploration of the topic should be built into the research process; for younger students, the research project should probably come after students have knowledge of subject-specific content or the teacher has provided background information on the topic or topics to be investigated.
- Teachers should discuss the use of journals in which students record their responses to the topics and their thoughts throughout the unit; in this way, students can use their recorded thoughts in selecting a topic and creating a research focus.
- The inclusion of regular checkpoints in structuring research assignments provides opportunities for teachers to monitor student progress in thinking about a topic as well as the research project as a whole.
- Students should have time to share their thinking, their ideas for a focus, and their feelings about the process with peers, teachers, and/or parents—a strategy that will facilitate conversations and make them more focused and productive.
- The structure of ISP tasks should include times for reading and reflection.
- Students should be encouraged to find personal links to research topics; where their thinking may be at concrete rather than abstract levels, student interest and enthusiasm might increase if they are able to select topics with which they have some prior knowledge or experience.
- The development of a focus is essential before students are allowed to move into the collection phase of the ISP; however, the focus may change during the process.
- Student research projects should allow for student individualization of the ISP. Insights and deep learning may result when students are permitted to experiment and devise strategies on their own rather than being made to follow a predetermined one-size-fits-all step-by-step research model.
- Motivating students at the outset of the information-seeking activity will help ensure sustained searching and deeper learning.
- Because students prefer searching for information through Google and Wikipedia, school librarians should teach students the critical thinking skills necessary to evaluate online information and show them the value of using online databases.

(21). In addition, study results provided some evidence that "girls chose topics about either males or females," while "males chose topics only about males."

In terms of student perceptions of the information-seeking tasks, girls in Burdick's (1996) study emphasized the exploration and formulation stages of the ISP, while boys showed more interest in collecting materials and completing the assignment. However, both boys and girls considered the completion of the assignment to be more important than the creation of a focus. Burdick's research also revealed that boys were less tentative than girls about "expressing a personal perspective" (22). While this quality may reflect gender differences related to self-confidence, Burdick suggests that there may also be developmental characteristics that have a bearing on students' abilities to formulate personal points of view, as in, for instance, whether students consider knowledge as something that is "given" or something that is "constructed."

Gordon's (2000) small study of grade 10 science students used Kuhlthau's ISP framework with special attention to task initiation and prefocus exploration. Using "think-alouds, interviews, and journals" as data sources, Gordon's quasi-experimental study compared searching efficiency and effectiveness of two groups, one of which had received direct instruction in concept mapping as a presearch activity and one of which had not. Interestingly, the concept mappers made greater use of print indexes in planning electronic searches and came to understand the dimensions and structure of their topics through their exposure to hierarchical arrangement of such topics and subtopics in indexes and in cross-references. The control group, on the other hand, immediately chose electronic searching as an information-seeking strategy, relying on key words. As a group, they were less able to determine the relevance of articles found and ultimately spent more time in searching than did the concept mappers. Other benefits of concept mapping for students included the ability to maintain their foci while searching, improved capacity to "relate new information to what they already knew to be meaningful," and greater gains in background knowledge important for successful focus formulation and information gathering.

In 2000, Broch reviewed the literature on children's use of the Internet as it related to each stage of Kuhlthau's ISP model. She determined that cognitive immaturity in terms of recalling prior searches and terms hampered their ability to modify their searches, while deficits in keyboarding skills, search term selection, sophisticated vocabulary, and Boolean logic led her to conclude that "some of the obstacles that Kuhlthau observed in information seeking are in fact potentially more burdensome on the web." Quoting Fidel et al. (1999), Broch noted that success at task initiation was compromised when students' faith in the Internet led them to conclude "that there was no need to plan ahead" and to rely on search results to guide subsequent searching activities. Searching in this way returned so many citations that students had a terrible time selecting a topic at all and were frequently distracted by the presentation of so many alternatives. By the same token, the easy availability of information was frequently used as the criterion for topic selection rather than any genuine interest on the part of students. "On the web," Broch opined, "it is almost impossible not to collect too much information."

If Broch's (2000) students experienced considerable difficulty selecting a topic, finding a focus at the formulation stage was equally problematic. This led Broch to conclude that efforts to locate pertinent sources replaced the thinking activities that one assumes will occur at this step, undermining the learning that is built in when one is asked to create a personal perspective. So too, at the presentation stage, the creation of the final report often defaulted to a cut-and-paste assembly of information from the sources chosen and the absence of any sort of individual understanding.

Harada (2002) used Kuhlthau's model as a framework for an action research study that looked at the utility of student journals in tracking thoughts, feelings, and actions of elementary school children aged 10 to 11 involved in a complex information-seeking task that grew out of content covered in the classroom. In order to understand the problems and feelings experienced by the children, the researcher used student journals, librarian logs, researcher observations, and teacher interviews.

Before beginning the information-seeking activities, the ISP model was presented as a useful approach to the task. However, students became confused at the exploration and collection stages of the ISP, and it became clear that additional instructional interventions would be necessary. To this end, a wall mural was created that provided a visual of the ISP process, and charts and discussion were also used as aids to understanding. As with students in the Pitts (1995) study, the student's lack of mental models led many to admit in their journals that they did not know "what they were doing." Having students create their own diagrams of the process later proved a useful strategy in addressing this issue, at least for the duration of the project. The actual internalization of the process by the students proved elusive, however, but journal keeping was shown to allow the teacher to assess the learning and plan appropriate interventions.

In 2004, Holliday and Li replicated Kuhlthau's research in an effort to understand the information-seeking behaviors of Millennials. In their study, Holliday and Li observed that students replicated behavior of students observed by Broch (2000) in choosing their topics based on quantity of information that was immediately available to them rather than on personal interest. In addition, these researchers found that students were also less interested in learning outcomes than they were in just completing the assigned task. Another finding was that having full texts of articles available online also resulted in less note taking on the part of students. According to Holliday and Li, "The students who do not go through all the stages of the model, especially focus formulation, have more difficulty conducting research and experience more uncertainty and frustration." They also noted that some students in their study "skipped altogether" a number of the steps, notably focus formulation, and "stopped searching for information in the prefocus stage and built their papers and bibliographies from what they had at hand" (364). Students noted frustration as well when they discovered "that research was not as easy or as seamless as they expected it to be" (363). Finally, students in the study appeared to represent the characteristics noted for Millennials in terms of reliance on the Internet and electronic resources and a "just-enough" rather than an exhaustive approach in searching for information.

Heinström (2006b) used Kuhlthau's ISP to study the information seeking of middle school students and the roles played by motivation (extrinsic and intrinsic) and intention (deep learning or task completion) in their searching behavior. She labeled the searching styles as "fast surfers" and "deep divers." Students this researcher characterized as deep divers tended to be intrinsically motivated to seek information because of an interest in what they were learning and were willing to keep a search open long enough to locate and examine information documents for use in obtaining deep understandings of the topic. Heinström also noted that for some students, the search strategies themselves were also compelling. These students made note of the processes involved in information seeking and evinced an interest in information handling that went beyond the skill level. "Extrinsically motivated students," on the other hand, "tended to adopt a surface approach to studying," relying heavily on the "reproduction of information through rote learning" and consulting "information sources only because they were required to do so" (1442). These students sought and used pieces of information to fill knowledge gaps rather than appreciating single items or documents as stepping-stones to more holistic understandings. Additionally, fast surfers were observed to put forth minimal effort, being preoccupied with task completion and using only the most readily available sources. In terms of Kuhlthau's moods, Heinström noted that motivation determined whether a student stayed in an invitational mood long enough to comprehend a topic or whether the student moved to an indicative mood, narrowing the search to bring the project to a swifter conclusion.

Hyldegård (2009) found that the ISP model was less useful in understanding the experiences of graduate students when seeking information as members of a small group. Using questionnaires, journals, and interviews to capture informants' experiences, Hyldegård explored collaborative projects, concluding that affective responses they reported were based on the motivation and expectations of individual group members rather than the group as a whole. While the study tended to confirm the general outline of the ISP, many participants continued to experience feelings of uncertainty and frustration no matter the outcome. Echoing Burdick (1996), Hyldegård's research seemed to suggest that contextual and social factors also play a role in information seeking not accounted for in the ISP.

Suggestions from the research studies based on Kuhlthau's model are summarized in Table 3.3.

ISP IN THE 21ST CENTURY

An article by Kuhlthau, Heinström, and Todd in *Information Research,* published in 2008, provided an opportunity for Kuhlthau herself to consider the efficacy of a 20th-century-based research process to a 21st-century "information environment," taking into account the findings in a number of the studies reviewed above and based on qualitative and quantitative data from a study of Millennials' seeking information within the context of digital technologies. The authors were reaffirmed in their confidence in the validity of the original ISP model to describe information seeking and use by students involved in constructing new knowledge in response to the demands of complex tasks and searches, as an instructional medium for guiding searching activities, and as an intervention model for diagnosing the process needs of students and pinpointing times and spaces for instructional focus. In addition, they assert that the model applies when researching involves both traditional and digital resources and venues (Branch 2003). However, improved access to Internet resources and the seemingly instantaneous information available has "changed students' conceptions of the research process, in that they expect to find information quickly and without effort" (Kuhlthau et al. 2008, 45).

Little (2012) also found that students preferred the ease of accessing information online through sources such as Google and Wikipedia, rather than subscription library online databases (Little 2012). "Unless instructed otherwise, students seem to abide by [the] principle of least effort when searching for information to use in their coursework and rely on free online websites that they located using a search engine" (Colon-Aguirre & Fleming-May 2012, 396). It is from this research that the authors determined school librarians should be responsible for teaching students the critical thinking skills necessary to evaluate online information. Results of a study by Todorinova (2015) also indicate the school librarian needs to take on the role of "information literacy educators" to ensure students have the skills needed to determine the credibility of online resources (211).

KUHLTHAU'S INTERVENTION MODEL: TAXONOMY OF SERVICE ASSISTANCE

Kuhlthau's research has contributed many insights to our understanding of the ISP and knowledge of how students learn from information. The fact that students not only need but also welcome such assistance, support, and encouragement, particularly during the initial stages of the ISP, is also an important finding (Kuhlthau 1993b). And this begs a number of important questions for school librarians. How can this intervention best be provided? When and what kinds of assistance would be most helpful? To address these questions, Kuhlthau created the "taxonomy" of assistance, which can serve to guide school librarians in providing instructional and emotional support for students involved in the ISP. In this way, it is hoped that students and librarians will come to understand that assistance is appropriate and necessary in providing intellectual as well as physical access to information resources.

The Theoretical Basis for Service Intervention

In building a model to guide instructional intervention levels in support of information seekers, Kuhlthau turned to the work of Lev Vygotsky (1896–1934), especially the construct of his theory of zones of proximal development. In Vygotsky's (1978) view, there are certain moments in the child's development when instruction is most effective, that is, times during which the child's cognitive elaboration is most likely to occur. Vygotsky called these moments "zones of proximal development." Specifically, each zone creates an instructional space that represents "the distance between" a child's actual "level of development as an independent problem solver and [his or her] potential level of development" (86). At the lower, or actual level, problem solving is achieved by the child working independently, and at the upper, or potential, level, the child can perform more difficult tasks with assistance provided by a more knowledgeable partner.

Vygotsky (1978) believed that through careful observation of a child's present level of functioning, a perceptive teacher should be able to identify, plan, and support learning activities to match each child's proximal zone. For example, the teacher first sets a goal and provides scaffolding in the form of directions, demonstrations, and strategies that the child can use in reaching the goal and then guides the child in enacting the activity. When this initial goal is reached, the teacher offers a new and more difficult one. The central mechanism of learning in such an approach is the transfer of responsibility from the teacher (or more knowledgeable partner) to the child as learning occurs and the task is completed. As the lesson proceeds, the teacher gradually eliminates the supportive explanations, hints, and demonstrations until, in the end, the skill is performed by the child alone. At this point, the child's newly internalized skill acquires its individual character and constitutes the new actual level of development—the foundational level for a new proximal zone. In this context, the teaching is dynamic and reciprocal, a negotiated division of labor aimed at increasing the learner's share of the burden for the attainment of the goal. Thus, in Vygotsky's view, the child does not alone possess a zone of proximal development (e.g., a set level of achievement or an IQ score) but rather shares one with his or her instructor.

Kuhlthau (1993b) has suggested five roles for library media specialists based on a taxonomy of five levels of intervention. These roles and levels are summarized in Figure 3.2 as organizer, lecturer, instructor, tutor, and counselor. The range of intervention techniques that Kuhlthau has devised are based on the "physician/patient interaction" model frequently used by medical professionals in choosing appropriate treatment levels (Kuhlthau 1993b, 156).

Inquiry Learning: A New Framework for Information Literacy Instruction

According to its proponents, inquiry learning centers on the research process (Kuhlthau 2001) but mimics real-life contexts where learners consider problems, develop strategies, and seek solutions. Donham et al. (2001) suggested that "[f]or children to own their own learning, they need to own their own questions" (vii); these include "What do I already know? What questions do I have? How do I find out? And finally, what did I learn?" (Kuhlthau 2001, 1). Kuhlthau continues, "Inquiry takes students out of the predigested format of the textbook and rote memorization into the process of learning from a variety of sources to construct their own understandings" (1). In short, "inquiry learning enables students to meaningfully accomplish the objectives of the curriculum by preparing them for living and learning in the world outside of the

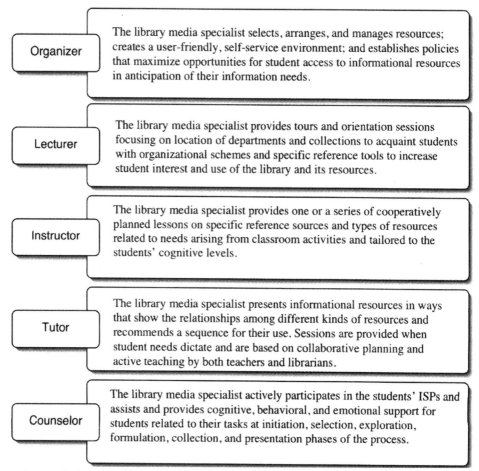

Organizer	The library media specialist selects, arranges, and manages resources; creates a user-friendly, self-service environment; and establishes policies that maximize opportunities for student access to informational resources in anticipation of their information needs.
Lecturer	The library media specialist provides tours and orientation sessions focusing on location of departments and collections to acquaint students with organizational schemes and specific reference tools to increase student interest and use of the library and its resources.
Instructor	The library media specialist provides one or a series of cooperatively planned lessons on specific reference sources and types of resources related to needs arising from classroom activities and tailored to the students' cognitive levels.
Tutor	The library media specialist presents informational resources in ways that show the relationships among different kinds of resources and recommends a sequence for their use. Sessions are provided when student needs dictate and are based on collaborative planning and active teaching by both teachers and librarians.
Counselor	The library media specialist actively participates in the students' ISPs and assists and provides cognitive, behavioral, and emotional support for students related to their tasks at initiation, selection, exploration, formulation, collection, and presentation phases of the process.

FIGURE 3.2 Kuhlthau's (1993b) Assistance Levels Available to Students during an ISP

school" (8). The emphasis on sharing what children learn "with others in the community" (9) sets inquiry-based learning apart from product-centered research projects. "Children as creators as well as consumers of online information products once seen as term papers exhibits or experiments, may now be shared in paperless fashion" (Bilal & Watson 1998).

THE IMPACT OF ONLINE RESOURCES

Since the 1990s, library and information science researchers have marked the revolution in information seeking made possible by increased access to the Internet. Mancall, Lodish, and Springer (1992) believe that online resources create authentic contexts for learning because their use replicates real-world complexities and provides access to perspectives and viewpoints that stretch students and encourage them to think critically. The availability of online resources in school libraries has also created opportunities for independent learning (Peck & Dorricott 1994). For example, Woronov's (1994) research indicates that computers have been useful in "supporting inquiry-based science teaching, inclusion of students with disabilities in regular classes, inter-district collaboration, [and] distance learning" (1). The potential that information skills and technological access provide for enabling students to engage in "active, self-directed learning" has also been noted by Kafai and Bates (1997, 104). Indeed, in Morton's (1996) view, access to technological resources provides students with an unparalleled opportunity to exercise critical thinking, create their own perspectives, and take charge of their own learning in ways that make computers "interactive learning extensions of the children themselves" (417).

Irving's (1990) study also confirmed that online resources facilitated children's independent pursuit of academic topics of individual interest, observing that their use provided information for personal decision making when the library's own collection offered little support. Since independently conducted activities allowed students a unique opportunity to control many aspects of their own learning, Bialo and Sivin-Kachala (1996) suggest that the use of electronic resources will enhance both the self-confidence and the self-esteem of students. In addition, Mendrinos (1994) reported that where resource-based learning initiatives were combined with electronic resources, students reported being able to exert a measure of control in meeting curricular objectives. In Irving's (1990) study, this sense of ownership seemed to arise from the children's ability to download information they themselves chose.

Making students aware of the possibility if not the likelihood of accessing information online that is false and/or created by unethical news websites is critical in an age when many adults as well as students rely on Google and Wikipedia as their primary sources of news and information. Students must also be aware of their own tendency to subscribe to confirmation bias, which can be defined as choosing and using only that information that supports one's own preexisting personal beliefs and biases. By teaching students to recognize both political and conformational bias, young researchers will be able to develop a personal awareness and begin to read sources strategically so as to become better consumers of information. As Wittebols (2016) suggests, "By building 'good habits' of assessing websites and news media, students become critical consumers of information in an information saturated world" (11).

GUIDED INQUIRY LEARNING: MOVING BEYOND THE ISP

Kuhlthau and her colleagues have paid increasing attention to the uses of a guided inquiry approach to teaching and learning (see Kuhlthau, Maniotes, & Caspari's monograph, *Guided Inquiry: Learning in the 21st Century*, published in 2007 and second edition in 2015). "In guided inquiry students are seen as active agents in construction of their own personal topical comprehension. This view of learning includes motivation and emotion as vital for lasting knowledge construction" (Heinström 2006a; Kuhlthau & Todd 2005a). A key concept in guided inquiry is "transformation," when a student's understanding of a topic translates into knowledge at a deeper level. The relationship between guided inquiry and information literacy is clear: guided inquiry effectively moves the teaching of information literacy skills to a higher level, instructing students to go beyond managing and analyzing information to the transformative level of understanding. As Heinström notes, guided inquiry casts learning in a "broader perspective . . . where 'students actively engage with diverse and often conflicting sources of information and ideas to discover new ones, to build new understandings, and to develop personal viewpoints and perspectives'" (Kuhlthau & Todd 2005a). It is widely held that the projects related to guided inquiry help students develop content knowledge as well as information literacy skills.

In a 2018 qualitative study by Garrison, FitzGerald, and Sheerman (2018), researchers looked at student perceptions of the guided inquiry process. Data collected through focus groups and survey questionnaires revealed that through guided inquiry, students liked the engagement and "independent nature, structure and pace, and focus on choice" (Garrison et al. 2018, 15). Students in the study also said that although they liked the independence, they still wanted the instructor or librarian to guide the inquiry, so they did the research correctly. It was revealed that young researchers felt unsure of their inquiry skills causing them to be anxious and insecure during the research project. Additional results from Garrison et al.'s study suggest that "students should be allowed to progress at their own rates" when engaged in guided inquiry (17).

Third Space

Perhaps the most compelling new building block for ISP work previously carried out by Kuhlthau et al. (2007), however, is the notion of "third space." The knowledge and nurturing of this concept lays the foundation for learners to successfully use the guided inquiry (GI) model. Developed for the ISP model from previous work by Maniotes (2005), third space represents the merging of first space (an individual's varied life experiences outside the school setting) and second space (the curriculum content of the classroom) (Kuhlthau et al. 2007, 31). Other researchers have also studied the concept of third space, especially in the area of discourse, as a way to examine the blending of informal and formal talk between teachers and students.[4] It is interesting to note that hints of third space can be seen in Dewey's (1915) discussions of the function of the school in the child's social life. Writing over a century ago, Dewey opined: "We all know how self-centered the little child is . . . his horizon is not large; an experience must come immediately home for him, if he is to be sufficiently interested to relate it to others" (18).

Tapping into Dewey's "organic connection," Kuhlthau et al. (2007) explained that inquiry for learning naturally includes all the worlds that the child inhabits. "Through this approach, what students learn in school helps them to understand what they then experience outside of school. And their outside experience is called upon to help them make sense of what they are learning in school" (30).[5]

The concept of third space specifically advances the GI model, helping students make sense and gain understanding as they encounter materials and ideas that they may then construe as part of their evolving schema. Within the model, Kuhlthau et al. (2007, 32) uses dotted lines to represent permeable boundaries wherein students cognitively (and verbally) cross the lines that separate aspects of their lives as they constantly reconstruct their worldviews within the hybrid classroom environment (see Figure 3.3). Essential to the success of this model are attitudes displayed by teachers and librarians as well as informal and formalized language structures.

The power of the ISP and GI models is demonstrated when digital age students, working with instructors, call upon prior knowledge as they encounter new information to reconstruct understandings and to create meaning in their worlds. Strategies that set the stage for and encourage these reconstructions are outlined in the GI model and include a reiteration of Kuhlthau's (1995) early recommendations for instructional strategies: collaborating, continuing, conversing, composing, and charting.[6]

The idea of learning in isolation is inconsistent with what we know about young learners today. If teachers can provide and nurture environments where the third space concept can flourish, might not their students also learn from the knowledge bases and new co-constructions articulated by one another? Todd (2008b) likens this setting to a "brave new world" and tells us that the school library is a place that provides "exciting opportunities for school librarians and classroom teachers to re-imagine the information-to-knowledge landscape for young people and chart meaningful approaches to instruction and information services" (32). A constructivist learning environment such as this demands collaboration between the classroom teacher and school librarian as

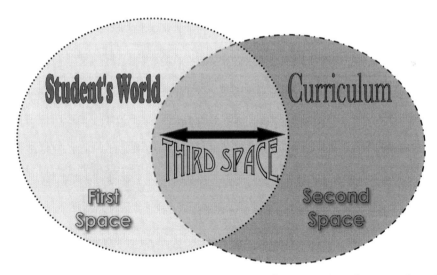

student centered <-------- learning centered -------> teacher centered

FIGURE 3.3   Guided Inquiry Model and Third Space (from Kuhlthau, C. C., Maniotes, L. K., & Casparti, A. K. [2007, 2015]. *Guided Inquiry: Learning in the 21st Century*. Westport, CT: Libraries Unlimited)

they pay attention to individual student learning needs while working through the inquiry process (Kuhlthau & Maniotes 2010).

Guided Inquiry: The Team Approach

Because of the complex nature of the inquiry process, Kuhlthau and Maniotes (2010) recommend that a team of educators lead students in the personalized process of ISP. This team should include the "school librarian who serves as the resource specialist, information literacy teacher and collaborator" (Kuhlthau & Maniotes 2010, 18). Along with the school librarian and classroom teacher, the GI teams should include at least one other educator, such as the learning specialist, literacy coach, gifted coordinator, tech specialist, or special education resource educator. "Three-member teams provide a synergy of ideas for developing inquiry learning" (Kuhlthau & Maniotes 2010, 19).

There is some research to show the value of using a team approach when utilizing the GI model, especially with regard to improving both student enthusiasm and searching competencies (Saunders-Stewart, Gyles, Shore, & Bracewell 2015). Saunders-Steward et al.'s study focused on student perceptions of inquiry when guided by teams of educators, finding that students were more engaged and felt they increased their knowledge and skills development in the process. Students also identified increased intrinsic motivation and a sense of autonomy with regard to their own learning. In short, "[t]he most student-centered, open-ended forms of inquiry observed in this study were able to motivate high school students to attend and invest in school, to want to learn and to employ high-level strategies to do their best" (308).

The National School Library Standards (2018) Feature Inquiry

Released in 2018, the new National School Library Standards' AASL Framework for Learners includes inquiry as one of the shared foundations of learning that supports the cognitive domains of think, create, share, and grow. In the shared foundation of inquiry, the key commitment is to "[b]uild new knowledge by inquiring, thinking critically, identifying problems and developing strategies for solving problems" (AASL 2018, 34). The AASL Framework for Learners identifies the domain and competencies for inquiry as:

- Think: Learners display curiosity and initiative by:
  1. Formulating questions about a personal interest or a curricular topic;
  2. Recalling prior and background knowledge as context for new meaning.
- Create: Learners engage with new knowledge by following a process that includes:
  1. Using evidence to investigate questions;
  2. Devising and implementing a plan to fill knowledge gaps;

3. Generating products that illustrate learning.
- Share: Learners adapt, communicate, and exchange learning products with others in a cycle that includes:
  1. Interacting with content presented by others;
  2. Providing constructive feedback;
  3. Acting on feedback to improve;
  4. Sharing products with an authentic audience.
- Grow: Learners participate in an ongoing inquiry-based process by:
  1. Continually seeking knowledge;
  2. Engaging in sustained inquiry;
  3. Enacting new understanding through real-world connections;
  4. Using reflection to guide informed decisions. (AASL 2018, 34)

National School Library Standards: AASL Standards Framework for Learners by the American Association of School Librarians, a division of the American Library Association, copyright © 2018 American Library Association. Available for download at www.standards.aasl.org. Used with permission.

AASL states that like other professional national learning standards, this framework does not constitute a curriculum, but rather can be integrated into instruction when targeting particular competencies. School librarians are the key to increased academic achievement as they collaborate with classroom educators to model and facilitate the inquiry process in learning (AASL 2018).

ALTERNATIVE FRAMEWORKS FOR PROCESS INSTRUCTION

Since the mid-1980s, a number of school librarians and library and information scholars have developed process models for use in teaching information literacy skills. These models are based on the experiences of practicing librarians and designed to improve the educational value of the kinds of information-seeking activities typically assigned in the classroom. Taken together, these models constitute a nexus of effective alternatives to stand-alone library "lessons," especially when they are aligned directly with classroom curriculum and delivered in response to students' immediate instructional needs.

As discussed previously, Kuhlthau's (1993b) information search process model is a seminal work that grew out of her observations of high school students involved in a complex research task. It is also the first model that explicitly acknowledged the "holistic" nature of information seeking, dealing directly with thoughts, feelings, and actions (Kuhlthau 1999). Kuhlthau's original ISP model described the search process itself, specifically that portion of research activity beginning at the initiation of the assignment and ending at the point when students are ready to organize their information and begin writing. The addition of an evaluation step made the model more comprehensive in its application.

Over time, a number of other process models have been created to provide more comprehensive guidance for students in completing school-based assignments. All of them are instructional in nature (Bates 1979); that is, they suggest an "effective practice" for students as they engage in information seeking and research projects, and all emphasize a "higher-order" of critical thinking skills and inquiry strategies. For this reason, school librarians, teachers, and students may find any or all of them useful at different times and under different conditions, depending on the context, the task or problem, and the student or students involved. Among the best known of these are the term paper and Stripling Model of Inquiry (Small et al. 2012), REACTS models created by Stripling and Pitts (1988), and Joyce and Tallman's (1997) I-Search model. As noted, both of these models provide a framework for research projects in their entirety, covering the writing of a paper or the creation of a project as well as the information-seeking processes that precede it.

Although the process approach proposed by Eisenberg and Berkowitz (1990) can also be applied to research paper projects, these authors believe that their models have applications beyond school-based student research. Eisenberg and Berkowitz regard their Big6 Skills model as flexible enough to use in many kinds of everyday decision making.

As with the reports of the research studies explored in this book, the descriptions of the models below are meant as introductions to the authors' ideas and frameworks and invitations to further reading. Full accounts of each model can provide school librarians and teachers with valuable strategies, and several also include lesson plans to extend understanding and suggest appropriate applications. For these reasons, readers are urged to read Eisenberg and Berkowitz's resources and materials at https://thebig6.org/resources-2; Stripling and Pitts's (1988) *Brainstorms and Blueprints: Teaching Library Research as a Thinking Process*; Small, Arnone, Stripling, and Berger's (2012) *Teaching for Inquiry: Engaging the Learner Within*; and Joyce and Tallman's (1997, 2006) *Making the Writing and Research Connection with the I-Search Process*.

Eisenberg and Berkowitz's Big6 Skills[7]

Eisenberg and Berkowitz's (1990) Big6 Skills is an instructional model currently being used by thousands of school librarians worldwide and "is a central focus of information literacy instruction on the K–12 level" (Newell 2010) in American school districts. Since it provides a straightforward summary of activities related to information seeking and project completion, the Big6 serves as an extremely user-friendly approach to what are often extremely complex tasks. Big6 creators emphasize the model's utility for teaching technology skills (Eisenberg, Johnson, & Berkowitz 2010) and have studied its application in academic settings (Cottrell & Eisenberg 2001).

According to Eisenberg and Berkowitz (1990, 1996), student assignments that require the use of multiple informational resources are essentially information "problems," which can be resolved through a systematic process of thinking about the task at hand, the activities and resources required for task completion, and the nature of and expectations about the project or product involved. For this reason, the Big6 works well as a cross-situational model in that the same process can be used for real-world decision making as well as for school reports and projects (see Berkowitz & Serim 2002; Eisenberg & Berkowitz 1996).

Essentially, the Big6 Skills approach ties cognitive levels (Bloom 1956) to various stages of the information-seeking process by identifying needs (knowledge level), relating resources to aspects of the problem (comprehension level), selecting channels and sources (application level), identifying salient elements within and across information sources (analysis level), restructuring and communicating information (synthesis level), and making judgments about the information obtained "in relation to specific needs" (evaluation level) (Eisenberg & Berkowitz 1990, 12). In effect, the model calls for application of a six-step strategy that requires students to define the task that has been set for them and the expectations in terms of the quantity and quality of the product that they will produce; select strategies and resources for finding the information they are going to need; locate and access relevant and appropriate information resources; use the information by "engaging" or extracting it through reading, note taking, and highlighting and by determining its relevancy for the task; synthesize the information in making a decision or creating a project, writing a paper, or producing a performance or exhibition; and evaluate the process and the project in terms of its effectiveness in meeting the criteria established by the teacher or school librarian in addition to the efficiency with which the project was carried out. The steps in the Big6 model are summarized in Figure 3.4.

Although the Big6 appears to be an iterative linear process with one step preceding the next, its creators argue that it can be used recursively as a student's searching activity progresses; for example, students' evaluations of what they are doing are activities appropriate at all stages, and location and access tasks may have to be repeated any number of times. The model's implicit

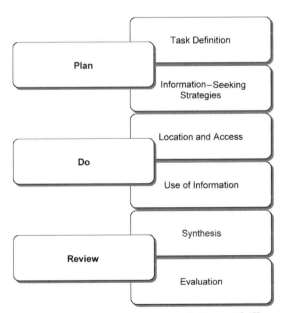

FIGURE 3.4   Summary Chart: Super3 and Big6 Skills Models for Information Problem Solving

understanding of information seeking as a recursive activity recognizes and accommodates variability in student learning styles.

The Big6 also emphasizes the importance of student-instructor interaction in brainstorming ideas and the desirability of using human as well as print and electronic information resources. The model also supports a variety of search strategies, making this an appropriate choice for teachers and librarians who hope to address the needs of a variety of student learners. Further, when truncated to the "Super3" ("plan, do, review"), the model can be used successfully with and by students at all grade and developmental levels.

Ideally, Big6 Skills lessons are created through collaboration between librarians and teachers to make the most of library resources and student research time. Indeed, one of the model's major advantages is its apparent simplicity, which helps students grasp the six steps quickly and in such a way that they can conceptualize the process as a whole as well as their own location within it at any given point in time.

Teaching inquiry through the Big6 is something that should happen across the curriculum. According to Marino and Eisenberg (2018), "(I)nquiry happens beyond the research project—inquiry happens every time a student uses information to answer a question, complete an assignment or solve a problem" (57). Students also apply school learned problem-solving techniques and inquiry in non-school-related situations. "This informal learning is influenced by student-driven motivation for learning and their control over the structure of the learning experience" (Marino & Eisenberg 2018, 58). When students take the Super3 and Big6 Skills outside the classroom to solve problems, they are honing a lifelong skill.

A longitudinal study published in 2017 also revealed the benefits of the Super3 and Big6 inquiry-based learning on students' memory and comprehension of the subject matter. This six-year study by Chen, Huang, and Chen (2017) focused on students in an elementary setting. Results of the study showed students of all academic levels improved their abilities to memorize curricular content and improved their comprehension of the subject studied (Chen et al. 2017). In addition, "Students engaged in such instruction have enhanced opportunities to become 21st century learners who are capable of critical thinking and participation in democratic societies" (Chen et al. 2017, 265).

First introduced in 1990, the Big6 Skills approach has proven so popular that it has spawned a variety of support structures, including a newsletter and an active website on the Internet (http://theBig6.org), which is devoted to answering Big6-related questions, providing news and research updates, providing information on Big6 conferences and workshops, identifying and describing exemplary Big6 programs, and listing articles published on Big6 model applications and success stories.

Stripling Model of Inquiry

Dr. Barbara K. Stripling, an award-winning library professional, educator, and research scholar, developed a six-phase model of inquiry, which is based on constructivist learning theory. Inquiry phases in Stripling's model (see Figure 3.5) include Connect, Wonder, Investigate, Construct, Express, and Reflect (Small, Arnone, Stripling, & Berger 2012). The initial Connect phase requires the learner to assess her or his prior knowledge, make a personal connection to a potential topic, and acquire background information on that topic. During the Wonder phase, students begin to formulate lines of inquiry, using questions to make predictions and create hypotheses. The third or Investigate phase requires the learners to locate and evaluate information as it pertains to their predictions and hypotheses. At this point, students can also entertain the idea of new questions and how these might relate to new hypotheses. During the Construct phase, learners connect what they have learned to prior knowledge and make inferences relating to the inquiry and hypotheses. In the Express phase, students apply the new knowledge to different situations by sharing and discussing their ideas with others. In the final Reflect phase, the learner reflects on the research process and uses the reflection to create and pose new questions (Small et al. 2012).

Joyce and Tallman's I-Search Model

Joyce and Tallman (1997) have also created a model to guide student research, but their approach differs in a number of significant ways. For example, in many of the earliest information-seeking models (e.g., Irving 1985; Stripling & Pitts 1988), there is an explicit or implicit assumption that the topics of research attention are either assigned by a teacher or chosen by students within the context of subject domains or curricular content and that the resulting reports and projects are formally and traditionally presented. In the case of the I-Search, the research topic is identified by the students on the basis of special personal interest or personal connection. In this respect, the topic can be seen to choose the student as well as the student choosing the topic. In addition, the resulting research report is presented not in the formalized style typical of academic writing but in the form of a first-person narrative, which not only presents the student's perspective on the specific topic but also chronicles his or her information-seeking and data collection strategies. The metacognitive aspect of this model requires students to think about the process as they go through the stages of research. By so doing, students maintain personal awareness of the process as their research activities proceed. Initially intrigued by the connections they saw between writing process models and contemporary research models and troubled by the student apathy that all too frequently accompanied the announcement of a research assignment, Joyce and Tallman (1997) set about finding an approach to the research process that would be personally meaningful for students.

Like Stripling and Pitts (1988), Joyce and Tallman were particularly interested in sense and meaning making and in the intellectual benefits to be realized for students engaged in metacognitive activities. The metacognitive aspect of their model required students to think about their personal journey through the development of the research as they proceed through the writing and

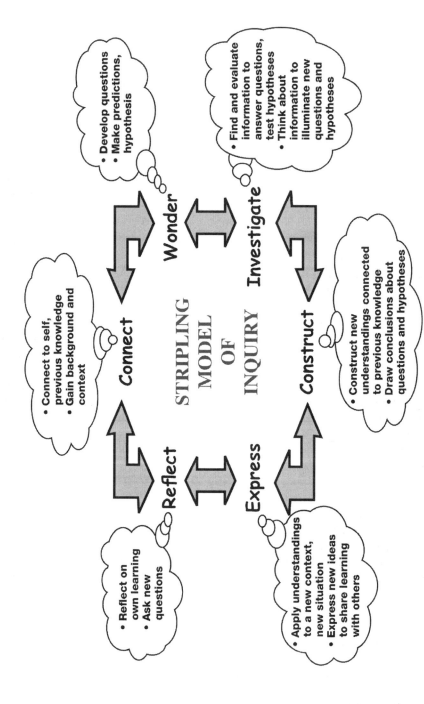

FIGURE 3.5   Stripling Model of Inquiry

research process. This reflection makes personal awareness a unique part of the I-Search model.

In the I-Search model, Joyce and Tallman saw a way to use writing and research "to foster critical thinking" (16) and personal investment on the part of their students. Although they reviewed a number of process models for writing and research, the authors eventually chose Macrorie's (1988, cited in Joyce & Tallman 1997) I-Search model, which asks students to select and research topics on a need-to-know basis and to write up the results in a narrative form. An important part of the narrative is the account of how the information students collected was "selected, evaluated and used" (17). In creating their model, Joyce and Tallman also drew on theoretical frameworks suggested by Murray (cited in Joyce & Tallman 1997) and Kuhlthau (1993b). In defining writing as a special case of information processing, Murray's process-writing model provided the conceptual link between writing and information-seeking tasks. According to the authors, Kuhlthau's research on the information search process was also particularly helpful, especially as her methodology had originally been based on models employed in process-writing research. In addition, Kuhlthau's emphasis on metacognitive activities, the importance she places on feelings as well as searching behaviors, and her use of interviews and conferencing techniques as a way of tracking individual student progress also became parts of Joyce and Tallman's approach. For example, the journals suggested in Kuhlthau's work were adapted by Joyce and Tallman, who asked students to maintain learning logs as records of their actions. Students used the logs to track their thoughts as their searches proceeded, and instructors used the logs in creating writing prompts and posing questions to stimulate student thinking and discussion. Joyce and Tallman also employed the use of webbing as a conceptual frame and a process device at several key steps. An I-Search Process Web involves four central tasks: selecting a topic, researching the topic, using the information found, and completing a research project.

Because of the personal nature of the research topics and the individual nature of student processes, school librarians and teachers play key roles in the I-Search process through conferencing activities. Instruction fits into the model at times when students need particular skills or specific resources in conducting their research activities. The major elements of the I-Search Process Web are summarized in Figure 3.6.

At Step 1, "Topic Choice," or topic selection, students explore their own interests through webbing activities and discussions with parents, peers, and teachers. The skimming and scanning of resources in the media center to identify items of potential use follow these activities. It is at this stage in the process that information skills can best be taught, with instructional approaches based entirely on student needs and skill levels. At Step 2, "Finding Information," students generate research questions, do background reading, create bibliographies of pertinent resources, and then enrich their knowledge through reading and interviewing. Step 3, "Using Information," can be undertaken in a number of ways, including highlighting and note taking. Reflection is encouraged at this stage and facilitated through conferencing and the use of learning logs. The final project is prepared at Step 4 and includes the opportunity to share the experience and the project with peers.

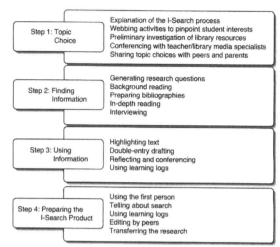

FIGURE 3.6   Summary of Steps and Activities in Joyce and Tallman's (1997) I-Search Process

From a motivational point of view, personal interest drives the selection of the student's research topic. The topic is then researched to answer the questions about the topic. Joyce and Tallman (1997) believe that the I-Search process creates the sort of authentic instructional environment that is most compatible with forms of assessment that are also considered authentic. In addition, the I-Search model stresses interaction and reflection with peers and parents as well as with teachers and the school librarian. All these strategies are consistent with the intent of authentic assessment, and inquiry approaches lend themselves readily to the creation of rubrics for evaluating the product and the process.[8] The I-Search process is compatible with many other information search models and can easily be incorporated when designing research assignments.

KWL-RAN©

KWL-RAN is a modification of the KWL model: the "what do I know, what do I want to know or find out, and what have I learned" strategy that has been used by many classroom teachers for decades, especially as a structure for information-seeking tasks in the early grades. In spite of its utility and the appeal of its simplicity, it is Stead's (2005) view that the KWL model may not help young information seekers when their knowledge of a topic is sketchy or nonexistent. In order to engage children in understanding topic content at a deeper level, Stead created the RAN© chart, an acronym for "Reading and Analyzing Nonfiction." Stead's (2005) model has been published in *Reality Checks: Teaching Reading Comprehension with Nonfiction K–5*.

Stead's (2005) model consists of a five-category chart that youngsters can use to record their understandings of a topic as the information-seeking task proceeds (see Table 3.4). Before reading begins, the student is asked to think

TABLE 3.4   Reading and Analyzing Nonfiction (RAN Strategy)

What I Think I Know	Confirmed	Misconceptions	New Learning	Wonderings
Children state information they think to be correct about the topic	Children research to confirm prior knowledge	Children research to discard prior knowledge	Children research to locate additional information not stated in prior knowledge	Children raise questions based on the new information gathered

about what he or she may already know about the topic. Once reading has commenced, students can begin to consider their initial understandings and sort out confirmed facts (information verified in nonfiction sources) from misconceptions (information that they initially believed to be true but that, on the basis of reading, they now learn is false or erroneous). Students enter new facts and understandings as new information in a fourth column, while in the fifth column, wonderings, students can record new questions they now have, sparked by their new understandings about the topic. The KWL-RAN strategy has been used successfully with both large and small groups of youngsters and can be interfaced with other research models.

CONCLUSION

Carey (1997) has argued that the most appropriate and valuable instructional role that teachers and librarians can have in creating students capable of becoming lifelong learners is to offer students an array of models and strategies so that they may construct for themselves a personal approach to solving information problems. This idea has found expression in Markless and Streatfield (2007), who urge librarians to encourage metacognitive activities that help students "think about their skills and how to apply them" in "plan[ning] activities to meet goals, anticipat[ing] obstacles, monitor[ing] their own progress, approach[ing] information critically, [and] evaluat[ing] information during the problem-solving process" so that "by these means" students can "develop a personal information style."

The importance of inquiry can be seen as institutions embrace this process. It is embedded in the educational philosophy of International Baccalaureate (IB) schools across the curriculum (Tilke 2011). "Inquiry, as a curriculum stance pervades all IB programs," explains Tilke (2011, 5). It creates collaboration opportunities for the school librarian, and students acquire knowledge through research instead of acquiring an assortment of facts, which may not mean anything to the student (Tilke 2011). This shows when students find meaning in their studies, they see the relevance of their learning and are more motivated to learn.

Jacobson and Ignacio (1997) have asserted that, especially in online environments, "librarians and teachers cannot follow a prescribed theoretical model" if they are "to teach students to be effective searchers" (793). Instead, Carey (1998) has suggested that teachers should provide problem scenarios that have intrinsic interest for learners, model information-seeking strategies, facilitate interaction among students as they collaboratively consider effective alternatives, and then provide "scaffolding" and support as solutions are developed.

The models reviewed in Chapter 3 offer attractive alternatives that librarians can use when they meet with teachers to collaborate on plans for research activities. Additionally, they constitute a rich array of tools from which school librarians can draw in helping students become independent learners. It is evident from this review that the models vary in emphasis, scope, and complexity. However, each one "assumes learning as an active and creative process, and each promotes the development of critical thinking skills" (Thomas 2000a, 1). Offering options as structures for information seeking is one way teachers and librarians can avoid applying a one-size-fits-all approach across children and contexts.

It is evident from this review of information-seeking models and strategies that changes they create in our understanding of teaching and learning in the library context are profound. It is also the case that the complexity and the sophistication of these ideas and approaches will serve school librarians well as they continue in pursuit of new strategies to inform practice and assist students in deepening understandings and enhancing information literacy competence.

NOTES

1. It is important to note that in Kuhlthau's studies, only the more successful students were observed to narrow or refine their topics in ways that provided the clarity needed to pinpoint information needs in preparation for the collection activities that followed (adapted from models provided in Kuhlthau, Maniotes, & Caspari [2007]).
2. It is also of interest to note here that Kuhlthau's assertion that where a personal effort at sense making and creating a point of view is neither part of a student's process nor an expectation of the instructor, plagiarism through the appropriation of another's words and thoughts is often the result.
3. Action studies represent an approach to research that is intended specifically to explore some aspect of professional practice. As Lindlof (1995) explains, action research in education is frequently employed when teachers wish to study new pedagogical techniques, such as "the introduction of new technology," in order to "diagnose problems, engage in collaborative analysis of data, and engender problem-solving skills" (110) so that instructional techniques can be modified or improved. Action research studies have certain limitations; they often although not always lack a theory base, and they are site specific, meaning that research findings are not transferable or generalizable to other situations or populations. However, such studies are extremely useful in that they often suggest new issues, topics, and avenues for other researchers to explore.
4. For a review of third space research, see Pane (2009).
5. Two other researchers recommend the same approach but do not label their assumption third space. Asselin and Doiron (2008) call for a merging of

literacies developed both in and out of school settings. "We know the new literacies are active in students' out-of-school lives, and we know the critical place of new literacies in the workplace. It is time to situate the new literacies of the real world in schools and make school libraries the bridge between in-school and out-of-school literacies" (15).

6. For a complete explanation of the concepts of GI and third space concepts, see Kuhlthau et al. (2007).

7. The "Big6™" is copyright ©1987 by Michael B. Eisenberg and Robert E. Berkowitz.

8. The value of creating a meaningful (to students) product as a result of the information search process is addressed by Oliver and Oliver (1997) in an experimental study involving 11- and 12-year-old schoolchildren. Specifically, the researchers studied the retention of information, "higher levels of knowledge acquisition" (519), and the learning that resulted from a research task when the task itself involved the creation of a meaningful information product. Drawing on Brown et al.'s (1989, cited in Oliver & Oliver 1997) model of situated cognition, the authors argue that "meaningful learning will only take place if it is embedded in the social and physical context within which it will be used" (521), preferably when the contexts have "relevance to the ways the information might be used in later life" (525). While the study results failed to find an increase in comprehension among students in the experimental group, they did note the "minimal cognitive processing" and retention of information when "the focus of research questions was not linked to any context or purpose" (525). "It is evident," state Oliver and Oliver, "that the factor underpinning the achievement gains experienced by the students . . . was the level of engagement and cognitive processing the activity encouraged" (525). Finally, "the context in which the activity was phrased was a significant factor in motivating the students to locate and retrieve information and to read and analyze that information for their own purpose" (525). On the other hand, "the lack of need to use the retrieved information for any purpose other than display for assessment purposes appeared to limit the degree to which the students [in the control group] engaged in reflective and cognitive processing" (525).

4

Cognitive and Social Frameworks for Teaching and Learning

[W]hen schools are organized and run in ways that fit the school to both the learning and developmental needs of children, both children and schools are successful; but when schools attempt to cram learning into students without regard to their developmental needs, children fail and so do schools.

—Howe (1993)

[Educators] can . . . intentionally learn more about their students' cultural backgrounds, individual needs, interests, and preferences. By using this knowledge, teachers help foster students' intrinsic motivation for information seeking in ways that work best for each individual, and thus guide them to bettering their lives in their own ways for their own reasons.

—Crow & Kastello (2017)

Although the instructional nature of the school librarian's job description emerged at a relatively early stage in the development of school librarianship, it did not achieve priority status until the American Library Association published *Information Power: Building Partnerships for Learning* (American Association of School Librarians & Association for Educational Communications and Technology) in 1988. *The National School Library Standards for School Libraries* continued this tradition by stating unequivocally that school librarians "bring teaching and learning to the core of the school library" and "provide leadership for a vision of learning centered on learner voice and choice" (AASL 2018, 44). This assertion is a succinct acknowledgment that, by empowering students to attain personal inquiry and curricular goals, school librarians

77

provide essential and foundational support for the learning process. In fact, the centrality of concern for the library user is a theme that runs through the contemporary research literature in library and information studies (LIS) (Jacobson 1997).

In school settings, where the library's mission is by definition responsive to the school's curricular goals, this concern has been shaped by theoretical frameworks defined as "constructivist." Indeed, LIS researchers who have come to consider information seeking as a cognitive process through which students create meaning and achieve understanding (Kuhlthau 1993b, 2004; Smith 1987) have adopted constructivism as a basis for redefining student information seeking and consequently for reframing information skills instruction.

Because of its assumptions of learning as an active, cognitive process, constructivism has become a primary theoretical basis for contemporary process models and information skills instruction. This chapter looks at constructivism and then considers other trends that mark contemporary practice, including the contextualization of library skills lessons, the value of process models, constructivist roles for teachers and students, and the contemporary emphasis on critical thinking and inquiry learning. Finally, the chapter discusses the critical importance of motivation to student learning outcomes and offers research-based suggestions for school librarians in their quest to foster motivation in today's learners.

CONSTRUCTIVIST PRINCIPLES DRIVE CURRICULUM DECISION MAKING

According to Von Glasersfeld (1995), constructivism is a theory of knowledge that has its roots in the domains of philosophy and cognitive psychology. Although constructivism has been variously defined in the literature, most scholars consider theoretical constructs in the work of John Dewey (1916, 1933), Jean Piaget (Inhelder & Piaget 1958), George Kelly (1963), and Jerome Bruner (1975, 1977, 1980) as seminal and recognize a set of assumptions they share. For example, constructivists generally hold that learning is "something which the individual *does*" (Dewey 1916, 390), that learning involves an act of personal construction, and that knowledge is the creation of meaning based on the experience of the learner. Thus constructivists assert that learners are active participants in their own learning rather than "passive receivers" (Kuhlthau 1993b, 24) of knowledge imparted to them by teachers and others. For this reason, constructivists consider the ability of the student to create a personal focus or "perspective" on a subject or topic as the hallmark of his or her understanding and learning. In fact, the ability to develop a personal viewpoint is, according to Sauer (1995), "the ultimate goal" (140) of education generally and of library instruction in particular. When viewed in this light, learning becomes less a matter of acquiring a set of skills than of developing a "deep understanding" (Von Glasersfeld 1995, 10). According to Kuhlthau (1997), "the constructivist approach seeks to foster deep learning that goes beyond the ability to respond to a text, to application in daily living" (710–711).

How Children Learn

Constructivists argue that, to be effective, learning activities must not only connect to what students already know but also have meaning for the learner at the time of the learning (Irving 1985). Indeed, most constructivists would argue that learning cannot occur in a vacuum but is inherently interactive and built on a knowledge base of previously learned concepts (see Table 4.1). Their emphasis also includes the social context and the role of learning communities (Bruner 1986) in the creation of knowledge structures. Bransford, Brown, and Cocking (2000) describe the community environment as a place wherein the learners develop the freedom to collaborate, are able to express a lack of understanding, and where competition between learners is diminished. Duckworth (2006) encourages critical exploration where learners "open out beyond themselves, and . . . realize that there are other points of view yet to be uncovered—that they have not yet exhausted the thoughts they might have about this matter" (140). Thus, an understanding of the social nature of teaching and learning provides important clues on how instruction may proceed within constructivist environments and thereby helps define the framework for instruction. For this reason, constructivist educators call on teachers to rethink their roles in the classroom and to implement models for instructional delivery in order to accommodate this understanding of how learning occurs.

As noted, constructivists focus primarily on the "cognitive" aspect of learning. However, they also recognize the importance of the "affective" (Kelly 1963) nature of learning tasks and recognize the need to provide emotional support for student learners. While these principles are sometimes advanced as something new in education, Von Glasersfeld (1995) reminds us that, in point of fact, "constructivism" actually supplies the theoretical grounding for activities and strategies that talented teachers have long employed without fanfare.

Contextualizing Instruction

Although constructivism is certainly not the only theoretical framework on which school librarianship draws, few would dispute the extent of its impact on practice or its value to the design of learning experiences in the school library. As we have seen, the acceptance of constructivism as "the fundamental theoretical foundation" (Kuhlthau 2001) for library programming has led most

TABLE 4.1 Constructivist Assumptions about How Children Learn

- Learning is an active and constructive process.
- Learning is the internalization and personalization of knowledge.
- Learning is the meaning that is made from experience.
- Learning involves understanding at a deep level.
- Learning involves the ability to apply new knowledge.
- Learning activities help students relate new information to past experience.
- Learning involves cognitive (thinking), social (interactive), and affective (feelings) dimensions.

school librarians to abandon context-free "scope-and-sequence" approaches to "bibliographic instruction" in favor of activities that promote information literacy (Walter 1994), critical thinking, information organization, and information use. Stand-alone library instructional sessions involving location and access skills have, in most places, been superseded by educational practices that call for the "contextualization" of skills within the curriculum, which is instruction presented at the point of need within the context of classroom content instruction. This means, for example, that instruction on the use of a particular library resource is not introduced until it is required for successful completion of curriculum-related tasks (Bowie 1990, cited in Callison 1994; Engledinger 1988). Perhaps more importantly, "contextualization" means that library skills are considered "information skills" that are taught within the framework of an overall process model for information seeking (Irving 1985; Kuhlthau 1993b). An essential value of implementing a process approach to information tasks is in helping students to understand "that knowledge is something" they themselves construct in "collaboration" with "the sources they find to inform their thesis" (Fister 1990, quoted in Sauer 1995, 142), rather than a collection of factoids they compile to satisfy a teacher or complete an assignment.

Disappointingly, although not surprisingly, research in the area of teaching information literacy has shown that instruction provided within a skills-based library curriculum has not provided sufficient learning to allow application to subsequent research projects undertaken in the same or different educational contexts (Goodin 1987, 1991; Kester 1994). Furthermore, Pitts's (1995, cited in Stripling 1995) research shows that "instruction in information seeking and use must be integrated within course content for subject matter learning to occur" (164); and there is a growing body of research evidence that substantiates this claim. For example, this finding was corroborated in Todd's (1995) study where, "for the specific students involved, integrated information skills interaction appears to have had a significant positive impact on students' mastery of prescribed science content and their ability to use a range of information skills to resolve particular information problems" (137). And in an experimental study of information seeking in research projects among primary school students, Brien (1995) found that teaching the complex skills of information seeking and use within the structure provided by class-related projects reduced the "cognitive load" for students and resulted in significant gains in student learning. In addition, a study by Todd, Lamb, and McNicholas (1993), cited in Todd (1995) suggests that "an integrated information skills approach to teaching and learning can have a positive impact on" such "learning outcomes" as test scores, recall, concentration, focus, and reflective thinking (133). These findings corroborate earlier studies indicating that integrated skills instruction results in higher achievement on library skills tests (Becker 1970; Nolan 1989) and an increase in student self-confidence (Nolan 1989).

THE FOCUS ON PROCESS: IMPLICATIONS FOR TEACHING AND LEARNING

As was evident in the discussion of process models in Chapter 3, the constructivist concern for "process" has created a shift in what is considered curricular content, that is, a concern for the processes involved in learning as well as—or, in some cases, as opposed to—a concern for the final "product" or project. For this reason, instructional designs that educational "constructivists" tend to employ the use of multistage curricular units. Implementing instruction in this way provides opportunities for students to engage in "authentic" problem-solving activities rather than through traditional and generic instructional sequences that proceed without reference to learners or context (Jonassen, Myers, & McKillop 1996). Loertscher (1985) and Eisenberg and Berkowitz (1990) have suggested the use of "collection mapping" as a way to target units and topics in all curricular areas and collect the resources to support them. Research indicates that this approach to instructional design is effective because it promotes comprehension, and promotes depth, and breadth in course content (Pappas, Kiefer, & Lewiston, cited in Winograd & Gaskins 1992).

Presenting information-seeking activities in the form of a comprehensive model is important in that it helps "students gain an understanding of the overall" process (Eisenberg & Berkowitz 1990, 15) as well as the relationship of specific subskills within the processes as "a series of instructional experiences" (17). This approach permits students to consider the "means" (e.g., steps in the process), not as meaningless hurdles or portions of the task to be "rushed" through, but instead as problem-solving skills that they can apply to other complex tasks in other contexts and situations.

Using a research model also creates a systematic approach to and structures for information seeking; in so doing, children develop a "vocabulary" to use in discussing the search process and their place within it. By the same token, an understanding of the process itself enables students to predict the activities that lie ahead and to visualize the goal of the research and the projects they will create. Research in LIS underscores the importance of this understanding to the meeting of curricular goals. For example, Pitts (1995) found that students' lack of a "mental model" of the steps involved in undertaking a curricular activity proved to be a serious obstacle to their success in completing their research projects. McNally's (2004) dissertation study of high school students engaged in online searching supports Pitts's conclusions. Given the complexity of most research tasks and the fact that teachers making the assignments may themselves be operating on outdated knowledge of available resource options or "flawed" models of information searching instruction (Tallman & Henderson 1999), it is not hard to understand why children and adolescents experience so many difficulties in completing information-seeking tasks.

MORE CONSTRUCTIVIST ROLES FOR LIBRARY INSTRUCTION AND SERVICES

Within a constructivist approach, the school librarian's primary responsibility is to provide structures and opportunities for learning and support and guidance for learners. Duckworth (2008) describes these responsibilities as fostering a culture of exploration, providing engaging problems and often taking on the role of researcher themselves, exploring and interacting with students as they learn. Although not denying the necessity or appropriateness of direct instruction in supporting specific learning styles, constructivism emphasizes the coaching role of the instructor in planning appropriate learner-centered activities, creating supportive environments, demonstrating important skills, modeling successful performance behavior, providing opportunities for student performances and reflections, motivating students, and providing feedback (Kuhlthau 1997; Means & Olson 1994). As noted in Chapter 3, this approach to instruction is based largely on the work of Russian psychologist Lev Vygotsky (1896–1934). In essence, Vygotsky (1978) viewed the process of education as a joint enterprise that involves both the teacher and the learner acting together. "Every function in the child's cultural development," Vygotsky believed, appears twice: first, on the social level, and later, on the individual level. This applies equally to voluntary attention, to logical memory, and to the formation of concepts. All the higher functions originate as actual relationships between individuals (57).

In the case of information literacy instruction, not only is learning the result of social interaction between individuals, but reading is also a social activity that occurs between the reader and the author (Black & Allen 2018). "Experienced readers conduct an internal dialogue between the author's words and their individual contextual understandings" (76–77). For this reason, Rosenblatt argued that the meaning of any text does not lie in the text itself, but in the reader's transaction with it, and that each transaction between the reader and text is unique because the reader brings their own set of experiences and store of knowledge to that particular transaction (1978). Bandura, in a broad sense, encapsulates this exchange in his social-constructive theory (1989), which posits that most of what we learn is through a process that involves our personal characteristics, our behavior, and the environment (including libraries, book collections, and other sources of information (Black & Allen 2018, 77).

Student-Centered Teaching

Effective instruction within Vygotsky's (1978) model is tailored to each child's "zone of proximal development," defined as that "distance between the actual developmental level as determined by independent problem-solving and the level of potential development" (86) that the learner may attain with assistance by a knowledgeable helper. At a first stage of a lesson framed in this way, the learner receives assistance in completing a task and comes to understand what is involved in carrying it out. At a second stage, the learner completes the task independently by following the directions and managing the process for herself or himself. In the third stage, the various aspects of the task are integrated, the learner having internalized the learning so that his or her responses and skills are automatic.

Within Vygotsky's approach, teachers prepare contexts for student learning by creating "scaffolds" or structures that take students beyond the limits of their own competence and experience. In effect, these structures provide the support necessary for the students to begin an activity or project; as each student's competencies and confidence grow, the teacher "withdraws," gradually relinquishing control so that the student can take over the responsibility for the project. Thus, for Vygotsky, learning is an interactive, interpersonal activity that involves the "transfer of responsibility" (Rogoff & Gardner 1984, quoted in Belmont 1989, 144) for "reaching the current goal" from teacher to student. This facilitative strategy creates opportunities for the teacher to learn how "the instructional activities are being interpreted" so that subsequent activities and practice are informed by what students are learning or failing to learn (Driver et al. 1994, 11).

When applied within a school library context, Vygotsky's (1978) framework provides strategies for planning and conducting instruction as well as a model for interventional support in information seeking and learning from information. The importance of student-instructor interaction has also been recognized by Kulleseid (1986), who describes as "dynamic learning situation[s]" those opportunities that involve instructors in modeling and "stimulating cognitive activity" (43). These kinds of learning contexts allow students to see firsthand those strategies that either work or fail to work and to talk through processes with others to "expose conceptual misunderstandings" (Jacobson & Jacobson 1993, 128). Such opportunities resemble the kinds of group activities that students are likely to encounter in real-world work environments.

Stripling (1994b) describes the facilitation role of the school librarian in terms of a six-step process for "effective teaching." The steps that Stripling advocates include conducting preinstructional activities, modeling the research process, and guiding student practice. In addition, Stripling suggests that teachers provide checklists for student evaluation and create additional projects that allow students to apply skills learned in new situations and different contexts.

Cognitive Apprenticeships

Activities that provide "real-life" tasks and situations reflect instructional strategies sometimes referred to as "cognitive apprenticeships and collaborative learning" (Jacobson & Jacobson 1993, 128). In these kinds of instructional approaches, teacher guidance is implemented through "situated modeling, coaching, scaffolding, and fading" in ways that support both interactive peer discussion and cognitive reflexivity. As Jacobson and Jacobson observe, conceptualizations of the information-seeking process that are "learned by students [only to be] repeated on tests" rather than to be applied in activities that necessitate their use are effectively "rendered inert [and] unavailable for application in new situations" (125).

According to Bertland (1986, cited in Mancall, Aaron, & Walker 1986), the zone of proximal development provides an ideal opportunity for the school librarian to demonstrate and model metacognitive behavior and show strategies for tackling unfamiliar tasks. These strategies might include estimates of difficulty, goals, action steps, and elaborative plans. In addition, the coaching role gives the instructor the opportunity to provide feedback, stimulate student questions, and prompt students to summarize their readings and monitor their own understanding of the material. In a study by Palincsar and Brown (1984, cited in Belmont 1989), the use of this sort of "reciprocal teaching" "resulted in improvements in children's daily independent reading comprehension" (146).

Own It, Learn It, Share It

Lee and Hannafin (2016) have identified autonomy, scaffolding, and audience as key constructs of student-centered learning outlined in their design framework: own it, learn it, and share it.

It is recommended that students: (a) develop ownership over the process and achieve personally meaningful learning goals; (b) learn autonomously through metacognitive, procedural, conceptual, and strategic scaffolding; and (c) generate artifacts aimed at authentic audiences beyond the classroom assessment. (1)

This learning design must be embedded in rich, organic learning environments that replace traditional direct instruction.

INFORMATION SEARCH PROCESS STRATEGIES THAT SUPPORT STUDENTS

As noted in the discussion of Kuhlthau's (1993b) information search process and intervention models reviewed in Chapter 3, Kuhlthau has invoked Vygotsky's (1978) model of zones of proximal development in creating a hierarchy of intervention strategies that provide direction for librarians operating in constructivist library environments. Interventional activities that Kuhlthau (1997, 2001) suggests as useful in framing support at the highest or counseling level include "collaborating, continuing, conversing, charting, and composing" (Kuhlthau 1997, 714).

Collaborating (Kuhlthau 1993a) acknowledges the value of social interaction in information seeking and critical thinking, as students brainstorm, mentor, coach, network, and learn together while working on joint projects. *Continuing* acknowledges the ongoing nature of information seeking within projects that extend over time and the series of cognitive events that students experience as they move from "uncertainty" to "personal understanding" (Kuhlthau 1997, 716). *Conversing* recognizes the importance of interpersonal communication to the process of information seeking. Student-teacher and student-student dialoguing helps teachers gauge student progress and encourages students to think aloud and to "think more deeply" (717) as they focus their research topics. *Charting* provides learners with a model or mental "picture" of the entire information search process as well as the stages from initiation to evaluation. Charting can be accomplished in a number of forms. Graphic organizers, including concept maps, semantic webs, and Venn diagrams, are tools that help students in categorizing ideas, understanding relationships among aspects of topics or steps in the process, and conceptualizing thinking processes. For example, a time line can provide students ways to predict events and structure activities. Finally, Kuhlthau (1993b) advocates *composing*, or journaling, as a strategy that allows students to track their thoughts, reflections, decisions, conversations, and readings in a systematic way. Of course, the use of student journals also allows librarians to monitor student progress (McNally & Kuhlthau 1994) and changes in their feelings as well. Providing encouragement when students experience uncertainty or anxiety and providing feedback on the process, as well as direction on "how to do it correctly" (Carson & Curtis 1991, 65), are also valuable strategies. By the same token, posing questions for students (Joyce & Tallman 1997; Mark & Jacobson 1995; Stripling 1995) in their journals can demonstrate for them the strategy of self-questioning, which, as Bondy (1984) concedes, is a skill that must be both activated and practiced if students are to embrace metacognition—the act of thinking about thinking.

The rationale for supporting students as they engage in active learning tasks is well established in the LIS research. For example, a number of studies indicate that the job of narrowing a topic called for within information process models such as Kuhlthau's (1993b) ISP may be very difficult for some students, suggesting that guidance, direction, and support for students engaged in this task are important services that school librarians can provide (Loerke 1994; Mark & Jacobson 1995). Irving (1985) has argued that "selecting appropriate information sources is impossible without some knowledge of which are available, accessible and relevant" (43). As this is the very area in which librarians have in-depth knowledge and expertise, Irving proposes that librarians share with their students the techniques they themselves use in acquiring this knowledge. Engledinger (1988) believes that this has been an important outcome of the constructivist movement in education. Within constructivism, collaboration is multidimensional, encompassing group activities for students, interactive relationships between students and teachers, and cooperative planning and team teaching between and among instructors. In short, collaboration in all its many and various iterations and configurations changes how education is "done."

Perhaps not surprisingly, the desire to make instruction more effective and learning more profound has led LIS researchers to advocate for collaboration in the planning and teaching of library and information skills (Kuhlthau 1993a; Stripling 1995). Indeed, there is research to suggest that library skills instruction is more effective when it is implemented to meet curricular goals and delivered in sessions that are collaboratively planned and cooperatively taught (Haycock 1992). Collaboration and cooperative teaching by teacher-librarian dyads also holds the promise of improving the nature of classroom assignments, particularly in terms of the kinds of questions/problems that students are asked to answer/solve. For this reason, school librarians must be "involved in the educational and developmental processes that begin and end outside the library door in the structure, use, and especially the creation of knowledge" (Sauer 1995, 137). Work by Kuhlthau, Maniotes, and Caspari (2007) suggests that, in guided inquiry activities, instructional teams should more properly include additional teaching specialists with relevant expertise.

Where collaboration has been successfully implemented (Kuhlthau 1993a), research indicates that a well-equipped library resource center, time for teacher-librarian planning, student motivation and time on task, administrative support, and an understanding and appreciation of a process approach to information seeking are all contributing factors. Elements that Kuhlthau (2001) identifies as enablers of collaborative projects include clarity in the roles that teachers and librarians will play as they team-teach "a mutually held constructivist view of learning," "a commitment to inquiry-based learning," and "competence in designing and implementing inquiry activities." Hartzell (1994) and others discuss the importance of professional trust and the value of personal relationships in creating and maintaining a culture that supports successful collaboration, because, in a very real sense, it changes fundamentally the way education happens. For example, true collaboration between teachers and librarians assumes shared responsibility for assessing student performance on research projects as well as joint teaching. Understood in this way, collaboration may appear "threatening" to some teachers where subject-specific curricula and self-contained classrooms constitute the norm. In such cases, school librarians must develop and use considerable sensitivity and social skills as well as professional expertise in enacting new models for teaching and learning.

An approach to engaging instructors in an academic library setting, as suggested in Engledinger and Stevens (1984), may provide clues for establishing productive relationships in secondary schools. These researchers found that instructors who were uncomfortable in teaching library reference skills actually welcomed assistance by academic librarians once they understood that their feelings were shared by other instructors. They also appreciated being given background information on library skills instruction and strategies to further cooperation between themselves and the members of the library staff. In addition, the researchers found that time for discussion allowed peers to create solutions to problems and that honest evaluation of cooperatively planned lessons resulted in "better projects" (598). Providing teachers with the experience of finding information for and by themselves in unfamiliar settings and on subjects about which they knew little was also an effective way to draw attention to the value of a librarian's assistance with information tasks.

Moving beyond the basic collaboration models described in the research is the vision of the guided inquiry team described by Kuhlthau et al. (2007), who comment, "Although two-member collaborations between one librarian and one teacher are commonly used, three-member instructional teams are highly desirable for the most productive collaborative planning and teaching" (48). They go on to note that this third team member might be an expert teacher, such as a reading specialist, technology specialist, and even subject-area specialists (e.g., art, drama, or music teachers).

MOTIVATING TODAY'S LEARNERS

Teachers have long understood the importance of motivation as it connects with student learning. Studies support this belief, showing that students who are motivated enjoy not only the benefit of higher academic achievement (Boggiano et al. 1993; Condliffe et al. 2017; Flink, Boggiano, & Barrett 1990;

Saunders-Stewart et al. 2015), but also other, less obvious benefits; these include more positive emotionality (Patrick, Skinner, & Connell 1993), higher self-esteem (Deci, Nezlek, & Scheinman 1981; Deci, Schwartz, Scheinman, & Ryan 1981), and greater creativity (Koestner et al. 1984). Certainly, motivating students to learn is an important part of the instructor's task. This is especially true in information seeking, as the tasks involved are complex and can be frustrating (Kuhlthau 2004); at the same time, we know that motivation is the key to creating independent, lifelong learners—and that goal is at the very core of the school library program's mission. But how can teachers and school librarians motivate learners? What motivational strategies does the research offer?

Motivation Theory: Two Approaches

Motivation theories address why people and animals think and act the way they do (Weiner 1992) and can be categorized into two basic approaches: *mechanistic* and *organismic.*

The Mechanistic Approach

The mechanistic approach to motivation began with the earliest motivational theories—the drive theories—which assumed that an organism's responses are governed by the interaction between its own physiological drives (such as sex, hunger, thirst, and the avoidance of pain) and the environmental stimuli around it (Freud 1925, 1957; Hull 1943). Over time, it became clear that people (and animals) exhibited many complex behaviors that could not be explained through drive theories, thus leading to the organismic approach to motivation theory.

The Organismic Approach

The organismic approach to motivation presumes an active role for the organism, one that is volitional and involves initiating behaviors. The organismic view sees outside stimuli not as causes of behavior, as did the mechanistic view, but rather as opportunities for the organism to satisfy its needs (Ryan & Deci 2017). It is this approach that led motivational theorists to create new definitions and concepts of motivation, specifically the concept of intrinsic motivation. Expectancy-value theory (Vroom 1964), curiosity (Berlyne 1960), flow theory (Csikszentmihalyi 1975, 1990), and self-determination theory (Ryan & Deci 2017) are all examples of intrinsic motivation theories.

LIS researcher Small (1998, 1999) took an organismic approach by using the ARCS model of motivational design (Keller 1987) to explore K–8 library media specialists' use of motivational strategies in library skills instruction and the consequential effects on the on- and off-task behaviors of their students. ARCS, founded on expectancy-value theory (Vroom 1964), identifies four components of instructional motivation: attention, relevance, confidence, and satisfaction. Keller, a professor of instructional systems, posited that instruction embedded with teaching strategies designed around these four aspects would be motivating to learners on an organismic level. In her early study, Small (1998) observed nine exemplary library media specialists teaching library skills to students in third to eighth grade. She found that the specialists used a significant number of motivational strategies during lessons (averaging 24 strategies per 30-minute lesson) and that middle school specialists used more motivational strategies than their elementary school counterparts. She also reported that only 2 percent of the motivational strategies used were considered to stimulate behavior based on *intrinsic* motivation (Small 1999).

In a study conducted in New York school libraries that continued LIS studies of motivation with an organismic lens, Small, Snyder, and Parker (2009) reported that there was a significant correlation between the school librarian's perception of the school library program's "ability to motivate students to learn and the importance he or she places on teaching basic information literacy skills" (8), and that the school libraries and librarians in the study positively influenced students' motivation for research and inquiry, their reading development, and their development of reading interest (Small, Shanahan, & Stasak 2010). They also found that elementary school library media specialists use "significantly more motivation strategies than either secondary or K–12 [school library media specialists]" (8); this finding is a reverse of conclusions drawn from data in the 1998 study. In a related finding, elementary and middle grade students saw the school library program as having had a greater total impact on their motivation than was reported by the high school students (Small & Snyder 2009).

Inquiry-based learning (IBL) is an organismic approach most commonly used in science and math classrooms but has also been used in school library settings for many years. IBL contains all or some of the following components: "1) a driving question 2) authentic, situated inquiry 3) learner ownership of the problem 4) teacher-support, not teacher-direction and 5) artifact creation" (Buchanan, Harlan, Bruce, & Edwards 2016, 27), all characteristics that support education based on a constructivist educational framework which strives to give the learner an active role. Forms of IBL include problem-based learning, self-regulated learning, and student-directed inquiry. IBL has been found to produce a range of benefits for the learner, including an increase of knowledge and skills, enhanced intrinsic motivation, more self-efficacy, greater commitment to the task, positive affect toward learning, increased perceived competence, and an increase in creativity (Buchanan et al. 2016, 27).

Interest in the Task

Because intrinsic motivation involves both a task and an organism, it can be defined in terms of the interest in the task and the satisfaction gained by the person when engaged in the task. Koch (1956, 1961) theorized that actions can be motivated by simple *interest in the task*, or engagement that is absorbing to the individual for the mere pleasure of doing it (Deci 1975). More recent theorists (e.g., Csikszentmihalyi 1975; Hidi & Baird 1986; Krapp & Fink 1992) have continued in the tradition of Koch to explore characteristics of activities that make them interesting, the individual interests of people, as well as the effect this "interestingness" has on the learner (Hidi & Ainley 2008; Linnenbrink & Pintrich 2002; Renninger, Hidi, & Krapp 1992).

A prominent theory based on interest in the task is *flow*. Csikszentmihalyi (1975, 1990) explored the characteristics of activities that cause flow, which can be understood as a state of complete absorption. He found that these activities have clear goals and rules appropriate to the activity and that usually flow activities provide feedback that is immediate and unambiguous. He also found that the skills needed for the activity align with the participant's abilities. His research indicates that the results of engaging in activities of high interest and flow are unselfconsciousness, serenity, joy, involvement, and happiness (Csikszentmihalyi 1975) as well as higher comprehension (Schiefele & Csikszentmihalyi 1995). Csikszentmihalyi and Hermanson (1999) applied flow theory to develop a "formula" for learning in museum experiences. The formula includes "the hook," opportunities for involvement, conditions for flow, and growth complexity in consciousness.

School library researchers have also found that interest plays a part in successful information-seeking behavior. Burdick (1996) noted that a majority of the youngsters she studied evidenced a bored attitude and a lack of interest in the research task, concluding that students' focus and involvement had a direct bearing on their success (or lack thereof) with information-seeking projects. Similarly, Heinström (2006a) reported that students in her study who employed a deep (as opposed to a surface) approach to information seeking found the research process to be easy and enjoyable because of interest in their topic. "What was striking among the students with a *deep* approach was the prevalence of topical engagement and ownership" (6).

Kuhlthau (2004) has theorized that, with the mediation of librarians and teachers, students can overcome the natural anxiety caused by the searching process and develop a personal interest in the topic being explored. Silverstein (2005), in her "Just Curious" study, reported that students (especially those of elementary and middle school age) using digital reference services to answer self-initiated questions were highly motivated to do so primarily because of the interest stimulated through informal learning environments. Lu and Gordon (2007) and Gordon and Lu (2008) found that high school students who participated in an online summer reading program read more than they had in previous summers when they were given traditional summer reading lists. They suggest that this increase was due partially to a greater number of books from which to choose, thus allowing for the likelihood students would find titles that were of interest to them. Crow (2011) found that upper-elementary-aged students who were identified as intrinsically motivated to seek information had undergone a point-of-passion experience, most at the age of or four or five. A point of passion is an interest-igniting episode that stimulates a child to explore more information on a specific topic for many years. Schmidt, Kowalski, and Nevins (2010) found that middle school students chose questions and topics with which they had a connection, either of personal interest or that held emotional ties to a societal issue.

Satisfaction of Needs

The other prong in intrinsic motivation research focuses on the satisfaction gained by the person when engaged in a task. White (1959) proposed that actions such as visual exploration, crawling, grasping, language and thinking, exploration, and manipulation of surroundings are motivated by the organism's psychological need to "interact effectively with his environment" (329), or its sense of *competence*. LIS researcher Bilal (2005) found that students experienced a high level of motivation while exploring the Internet, primarily because they enjoyed the challenge of searching and discovering new information. Another study (Arnone & Reynolds 2009; Arnone, Reynolds, & Marshall 2009) suggests that eighth graders' perceived competence in their information literacy and reading skills contributed to their intrinsic motivation to do research, and that "school librarians play a key role in building students' confidence in information skills and intrinsic motivation to engage in research" (Arnone, Reynolds, & Marshall 2009, 128). Gordon and Lu (2008) reported that average achievers and honors students acknowledged the benefit of summer reading because of the new knowledge they gained from reading self-chosen nonfiction books, perhaps suggesting a newfound sense of competence.

Additional research studies into intrinsic motivation based on the satisfaction of the person's needs are those by Harter (1980, 1981) and Lepper, Corpus, and Lyengar (2005). Harter's studies focused on five dimensions of students' needs, and her findings indicate that there is a significant and progressive decline in intrinsic versus extrinsic motivation across elementary and middle school years, perhaps because the needs that stimulate intrinsic motivation (such as curiosity, challenge, independent mastery, and independent judgment) are not being met. Lepper et al. (2005), in a large study of ethnically diverse third- through eighth-grade public school students, found that extrinsic motivation for academic activities remained relatively stable across grade levels, whereas intrinsic motivation—positively correlated with higher grades and test scores—steadily and significantly decreased throughout the grades. LIS researchers Fourie and Kruger (1995) identified the psychosocial, cognitive, and affective needs behind the information-seeking behavior of secondary school students. They theorized that the fulfillment of these developmental needs is the basis of adolescents' motivation to choose particular books and media. Agosto and Hughes-Hassell (2006a, 2006b) similarly found that urban teens seek information in order to facilitate fulfillment of their developmental needs in seven areas: social self, emotional self, reflective self, physical self, creative self, cognitive self, and sexual self.

Self-Determination Theory

Many studies about intrinsic motivation and youth are based on the self-determination theory (Ryan & Deci 2017). Self-determination theory is an organismic theory that categorizes motivation into three basic types spread across a spectrum: *amotivation, extrinsic motivation,* and *intrinsic motivation.* The theory points to three innate psychological needs: competence, autonomy, and relatedness; it posits that people living in social contexts that provide opportunities to meet these basic psychological needs are optimized not only for motivation but also for performance and development (Ryan & Deci 2000).

An LIS study conducted in Colorado Springs, Colorado, based on the self-determination theory examined the experiences of students who were self-motivated to explore information about the world around them (Crow 2009). Using the Self-Regulation Questionnaire for Information Seeking, Crow identified fifth graders who were indicated as highly and distinctly intrinsically motivated to seek information. Based on student interviews and analysis of the children's artwork, Crow found that all the students exhibited an affinity for play, tended to be creative, and were noncompetitive in nature. They all perceived themselves to be competent (though not always in school subjects), and the study suggests that their relatedness needs were met through "anchor" relationships—people who supported their information-seeking interests.

An important principle espoused in self-determination theory is that extrinsic motivators, while effective in promoting motivation for rote and routine tasks, actually results in decreased levels of intrinsic motivation (Ryan & Deci 2017). Several authors have examined the motivational aspects of Accelerated Reader (AR) (e.g., Biggers 2001; Huang 2012; Krashen 2003; Mallette, Henk, & Melnick 2004; Robbins & Thompson 1991; Schmidt 2008), a computer-generated reading program in which students select a title based on reading level and then are awarded points upon successful completion of an electronic comprehension quiz about the book. Schools traditionally offer prizes when students reach point goals. Biggers (2001) sees the program's focus on external rewards as a "Skinnerian . . . system of literacy learning that poses the threat of extinction once the rewards are withdrawn" (73). In a study of the school librarian's role in managing the program, Everhart (2005) explored the relationship between the implementation of AR and student motivation, then applied her findings to the leadership role that school librarians can play in the program's administration. She recommends that those school librarians who already work in AR schools can be instrumental in its proper implementation, "particularly in the area of book selection, reading guidance and motivation, organization of materials, and teacher professional development" (12). She recommends that school librarians in non-AR schools use her study to support collaborating directly with teachers to help students set reading goals outside the AR program. Studies (Crow 2004, 2010; Maliszewski 2018) suggest that children's choice book award programs are preferable to AR as motivational tools because students are empowered by the act of voting for their favorite book, the programs are based on student choice (a powerful intrinsic motivator), celebratory events and author visits incorporated into the programs increase excitement for reading, and the act of reading a common list of books creates a sense of camaraderie, all factors that build intrinsic motivation (see Table 4.2).

The Effect of Culture on Motivation

A key premise of self-determination theory (Ryan & Deci 2017) is that the three psychological needs of autonomy, competence, and relatedness are

TABLE 4.2 What School Librarians Can Do to Foster Intrinsic Motivation

- Provide students with individualized opportunities, not a one-size-fits-all approach to learning.
- Use teaching strategies and exhibit an attitude based on play (including a sense of humor) and create playful environments.
- Offer creative outlets for project completion, collaborate with music and art teachers, and provide access to materials about creative people and pursuits.
- Provide choices to various media (including authentic objects).
- Educate parents/guardians in the role of information-seeking "anchors," and notify them when a child is showing an affinity for creativity or a particular interest.
- Pay attention and be proactive in connecting students to resources (including people) based on their interests.
- Initiate low-key research experiences with the very young.
- Use constructivist teaching methodologies (such as problem-based learning and inquiry strategies).
- Reduce extrinsic motivators in the learning environment.
- Be sensitive to the differing relational needs of individual students.

Source: Adapted from Crow (2011, 2015) and Crow & Kastello (2017).

universal; that is, they apply to all people regardless of their culture or cultural upbringing. However, when examining the three needs, there would appear to be a tension between autonomy (the individual's need for volition) and relatedness (the individual's need for community). Heine, Lehman, Markus, and Kitayama (1999) theorized that people of individualistic cultures (e.g., United States, Australia, Great Britain, Canada, the Netherlands, and New Zealand) have more need of autonomy support, and that people of collectivist cultures (e.g., Japan, China, Korea, Taiwan, Uganda, Venezuela, Guatemala, Indonesia, Ecuador, Argentina, and Brazil) have more relatedness needs. Conversely, other studies posit that autonomous-based motivation is universal across time and cultures (Chirkov & Ryan 2001; Chirkov, Ryan, Kim, & Kaplan 2003; Grouzet, Otis, & Pelletier 2006; Roth, Asor, Kanat-Maymon, & Kaplan 2006). In the field of education, studies have shown that autonomy-supportive strategies are successful in collectivist cultures (Jang et al. 2009; Vansteenkiste et al. 2005), supporting the premise that instructional approaches that foster intrinsic motivation benefit people of multiple cultures.

Crow, and Crow and Kastello, in two follow-up studies to the Colorado Springs study (Crow 2009), examined the experiences of students who were self-motivated for information seeking from (1) a collectivist culture (Kampala, Uganda) and (2) from a culture that is both individualistic and collectivist (Mysore, India). The findings indicated that the students from all three cultures had the same affinities for play and creativity, and that all enjoyed competence-building activities. Interest and relevance were also the predominant factors in all three groups of students' favorite information-seeking experiences. However, the Ugandan and Indian children were more apt to ask people when seeking information than the students from the United States. Interestingly, a similar percentage of the students from all three cultures were readers and book users (23 percent for Colorado, 18 percent for both Uganda and India), even though there were far fewer reading materials available for the students in Uganda. Recommendations from the three studies are to allow choices when developing information-seeking assignments, to provide creative alternatives of presenting information, and to be sensitive to the differing relational needs of individual students regardless of their cultures (Crow 2015, Crow & Kastello 2017).

It behooves librarians to invest the time needed to intentionally learn about their students' interests, needs, families, preferred information-seeking methods, and cultural backgrounds. Students from war-torn or refugee situations may not know how to find information in conventional ways, but they have developed their own survival skills. Students from collectivist family cultures may not work well individually but excel when working in groups. By understanding and respecting students, showing them the practicality of enhancing their information-seeking abilities, and fostering their desire to use newfound skills, school librarians can affect students' lives and the lives of their families for the betterment of all society.

5

Diagnosing Informational and Instructional Needs

We need to begin asking the "why questions" about youth and information-seeking behavior and taking young people more on their own terms than exclusively on terms dictated to them.

—Bernier (2007)

Students with disabilities should have at least an equal opportunity to participate in library programs as their nondisabled peers. . . . Unfortunately research demonstrates that many school libraries do not fulfill this obligation.

—Small & Stewart (2013)

Teachers are being challenged as never before to tailor instruction to meet the educational needs of an increasingly diverse population of young learners and to make sense of the differences in cognitive development and ability, cognitive style, social and cultural experiences and traditions, as well as language variations.[1] Diagnosing instructional needs and customizing instructional approaches for information literacy education assumes the presence of "reflective practitioners" (Schön 1983) who are able to apply educational theory to practice. As has been noted in previous chapters, school librarians have proven themselves to be both reflective and resourceful in reframing resource-based "library skills" to focus on information seeking, process learning, critical thinking, problem solving (Bodi 1992; Kuhlthau 1993b), and guided inquiry (Kuhlthau et al. 2007).

There are, of course, many ways to differentiate instruction. In the research literature of library and information science, individual differences have frequently been viewed in terms of "user needs" and information-seeking behaviors. Within the educational literature, differences are seen to relate to cognitive and personal development and learning styles. Research in sociology, communication, and other disciplines suggest worldview, culture, socioeconomic status, and gender as foundations of difference. Understanding each of these dimensions can help school librarians design effective learning sessions.

GROVER'S DIAGNOSTIC MODEL

In the 1990s, Robert Grover (1993, 1994) proposed a useful approach to instructional customization that takes account of differences in thinking and learning. In essence, Grover's model reframes the standard reference interview as a "cycle of service" that shifts the focus of attention from the characteristics of the library's resources to a concern for the information seeker and his or her particular information needs. Originally aimed at re-creating reference interactions as user-centered activities in public and academic libraries, the model can be used by school librarians in lesson planning because, as Grover (1994) suggests, "information skills instruction is an educational service" (176).[2]

In creating his model, Grover (1993, 1994) invoked a clinical approach developed by doctors to diagnose, prescribe for, and treat their patients. In Grover's adaptation, the service cycle begins when a librarian and an information seeker first encounter each other and ends with the librarian's evaluation of the services provided. Two elements in the model specifically address accountability issues and deserve special notice. The first is that, from the outset, the librarian assumes responsibility for the successful outcome of the service interaction or information search process. The second is that it is the library user, not the librarian, who determines what constitutes "success" in terms of service or search outcomes.

The four steps in Grover's (1993, 1994) model are diagnosis, prescription, treatment, and evaluation (see Figure 5.1). At *diagnosis*, the information provider must inquire into the what, where, and when of the user's information topic or need. However, the central question to be answered is "who?" According to Grover, factors to consider include the individual's literacy level, developmental level, cognitive style, worldview, format preference, culture, and technological skills. Age, gender, communication style, and English-language proficiency may also be germane at the diagnosis phase. This information is then used in the second, or *prescription*, stage of the model in determining the relevance and appropriateness of specific resources (available in the collection, online, or in another library) that will meet the user's need.

The information seeker and the resources identified by the librarian are brought together at the *treatment* stage of the cycle; at *evaluation*, the librarian assesses the service process in light of the user's satisfaction with the resources provided. The questions to be addressed at evaluation include: Has the user's need been met? Has the user's problem been resolved? If the answer to these questions is "no," the diagnostic process begins over again and is repeated until the user is satisfied.

When applied in a school context, diagnosis of a student's needs must additionally involve initial assessments of his or her reading level, prior knowledge of the topic or subject, and preferred learning style (Grover 1994) so that lessons that address specific curricular objectives and standards and that meet

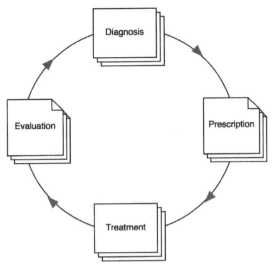

FIGURE 5.1   Grover's (1993, 1994) Model for Diagnosing Information Needs

the instructional needs and preferences of individual students can be created. The implementation of the lesson corresponds with the treatment stage of Grover's model. Evaluating the outcomes of instruction concludes the cycle; at this stage, the school librarian and teacher can assess student learning in relation to the objectives established earlier. This assessment can then serve as a basis on which to plan further activities or make necessary modifications to instructional strategies.

Student progress and learning may be assessed through observation, interviewing, student journals or learning diaries, portfolios, student projects, paper-and-pencil tests, and teacher-, peer-, and self-evaluations. In the event that assessment measures show that objectives have not been met or that skills have not been learned, a new round or rounds of planning, instruction, and assessment can be carried out until such time as students achieve mastery. In sum, Grover (1994) proposes *diagnose, design, teach, assess, reteach,* and *reassess* as steps in an instructional adaptation of his service cycle.

DIMENSIONS OF DIFFERENCE

Successful implementation of Grover's (1994) model calls for a theoretical grounding in library and information studies (LIS) and related disciplines as a way to advance student learning and individualize instruction. In the LIS research literature, individual differences have frequently been viewed in terms of user needs and information-seeking behaviors as conceptualized by Taylor, Belkin, and Dervin. Within the educational literature, differences have been identified related to psychology (Maslow), cognitive development (Piaget, Bloom, & others), cognitive processing and activity (e.g., laterality) (Buzan), an environmental-systematic approach (Tomlinson), multiple intelligences (Gardner), learning modes and approaches (e.g., Kolb & Pask), worldview (Anderson), and gender (Gilligan). Understanding each of these dimensions can help school librarians design effective learning sessions. In a very real sense, they also reveal the layers of complexity embedded within activities that may appear, on the surface, to be straightforward and unproblematic.

Information Needs

A useful place to begin an examination of approaches to library and information skills instruction is a discussion of information needs. Theorists in LIS (Taylor & Belkin) and communication (Dervin) have made major contributions to our understanding of needs as an important aspect of information behavior.

Taylor's Levels

In one of the foundational articles in the literature of LIS, Taylor (1968) explored the process through which information *needs* of users are transformed into the kinds of questions or *queries* that can be successfully addressed in a library setting. To this end, Taylor described information needs as a set of hierarchically arranged levels based on the seeker's ability to express the need and the clarity of that expression. According to this taxonomy, Taylor identified as *visceral* those needs that are unexpressed and inexpressible; needs at this level may be experienced simply as a sense of uneasiness or dissatisfaction with a situation. In the event that the feelings persist, they will eventually come to the surface; needs at this level Taylor identified as *conscious*. Users with conscious needs can articulate or talk about them and relate them in a general way to specific subjects, topics, or situations (e.g., "I need information about . . ."). As the need becomes clearer in the user's mind, it becomes more focused and can be *formalized* as a rational statement or a specific question (e.g., "I need specific information on . . ."). Once the information need can be stated in this way, it can be reformulated or *compromised* into vocabulary (e.g., key words or Library of Congress subject headings) to which an information system can respond. Taylor's model is useful in that it raises awareness of the difficulties that users may experience in expressing their needs in a library setting. At the same time, it suggests that librarians have a role to play and expertise to offer in helping users articulate their needs, especially at formalized and compromised levels. The traditional reference interview was an acknowledgment of and framework for this role.

Belkin's Information Problems: Anomalous States of Knowledge

For Belkin and his colleagues (Belkin 1980; Belkin, Oddy, & Brooks 1982a, 1982b), the information problems that individuals experience are best described as *anomalous states of knowledge* (or *ASK*). An information science theorist interested in the design of electronic information retrieval systems, Belkin argues that information needs can more usefully be addressed if they are considered information "problems" that arise when a person realizes that "his or her state of knowledge" is not sufficient to make a decision, solve a problem, or reach a goal. The challenge this poses for the information seeker is that the specific information or resource necessary "to resolve the anomaly" (Belkin 1978, quoted in Dervin & Nilan 1986, 13) may not be known. As it is difficult for people to request assistance when they themselves are unsure what it is they are seeking, Belkin suggests asking users to describe what they do know about the topic or situation to determine what is "missing." When the information seeker is allowed to tell his or her own story in a reference interview, it may be possible for the information professional to understand and thus address the need and identify relevant resources to satisfy the unarticulated question.

Dervin: Information Seeking as Sense Making

One of the first theorists to introduce the idea of customized services as a goal for reference librarians was Brenda Dervin (1983, 1989). A communication scholar, Dervin sees information seeking as sense making. Within this framework, information seeking is initiated when individuals encounter gaps in their knowledge sufficient to impede, prevent, or stop their forward progress through time and space (see Figure 5.2). These gaps may be perceived as dilemmas, confusions, or uncertainties of the sort that people face as a part of daily life. The "sense" or understandings that they ultimately construct from the information they obtain in information encounters provide the "bridge" that enables them to proceed with their activities or decision making.[3]

In Dervin's view, what people require when they find themselves stuck in an information gap is personalized information based on their interests, their views of the problem, and whatever barriers they expect to encounter. As information problems do not arise in a vacuum but are tied to situations in which people find themselves, Dervin suggests that librarians create and pose one or a series of neutral questions (Dervin & Dewdney 1986) that will uncover the seeker's situation, the gaps in understanding, and the intended use. Neutral questions are a subset of open-ended questions that professionals can use to

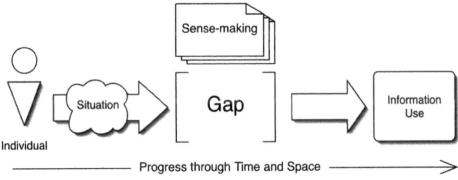

FIGURE 5.2   Dervin's (1983) Situation-Gaps-Uses Model

guide information seekers in explaining their information needs, their situations, their knowledge gaps, and their intended plans of action in their own words.

Maslow's Hierarchy of Needs

Abraham Maslow (1908–1970) conceptualized individual needs as psychological or "human" rather than strictly informational. In Maslow's (1970) model, needs are ranked hierarchically, with the physiological and physical dimensions of human experience at the base or bottom levels and self-actualization at the highest or top level. Originally, Maslow posited only five levels of needs; later, he added two dimensions to self-actualization: the need to know and the need for beauty and order. Maslow holds that failure to have needs met at any of the first four levels compromises an individual's successful achievement or fulfillment of needs at higher levels (see Figure 5.3).

The lowest or base level of needs comprises those *physiological* elements that support and sustain life: the need for food, water, rest, warmth, and shelter. Needs at the next higher level involve personal *safety*, including the needs for environmental and personal stability and physical and psychological *security*. At a third level are *love and belonging* needs, which are fulfilled in family relationships, friendships, and acceptance by one's peers. *Esteem* needs occupy a fourth level and are realized in acknowledgments of our personal competence by others and resulting feelings of self-respect and self-worth. *Self-actualization* needs arise in feelings of self-acceptance and frequently are expressed in self-enhancement activities and activities that allow the exploration of personal values. The *need to know* and the *need for beauty and order* often translate into love of learning and the pursuit of personal interests, while the need for beauty is often realized in art appreciation, literature, and music. Maslow conceptualized this highest state as episodic rather than static and characterized by peak experiences of creativity, spontaneity, happiness, and the fulfillment of

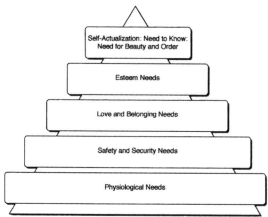

FIGURE 5.3 Maslow's (1970) Hierarchy of Needs

potential that punctuate our existence. Maslow's hierarchy of needs makes acutely apparent the reasons why a hungry child may not demonstrate much intellectual curiosity or why one who has been belittled at home or is worrying about the acceptance by peers at school may not take an interest in abstract notions of beauty or justice. Comer (2001) acknowledged the continuing value of understanding children's needs in school settings. "Despite massive and rapid scientific, technological, and social change," Comer writes, "children have the same needs they always did: They must be protected, and their development must be guided and supported by the people around them. They cannot rear themselves."

APPLYING THEORIES OF INFORMATION NEEDS
IN THE SCHOOL LIBRARY

In her studies on the expression of information needs by school-age children, Gross (1995, 1997) drew on the work of Taylor (1968) and his conceptualization of levels. Her findings suggest that although the ways in which information needs have been understood in the literature of LIS illuminate the evolutionary process through which self-generated questions pass as they move from visceral to compromised levels, the information questions that teachers pose for students to answer present entirely different kinds of problems. If, for example, the question the student brings to the librarian is stated unclearly, it may be because the student lacks the background knowledge (possessed, presumably, by the teacher who created the question) to clarify the nature of his or her information need. Under these circumstances, the task of helping the student formalize the need (restate the need as a question) may be extremely difficult no matter how well or compassionately the librarian conducts the interview. Indeed, the question that the student poses when seeking assistance will reflect his or her *interpretation* of the teacher's intent, an interpretation that may or may not reflect the teacher's understanding of the task or question. Obviously, relevance judgments of resources and information provided to answer these kinds of requests are compromised as well. This is particularly true when information that matches the question cannot be found in student-appropriate resources.

Furthermore, the student's request or question is also interpreted by the school librarian through layers of meaning based on the librarian's prior knowledge of the teacher, the subject, or the assignment. When both the teacher and the assignment are unknown to the librarian and the student's understanding is incomplete, both the librarian and the student will be left to speculate on the teacher's intent.

Gross (1995, 1997) believes that understanding the ways in which a teacher-imposed question differs from a self-generated question will assist school librarians in providing guidance to students. For a start, it demonstrates how sensitive librarians must be to the *possibility* that the students themselves lack an understanding of the very questions they are asking. In her study with elementary school students, Gross found that determining the origins of their requests was not at all straightforward because the children in the study interpreted even this question in a variety of ways.

The sorts of confusion that assigned questions can engender can be ameliorated to a great extent if the school librarian and the classroom teacher work together to establish assignment objectives and create potential research questions. Another, perhaps better solution would be to make the students part of decision making so that the objectives of the assignment are understood by all parties before the library activity actually begins. But even in cases where the questions appear to adults to be clearly and unambiguously stated, the school librarian must check for student understanding before acceding to requests for help. Indeed, Gross (1995) argues that librarians need to interview "all students who come to the reference desk regardless of whether they are the first, fifth or twentieth person to make that request in a given day" (242).

Whereas Gross's (1995, 1997) research considered children's information seeking and needs related to instruction, Walter's (1994) study was concerned with identifying the information that children need for daily living (e.g., personal safety and life choices). Citing the richness of the LIS literature on adults as information seekers and the lack of research on children's information needs, Walter set out to explore this issue. At the outset, she made two assumptions: first, that, like adults, "children have information needs that, if met, would enable them to solve problems and resolve particular difficulties" and, second, "that children are frequently unaware of their needs" (115).

In the absence of field-tested strategies and guidelines as to how to implement such a study, Walter (1994) organized her research around interviews that she conducted with 25 adults (other than parents) who were involved in working directly with and/or planning services for children. In each case, the adults were asked to discuss what information they thought the children should have, how they thought the children were getting their information, and what information gaps existed for children.

Walter (1994) justified her decision to interview adults rather than children about children's needs because, in many instances, children lack the experience necessary to know that an information need exists. Kuhlthau's (1993b) research confirms that children are often unable to express their needs in ways that will help them initiate the search process, while Moore and St. George's (1991) study demonstrated the problems children have in extracting and using information they find, even when the research topics themselves are preselected. "Imagine the obstacles," as Walter (1994) directs, "when children must also" (115) initiate information seeking and explain the original information need. It is for this reason that Walter asserts that "adults must articulate those needs for them" (113).

Walter's (1994) study revealed that, indeed, school-aged children do have information needs and that many of these needs are not being met. In reviewing the interview data, Walter determined that the articulation of needs closely resembled the hierarchy identified by Maslow (1970). Specifically, Walter found that children's needs for information on health, hygiene, and disease (AIDS) prevention, substance abuse, and child abuse[4] are expressions of needs experienced at a physiological level. Lu (2010), in her study of fifth- and sixth-grade students in an urban public school, found that nearly two-thirds of the youth in the study used information seeking to cope with daily-life problems. This coping took on the form of problem solving, escapism, learning about transitions, desire to change moods, and information avoidance.

Children's safety needs were reflected in information on avoiding crime, safety procedures of various kinds, literacy skills, and traffic laws. Belonging needs identified in the study related to information on interpersonal relationships, multicultural issues, emotional awareness, and recreation. The esteem needs that Walter (1994) reported related to "multicultural awareness, emotional awareness, social system knowledge (legal, economic, etc.)" (120) and to information on values and ethics. Finally, at the level of self-actualization, Walter noted children's needs for education, recreation, values and ethics, and "cultural" opportunities related to reading, art, and music.

In Walter's (1994) work, sex education was mentioned by so many of the interviewees as being related to "so many different contexts" (122) that she considered this an information need at every level except self-actualization. Of interest as well was Walter's finding that adults in the study emphasized physiological and safety needs as being of primary importance for the development of skills necessary for basic survival. They also mentioned the *misinformation* supplied to children through the media and from uninformed or ineffectual caregivers, service providers, and peers as a central problem.

In addition, Walter (1994) identified a number of barriers to children's information seeking; these included inadequate services, absence of adult-child interaction, and ineffective information programs and providers (especially noted were lack of rapport between service providers and children and failure to provide appropriate instructional approaches). It is significant to note that some adults in Walter's (1994) study considered children's needs as relational rather than informational and did not see a role for the library to play in improving the situation. But if, as Walter asserts, all children are "information poor" (126), is there not a role for library professionals to play in helping children meet these unmet information needs? Harris and McKenzie (2004) believe there is. In their study of public library users aged 7 to 11, they found that many of the barriers children face can be overcome by using developmentally appropriate practices, such as student language in point-of-use labeling, picture-oriented spine labels on books of various genres, library "buddies," and library orientations that are hands-on and use "kid-friendly" terms.

Although Walter (1994) and Harris and McKenzie (2004) are interested mainly in improving public library services, school librarians, most of whom have direct access to children on a daily basis, are in an excellent position to address these needs. In addition, they can do so through the information skills curriculum. For example, creating "authentic" information tasks directed at addressing the information gaps children have could be easily incorporated into various content or subject areas assigned to meet classroom objectives. In addition, collecting pamphlets, periodicals, and magazines as well as nonprint resources that support such an information-rich and authentic curriculum and making them easily available to children through the library, the classroom, and wherever children congregate would serve as well. Secondary school librarians often provide such pamphlets as a matter of course, but the availability of such information products has been observed less frequently in elementary school libraries.

Harmon and Bradburn (1988) discuss information needs of adolescents in terms of developmental tasks. Citing the work of Havighurst (1953) and Abrahamson (1979), these researchers suggest that the needs unique to teenage youth pertain to social and gender identity tasks, the need to establish both emotional and economic independence, intellectual skills and ethical values, life skills, self-control skills, and coping skills. From these tasks, Harmon and Bradburn have identified three categories of needs: research needs (for academic and personal intellectual use), recreational needs (media resources in all formats), and information needs (life skills and coping skills). In their view, a problem with meeting all these information needs is the complexity of the adolescent tasks themselves.[5] It is interesting to note that the information needs that Harmon and Bradburn identified in 1988 as needs of adolescents did not include the concerns for survival or personal safety identified by the informants in Walter's (1994) study.

SOCIOECONOMIC ISSUES AND CHILDREN'S INFORMATION NEEDS

Jonathan Kozol (1994, 1996, 2000, 2006) has written extensively about the needs of children in low-income neighborhoods where deficits in the availability of print resources and access to knowledgeable adults who can stimulate reading interests and guide information seeking are continuing problems. In discussing the importance of school libraries, Kozol notes that, without them, the children "who ha[ve] the least to stimulate their reading appetites at home . . . find much less to stir their love of learning in their public schools." He speaks of this kind of deprivation as a "theft of stimulation, cognitive excitement, and aesthetic provocation" that is catastrophic. He writes that school libraries developed with the artfulness of skilled librarians—remain the clearest window to a world of noncommercial satisfactions and enticements that most children in poor neighborhoods will ever know. To shut those windows is to close down one more opening to democratic amplitude and one more opportunity for fully realized cultural existence. Such an eventuality clearly limits underprivileged children's access to the higher levels of Maslow's hierarchy.

Neuman and Celano (2001) studied access to print resources in middle- and low-income neighborhoods. In particular, they looked at the nature of the kinds of texts available in each of these environments. Drawing on the work of Rogoff, Bronfenbrenner, McCloud, and others, Neuman and Celano believe such texts "shape children's first literacy experiences." As such, they constitute the very "architecture of everyday life," which "embed opportunities for children to learn and develop through observation and apprenticeship" (11). Their intent was to examine "access to literacy as a potential contributing factor for explaining differences in interaction, behaviors, and ultimately achievement for these children" (11).

Particularly germane to some of the issues addressed in this book were Neuman and Celano's (2001) descriptions of the disparities between the school libraries in the neighborhoods included in their study. Chief among these differences were numbers of resources per capita, condition of print collections, availability of computers, presence of a certified library media specialist, and hours of operation. Statistical significance was observed in the number and condition of books, the number of days open, and the availability of computers. School libraries in low-income neighborhoods lacked certified librarians; school librarians in middle-income neighborhoods held master's degrees. Their data suggest that "children who live in already print-rich environments tended to have school libraries that offered more books, more computers for research, better trained librarians with more experience, and more hours to visit during the day" (22).

Although clearly family interactions are immensely important to children's access to resources, the larger social settings within which families live exert tremendous pressures as well:

> Pervasive poverty, institutional settings like the workplace, and social welfare systems act as indirect environmental influences on children's interactions. They may affect the physical and emotional resources provided to the child (e.g., stress levels due to lack of work), adult responsiveness, and involvement in daily activities (Hart & Realey, 1995; McLoyd, 1990). (Neuman & Celano 2001, 23)

When it comes to content on the Internet, a report by The Children's Partnership (Lazarus & Mora 2000) provides some insights into what children of "under-served Americans" (defined as low-income, rural, limited education, or racial or ethnic minorities) want the Internet to provide. Included on the list were participation and self-expression, high-impact packaging with interactivity, multimedia, and youth-friendly tutorials, easier searching and usability, encouragement, and involvement. With regard to people in situations of information poverty (Chatman 1996), a study by Hasler et al. (2014) found that they are turning to online newsgroups and other discussion groups to meet their information needs. The posts they read and write range in topic from health conditions (51 percent of all posts in the study) to schoolwork (.5 percent of posts). The largest topic of need was mental health (38 percent). Clearly, the Internet is providing information to the information poor, but of what quality? Now more than ever the role of the school library in providing access, instruction, and guidance in information use to all students, but particularly the information poor, is crucial to the searching success of today's youngsters.

Of special interest with regard to children's everyday information needs is the work of Agosto and Hughes-Hassell. In their study of inner-city youth (2006a, 2006b), they found that the informants' developmental needs drove their information seeking and that this finding was similar across contexts for advantaged, nonminority youth (2006b) as well as for minority children. Their research suggests that information needs of youth are universal across socioeconomic, geographic, and cultural lines.

THEORIES OF COGNITIVE DEVELOPMENT AND COMPLEXITY

Although, as Kuhlthau (1993b) argues, information seeking and learning from information have behavioral and affective as well as cognitive dimensions, the primary concern of information models in LIS is with children's capacity to think critically. For this reason, Grover (1993) and others recommend that school librarians consider theories of learning as they plan for information literacy instruction. Of particular value in this regard are the frameworks provided by theorists Jean Piaget (Inhelder & Piaget 1958) and Benjamin Bloom (1956).[6]

Piaget's Theory of Cognitive Development

Piaget (Inhelder & Piaget 1958) believed that cognitive development is dependent on physical maturation and interaction with the environment and proceeds for all children according to an orderly succession of learning states. Within Piaget's framework (see Figure 5.4), learning structures or schemata develop in response to the child's concrete experience of his or her world and are extended with each new experience through the mechanisms of accommodation and assimilation. Accommodation involves modification of schemata in response to new information. Assimilation is the integration of new knowledge into what is already known. For Piaget, maturation can best be understood in terms of developmental stages, which are thought to be invariant across culture and gender, although children may pass through them at different chronological ages and at different rates.

Piaget (Inhelder & Piaget 1958) described the development of children's intellectual skills or "mental operations" as a progression of accomplishments related to perception (the ability to detect and organize information through the senses), memory (the storage and retrieval of information), reasoning (the ability to use knowledge to make inferences and draw conclusions),

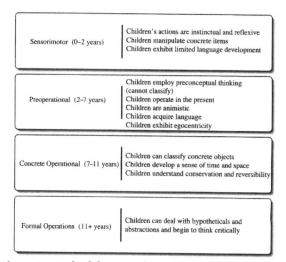

FIGURE 5.4   Piaget's (Inhelder & Piaget 1958) Stages of Cognitive Development

reflection (the ability to evaluate the quality of ideas), and insight (the ability to see patterns and to recognize and understand relationships among ideas). As they grow biologically, children move from a sensory stage where learning is accomplished through direct experience and the manipulation of physical objects in an egocentric universe to a state of formal thinking wherein a child is able to consider perspectives different from his or her own and to do mentally (by thinking) what as a younger child he or she had to do physically (by doing).

During the *sensorimotor* stage, the largely reflexive behavior of the newborn progresses to include responses to observed objects and the differentiation of self and other. Children at this stage become increasingly able to explore the world through their senses and begin to learn language. During the *preoperational* stage, language development continues, and children grow in their ability to classify or group objects. Preoperational children are egocentric, however, seeing everything from their own points of view. They learn by imitating the behavior they observe in others, and they are very busy exploring the environment. During the *concrete* operational stage, children continue to learn through the manipulation of tangible objects; but they also begin to develop a sense of time, and their thinking becomes increasingly logical. They begin to understand cause-and-effect relationships and can classify objects based on more than one characteristic. As their cognitive "operations" become increasingly "formal," children learn to take the point of view of others and to think abstractly and critically. It is at this stage that they become able to consider a number of solutions in solving a problem and develop the capacity to compare alternatives and consider hypotheses. As *formal* thinkers, children are able to consider their own lives from different perspectives and to think about and evaluate their own thinking (metacognition).

Bloom's Taxonomy

Whereas Piaget considered the development of thinking skills as maturational, Benjamin Bloom (1956) proposed a taxonomy of mental activities, independent of physical development, which ranked thinking tasks on the basis of mental complexity or cognitive load. These levels are summarized in Figure 5.5. Bloom ranked *recognition* at the basic or beginning level. As explained by Bloom, thinking at the level of recognition allows an individual to distinguish one entity from another and to give the entities names or labels. Thinking at the second level, *knowledge*, constitutes the ability to recall information or report facts. At the next level, *comprehension*, thinking is described as an understanding of concepts. At the fourth level, *application*, thinkers are able to take what is known or has been learned in one situation and use it to solve problems in a variety of other situations. *Analysis* is the ability to look at a whole by examining its constituent parts, while *synthesis* is the ability to construct new knowledge or new understandings out of disparate ideas or facts. At the highest level, *evaluation*, thinkers are able to make judgments regarding the value of an idea, an activity, or a project. "In this model," as Fitzgerald (1999) notes, "each skill potentially exercises all of the ones below it in the hierarchy."

Recognition	Remembering and labeling
Knowledge	Recalling facts
Comprehension	Understanding important concepts
Application	Using what is known in a variety of situations
Analysis	Understanding the whole through an examination of its constituent parts
Synthesis	Making something new out of separate ideas or facts
Evaluation	Judging the value of an idea, concept, or project

FIGURE 5.5   Bloom's (1956) Taxonomy

Revising Bloom's Taxonomy

Recognizing changes in how students interact with technologies and considering research demonstrating best practices for educating students, Marzano (2000) has provided an update for Bloom's Taxonomy that takes into account motivation and metacognition. His revised system does not necessarily proceed in a linear fashion, and it mirrors the learning processes that students undergo. Whereas Bloom's Taxonomy includes the ordered steps of *knowledge, comprehension, application, analysis, synthesis,* and *evaluation,* Marzano (2000) has created a nonlinear model, labeling his conception "A New Taxonomy of Educational Objectives," comprised of three main systems and a *knowledge domain.* His model, which builds on earlier work that he completed on a "dimensions-of-learning model" (Marzano 1992), posits that five dimensions of thinking influence the learning process and proceeds in a nonlinear fashion. These dimensions are (1) *positive attitudes and perceptions about learning,* (2) *acquisition and integration of knowledge,* (3) *extension and refinement of knowledge,* (4) *meaningful use of knowledge,* and (5) *productive habits of the mind.* Marzano's model holds that, in fact, learning categories do not build on each other in a linear way but instead exist with equal importance in the overall learning process. He explains,

> The three systems are the Self-System, the Metacognitive System, and the Cognitive System. When faced with the option of starting a new task, the Self-System decides whether to continue the current behavior or engage in the new activity; the Metacognitive System sets goals and keeps track of how well they are being achieved; the Cognitive System processes all the necessary information, and the Knowledge Domain provides the content.

Other researchers have also proposed changes or updates to Bloom's Taxonomy. Anderson and Krathwohl (2001) recommended combining both the cognitive processes and the knowledge dimensions originally described by Bloom. They list the following items, among others, as key to their "upgrade" of Bloom's work: *recognizing, recalling, interpreting, exemplifying, classifying, summarizing, inferring, comparing,* and *explaining.* Wiggins and McTighe (1998) proposed "Six Facets of Understanding" as a model for curriculum design processes in an effort to bolster student understanding of content. They label these facets as *explanation, interpretation, application, perspective, empathy,* and *self-knowledge* and include specific performance indicators as well as common vocabulary for assessment of learning.

LEARNING STYLES AND LEARNING MODES

While it is useful to consider thinking in terms of developmental stages and complexity levels, approaches that focus on styles of learning and knowing can help school librarians create activities that take advantage of students' preferences, "potentials," and strengths. The inclusion of alternative ways of knowing and being in the world (McCarthy 1996) within curricular assignments also raises teacher and school awareness and appreciation of the many kinds of intellectual gifts that students possess while honoring differences in ways that enhance both the learning and the learner. The following sections consider cognitive diversity in terms of learning styles (Kolb 1983), problem-solving skills (Pask 1972, 1975), hemisphericity (Bogen 1969; Buzan 1991), the interaction of intelligences (Sternberg 1985), and multiple intelligences (Gardner 1996, 1999, 2003).

Kolb's Learning Modes

Kolb's (1983) theory of learning styles is based on the work of the Swiss psychologist and psychoanalyst Carl Jung (1875–1961), who theorized that people function in the world in four different ways: by thinking and reasoning, by feeling and relating, by perceiving and sensing, and by intuiting and imagining. As interpreted by Kolb, the ways in which people implement these "vantage points of human consciousness" (McCarthy 1996, 47) create for them individual patterns or "modes" of thinking, which Kolb labeled as concrete experience, reflective observation, abstract conceptualization, and active experimentation. Kolb and Fry (1975) argue that effective learners possess all four learning modes to some degree. Indeed, there are no age levels attached to these different patterns of functioning, and there is no intimation that one way of thinking is better than another. For this reason, Kolb's theory is considered "experiential" rather than "developmental."

According to Kolb (1983), every person has the capacity to function in all four modes. However, individuals develop preferences for one mode over the others and find that operating in that mode seems entirely ordinary and natural. Indeed, when individuals are asked to think outside their preferred modes,

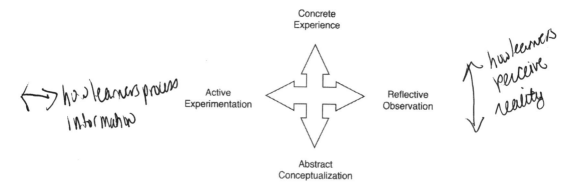

how learners process information

how learners perceive reality

FIGURE 5.6   Kolb's (1983) Modes of Learning

Kolb believes that they have to work harder to make sense of the learning task at hand. On the other hand, many individuals have the cognitive flexibility to use alternative modes, depending on the subject, the situation, or the level of stress. Figure 5.6, which is based on Kolb's theory, shows the relationship of the modes to one another. Here, ways of thinking and learning are represented as two continua of experience. The horizontal axis, extending from action/participation (doing) to reflection (watching), represents how learners process information. The vertical axis, extending from concrete (sensing and feeling intuitively) to abstract (analyzing and reasoning conceptually), represents how learners perceive reality. Kolb maintains that the intersection of the two continua not only defines four distinct learning abilities but also creates a four-part or four-step model of learning (see Figure 5.7). Kolb argues that learning can begin in any of the steps in the cycle.

In Kolb's view, *concrete experiencers* enjoy problem solving in real-world situations, and they tend to personalize task experiences, emphasize feeling over thinking, rely on intuition, and enjoy creative approaches to decision making. People who prefer this approach tend to relate well to others and enjoy working under flexible as opposed to highly structured conditions. Kolb's *reflective observers* like to learn by watching others and observing situations and events. Individuals who take this approach to learning are thoughtful rather than pragmatic, frequently seeking understanding, meanings, and truth rather than "what works." Reflective observers prefer contemplation to action in problem solving, and they frequently excel at being able to see the implications of situations or actions within a wider context of frame. Reflective observers are self-reliant, preferring to work alone and depending on their own judgment rather the opinions of others when making decisions. The mode of learning used by *abstract conceptualizers* emphasizes logic and thinking rather than feeling, favors analysis and quantification types of activities, and approaches problem solving in scientific and systematic ways. These kinds of learners are often task oriented and highly productive. Finally, Kolb's *active experimenters* learn by doing and favor hands-on activities that allow them to use the ideas and theories they encounter for practical tasks and pragmatic problem solving. Active experimenters are often risk takers and change

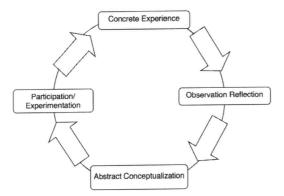

FIGURE 5.7   Kolb's (1983) Four-Part Learning Cycle

agents, and, since they are often results oriented, they enjoy setting goals and completing projects.

Few learners actually exhibit the "ideal" behaviors implied in Kolb's (1983) model, tending instead "to develop [an] orientation to . . . one of the poles of each dimension" (Smith 2001). To take this into account, Kolb and Fry (1975) acknowledge the existence of four learning styles (see Figure 5.8), which mark positions people can take between concrete and abstract thinking and between action and observation. In brief, these characterizations describe four ways in which people like to learn. *Convergers* are pragmatists who combine active participation with an ability to think abstractly. *Divergers* are watchers, who enjoy learning through observing real-world activities. *Assimilators* are thinkers who learn best through reflecting on abstract concepts, while *accommodators* like to learn by doing.

While many educators acknowledge the value of Kolb's models to the creation of instructional strategies, critics have pointed to a lack of research verification for the theory itself (Schenck & Cruickshank 2015). In addition, they argue that the model fails to account for individual motivation, cultural characteristics, aspects of the task, and contextual differences experienced by specific learners. Dunn, Beasley, and Buchanan (1994) have reviewed the educational literature on learning styles and achievement and assert that "most students can learn anything when . . . they are interested in the topic, begin learning with their preferred processing style," receive reinforcement through their "secondary or tertiary modality," and "apply new information" to the development of "a new instructional service," such as the creation of a game, play, poem, or "set of task cards" (12). Still, Kolb has contributed a great deal to our understanding of the very real differences that exist in the ways people learn.

Sternberg's Triarchic Theory of (Successful) Intelligence

Sternberg's triarchic theory of (successful) intelligence posits that there are three collaboratively functioning intelligences: *analytical, creative,* and

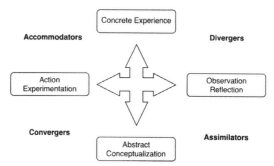

FIGURE 5.8 Learning Styles Identified by Kolb and Fry (1975)

practical (Sternberg 1985, 1997, 1999). *Analytical* intelligence results in the abilities to analyze, to compare and contrast, and to evaluate information. *Creative* intelligence allows people to invent, discover, and do other creative activities. *Practical* intelligence incorporates applying what the person has learned in appropriate settings. In order to be successful, individuals know and use the strongest of their intelligences, and learn how to compensate for their weakest. This can manifest in people seeking contexts (such as education or employment) in which they use their strongest intelligences or may mean individuals use their strengths in finding ways to avoid or overcome their weaknesses. An important feature of Sternberg's theory is adaptability, both within persons and within their sociocultural contexts (Cianciolo & Sternberg 2008). The Sternberg Triarchic Abilities Test (STAT Level-H), developed by Sternberg (1992), can be used to measure triarchic intelligence and has been proven empirically to be a valid test (e.g., Momani & Gharaibeh 2017; Sternberg et al. 2001) though some researchers dispute that it is a valid measure of intelligence per se (e.g., Chooi, Long, & Thompson 2014; Visser et al. 2006). The specific usefulness of the STAT is that it can be used to "identify children who are gifted in unconventional ways, or who would appear mentally [disabled] by a conventional test but not by this one, which considers practical as well as academic intellectual skills" (Sternberg 2002). In this way, teachers and librarians can use the STAT to identify students' strengths and weaknesses, and differentiate instruction accordingly.

Pask's Holistic and Serialistic Problem Solvers

Pask (Pask & Scott 1972) construes differences in thinking and learning in terms of problem-solving orientations. In brief, Pask suggests that people prefer to think either holistically or serially when considering information to resolve an issue or dilemma. Holists take a global view of a problem, seeking to understand "the whole" and how a problem may be linked to other problems or topics. As information seekers, holists are top-down processors who survey systematically and exhaustively all possible information resources and then examine each in turn (Eisenberg & Berkowitz 1990). Holists tend to thrive on complexity and enjoy hypothesizing. Serialists, on the other hand, reach understanding through an orderly process of sequential steps, identifying constituent elements and focusing on specific details.

These learners favor simple and straightforward solutions to problems they face. As information seekers, serialists may find and use resources in a linear fashion, viewing a succession of items and quitting when they perceive that they have found a sufficient number.

CEREBRAL LATERALITY AND MULTIPLE INTELLIGENCES

A number of learning theorists consider structures in the brain the foundation of differences in thinking and learning. Major frameworks anchored in physiology include cerebral laterality theory and split-brain theory, left-brain/right-brain dominance theory (Bogen 1969; Buzan 1991), and multiple-intelligences theory (Gardner 1983, 1996, 1999, 2003).

Theories of difference involving left-brain and right-brain orientation are anchored to scientific evidence that locates mental functions and patterns of cognitive activity within specific areas of the left and right hemispheres of the brain. Stated briefly, split-brain theory recognizes that for most right-handed people, the left side of the brain is responsible for analytical tasks, such as separating a whole into its constituent parts. The left brain thinks logically, rationally, and sequentially. Verbal and computational skills are also considered left-brain functions in these individuals. By the same token, the right brain manifests abilities to integrate elements into a whole, to find patterns and relationships, and to perform spatial and visual tasks. Aesthetics and intuition are considered right-brain activities, as are the abilities to recognize faces and remember tunes. The two sides of the brain work together to perform mental tasks, "shifting back and forth" (Gedeon 2000, 260), depending on the skills required to complete the task at hand.

The theory of cerebral laterality was first posited in the 19th century by pathologists and neurologists who were treating patients who had sustained brain injuries. Twentieth-century advances in medicine and neurology allowed researchers to observe and study the brains of normal people as well as split-brain patients who, from injury or surgery, have lost function of the corpus callosum, a band of tissue that links the two hemispheres.

Brain or cerebral dominance theory holds that the left side of the brain is the leading or dominant hemisphere because it controls language and speech (Springer & Deutsch 1993). However, Gedeon (2000) explains the theory of brain dominance in this way: "As one grows intellectually, tendencies develop for hemisphere preference. These tendencies, influenced by an assortment of social and genetic considerations, generally become more entrenched with maturation" (260). Although the preference of one hemisphere over the other can be very strong, Gedeon cites Johnson and Daumer (1993) in suggesting that "it is possible to cultivate use of the less dominant hemisphere" (260). Psychopathologists have noted the relationship between hemisphere dominance and illnesses such as schizophrenia and bipolar disorder.

Research in cerebral laterality offers practitioners some suggestions for tailoring direct instruction to the needs of individual learners. As discussed above, left-brain learners tend to think analytically, rationally, logically, and critically; possess special facility in the use of language; prefer verbal and written instructions; like hands-on activities; enjoy learning facts and details; and excel at classifying, comparing, contrasting, and sequencing. They appreciate structure and understand processes best when they are presented in terms of a sequence of orderly steps. As noted above, those for whom right-brain functions are dominant tend to think holistically, creatively, and intuitively, rather than analytically, and are especially adept at creating visual images, recognizing patterns, making connections, and pulling ideas together. They enjoy inventing, predicting, and imagining alternatives. Such learners like to use metaphors and are talented at synthesizing activities.

Research in brain function recognizes hemisphericity as it is related to the task, to the individual, and to culture. Task hemisphericity recognizes the specialization of functions within areas of the brain. Individual hemisphericity relates to an individual's preference in performing a specific task. Cultural hemisphericity acknowledges cultural preferences in thinking styles that typify specific groups (Gordon 1996). While it is safe to say that the complexities of brain functioning are masked in models that sort functions into neat arrays of abilities and capacities, the simplicity of such models does assist in making them comprehensible to nonspecialists.

Another cognitive model identifies four *cerebral modalities*: visual, auditory, kinestheic, and tactile (Dunn & Smith 1990). Characteristics of *visual learners* include the ability to recognize words by their shape; an interest in visual display, graphics, and media; the tendency to concentrate attention on faces; the practice of making of lists; and recall based on the location of information on a particular page. *Auditory learners* prefer verbal instructions, class discussions, and talking through problems and issues, and they often use music and rhythms as mnemonic aids. Storytelling and group work appeal to these learners. Individuals who enjoy role playing, dramatics, and games and find sitting for extended periods a hardship are exhibiting behaviors of *kinesthetic learners*, while *tactile learners* enjoy hands-on activities and use the act of writing—as in note taking or outlining—as an aid to memory.

Gardner's Multiple Intelligences

One of the most influential of the "cognitive theories" in contemporary psychology and education is the theory of multiple intelligences. In *Frames of Mind*, Gardner (1983) challenged the conventional wisdom shared by supporters of Binet's testing methodology that IQ is a genetically based and stable characteristic, retrievable and measurable through an examination of a person's verbal and analytical skills. On the contrary, Gardner defined intelligence as the *ability to solve problems* and *to create intellectual products* that closely reflect skills valued by families and communities that surround the learner. Thus, for Gardner (1996), frames of intelligence represent "biological and psychological potentialities"—"relatively autonomous intellectual capacities" that can be "realized to a greater or lesser extent as a consequence of the experiential, cultural, and motivational factors that affect a person" (2).

Gardner originally identified seven intelligences (Lazear 1991). *Linguistic intelligence* is shared by writers, poets, and debaters, whose verbal gifts and interests in words and grammar make them good readers and articulate communicators. *Musical intelligence*, which emerges earlier in a child's development than other forms, includes the ability to sing, to detect perfect pitch, to discern rhythms, and/or to create original compositions. *Logical-mathematical intelligence*, which is traditionally tested and thought to measure "intelligence," includes the ability to reason and to think through problems in logical and sequential ways. Individuals with *visual-spatial intelligence* possess the ability to visualize patterns, to create maps and diagrams, and to use flowcharts. This group includes architects, designers, and artists. According to Gardner's (1983, 1999) theory, dancers, athletes, actors, and others who can use their bodies in skilled ways or who have highly developed fine and gross motor skills exhibit *bodily-kinesthetic intelligence*. Gardner also identifies sensitivity to others and sensitivity to self as forms of intelligence. Thus, those with *interpersonal intelligence* have a keen sense of the moods of others and are adept at both personal communication and group facilitation processes, while those with *intrapersonal intelligence* are highly self-reflective and especially good at metacognitive tasks.

Although individuals vary to the extent that they exhibit to a high degree one or several of the intelligences, Gardner (1996) asserts that everyone possesses some ability in each of the "intelligence" areas and that these constitute potentialities that can be strengthened in children if they are exposed to appropriate educational strategies and support. While Gardner argues that multiple-intelligences theory can be productively used to alter instructional approaches in ways that "reach more students, and give those students the opportunity to demonstrate what they have understood" (3), he does not suggest them as a replacement for curriculum nor as a shortcut to learning. The central task for teachers, as Gardner sees it, is to provide support for learners so that they can use their own unique sets of capacities in mastering the tasks and skills that will allow them to succeed in contemporary society.

Gardner's theory has been widely accepted and used by educators in differentiating instruction to best "fit" students who exhibit the various intelligences (Chen 2004). However, there has been debate on the validity of the theory in academic circles, largely because there is a lack of empirical evidence for it (Waterhouse 2006).

THEORIES OF SOCIAL AND CULTURAL DIFFERENCE

Many researchers look to culture, ethnicity, and social status as frameworks for considering individual differences. Some scholars believe that ethnicity and culture shape not only the development of cognitive skills in children but also their approaches to school tasks and behaviors (Hale-Benson 1982). Others have pointed to the impact of social and economic contexts as keys to understanding the different ways that children learn. As will be seen later in this chapter, cultural, social, and ethnic dimensions of learning have tremendous implications for teaching and learning in an information skills curriculum. It is important to note at the outset that any general statements made about groups is always tempered with the realization that no group is monolithic—that there are differences among members of any one cultural or ethnic group just as there are among members of disparate social groups.

Anderson (1988) understands differences in thinking and learning as differences in "worldview" and relates these differences to cultural traditions and values, which he characterizes as "Western" and "non-Western." Among groups Anderson classifies as Western thinkers in the United States are most American males of Anglo-European descent and those members of various minority groups, including women, who have become acculturated into the dominant Anglo-European traditions and value systems to a high degree. In Anderson's analysis, populations considered non-Western include American Indians; Americans of Mexican, African, Vietnamese, Puerto Rican, Chinese, and Japanese descent; and many Anglo-European females. Anderson frames his comparison of the two groups on a variety of dimensions, involving values, social orientation, and cognitive style; these dimensions are summarized in Table 5.1.

According to Anderson (1988), the differences in worldview he has identified are expressed in the classroom in a number of ways. For example, non-Western thinkers tend to perceive separate elements of a phenomenon holistically—that is, as the constituent parts of a complex picture; for this reason, they prefer to begin learning tasks with an overview of a topic or project so that they can see how the subsets or elements are related to each other and to the whole. This orientation is sometimes referred to as field dependence. In addition, they value "affiliation and conformity" in classroom activities over "individuality and competitiveness" (Clark & Halford 1983, 281) and perform best on verbal tasks. Hale-Benson (1982) points to African traditions as the wellspring for the importance of personal connections and social interaction in the learning preferences of black children. Learning that is personally situated and that involves a human aspect is preferred by many non-Western students to the more impersonal, objective, and detached view that typifies the

TABLE 5.1 Anderson's (1988) Dimensions of Non-Western and Western Worldviews

Non-Western	Western
• Emphasis on cooperation/ group achievement	• Task orientation
• Emphasis on individual/ competition	• Emotional expressions are limited
• Social orientation	• Strong nuclear family orientation
• Emotionally expressive	• Values mastery and control of nature
• Strong extended family relationships	• Time provides an invariant structure
• Values harmony with nature	• Religion is separate from culture
• Time is relative	• Believes that the Western worldview is superior
• Religion permeates culture	• Analytical thinking
• Accepts worldviews of others	• Field-independent thinking
• Holistic/relational thinking	
• Field-dependent thinking	

Western approach to topics and subjects. Finally, for many non-Western students, performance in school is highly influenced by authority figures. This may make them especially sensitive to expressions of confidence and expressions of doubt from teachers, administrators, and other adults in the school environment.

Western thinking, on the other hand, is analytical, with elements perceived as separate from the background or "whole" and distinct from one another, an orientation that is known as field independent. Students who exhibit a Western worldview tend to enjoy working more independently and are less likely to be affected by the opinions of others.

Claxton (1990) also recognizes the differences between Western and non-Western worldviews, which he characterizes as two distinct "ways of knowing" (7) that have both sociocultural and cognitive dimensions. Echoing Anderson (1988), Claxton characterizes the Western way as intellectual, detached, and analytical; while the non-Western way is affective, relational, and attached. While Claxton believes that most people feel fairly comfortable with the idea of *learning styles* related to cognitive development, discussions of learning differences related to the social, cultural, and ethnic experience of learners tend to make many educators, community groups, and politicians uneasy. In Claxton's view, educators fear that calling attention to the learning styles of "minority students" will contribute to racial and ethnic stereotyping in ways that undermine demands for educational equity or that justify educational "tracking." However, Claxton argues that a teacher's understanding of the instructional needs of individual children can be deepened through an appreciation of and regard for the differences created by culture and experience. Indeed, he maintains that, as long as educators realize that individual differences within groups negate generalizations across groups, they can employ alternative approaches to learning that can work in each child's environment, and ultimately improve their school performance (Claxton 1990). Understood in this way, knowledge of learning styles can actually validate learning-style differences among students while helping teachers individualize teaching and learning.

Crow (2015) and Crow and Kastello (2016, 2017) used the Hofstede-Bond Model of Five Cultural Dimensions (Hofstede & Bond 1988) in their intrinsic motivation cultural studies (see Chapter 4). Going beyond the Western and non-Western worldview dichotomy, the five dimensions described in the model are *power distance, individualism versus collectivism, masculinity versus femininity, uncertainty avoidance,* and *long-term orientation versus short-term orientation.* Hofstede, called "the founder of comparative intercultural research," conducted a comprehensive study between 1967 and 1973 on how culture influences values in the workplace in more than 70 countries (Hofstede Insights 2019). The original research was expanded to more countries and respondent groups (including students) and now includes cultural dimension comparisons of 76 countries. Additionally, the model now incorporates a sixth dimension, *indulgence versus restraint,* and was renamed the six dimensions of national culture (Hofstede, Hofstede, & Minov 2010). Crow and Kastello used the model to determine the individualism versus collectivism dimensions of the societal context for the students in their studies from

Colorado Springs, United States; Kampala, Uganda; and Mysore, India (Crow 2015; Crow & Kastello 2016, 2017).

One of the most outspoken and influential psychologists in the United States is Carol Gilligan, who was among the first to call attention to the fact that the major developmental theorists based their descriptions of human development exclusively on research from which females and female experience had been excluded. Since the appearance of Gilligan's (1982) book *In a Different Voice*, many scholars have developed a research interest in the experience of women and girls (e.g., see Burdick's research discussed in Chapter 3).

The importance of providing "culturally responsive instructional techniques" has been addressed by a number of scholars who have studied the instructional needs of African American, Hispanic American, and Asian American youth. Irvine and Irvine (1995) have outlined the difficulties that exist for African American and other minority youngsters when schools fail to take their differences in worldview and culture into account. As "Black children's ways of doing and knowing often conflict with and are antithetical to the ways in which schools do and know" (133), the kinds of cultural discontinuities that can occur in the classroom can lead these children to experience both "psychological discomfort and low achievement" (134). In particular, Irvine and Irvine argue that where cultural "otherness" in learning and knowing is "not recognized" or is "rejected," educational contexts can prove alienating and diminishing to minority youngsters. On the other hand, research indicates that where teachers personalize the educational experience, encourage active participation, contextualize instruction, and link curriculum concepts to the "social, cultural, historical and political reality" (138) of "students' everyday experiences" (137), minority youngsters thrive.

Specifically, Irvine and Irvine (1995) argue that minority youngsters who are "predisposed to learning" through "movement, variation, creativity, divergent thinking approaches, inductive reasoning, and a focus on people" are especially at risk where classroom activities and assignments promote only an "analytical style" and emphasize "rules and restriction of movement, standardization, conformity, convergent thinking approaches, deductive reasoning, and a focus on things" (135). In explaining the sorts of misunderstandings that can arise when teachers view stylistic differences in a negative light, the authors offer as an example the elaborate "stage-setting behaviors"—such as "looking over the assignment in its entirety; rearranging posture; elaborately checking pencils, paper, and writing space; asking teachers to repeat directions that have just been given; and checking perceptions of neighboring students" (135)—that often attend initial task engagement for field-dependent students. Such activities are often misconstrued as "avoidance tactics, inattentiveness, disruptions, or evidence of not being prepared to do the assigned task (Gilbert & Gay 1989, 277)" (136).

Understanding behaviors and being sensitive to cultural patterns and preferences will make school libraries safe and supportive places for all students. Group projects, class discussion, and allowing time for student storytelling and the relating of personal experiences as well as positive feedback and interaction with instructors are strategies that will support African American students. In stressing the need for culture-appropriate teaching strategies, Hale-Benson (1982) noted that classrooms that depend primarily on technology, texts, learning centers, drill and practice sessions, television, and programmed instruction at the expense of socially interactive learning activities and people-oriented learning place many children of African heritage at educational risk (Kuykendall 2001).

Finally, teacher expectations are particularly important in the development of positive self-images in minority students. Positive racial attitudes by teachers are associated with higher minority achievement (Forehand, Regosta, & Rock 1976). Conversely, teachers' low expectations based on racial stereotypes lead to lower academic achievement (Pringle, Lyons, & Booker 2010; Sirota & Bailey 2009; Tyler & Boelter 2008). Perhaps even more disturbing are the findings by several researchers that teachers' lowered expectations of minority students begin when reading of their ethnic and social backgrounds, even before the students are "out of the starting gate" on the first day of class (Kleen & Glock 2018; Tenenbaum & Ruck 2007; Tobisch & Dresel 2017).

USING COGNITIVE, CULTURAL, AND SOCIAL THEORIES IN A LIBRARY CONTEXT

The theories presented above have important implications and applications for school librarians in crafting information skills programs and tasks. For example, many of the process models created to guide information seeking and student research are highly sensitive to students' cognitive levels as described by Piaget, Bloom, Marzano, and others. That is, most require students to have achieved formal operations and be capable of higher-level thinking in that they demand that learners examine information sources critically, synthesize information, and evaluate their own thinking as well as their own projects. Assignments that require students to explore a topic, construct research questions, narrow a topic, create a focus, and evaluate the process and its outcomes are complex indeed, and librarians and teachers need to be especially concerned that the complexities of their assignments do not so far exceed a child's present level of cognitive functioning that frustration and failure result. Used by reflective practitioners, knowledge of developmental levels helps school librarians diagnose instructional needs and create scaffolding activities that will support the children in doing with assistance what cannot be managed by the child acting alone.[7] Finally, expectations that students will learn the information search process within the context of a single research project are also bound to end in disappointment (Harada 2002).

Bloom's (1956) Taxonomy provides an extremely useful tool to use when considering the levels of thinking required in carrying out instructional tasks and activities of any kind. Indeed, taking the taxonomy into account is especially important in implementing a successful information skills curriculum, as the processes involved in information searching and the creation of research projects are specifically intended to provide opportunities for students to develop and practice critical thinking skills.

Especially relevant to school librarians has been the work of Hensley (1991), who has applied Kolb's (1983) model of the four learning modes in the library context. Thus, for Kolb's *concrete experiencers*, librarians might want to provide affirmation for the user's request for assistance and respond to requests in empathetic and personalized ways. As *reflective observers* enjoy consider-ing alternatives, librarians should be prepared to listen with patience to the students' explanations and thought processes as they work through assign-ments and projects. Because Kolb's *abstract conceptualizers* often like to work independently, Hensley suggests preparing printed instructions that describe searching techniques and resource options. In providing personal assistance to these learners, Hensley suggests that librarians offer a rationale for sugges-tions they make and provide a number of alternatives. For *active experiment-ers* who enjoy learning by doing and prefer practical and simple explanations, librarians can offer instruction at the same time that they demonstrate or pre-sent appropriate resources.

Matching Learning-Style Preferences to the Information Search Process and Information Search Process Models

In planning instructional interventions and in choosing process models to help guide students in information-seeking activities and research projects, it is important to be sensitive to the different approaches students use in solving real-world problems and to consider allowing students a range of choices. In fact, it is interesting to consider the process models described in Chapter 3 in relation to preferences for teaching and learning. Indeed, when taking into con-sideration Kuhlthau's (1993b, 2004) information search process model, which emphasizes reflection and meaning making; Eisenberg and Berkowitz's (1990) Big6 Skills model, which provides a conceptually neat, analytical, and scien-tific emphasis; Joyce and Tallman's (1997) I-Search model, which focuses on the personal experience of the student in determining topic and format for the project as well as in presenting the final project—all can be seen to reflect dif-ferences in approach similar to the learning modes described by Kolb (1983).

Library Applications for Gardner's Multiple Intelligences and Sternberg's Triarchic Theory

Knowledge of Gardner's (1983) theory of multiple intelligences and Stern-berg's triarchic theory (1985 1997, 1999) certainly argues for school librarians to move beyond the more traditional forms of instruction to provide multimodal approaches to teaching and design information projects that permit students to present their learning in different ways so that students can learn to build on their strengths while at the same time learn to compensate for their weak-nesses (Denison & Montgomery 2012). In so doing, students can build their competence in all areas and demonstrate those gifts not ordinarily valued in school or in school-related assignments and assessments (Lazear 1999).

The move to permit students to present their learning through project options beyond the written report or term paper has made it possible for children and youth with special abilities to maximize their own interests and talents. Other strategies would include the use of games and role playing, graphics and visu-als, manipulatives, class discussions (small and large group), journal writing, graphic organizers, flowcharts, time lines, as well as a myriad of open-source websites and applications and group activities and cooperative learning opportunities in addition to individual activities. These strategies naturally take into account the visual, auditory, and kinesthetic preferences of students and create a context of support for all kinds of learners. It is well to note also that accommodating children's differences in these ways is "culture-fair" (Ford 1996, 19).

Services to Children with Disabilities

An important difference to be accounted for within the context of information seeking and information skills instruction relates to cognitive, physical, or sensory ability levels of students in contemporary classrooms. In 2015–2016, 13 percent of American students received some sort of "special education" support for conditions that included speech or language impairment, autism, developmental delay, intellectual disability, emotional disturbance, hearing impairment, orthopedic impairment, other health impairments, and learning disabilities of various kinds (National Center for Educational Statistics 2018). Since the mid-1970s when Congress passed the Education of All Handicapped Children Act (Public Law 94–142, amended in 1986 by Public Law 99–457), the Elementary and Secondary Education Act of 2001, and the Individuals with Disabilities Education Act in 2004, providing for children with special needs has been a mandate for public education. In effect, these laws required schools to create instruction for children with disabilities in the least restrictive environment possible in accordance with the Individualized Education Program (IEP) created for each exceptional learner. This practice assumes that each adult with whom the child interacts within the school setting has an opportunity to contribute to the child's educational experience.

Two approaches used to structure education for children with disabling conditions are mainstreaming and inclusion. Mainstreamed youngsters spend a portion of the school day in a regular classroom. Inclusion provides all children an opportunity to have their instructional needs met within the regular classroom regardless of disabling conditions. Inclusion presupposes that special needs students may receive support within that setting. Research indicates that the mainstreaming/inclusion of exceptional students results in an improvement in student performance when instruction is tailored to the cognitive and social needs of these students and cooperative learning techniques (peer tutoring, learning buddies) and technology are part of the instructional repertoire (Slavin 1990).

Within both the mainstreaming and inclusion approaches, Universal Design for Learning (UDL; Meyer, Rose, & Gordon 2014) is a newly founded, practical framework which takes a proactive approach "to maximize learning opportunities for all students" (Blue & Pace 2011) primarily with the intentional and targeted use of technology. The framework calls for creating instruction from the outset that provides:

- *Multiple means of representation* to give learners various ways of acquiring information and knowledge;
- *Multiple means of expression* to provide learners alternatives for demonstrating what they know;

- *Multiple means of engagement* to tap into learners' interests, challenge them appropriately, and motivate them to learn. (Center for Applied Special Technology [CAST], 2019)

The UDL approach in libraries underscores not only the importance of developing a rich and diverse library collection, but also provides means through which all learners are able to "attain, engage, and express ideas and information" (Blue & Pace 2011, 51). Knowledge of technology resources and instructional approaches are essential for school librarians to provide these types of comprehensive services.

Callison's (1990) review of the research literature in school librarianship and special needs children in the early 1990s cited a number of unpublished doctoral dissertations that dealt with the library collections for special needs students (e.g., Davie 1978; Vinson 1983) and the practice and perceptions of school librarians with regard to exceptional students (Buckley 1978). At that time, Callison called for increased attention in this area of school librarianship. That call, at least to some extent, has been answered with studies conducted in the ensuing years, but the news is still not satisfactory with regard to school library services for students with disabilities.

Studies on collaboration between SPED teachers and school librarians, as well as the inclusiveness of the library program's collection and services have surfaced (Allen & Hughes-Hassell 2010; Ennis-Cole & Smith 2011; Perrault 2011; Small, Snyder, & Parker 2009; Subramaniam, Oxley, & Kodama 2013). The research on the training and preparedness of school librarians to teach students with disabilities paints a bleak picture (Cox 2004; Ennis-Cole & Smith 2011; Murray 2001; Perrault 2011; Small, Snyder, & Parker 2009; Subramaniam, Oxley, & Kodama 2013). While the research shows that school librarians understand the importance of and desire to provide specialized services for students who need them (Allen & Hughes-Hassell 2010), they simply have not been trained to do so. Very few LIS programs provide or require course work in library services and exceptionalities (Ennis-Cole & Smith 2011; Small, Snyder, & Parker 2009; Subramaniam, Oxley, & Kodama 2013).

There have been some bright lights in the dim picture portraying the support of students with disabilities in school libraries. Ennis-Cole and Smith (2011) found in their national study on the use of assistive technology (AT) used to assist students with autism that school librarians "do have the foundational knowledge to implement AT" (95) but that in order to be leaders in school implementation they need training to be able "to think of the application of technology in a specialized manner" (95). In their study of the implementation of response to intervention (RTI, Gersten et al. 2009) in Missouri schools, Robins and Antrim (2012) found that 62 percent of the librarians had found ways to contribute to the RTI initiative in their schools, including opportunities for more collaboration. Blue and Pace (2011) include a table of media formats and a simple checklist school librarians can use to make "strategic steps forward toward inclusion and independent use of library resources," including the implementation of UDL (54). In the spring of 2019, the American Library Association offered "Serving Children with Autism Spectrum Disorder Workshop" taught by Dr. Lesley Farmer. Small and Stewart (2013) reported on Project

ENABLE (Expanding Non-Discriminatory Access by Librarians Everywhere), an initiative by the Center for Digital Literacy at Syracuse University and backed by the Institute of Museum and Library Services (IMLS), which provides "free and accessible professional education to librarians who seek to deliver effective, inclusive library and information services and programs to their students with disabilities" (12). The project began with workshops in the summer of 2011 to 45 teams from New York State school districts. The teams consisted of a librarian, a special educator, and a general educator who participated in the five-day face-to-face workshops. In the summer of 2013, the project expanded to include teams nationwide. Currently, the project provides a free and accessible training website designed to accommodate groups or individuals (13).

The National School Library Standards (AASL 2018) incorporates "Include" as one of the Shared Foundations, based on the key commitment to "demonstrate an understanding of and commitment to inclusiveness and respect for diversity in the learning community" (76). Project ENABLE (Small & Stewart 2013) and "Serving Children with Autism Spectrum Disorder Workshop" taught by Dr. Lesley Farmer are both forward-thinking and courageous beginnings, but in order to meet this mandate more training is needed, both in LIS programs and through other forms of professional development for school librarians.

RELATING CULTURAL AND SOCIAL DIFFERENCES TO INSTRUCTIONAL DESIGN

In dissertation research that sought to test a variety of instructional approaches to the teaching of library skills, Bobotis (1978) compared the effectiveness of oral (lecture), visual (overhead transparencies), and performance approaches to instruction with 21 classes of Hispanic (Mexican American) and Anglo-American seventh graders. Her findings revealed that Mexican American students in her study learned more when information was presented using performance-based methods that more clearly reflected "real-world" types of activities. For this reason, she concluded that there might be a relationship between ethnicity and learning-style preferences in the acquisition of library skills. Lin (1994), who studied cultural differences in an academic library, reached a similar conclusion. Lin's research suggested that Asian (Chinese) and other non-Western, holistic thinkers might benefit for an overview of the library as a system before being introduced to library routines, library resources, and searching skills. Adeoye's research of Nigerian university students taking online classes also found that their learning styles varied according to their tribal backgrounds and gender (2011).

Citing studies that indicated that there are gender differences[8] (Canada & Brusca 1991; Diem 1986; Freedman 1989) and ethnic differences (DeVillar & Faltis 1991) related to attitudes and the use of computers, Freedman and Liu (1996) found that there were "cultural differences in learning with computers" (57) when they studied a group of middle school Hmong youngsters. In observing the exchange of e-mail messages between their informants and minority students in other cities involving their ethnic traditions, family life, and school experiences, the researchers found that cultural values of the Hmong students created difficulties related to course content, the role of the instructor, and inquiry learning strategies. Content issues related to the assignment surfaced because the students in the study had been raised according to "a strictly patriarchal system" within which males are regarded as "keepers of cultural knowledge" (48) of the sort that students were supposed to investigate. Since the possession of this kind of information is exclusively a male prerogative, "both boys and girls were concerned about the girls learning things about Hmong culture traditionally outside of their accepted range of knowledge" (54). In addition, restrictions on access to cultural traditions meant that in many cases Hmong students lacked knowledge of their own culture to share in response to questions that their "key pals" asked of them. Negotiation with students and parents was necessary to overcome these impediments to information seeking and learning.

The role of the teacher in the learning process also proved problematic for this group of youngsters. For example, even though learning the use of the computer was the intent of the course, many students were reluctant to ask for assistance because to do so would have been to admit that they "lacked computer knowledge" (Freedman & Liu 1996, 52). Rather than "lose face" in this way, students tended to ask one another for help. Similarly, the Hmong students did not like others to watch "over their shoulders" while they were working, lest they be observed making errors. Finally, whereas Anglo students tended to jump into assignments and use a trial-and-error method when using computers, Asian students were reluctant to undertake an assignment without specific direction.

These kinds of differences pose challenges for teachers and librarians in planning instruction for groups of minority students unless they have knowledge of approaches to learning that are part of the cultural experience of these students. Where there are differences between the content and processes of instruction and the ways of knowing and learning, the differences will have to be discussed so that students and parents see the value of the assignments and develop a level of comfort with what may be for them entirely novel instructional situations. By the same token, changes in practice to ensure the personal and cultural confirmation of minority students are also appropriate; these might include the use of same-sex grouping, turn taking with regard to leadership roles in group activities, and the explanation, modeling, and implementation of peer tutoring activities.

Clearly, the challenge of differentiating information skills instruction is multidimensional, and much more research on information-seeking behavior will have to be done before there will be definitive answers about how differences in learning styles can be best accommodated in instruction and supported in action. However, the research reviewed above provides a foundation and a rationale for the development of user-centered instruction. Students need to be made aware of the processes that underlie information seeking and to have opportunities to discuss with others the projects in which they are involved (Irving 1985; Kuhlthau, Goodin, & McNally 1996). Indeed, many scholars believe that the reflection on the process is essential for the retention and application of learning across situations and settings. Others would argue, with Delpit and Kohl (2006), that attention should also be paid to the products created by students in demonstrating their learning as well since in many cases it is by project completion that adults are evaluated in the larger world outside the school. School librarians who can take individual differences into account will be able to make a genuine contribution to the success of all students and model a type of inclusivity that honors "the many different ways students learn and process information" (Teele 1996, 65). Indeed, the library should be a safe place for the expression of these differences.

DIFFERENTIATING RESEARCH TASKS

A useful way to accommodate the learning styles and capitalize on learning strengths that individuals bring to learning tasks within the context of library-based information-seeking tasks is to reframe or have students reframe research questions based on their own preferences. Handling research assignments in this way ensures that students actually have to interact with and apply the information they find to resolve a specific issue and present a synthesis in their own words. Planning a variety of questions to guide student research will accommodate learning-style differences because alternative questions permit students to investigate a subject or engage a topic based on personal interests and perspectives (Thomas, Vroegindewey, & Wellins 1997). Such an approach has the added advantage of promoting a type of inquiry learning that is "founded in gathering information for the purpose of seeking various perspectives, not just a single conclusion" (Callison 1994, 55) and to do so in ways that reflect "the way we learn in 'real life'" (Donham et al. 2001). Kuhlthau, Maniotes, and Caspari (2007) promote the seeking of many perspectives rather than a transmission approach to teaching that "emphasizes the right answer, memorizing specific facts, and repackaging information" (14). Such an approach also reduces the likelihood that students will find either useful or relevant information that they simply copy or download from print or online sources.

However, it should be noted that generating research questions is often a very difficult task and requires practice (Irving 1985). For example, the ability to consider alternative points of view will pose a considerable challenge for concrete thinkers. For this reason, it is appropriate to offer younger students an array of alternatives in research approach from which students can choose. On the other hand, changing the ways that questions are asked may provide students with practice in creating a focus for their topics (Irving 1985), which Kuhlthau (1993a, 1993b) considers *the* crucial element in the successful implementation and completion of the information search process.

When generating a thesis statement and developing a personal focus are objectives within the overall assignment, teachers can assist students by providing models to serve as catalysts for student thinking. By assisting teachers in the development of alternative questions, librarians can use their expertise as instructional consultants to add value to the projects students create. Past research has tended to focus on two-member collaborative teams consisting of the teacher and school librarian. However, Kuhlthau et al. (2007) recommend three-member instructional teams (consisting of the teacher, school librarian, and an additional specialist) as "highly desirable for the most productive collaborative planning and teaching" (48).

Collaborating with teachers in creating research projects for students that permit student choice in terms of topics and approaches is a way of ensuring culture-fair practice in information skills instruction. Moreover, providing an overview of the search process and a rationale for its use are strategies that will be appropriate for many minority youngsters whose thinking is consistent with non-Western cognitive patterns. Finally, making sure that minorities and minority history and traditions are fully represented in the topics chosen as vehicles for student learning as a standard part of the curriculum (not just the focus of Black History Month) and in the organization and patterns of classroom activity will help subvert institutional racism, which many educators see as compromising the ability of minority youngsters to achieve at high levels.

Insights from the research in education and LIS can be summarized as including the following themes: that learning involves personal construction, that learning builds on prior experience or knowledge, that learning proceeds in a nonlinear fashion, that learning is inherently social as well as psychological, that children can understand at a number of levels, that they can perform at higher levels if they are assisted by knowledgeable others, that they learn differently, that intelligence can take multiple forms, and that differences in learning styles are related to biology, culture, motivation, and experience. To create assignments supportive of only one style of information behavior is a discriminatory practice that works to disadvantage students whose cognitive styles and strengths reflect other orientations and interests. This fact demands that school librarians consider multiculturalism and its complexities in ways that truly support and extend learning rather than merely to engage in cultural "tourism" of the type represented by sporadic, once-a-year tributes to ethnic heroes, multicultural food festivals, and multiethnic literature fairs. Although these gestures no doubt make multiculturalism objectives visible, their use addresses the artifacts of culture rather than reflecting cultural values and alternative ways of knowing[9] and constitutes a nod in the general direction of minority students rather than an invitation for them to dine at an educational table prepared with their instructional needs in mind. "We can continue to view diversity as a problem," Delpit (1995) writes, or "we can recognize that diversity of thought, language, and worldview . . . can not only provide an exciting educational setting, but can also prepare our children for the richness of living in an increasingly diverse national community" (66).

MODELING SUPPORT FOR ALL STUDENTS IN LIBRARY DESIGN AND INSTRUCTION

Support for the use of individual differences in planning library spaces for library instruction appears in research by Dunn and Smith (1990). In their study, these researchers employed a 23-element construct of learning styles developed by Dunn, Dunn, and Price (1985). The elements, which can "affect a person's ability to absorb, process, and retain information" (Dunn & Smith 1990, 33), can be grouped along five dimensions: (1) environmental (sound, light, temperature, and design), (2) emotional (motivation, persistence, responsibility, and structure), (3) sociological (social ability in terms of self, pairs, peers, teams, adults, and variety), (4) physical (perceptual, nutritional, temporal, and mobility), and (5) psychological (hemisphericity, impulsivity and reflexivity, and analytical and global). According to Dunn and Smith, "the most important aspect is the potent contribution to individualizing instruction" (36) made possible through applications of this construct. More recently, Lovelace has affirmed that the Dunn and Dunn Learning-Style Model (1993, 1999) improves both students' academic achievement and attitudes toward learning by "matching students' learning-style preferences with complementary instruction" (2005, 1). In the same way, Blue and Pace (2011) outline the importance of using Universal Design (UD) in school library environments to enable "access to the

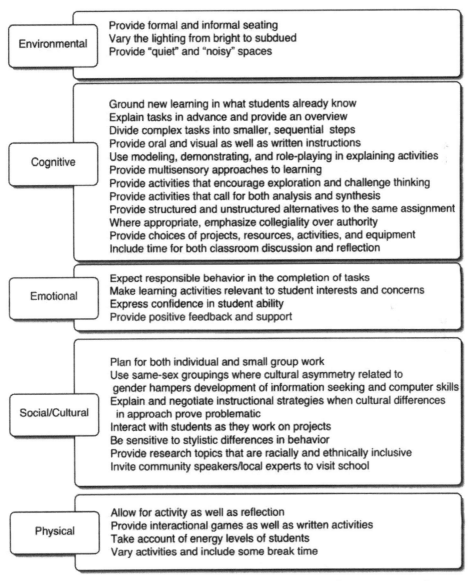

Environmental
Provide formal and informal seating
Vary the lighting from bright to subdued
Provide "quiet" and "noisy" spaces

Cognitive
Ground new learning in what students already know
Explain tasks in advance and provide an overview
Divide complex tasks into smaller, sequential steps
Provide oral and visual as well as written instructions
Use modeling, demonstrating, and role-playing in explaining activities
Provide multisensory approaches to learning
Provide activities that encourage exploration and challenge thinking
Provide activities that call for both analysis and synthesis
Provide structured and unstructured alternatives to the same assignment
Where appropriate, emphasize collegiality over authority
Provide choices of projects, resources, activities, and equipment
Include time for both classroom discussion and reflection

Emotional
Expect responsible behavior in the completion of tasks
Make learning activities relevant to student interests and concerns
Express confidence in student ability
Provide positive feedback and support

Social/Cultural
Plan for both individual and small group work
Use same-sex groupings where cultural asymmetry related to
  gender hampers development of information seeking and computer skills
Explain and negotiate instructional strategies when cultural differences
  in approach prove problematic
Interact with students as they work on projects
Be sensitive to stylistic differences in behavior
Provide research topics that are racially and ethnically inclusive
Invite community speakers/local experts to visit school

Physical
Allow for activity as well as reflection
Provide interactional games as well as written activities
Take account of energy levels of students
Vary activities and include some break time

FIGURE 5.9   Strategies for Multidimensional, Student-Centered Learning

facility and its services for the widest number of users, including people with a range of differences (e.g., disabilities, age, reading ability, language, and culture) (49). Not to be confused with Universal Design for Learning (Meyer, Rose, & Gordon 2014), UD espouses the need for "the design and composition of an environment so that it can be accessed, understood and used to the greatest extent possible by all people regardless of their age, size, ability or disability" (National Disability Authority 2014). This seems entirely consistent with the goal of customization promoted in most contemporary school libraries and many schools.

CONCLUSION

The work of the many theorists and research scholars reviewed in this chapter offers school librarians a variety of approaches and strategies to use in tailoring instruction to the needs of individuals and groups they serve. Some practical suggestions gleaned from this review are presented in Figure 5.9.

NOTES

1. The contemporary term for individualizing instruction is "curriculum differentiation," a strategy that calls on teachers to alter course content and processes, instructional environment, learning products, and assessment measures in response to the interests and abilities of individual students. Interdisciplinary approaches to content, independent activities, critical thinking, active exploration, and challenging assignments are current priorities in curriculum differentiation.
2. When employed in this context, the model assumes that lessons proceed within the context of ongoing classroom activity and draws attention to the necessity of project coordination and cooperative planning with the classroom teacher.
3. In recent thinking and writing on the topic of sense making, Dervin has moved from conceptualizing gaps as obstacles in everyday life to an emphasis on the "hows" of sense making as a "methodological tool" (Savolainen 2003, 697). For a complete explanation of Dervin's current use of sense making, see Dervin (1999).
4. Of interest in this regard is a recent (2002) Kaiser Family Foundation study presented ("See No Evil: How Internet Filters Affect the Search for Online Health Information") citing Generation Rx.com's report that 75 percent of young adults (ages 15–24) relied on information obtained online to fulfill their health-related information needs with fully 44 percent seeking information on birth control and sexually transmitted diseases. The Kaiser report studied three levels of Internet filters (least restrictive [blocking pornography] to intermediate [blocking pornography, nudity, and discrimination] to most restrictive [blocking these categories in addition to profanity, drugs, and alcohol]). Filters assessed to be most restrictive incorrectly blocked 50 percent of sites dealing with safe sex and sexual health issues (as opposed to 9 percent for least restrictive filters) and 60 percent of gay health sites. Significantly, the kinds of information most often blocked related to sexually transmitted disease, pregnancy and birth control, and safe sex.
5. Julien's (1999) study of adolescent career decision making supports this view. In addition, career decisions, as well as health decisions, require youth to make

sense of information from an often bewildering array of sources: "parents, siblings, other family members, family friends, peers, guidance counselors, teachers, school and public library resources, the mass media, and government career centers" (38). Add to this the social pressures, socialization patterns, and lack of self-confidence that accompany children into adolescence and one begins to understand the complexities of information-based decision making.

6. The theoretical frameworks related to moral and social development in the writings of Lawrence Kohlberg, Erik Eriksen, and others are also relevant to issues of differentiation of instruction. Readers are encouraged to explore these theories in Lawrence Kohlberg's Stages in the *Development of Moral Thought and Action* (New York: Holt, Rinehart and Winston, 1969); and Erik H. Eriksen's *Identity, Youth, and Crisis* (New York: Norton, 1968).

7. A study by Cooper (2002) takes into account frameworks created by Piaget, Vygotsky, and Kuhlthau in exploring the information-seeking behavior of second graders. Specifically, Cooper was interested in observing how students, operating cognitively between preoperational and concrete-operational levels, find information in a school library. The research tasks undertaken by the youngsters included searching for books on general and specific topics on the library shelves and for information on the same topics in a CD-ROM encyclopedia. Cooper found that scaffolding techniques of encouragement and suggestions provided by the school librarian as the electronic searches proceeded enabled preabstract thinkers to operate more successfully and confidently in the "metaphysical world" of electronic searching. In addition, computerized searches, which channeled the seekers directly to relevant information, reduced the cognitive demands experienced when new readers negotiate finding aids such as titles, indexes, and tables of contents before actually locating information. Cooper's work also provided evidence for Kuhlthau's (1993b) assertion that feelings are an important aspect of the ISP for "novice information seekers." Her observations led Cooper to conclude that "children tend to favor browsing types of strategies in their information seeking"; that they "rely on visual information if it is available to them rather than using textual information"; and that they can use "meta-information in textual format to find information if it is presented in a very directed manner."

8. Cai, Fan, and Du (2017) affirmed in a meta-analysis that such gender differences still exist.

9. Ford (1996) presents Boykin's (1994) list of cultural values and styles as follows: spirituality ("the conviction that nonmaterial religious forces influence people's everyday lives"), harmony ("the notion that one's fate is interrelated with other elements in the scheme of things so that humankind and nature are harmonically conjoined"), movement ("a premium placed on the amalgamation of movement, (poly)rhythm, dance, and percussion embodied in the musical beat"), verve ("a propensity for relatively high levels of stimulation and for action that is energetic and lively"), affect (the centrality of affective information and emotional expressiveness and the equal and integrated importance of thoughts and feelings"), communalism ("a commitment to the fundamental interdependence of people and the importance of social bonds"), oral tradition ("the centrality of oral and aural modes of communication for conveying full meaning and the cultivation of speaking as performance"), expressive individualism ("the cultivation of a distinctive personality and a proclivity for spontaneity and genuine personal expression"), social time perspective ("a commitment to a social construction of time as personified by an event orientation") (85–86).

6

Building Information Competence
Designing Instruction for Today's Learners

The solution is not just helping people develop simple, common-sense web evaluation habits. It's also helping them determine what they are going to trust, since the vast majority of sources lie in the gray area between unimpeachability and fake news. Being able to make sound decisions about information sources is both a skill and a habit of mind, one that requires practice to develop. Libraries can play a vital role in building better communities by supporting our patrons in becoming savvy information consumers.

—Farkas (2018)

The profound changes wrought by digital technology have created opportunities for students unparalleled in the history of education. Our ability to connect students with an ever-expanding, increasingly "interactive informational universe" (Huston 1989, 19) has transformed the concept of "library" from a place to a "function" (Ely 1992) and has vastly increased the contributions school libraries can make to teaching and learning. Indeed, late-20th-century preoccupations with library automation, Internet access, and expanding electronic resources (Kafai & Bates 1997) have given way to millennial efforts to integrate technology across the curriculum and help students make sense of Web 2.0 technologies within a climate of school reform characterized by both severe budgetary limitations and demands for increased accountability. At the same time, the ability to access electronic resources has brought into sharp relief the layers of complexity surrounding online searching and the challenges that confront school librarians when helping students find and use information to meet academic and personal needs.

CREATING COMPETENT STUDENTS: AN INSTRUCTIONAL IMPERATIVE

Basic to research in the area of technology and information skills instruction is the assumption that a contemporary definition of information literacy must include the ability to locate, retrieve, and use electronic as well as print-based resources and that, in addition to information literacy, students must also "develop and satisfy personal curiosity by reading widely and deeply in multiple formats and write and create for a variety of purposes" (AASL 2018, 38). While our commitment to helping children learn the skills they need to be successful in school still holds strong, school librarians must also ensure that students can succeed in the workplaces of today and of tomorrow (AASL 2009; Kuhlthau 2001).[1]

In an article in *Forbes'* electronic journal, columnist Mark Moran (2010) cited a *New York Times* story that "chronicled the 21st century school librarian as web curator and information literacy specialist" for the nation's children. While it is indeed good news that the contributions to education that school librarians make on a daily basis has been so publicly acknowledged, Moran's article went on to bemoan the prevalence of "clueless administrators [who] persist in maintaining that a search engine is an adequate substitute for a trained research teacher." Writing for a lay rather than a professional audience, Moran made his case in this way:

> In the libraries of old, the Dewey Decimal System got you started in research. But there is no card catalog for 2.0. To use the Internet as a library you need new research skills: the ability to pick out reliable sources from an overwhelming heap of misinformation, to find relevant material amid an array of options, to navigate the shifting ethics of creative commons and intellectual property rights and to present conclusions in a manner that engages modern audiences. . . . In addition to learning how to phrase a search query, students need to learn how to protect themselves online, and how to share their work through wikis, videos, and other interactive media. Without a dedicated guide, they end up, in the words of professor Henry Jenkins, as "feral children of the Internet raised by Web 2.0 wolves." (para. 4, 7)

In a nutshell, Moran has summarized the new competencies needed by contemporary youngsters in navigating the dynamic and complex information landscape that the Internet represents while also articulating what is most problematic in using the very resources that so many school administrators are apparently counting on as substitutes for school libraries.

The new standards introduced by the AASL in 2018 were created to meet the challenges of contemporary and evolving information environments and together identify the technological competencies that students need to develop not only in today's school, but in our increasingly global society. The instructional imperative, which Moran (2010) so clearly articulates, also sets a high bar for library professionals in engaging students of Generation Z and helping them overcome the issues and challenges manifest in obtaining the benefits of technology set forth above. Research studies have identified the many challenges that technology poses for young searchers. It is hoped that the review provided below will initiate discussion, drive objectives, and identify outcomes for instructional programs that will directly address the learning needs of students for whom Moran advocates so passionately. Because most contemporary observers consider today's learners as a unique group with needs and perspectives that differ in significant ways from those of students in preceding generations, this chapter begins with a description of the Net Generations (Generations X, Y, and Z) and how these contemporary youngsters understand and use digital technology and behave when seeking information online. Also considered are the ways in which technology has revolutionized teaching and learning in classrooms and school libraries and the need for new and sophisticated skill sets and research-based instructional intervention to ensure searching success. Strategies for helping students deal with the ethical uses of information found online are included. A concluding section discusses issues relating to hardware, software, and maintenance of computer equipment and the challenges these may present in running the school library.

THE DIGITAL AGE OF GENERATIONS X AND Y

Members of Generation X (born 1965–1979) are digital immigrants but are heavy TV and Facebook users. According to KASASA (2019) Generation X are savvy computer users and consumers of digital information. They spend approximately seven hours a week on social media, being the highest Facebook users compared to Generations Y and Z (born between 1995–2019). This generation was born at a time when there was also a rise in personal computing.

Generation Y, or the Millennials (born between 1980–1994), is the largest generation in America today, with a population of 95 million. "This generation is extremely comfortable with mobile devices but 32% will still use a computer for purchases. They typically have multiple social media accounts" (Kasasa 2019, para.19). Whereas their parents may have been content to be information consumers, Millennials prefer to construct their own knowledge and distribute it using a dazzling array of Web 2.0 tools. This means, of course, that "the literacy education provided in the past by parents and teachers will no longer equip [them] for success in the altered world in which [they] live" (Selfie & Howisher 2004, cited in Asselin & Doiron 2008, 1). What was necessary and sufficient to know and understand in a print-based and often finite set of information resources is today not in any way helpful for students who must navigate constantly evolving networks, evaluate websites, choose search engines, select hyperlinks, and compare "information across sources" (Asselin & Doiron 2008, 2).

It is interesting to note that Generation Y members were among the first to embrace the use of computers in the school library. While some of their elders were mourning the passing of the "card catalog," youngsters were eager to search the library collection electronically (Armstrong & Costa 1983) and could do so successfully (Borgman et al. 1995; Marchionini & Teague 1987; Solomon 1994) from an early date. As long ago as the 1990s, for example, Tapscott (1998) sensed a change in computer expertise that often made teenagers more technologically adept than their parents and teachers. In the years since, student access and comfort with technologies of all kinds have increased, just as the ages at which children are developing relatively sophisticated skill sets continue to decrease.

Tapscott followed up his original work *Growing Up Digital* (1998) with a large-scale mixed-methods research study that examined the habits and activities of the Net Generation. His team interviewed Generation Y (Millennials) as well as members of the Generation X population. In *Grown Up Digital,* Tapscott (2009) addresses those who would bemoan the potential issues displayed by this generation who daily interact with digital technologies—that is, a possible lowering of intelligence, a growing lack of social skills, the blurring of concept of privacy within evolving social conventions, interference by so-called helicopter parents, the violation of online intellectual property rights, cyberbullying, online violence via gaming behaviors, the lack of a work ethic, increased narcissism, and an overall lack of moral and civic values. Instead, Tapscott (2009) describes eight characteristics of today's digital age learners, which he terms "net gen norms." In his view, these learners prefer freedom to create and perform work when and where they please. They customize hardware and software to make their preferred technologies work in ways that suit their personal needs. They use *scrutiny* to determine the worth of information and goods: "They compare and contrast product information online and look for the cheapest price without sacrificing value. They read blogs, forums, and reviews. They're skeptical about online reviews. Instead, they consult their friends" (81).

Tapscott describes integrity for Generation Ys as meaning that they are tolerant, open to alternative viewpoints, and quick to examine corporate misbehavior. (It is interesting to note, however, that here Tapscott provides several statements from students and young adults who comfortably provide justification for illegally downloading music, videos, and other content from Internet sources.) These students also express a need for collaborative experiences, whether they occur in an actual, physical place, or in online environments where many users from different geographical locations may come together to work on projects or gaming. These preferences argue for flexibility and creativity of instructional design. However, as Tapscott warns, "The current model of pedagogy is teacher focused, one-way, one size fits all. It isolates the student in the learning process" (91).

Tapscott goes on to advise us that Net Gen students also have a need for entertainment both in personal and in work situations, which in part explains their proclivities toward engaging in many activities at once. These same students also greatly value speed in terms of connectivity and response time for instant messaging and social networking. Additionally, they seek out innovation, looking for newer and better ways to conduct the business of their lives. Tapscott tells us that it is not unusual to see young people upgrade media players, for example, every time a newer generation with more features is released for sale.

A journal article by Donald Secreast (2013) questions Tapscott's positive prediction of Generations X, Y, and Z. He questions the Net Gen's ability to think critically. "As convenient as it might be to have 24-hour access to journals, books, and specialized websites, at some point we must climb out of that information hot tub and let our brains do their work" (26).

That said, it is clear that the technological expertise that today's students bring to the classroom and library has changed the dynamics and direction of instruction in both settings. While as individuals the youth of the digital age are remarkably diverse, school librarians can capitalize on the technological prowess many members of this group of youngsters display in the development of dynamic teaching models that will assist these learners to develop 21st-century literacy competencies.

UNDERSTANDING GENERATION Z

When understanding the different generations, one must note that new technologies are usually first embraced by members of the youngest generation, currently Generation Z (born between 1995 and 2020). A statistic that supports this assertion is that 95 percent of all Americans own a smartphone; however, the members of the Generation Z population is the highest user group of this device (Kasasa 2019). Gen Z (also known as iGen) has grown up in a "hyperconnected world and the smartphone is their preferred method of communication" (Kasasa 2019, para 22). It is estimated that Gen Z members spend three hours daily on their mobile devices. With this information, what kinds of preferences and enthusiasms does this generation exhibit, and how can our understanding of their worldview assist us in providing learner-centered programs and services?

While there is not yet a great deal of research on the information literacy tendencies of Generation Z, a 2019 study developed by researchers at *Library Journal* revealed that Generation Z is the user group that most reads for pleasure (Vercelletto 2019). According to Vercelletto (2019) after reading a book, "A little more than a third of Gen Z readers are 'very likely' or 'likely' to rate or review that book online or to post their thoughts about it on social media, slightly down from Millennial rates" (27). This research also revealed that 65 percent of Generation Z readers preferred reading fiction books with their favorite genres being "young adult fantasy, romance, horror and graphic novels" (28).

It will be interesting to see what future research reveals about the current generation of students now in school, but the findings to date show great promise in the area of reading and information literacy.

WEB 2.0: AN INFORMATION SPACE FOR CHILDREN AND YOUTH

If there is one single behavior that typifies technology use by today's young people, it is their obsession with social networking sites (e.g., Facebook/Messenger, Instagram, Twitter, Pinterest, WeChat, Snapchat, Tumblr, LinkedIn, Vine, TikTok, and Yik Yak), virtual worlds (e.g., Worlds Away, Farm World, Habbo Hotel, Dreamscape, and Cityscape), multiplayer gaming (e.g., Call of Duty, World of Warcraft, Minecraft, and Halo) online collaboration (e.g., wikis and

Google Docs), and journaling (e.g., blogging, Tumblr, and Ghost, mashups, zines, and video sharing, to name a few, and the seemingly seamless ways in which these are integrated "into all aspects of their lives" (Asselin & Doiron 2008, 1).

Finally, graphics and the interactive features of Internet searching are particularly popular among today's Web-surfing youngsters. Interactivity and animation reflect the active learning style of many children, while the graphics help them to make sense of the information, especially when a child's interest level exceeds her or his cognitive ability and reading proficiency.

HOW STUDENTS THINK ABOUT AND USE THE INTERNET IN INFORMATION SEEKING

What does the research tell us about Internet use by children and youth of the latest generations? Almost 20 years ago (2001), the Pew Internet and American Life Project (Simon, Graziano, & Lenhart 2001) interviewed students from across the country to determine information-seeking behaviors and experiences. The studies provided statistical evidence for what most educators already suspected—students were using the Internet in ever-increasing numbers, and most of them were thoroughly enjoying the experience. For example, 94 percent of the teenagers who reported having access to the Internet indicated that they relied heavily on online information for research tasks; 71 percent of them used "the Internet as the major source for their most recent school project"; "58% had used a Web site set up by school or a class; 34% had downloaded a study guide; and 17% had created a Web page for a school project." As Bilal and Watson (1998) observed, "[T]he Web's ease of access, speed of finding information, convenience of access from home and richness in graphics" so appeal to 21st-century youngsters that their continued participation online for school-related research, personal information seeking, and entertainment is virtually guaranteed.

A number of earlier studies also demonstrated the popularity of electronic and online resources and preferred searching strategies. For example, a study by Newbold (1993, cited in Bialo & Sivin-Kachala 1996) reported not only that children preferred researching the electronic encyclopedias to their print counterparts but also that the use of these electronic sources was related to positive attitudes about the library and about writing. Interestingly, Large and Beheshti (2000) found that their informants preferred using the Web as a research resource even though they reported that it was harder for them to use than print sources. In addition, Sutton's research (1991, cited in Martinez 1994) found "some evidence that [for] disadvantaged students" "computer technology [was] especially engaging" (399). It is perhaps for this reason that students surveyed by Todd and Kuhlthau in the Ohio Research Study (Whelan 2004) emphasized technology support and instruction as such important aspects of their school's library program.

Although many researchers have frequently commented on the motivational value of Internet use and electronic searching capabilities, this does not necessarily mean that today's youngsters have abandoned print resources. In fact, not all research supports the notion that students uniformly prefer the use of the Internet to books and other media for information seeking. Latrobe and Havener (1997) found that books, magazines, and television all were used more often than were electronic resources by high school honor students in meeting their information needs. Both Large and Beheshti (2000) and Gross (1999) found that younger students did not have the same affinity for using the computer for information seeking as their high school counterparts. A study by Crow (2009) found that upper-elementary students who were intrinsically motivated for information seeking were all users of computer technology, but fewer preferred electronic information sources over print materials.

A 2017 mixed-methods study by Baron, Calixte, and Havewala involved 429 college students from the United States, Japan, Germany, Slovakia, and India. This study examined students' preferences of print or digital media. Results continued to show students preferred reading print materials. "Nearly 92% said they concentrated best when reading in print, and more than four-fifths reported that if cost were the same, they preferred print for both schoolwork and pleasure reading" (Baron et al. 2017, 590). The study went on to report that student participants had a propensity to reread printed information compared to digital, and they also reported a tendency to multitask when reading digital information onscreen. Students in the study were also asked to report what they liked most and least about reading in print and digital formats. "Advantages reported for print included ease of annotation and paper's tactile properties, while among the disadvantages were lack of convenience and expenditure of environmental or monetary resources. The biggest advantage of screen reading was convenience, while the primary disadvantages were eyestrain and distraction" (Baron et al. 2017, 590). Data from a 2018 Pew Research Center survey (Anderson & Jiang 2018a) of U.S. teens show students in the digital age are knowledgeable about Internet challenges, but also see the advantages of growing up in a digital world.

It remains to be seen if future studies will confirm these patterns and preferences.

THE EXPERIENCE AND MEANING OF THE INTERNET FOR CHILDREN AND YOUTH

Research indicates that children's search experience online is multidimensional, engaging them in cognitive, behavioral, affective, and social activities. For example, the thinking about and choosing of a topic and coming up with search terms to describe it, as well as keeping track mentally of search options and determining relevance of retrieved items, are tasks that engage children on a number of cognitive levels. At the same time, behavioral demands of Internet use relate to eye-hand coordination, keyboarding and typing, mouse management, and operating peripherals (e.g., printers, web cams, and jump drives). Children are also engaged on an emotional or affective level, particularly when screens freeze, printers jam, and searches result in an avalanche, or a dearth, of "hits." Perhaps because they have been conditioned by technological advances and/or media hype to expect near-instantaneous responses from information systems, speed seems to be an issue and an expectation for many technology natives. Outdated equipment and insufficient bandwidth can combine to produce slowdowns in retrieval that exasperate students, especially when connection time in school is limited to one or a portion of a class period.

Finally, children's use of the Internet has a dynamic social dimension in that they enjoy assisting one another and sharing ideas, information, and websites. Facebook once dominated social media, but current teens identified YouTube, Instagram, and SnapChat as their preferred social media applications according to a 2018 Pew Research Center survey (Anderson & Jiang 2018a). "When it comes to which one of these online platforms teens use the most, roughly one-third say they visit Snapchat (35%) or YouTube (32%) most often, while 15% say the same of Instagram" (Anderson & Jiang 2018a, para. 9). Facebook followed with 10 percent using this online social platform.

In addition, data from a recent Pew survey show 95 percent of teens have access to a smartphone. These mobile devices facilitate a constant online presence with "45% of teens now say[ing] they are online on a near-constant basis" (Anderson & Jiang 2018a, para. 2). With this persistent online presence and the threat of cyberbullying, one might question if teens view social media negatively. But according to Anderson and Jiang (2018a), "Minorities of teens describe that effect as mostly positive (31%) or mostly negative (24%), but the largest share (45%) says that effect has been neither positive nor negative" (para. 3). The Pew survey revealed that teens appreciate how social media facilitates an ease of communicating with friends and family as well as allowing them to connect to new people.

Yet, the threat of cyberbullying is real, and it is dangerous. "Cyberbullying includes tactics like posting vicious comments (including text messages), spreading rumors, making threats, telling people to kill themselves, impersonating someone through a fake account and creating a social media account to harass someone" (Valencia 2019, 1). Such behavior is becoming all too common and poses a significant social threat, yet many schools have not felt compelled to intervene either because much of the activity goes on outside of the classroom, or because they "didn't have the legal authority to do so" (1). Where this is the case, school librarians can work to educate students in ways to combat cyberbullying, such as advising students to take screen shots of the negative posts and any identifying sources they may include and sharing them with adults. Such tips should be more than an occasional remark or lesson but should be part of an intentional curriculum to teach students the responsibilities and rights of digital citizenship (Maughan 2017).

The negative influences of social media on youth today is a concern, but the Pew survey shows teens are aware of the challenges along with the benefits of the digital world. A Pew Research Center survey in 2018 revealed, "Roughly eight-in-ten teens ages 13 to 17 (81%) say social media makes them feel more connected to what's going on in their friends' lives, while around two-thirds say these platforms make them feel as if they have people who will support them through tough times" (Anderson & Jiang 2018b, para. 3). Survey responses also indicate teens believe social media exposes them to people from diverse backgrounds and worldviews (Anderson & Jiang 2018b).

Teens in Generation Z said they feel pressure to "post content on social media that makes them look good to others (43%) or share things that will get a lot of likes or comments (37%)" (Anderson & Jiang 2018b, para. 6). The previous Generation Y is known as the "selfie generation," but Gen Zs indicated they rarely or never post social media selfies (Anderson & Jiang 2018b).

RESEARCH FOCUS ON INFORMATION SEEKING IN ELECTRONIC RESOURCES

Research interest related to technological issues in library and information studies has been very high, for there is still much to be learned that will help designers create more user-friendly systems in the "brave new world" of high-tech school libraries. Over time, research on children's information seeking online has progressed to keep pace with the new and emerging technologies. Thus, studies that once centered on children's use of automated catalogs (online public access catalogs) have given way to research into their use of online encyclopedias, electronic databases, search engines, the Internet, and social media.

Online Searching Behavior of Students

Pew Research Center studies in 2012 investigated how teens do research in the digital world. "Teachers characterize the overall impact of digital technologies on students research skills as 'mostly positive' but observe mixed effects" (Purcell et al. 2012, para. 2). Teachers opined that while search engines definitely facilitate the research process and have made students feel they can access information rapidly and easily, the use of these resources did not necessarily increase the quality of the student's final research product (Purcell et al. 2012).

Taking a closer look at the Purcell et al. (2012) study, 99 percent of teachers said students were able to find and use resources for the research that would not normally be available to them. "A majority (65%) also agree with the idea that the internet makes students more self-sufficient researchers who are less reliant on adult help, though only a small portion 'strongly agree' with this statement (18%)" (Purcell et al. 2012, para. 5). Teachers of research also felt that "digital technologies foster deeper learning and expanded worldview" (Purcell et al. 2012, para. 9). On the other hand, 83 percent of the teachers surveyed felt the amount of information students could access online could be overwhelming, and 60 percent of the teachers concluded that "today's digital technologies make it harder for students to find and use credible sources of information" (Purcell et al. 2012, para.7).

Two open-ended questions were posed to the teacher participants in the impact of digital technologies on student research survey (Purcell et al. 2012). The first question asked what teachers perceived to be the most positive aspect of students' researching online. Responses to this question included:

- Students have quick access to some of the best available research online, especially if they have access to databases and are taught how to use them to do research. Also, when students do come across information they don't understand in the course of research, the Internet allows them to conduct quick, tangential searches to learn needed information in support of their primary search;

- The nearly infinite possibilities for information retrieval make for animated research;
- Students are WILLING to research online because things are easier to find with search engines. Researching with books, journals, etc., is more tedious and time-consuming. Students are not willing to put in that kind of time and effort;
- Easy accessibility to a variety of sources and access to things like museums or archeological sites worldwide they would most likely not be able to travel to on their own;
- Students can use the worldwide web as the best library ever built and as the largest public forum. They can read articles of every opinion and often discuss those opinions on the same page;
- If students have access to the internet and will take the time to do the research it lessens the gap, in other words all students have equal access to the information, and it is portable. (Purcell et al. 2012)

The second open-ended question asked what teachers perceived to be the most negative aspect of student researching online. Responses to this question included:

- Same as the positive! They have access to a seemingly endless amount of information, and they can get to it quickly. They don't know how to filter out bad information, and they are so used to getting information quickly, that when they can't find what they are looking for immediately, they quit;
- Plagiarism has increased, as has a student's ability to locate answers online, circumventing thereby the need for personal cognitive activity or effort;
- Students cut and paste without reading or evaluating the information;
- Students have difficulty sorting through all the information that they access. Because of the opportunities for leading the student to other subjects I think that students many times become diverted to other topics and have difficulty staying focused on the current work. Also, students have trouble with documentation of the sources of their information;
- Students have become lazier about research, relying on the first selection of sources, rather than digging deeper into subject matter;
- They click on the first Google link that comes up. They rarely look farther down, or at subsequent pages. They don't judge the quality of the information they find. They have lost the ability to do any non-Internet-based research;
- They can find information quickly and independently but they do not have the evaluative skills to determine if the information is accurate, they do not have the patience or determination to check the

information with an alternate source (second opinion) and when we spend time in class using the Internet to do research, they assume once they've found a site, they can print and be "done"; in reality, they should print and read, think, analyze, and reassess whether they will need more or different information. Students also have a very hard time reading online for extended periods of time. They get distracted so easily with the computer screen as opposed to salient, extended reading in books/texts. (Purcell et al. 2012)

Technology and Learning: Benefits and Challenges of Online Access

Many studies conducted since the 1980s have led educators to conclude that the use of technology can benefit students in a number of important ways (see Table 6.1), including the promotion of critical thinking skills, the development of writing skills, enhanced opportunities for language development, and an increase in student motivation. Although it is useful conceptually to consider these benefits as separate entities, research shows that they are interrelated.

While the potential for learning in the classroom and the library in tapping the information resources on the Internet cannot be overstated, researchers have identified a litany of problems children encounter online. In spite of E-Rate funding and an expansion in Internet access in the nation's schools, there are still inequities and barriers that jeopardize the ability of many children to make educational use of online information. And in spite of increased computer skills, children still encounter search failure based on skill deficits of one kind or another.

Barriers to Information Seeking: Ethical Issues

Inequities in educational opportunities due to community socioeconomics directly affect students' access to information in print and online sources (Kozol 2000; Neuman & Celano 2001) and to the use of the Internet for school research

TABLE 6.1   Educational Benefits of Access to the Internet and Electronic Resources at Home and School

- Fosters motivation in students
- Improves attitudes toward reading and writing tasks
- Improves language skills (reading, writing, spelling, and vocabulary)
- Provides an audience for student work outside the classroom
- Creates opportunities for inquiry learning, student independence, and differentiated instruction
- Increases student choice and sense of control of their own learning
- Provides immediate access to resources not available locally
- Provides access to other points of view and invites critical thinking and evaluation
- Promotes collaboration between and among students

tasks. Even though nearly 100 percent of U.S. classrooms have Internet access (Wells & Lewis 2006) and have had for over 10 years, the disparities between those with easy access to computers and the Internet and those without persist. Equality in home access to the Internet, often called the "digital divide," has narrowed in recent years, but not by much. In 2015, a report from the U.S. Department of Education released the percentage of students with access to the Internet and digital learning outside of school. "As of 2015, 61% of children had internet access at home. That figure was up from 58 percent five years prior" (Herold 2018, para. 6). This result has spurred education advocates to call for "federal programs intended to increase home broadband access and close the 'homework gap' afflicting students without reliable internet service outside of school" (Herold 2018, para. 4). This survey also showed the breakdown of students with home Internet access by ethnic group: white 66 percent, Asian 63 percent, Hispanic 52 percent, and American Indian/Alaska Native children 49 percent (Herold 2018).

Another aspect of the "digital divide" relates to online content. For example, a significant barrier to information seeking for some students is the predominance of English as the language of the Internet. In 2000, Lazarus and Mora reported that fully 87 percent of the content on the Web was in the English language and that only 2 percent of the sites surveyed were multilingual. As of February 2019 the percentage of websites in English had decreased to 54.4 percent, but English was still far and away the dominant language (followed by Russian, 6.7 percent, German, 5.3 percent, and Spanish, 4.9 percent (W3Techs 2019).

The language disparity coupled with the fact that the Internet is primarily text-based makes successful information retrieval online a problem for all children but especially for those for whom English is a second language. To help mediate this problem, librarians and teachers can use tools like Google Translate (https://translate.google.com), which can instantly translate a website to more than 100 languages. Released in 2006, Google Translate was originally criticized and even ridiculed for its lack of accuracy, but in November 2016, Google announced that Google Translate would switch to a neural machine translation engine—Google Neural Machine Translation (GNMT)—which translates "whole sentences at a time. . . . It uses this broader context to help it figure out the most relevant translation, which it then rearranges and adjusts to be more like a human speaking with proper grammar" (Turovsky 2016).

In an article championing the professional resource embodied in each school's librarian, Moran (2010) has drawn attention to ethical issues surrounding information access and has reframed the digital divide in terms of access to media literacy instruction. In fact, Moran's own experience of corporate America has led him to conclude that "[s]tudents do not know how to find or evaluate information they need on the Internet." Yet "I know that without adequate media literacy training, kids will not succeed in a 21st century workplace." The stakes in the kind of administrative myopia that results in a school district "abandon[ing] its professional guides," as Moran suggests, are high.

Ineffective Searching Strategies and Techniques

Having readily accessible information through the Internet has not meant that students automatically understand how to search. As long ago as the 1990s, Chen (1993) noted the failure of students to extend searches beyond the terms originally chosen and to use subject headings and tracings as keys to appropriate alternatives. Students in Neuman's (1995) study also noted failure to "switch" approaches or to employ other terms when their searches got "stuck" or when their search terms produced an insufficient number of "hits." These results were confirmed by student search behavior by Fidel et al. (1999), who noted that students frequently changed their topics rather than do the intellectual work of finding suitable alternatives to describe the topics originally chosen. This would seem to support Eaton's (1991, cited in Fidel et al. 1999) finding that successful searches may rely on the searchers' abilities to change and detach themselves from unsuccessful strategies and then to continue the original search in a different manner. It also suggests that the invitational (open) mood, essential to continuing the information-gathering phase of the information search process (Kuhlthau 1993b), demands a degree of cognitive flexibility not usually acknowledged.

Lack of computer skills as well as an inability to create effective "search statements" by students observed by Nowicki (2003) inhibited their retrieval of relevant information. This led Nowicki to conclude that "[i]f users cannot define the information for which they are searching, no search engine will return relevant results." Thus, it is important that searchers learn the nature and capabilities of specific search engines as resources of value in addressing specific kinds of information questions.

As one might expect, not only do youngsters use the Internet as the court of first resort, but studies indicate that they "tend to rely almost exclusively on Google as their search engine, and use natural language as search terms" (Asselin & Doiron 2008; Rowlands & Nicholas 2008) and browse serendipitously through Internet texts in what Asselin and Doiron describe as "digital grazing" (7).

Handling Search Output

Since information overload frequently leads adults to premature abandonment of online searches (Wiberley & Daugherty 1988, cited in Oberman 1995), it is fair to assume that less experienced information seekers will find excessive search output intimidating as well. In point of fact, managing search results has indeed proved to be a daunting task for many students (Liebscher & Marchionini 1988). Studies show that the sheer volume of search "hits" (Oberman 1995), as well as the prospect of reading through long texts online (Irving 1991), makes selecting relevant items difficult. Perhaps for this reason, student searchers frequently stop with the first screen they encounter, using it as a sort of index or abstract of the site rather than scrolling though successive screens to locate the information they need (Fidel et al. 1999; Schacter, Chung,

& Dorr 1998). Information overload and students' strategies to cope with it have also been documented in studies by Akin (1998), Gordon (2000), and Agosto (2001). Asselin and Doiron (2008) describe Generations Y and Z's handling of retrieved information in this way:

> They approach the results list with a "click and grab" strategy by most often selecting the first source on the list with minimal or no review and evaluation of its relevance or quality. . . . (Guinee, Eagleton, & Hall 2003; Henry 2006). Students spend little time in reading the source; instead skimming and scanning are typical reading processes. . . . Once within a website, becoming distracted by both internal and external hyperlinks is a greater risk than in print sources of information. Finally, cutting and pasting rather than rewording and recording are dominant processes when students are taking notes from online information sources. (3)

Evaluating Online Information Sources

Many youngsters lack the conceptual skills to understand that the Internet sites and resources are not centrally created but are the work of different providers with different motives (Asselin & Doiron 2008). This leads many youngsters to accept what they find online without question. In fact, a concern for determining the authoritativeness and factual accuracy of online information does not characterize the mind-set of most young information seekers (Watson 1998), who are often oblivious to the need to question the origins of resources they locate via electronic searching. Schacter et al. (1998), Todd (1998), Kafai and Bates (1997), and Shenton and Dixon (2003) reported similar behavior on the part of their informants. "As with books," Shenton and Dixon found that "the children were quick to assume everything they found about their topic on the Internet was correct just because it was there" (101). However, with guidance and experience, many students were eventually able to "distinguish sales and marketing sites from more neutrally informational sites" (109).

Kuhlthau (1997) believes that the sheer amount of information on the Internet is a barrier to evaluation. In Kuhlthau's view, when information is available in such "abundance," it is "particularly challenging for a school librarian or teacher to convince an unmotivated student to distinguish between an adequate and a better than adequate source" (Broch 2000).[2] In their study, Kafai and Bates (1997) found that children under 10 years also experienced difficulty with evaluation tasks, including the ability to articulate evaluative criteria. However, once criteria (e.g., "easy to read") were suggested, these students could evaluate the sites they visited. It might be well to note that unless youngsters are taught and also expected to appraise critically the resources they find on the Internet and pursue research questions rather than fact-finding tasks, the potential for inspiring the development of higher-order thinking skills represented by the activity of Internet-based searching will remain largely unrealized.

The Importance of Critical Review of Internet Resources in an Era of Fake News

There is a common assumption that today's students of Generations Y and Z are tech savvy and have a great ability to locate information. According to Bowler, Julien, and Haddon (2018), there is no empirical research to support this assumption. Particularly concerning is their observation that in using their mobile devices to follow news stories of the day students were not able to differentiate between stories posted by credible news sources and information posted on social media. This failing is one that is likely mirrored in kind among adults who have also become reliant on cell phone technology in communication. Given that school librarians include resource evaluation as part of any Internet curriculum, they should also take pains to call attention to the necessity of applying these same critical skills to seeking information for everyday uses and tasks.

Beginning almost as soon as he was elected in 2016, President Donald J. Trump used the phrase "fake news" when he felt the media presented his administration and its activities in a negative and therefore unfair light. Given the preponderance of its current use, one might think this was a phrase coined by this POTUS, but fake news was originally used to describe the tabloid wars of the rival tabloid newspapers in New York at the end of the 1800s vying for subscribers. According to Heather Duby (2018), library director for the Sullivan County Public Library System in Tennessee, "This phrase (fake news) is so neatly woven into our media consumption that most of us have become inured to it" (4). Duby (2018) challenged librarians to teach patrons critical thinking skills and provide them with the most accurate information possible, and then let the consumer determine the credibility of the source.

"The solution is not just helping people develop simple, common-sense web evaluation habits. It's also helping them determine what they are going to trust, since the vast majority of sources lie in the gray area between unimpeachability and fake news" explains Meredith Farkas (2018, 78). Evaluating Web information is a skill along with being a habit of mind school librarians need to teach their students. "Libraries can play a vital role in building better communities by supporting our patrons in becoming savvy information consumers" (Farkas 2018, 78).

According to the *Common Core State Standards* (CCSS), we need to teach students "to be ready for college, workforce training, and life in a technological society, students need the ability to gather comprehend, evaluate, synthesize, and report on information and ideas" (CCSS Initiative 2019). Evaluating sources became a key element of high school research dictated by the new CCSS. With online Google searches being the norm, school librarians were given the task of teaching students website evaluation. Berg (2017) describes the ability to effectively evaluate websites as a "lifelong learning skill" (9). Just because something is available on the Internet does not make it bad or good. "That judgment needs to come from evaluation itself and (the researcher needs to realize) that biases exist even in what appear to be credible sources" (Berg 2017, 9).

In 2010 California State University in Chico developed a strategy for evaluating websites that is used in many secondary schools and universities in teaching the skills needed to evaluate research information. The strategy uses the acronym CRAAP and directs students to evaluate websites for currency, relevance, authority, accuracy, and purpose (Berg 2017). "With the students using websites for both academic and personal use, we want them to critically understand the information they are seeking" (Berg 2017, 10). Information on the CRAAP text is available at https://library.csuchico.edu/help/source-or-information-good.

Judging Relevance

In their evaluation of information sources, "relevance" seems to be a particularly difficult concept for children to determine, though there is indication that some are able to learn this skill especially when their interest levels are high. Hirsh's (1998) study indicated that children can articulate criteria for relevance, although these may differ significantly from those that adult or expert searchers might use. The three most mentioned criteria identified by Hirsh's students included topicality, novelty, and interest. Novelty as a relevance category translated as "new information" for Hirsh's informants. In other words, if a source provided facts not previously encountered that they needed to complete a research assignment, the information was considered "new." By the same token, an assessment of "interesting" in terms of texts and (especially) graphics was taken to mean that the information was of personal interest to the searcher. Some students also considered peer interest as a mark of relevance. Following Kuhlthau's (1993a) finding that student interest increases during the information-searching process, Hirsh noted that relevance judgments changed as the research proceeded with "interesting" replacing "topicality" as the information search neared completion.

Hirsh's (1998) study (as mentioned above) showed that highly motivated fifth graders "were generally able to articulate their reasons for selecting relevant information in both text and graphic formats." These students made use of "metadata and other descriptive elements" in searching in "an online catalog, an electronic encyclopedia, an electronic magazine index, and the Internet" (58), at home, and at school. As concrete thinkers, Hirsh's fifth-grade informants judged topical relevance on the basis of "exact matches" between search terms they used, and the vocabulary used by the teacher and the retrieved documents. Students also had difficulty in recognizing the larger categories within which their topics or subjects might fit. For example, "when the book titles [reviewed] did not include their athlete's name," they did not identify the book as relevant. This behavior mirrors that of students in Wallace and Kupperman's (1997) study (cited in Hirsh 1998) and Hirsh (1996, cited in Hirsh 1998), where children looked for matching terms in the subjects of retrieved bibliographic records.

Agosto's (2002) informants also considered relevant any information they found that fit with personal convictions, opinions, and beliefs and also made choices of relevance and usefulness based on the tone of the site (e.g., friendly, patronizing, humorous). This led Agosto to conclude that "personal preferences are an aspect of the affective side of information seeking, as these preferences

TABLE 6.2   Challenges for Students When Searching Electronically

- Limited knowledge of databases and their arrangement
- Lack of understanding of the Internet as a collection of resources
- Difficulties in evaluating online sources
- Difficulty in determining relevance of resources to research question
- Lack of knowledge of searching strategies
- Lack of Internet sites available in students' native languages
- Difficulties in handling search results or output
- Lack of basic literacy skills

are based on personal feelings (such as personal dislikes for particular colors), rather than on cognitive or behavioral information seeking" (18). For this reason, Agosto sees a role for "adult intermediaries who work with young people and information" (25) in explaining evaluative criteria and providing search training (see Table 6.2).

IMPROVING CHILDREN'S CHANCES OF SEARCHING SUCCESS

Although at least some of the difficulties that students encounter clearly relate to the idiosyncrasies of specific online resources, the good news is that most student-centered problems can be overcome through instructional intervention and careful planning on the part of teachers and school librarians. It is clear that students need to develop skills related to the mechanics of searching, including at least some knowledge of search commands and basic keyboarding moves. Of equal importance, however, is an awareness of how information is organized and represented in online search environments. This awareness will aid them not only in selecting appropriate databases but also in finding information in useful formats (e.g., titles, abstracts, extracts, or full text). In addition, providing instruction in terms of process models, new conceptions of the library and its resources, and attending to domain knowledge will greatly improve children's chances of searching success (see Table 6.3).

Process Models as Structures for Learning

A process approach to the teaching of research, particularly as provided in models created by Kuhlthau (1991, 1993b, 1994), Eisenberg and Berkowitz (1990), Irving (1985), Stripling and Pitts (1988), Pappas and Tepe (1997, 2002), and others, constitutes a useful structure within which online searching activities can be planned and implemented. Kuhlthau's model is valuable in its specific emphasis on gaining a view of the topic through exploration as a prerequisite for data collection. In addition, its consideration of affective, behavioral, and cognitive aspects of information seeking makes it a useful tool for teachers and librarians in helping students plan and cope with the frustration and stress—as well as the high cognitive demands—created by the use of electronic resources. Eisenberg and Berkowitz's (1990) Big6 Skills, having been

TABLE 6.3 Key Competencies for Searching Success

- Knowledge of the library and its print and online resources
- Knowledge of the information search process as a structure for searching
- Knowledge of database organization and design
- Background knowledge of the topic of the research question
- Time for information seeking online

successfully applied to searching in electronic environments, is particularly useful in matching particular databases to specific topics at the point of planning information-seeking strategies, a stage which research indicates has been a problem for student searchers in the past. However, it is well to note that in the final analysis, students will have to create their own mental models as frames for independent problem solving online. Providing students with an overview of the options is a place to start in engaging students in this crucial information-seeking activity.

Another useful strategy within the context of an overall process of information seeking is understanding how much information is "enough" to create the understandings that the tasks were assigned to accomplish. Of course, how much information is too little, too much, or just right depends in large part on the learning style and the cognitive level of the information seeker, the demands of the task, and the information context. In considering information seeking online, Kuhlthau (1999) notes the changes created by access to the Internet. "What is enough [information] may have been a fairly straightforward notion when a person could gather all there was to know on a problem or topic in a contained collection. The concept of enough is quite a different matter in the present information environment" (6). "Enough," then, is an individual determination based on "what is enough to make sense for oneself within a context and to accomplish the task at hand" (6) and should be considered at each stage of the information search process. In a very real sense, the ability to assess for oneself "what is enough" is an important information skill that children need to acquire and relates directly to the ability to bring closure to a search task. To a certain extent, the concept of enough may help to answer the question often heard in the classroom and library: "How many sources do I need to use?" Depending on the situation, the concept may turn out to be liberating for both instructor and learner.

Understanding the Library and Its Online Resources

In the days when children's research tasks were based solely on resources available in the school library, information seeking was relatively straightforward. Children used standard "tools" to locate information in print and media formats on hand. The library was "a collection" in its strictest sense, for in most instances the resources had been painstakingly, even lovingly, selected by highly informed professional adults with the developmental needs, domain knowledge, language requirements of students, and the specifics of the curriculum in place at a particular school in mind. In such an environment, students could assume the authority, accuracy, and truthfulness of the resources they used. Online catalogs and electronic encyclopedias that signaled the library's entry into the information age were essentially extensions of this early controlled, well-structured library environment (Hirsh 1998).

Searching on the Internet today assumes none of these characteristics (with the exception perhaps of websites created to offer a number of carefully selected links for children's use). In fact, it is an activity of an entirely different sort. The old saying that "on the Internet no one knows you're a dog" seems particularly apt in this regard. Today, anyone can create a website or other Web-based information space and represent him- or herself in any way for any purpose. Many websites that appear informational are, in fact, commercially produced and purposed. By the same token, even informational websites "sell" a point of view by selecting to focus on a specific slice of the experiential pie; in this context, reality is what the creators of the site say that it is, complete with inherent and often hidden biases. In addition, search engines tend to provide access to a unique and limited portion of the websites out there. For learners who expect to search exhaustively online, the information scatter that characterizes the Internet may be especially perplexing.

To help with sorting out the useful from the harmful websites, public schools receiving federal funds are required to incorporate an Internet filter into their network. "The Children's Internet Protection Act (CIPA-2000) does not require that all schools and libraries install filters, only those that accept certain types of federal funds or discounts for the provision of Internet access" (Batch 2015, 61). Each school has the discretion to filter as much or as little as is determined by the school district, but according to Batch (2015), "Filtering beyond CIPA's requirements results in missed opportunities to prepare students to be responsible users, consumers, and producers of online content and resources" (62). It can also result in frustration when searching on topics with words that are typically filtered, such as "breast" cancer.

The Importance of Background, Domain, or Topical Knowledge

Research related to online searching underscores the importance of domain knowledge and generally holds that students who "jump into" online searches without taking time to develop some familiarity with topic-related concepts and topic-related vocabulary (Fidel et al. 1999; Irving 1991; Solomon 1993, 1994) severely compromise their chances of a successful search experience (Gross 1997; Hirsh 1997; Loerke 1994). Because background knowledge enables students "to recall more concepts and integrate these concepts more readily into their cognitive structure" (Chi, Hutchinson, & Robin 1989, cited in Borgman et al. 1995, 666), "building adequate content knowledge [is] a critical first step in successful information searching" (206), regardless of whether the research tasks are self-selected tasks or imposed by others.

Research indicates that when children lack essential frameworks, they experience difficulties in identifying an interest to pursue and later, in narrowing, focusing, or refining their topics (Kuhlthau 1993b; Oberman 1995; Scott & VanNoord 1996). For this reason, Kuhlthau in particular recommends that students explore their topics thoroughly before beginning the tasks of collecting sources and gathering information. Domain knowledge as a preliminary to successful information seeking was also addressed by Neuman (1995), who noted that a student's understanding of the topic determines not only the types of the resources that the student needs most but also the relevance of the information and resources eventually located.

Indeed, a lack of background knowledge sets the stage for a variety of problems. For example, Solomon (1993), Moore and St. George (1991), and Irving (1985) found that children who lacked knowledge of their topics were unable to pose appropriate research questions or select appropriate search terms. These findings underscore the emphasis that Chen and Kuhlthau (1994, cited in Nahl & Harada 1996) place on identifying "descriptors and alternative subject headings" (200) as prerequisites to a successful search process.

Irving's (1985) research indicates that teaching subject knowledge alongside online searching is one way to ensure that students know enough about topics to undertake initial searches. Widely appreciated in other kinds of instruction, this strategy has been successfully applied to searching tasks described by Ruggiero (1988, cited in Bodi 1992) and Mark and Jacobson (1995). Hayes (1994, cited in Mark & Jacobson 1995), for example, found that getting students to consider all the areas that could be covered within particular topics made students more aware of "how broad" their topics actually were.

Selecting Topics and Tasks That Are Developmentally Appropriate

It is clear from the research that difficulties in accessing and using online information sources are related to cognitive development. Oberman (1995) noted problems her informants experienced in dealing with abstractions, whereas Walter et al. (1996) found that "the only topics that were consistently easy for children to find were concrete subjects that were [also] easy to spell" (108), though the ability of search engines to "fill in" and correct spelling has helped in this area. Related to concrete operational thinking is the assumption that many youngsters think that the title of a book or article reveals its content in a straightforward way. Yet many books and magazine articles carry "catchy" titles that give no hint as to what they are actually "about." The obscurity of titles was found to be a problem for searchers in a study by Kafai and Bates (1997), and Hirsh (1998) confirmed that when her informants used titles as indicators of relevance, their ability to evaluate retrieved items for relevance was seriously diminished.

Allowing Time for Information Seeking

For more than three decades, Irving (1990, 1991) and others have noted the importance of class scheduling for online searching, because children need time for learning how to search; for practicing search techniques, protocols, and procedures; and for applying newly acquired searching skills to research tasks; once-a-week class sessions were simply insufficient to provide students the time needed to develop searching competence. Not only did this sort of scheduling magnify the impact of system failures and mechanical difficulties, but the intervals between library sessions also increased student forgetfulness of procedures and strategies, which necessitated the repetition of instruction.

Access to high-speed Internet is still an issue for students in rural areas according to a Pew Research Center (2018) study. The survey showed "24% of rural adults say access to high speed internet is a major problem in their local community" (Anderson 2018, para. 1). This has an impact on the time needed for rural students when accessing information online. According to the Pew Research Center (2001) study, youngsters reported that even when there was sufficient school access to computers, their involvement in curricular activities in the classroom left little school time for online research (Simon, Graziano, & Lenhart 2001). The time issue surfaced as well in Broch's (2000) review of search engines designed for children's use. Specifically, Broch discussed the time it takes students to review the potentially large number of "hits" that sometimes result when searching online.

DEVELOPING COMPETENT SEARCHERS: INSTRUCTIONAL STRATEGIES

The research related to student searching provides some insights into the skills students need and the kinds of lessons that may be the most valuable in helping students reap the positive outcomes that can be gained by accessing electronic resources. Given the range of problems that children encounter in searching online, Chen's (1993) insightful observation that "merely emphasizing the mechanical aspects of online technology will probably not serve students very well" (38) seems particularly appropriate. Clearly, as Moran (2010) argues, when left to their own devices, students will not develop information competencies on their own. Professional instruction and guidance is clearly necessary. Thus, it is up to school librarians to apply their expert knowledge of information resources and search techniques, curricular goals, instructional design, and student abilities in planning instruction and guiding students in seeking information. In addition, they must create and sustain a climate for searching success while also documenting problems so that their own instructional strategies (and perhaps even the systems themselves) can be redesigned to reflect a more student-centered, child-friendly, and differentiated focus. These are complex responsibilities indeed.

Fortunately, lessons learned from research studies provide many clues to student information needs in electronic environments and can help school librarians develop curricular strategies. As noted above, we cannot expect students to pick up the information skills they need without instructional intervention (Entwistle 1981; Nahl & Harada 1996) no matter how computer savvy they may appear (Moran 2010). In addition, studies by Irving (1990, 1991), Kuhlthau (1993b, 1997), McNally and Kuhlthau (1994), Fidel et al. (1999), Childress and Benson (2014), and others repeatedly underscore the need for school librarians to play an active role in assisting youth in information seeking and learning from information sources.

The Importance of Personalized Learning

Providing a student-centered approach to learning is key to increasing student academic achievement. "Personalized learning can meet all students where they are, motivate them based on their interests and academic level, accelerate their learning and prepare them to become true lifelong learners" (Childress & Benson 2014, 34). Giving students the skills to navigate their own learning in a research project is motivating and makes them autonomous in their learning (Childress & Benson 2014). School librarians need to meet the challenge of teaching students research skills by planning and implementing a coherent program of instruction that not only meets the needs of students with vastly diverse computer skills, search experience, and interests but also encourages "deep" as opposed to "surface" understandings of the processes involved (Entwistle 1981). Tailoring instruction to fit skills levels will be increasingly complex as the range of student experience with computers and Internet searching continues to widen. Sitting through instruction on basic computer operations will be every bit as frustrating for experienced "surfers" as advanced instruction would be for already angst-ridden novices. The basis of instruction at any level must be the enactment of active learning, which requires learners to relate new information to what they already know, link abstractions to experience, and evaluate the ideas they encounter in light of their relevance and utility (Entwistle 1981).

For their part, Nahl and Harada (1996) believe that students need direct instruction and activity for learning the skills required to conduct successful searches and that written instructions may not be as effective an instructional approach as face-to-face interaction. Irving (1990) came to the same conclusion in noting that the children in her study proved reluctant "to read manuals and detailed handouts before searching computerized files" (Norton & Westwater 1986, cited in Irving 1990, 14). In order to increase the educational value of online information tasks, these researchers also recommend that students justify their choices of relevant materials and demonstrate an understanding of the differences between academic and technical journals, popular magazines, and ideological tracts.

Collaboration as an Information-Seeking Strategy

Just as an improved knowledge of information and use in electronic environments creates new kinds of models, formats, and levels of interaction for school librarians, new instructional models may be needed in teaching students how to navigate the sometimes treacherous technological waters. According to Neuman (1995a), collaborative searching involving both librarians and students as well as peer mentoring can be effective additions to the librarians' repertoire of instructional strategies. Morton (1996) asserts that allowing students to take the lead in pursuing personal lines of research enables librarians and teachers an opportunity to participate as colearners: intellectual sojourners "who also [do] not know the answers" (Irving 1990, 115).

Studies related to student use of electronic resources and online searching suggest that essential elements of a dynamic and effective information skills curriculum include instruction about the information search process, an emphasis on the presearch phase of the process, a through exploration of the research topic, instruction on critical strategies for evaluating Web-based information, attention to basic literacy skills, attention to searching strategies, and an emphasis on information-handling skills and information use.

Presearch/Inquiry: An Essential First Step

It seems evident that the activities that precede actual searching are more than simply opening moves in the analysis of the research task at hand. School librarians are responsible for teaching inquiry skills before the research begins (Stripling 2010). The Stripling Model of Inquiry (see Chapter 3) requires students to Connect to their prior knowledge of the research topic and Wonder about the questions this research will answer. This is done prior to actual research activity. "True inquiry should result in new understandings for learners, but not final answers, because during the process, learners should naturally discover new questions and intriguing areas to pursue in future investigations" (Stripling 2010, 17). Over and over again, studies of electronic searching portend the importance of presearch planning (Nahl & Harada 1996), question creation, search term generation, and strategy selection. In addition, providing a presearch "space" in the overall project makes good instructional sense in that it allows students the opportunity to capitalize on what they already know and make personal connections with important aspects of topics before proceeding.

It is also possible that the presearch phase of information-seeking assignments should include time for librarians and teachers to review the specific process model that youngsters are going to use in carrying out research tasks. Newell (2010), for one, has also pointed to the necessity of direct instruction by school librarians on the overall process of information seeking as a basis for enacting coaching and facilitation roles that are helpful later on.

Instructors can help students learn to become planners by providing activities that stimulate thinking about the topic and the research process and that allow students to practice making research decisions. For example, Irving (1990) found brainstorming to be valuable for both librarians and students in that these activities helped the instructors consider the informational dimensions of the research task, the kinds of resources that would be needed, and the "range of topics in which the students were interested" (64). Graphic organizers and other types of "visual representations," which allow students to "see" facts from a content area in meaningful patterns (Clarke, Martell, & Willey 1994, 70), have also been found helpful to students in exploring possible search topics, formulating search questions, and selecting search terms when used as a part of the presearch planning (Irving 1990) process. In fact, Irving concluded that these activities enhanced the opportunities for successful searching and for information seeking in general. Today's educators have at their fingertips a plethora of electronic brainstorming tools, such as Prezi, Bubbl.us, and MindMap.

The importance of creating a focus or narrowing a topic has proven to be of even greater importance as a presearch strategy in online environments because within this context, the possibility of retrieving literally thousands of items is assured. According to Creanor et al. (1995), "The sheer volume forces users to think more precisely about the topic and about their own needs, to make qualitative decisions on the nature of the material at every step, [and] to rely on their own judgment to a much greater extent" (5) than was necessary before. The axiom "looking for a needle in a haystack" is quite appropriate when applied to searching electronically, and indeed, the Internet adds more hay than the searching environment has ever had.

Creation of focused questions assumes that children can discern the difference between broad and narrow topics or questions and between objective and subjective questions (Oberman 1995). A group exercise that provides practice for students in recognizing the differences might include presenting students with a list of focused and unfocused research questions and asking them to identify and discuss them as alternatives to a topic, then to select broad and narrow search terms based on the questions. The identification of key words, which is an important strategy in creating search protocols or "strings," can be facilitated by providing practice in main idea identification (e.g., underlining the nouns in a passage, crossing out unnecessary words, and identifying key concepts) and the selection of key words. The expansion of this key word list through the use of synonym finders and the matching of search terms with descriptors are also useful presearch activities.

Once children have a general understanding of the topic and have generated key words to use in searching particular aspects, they will require assistance in constructing effective search statements and browsing techniques. Although Boolean searching can be a difficult concept for young children to grasp initially, school librarians and teachers have found creative and "concrete" activities to allow children to conceptualize the strategy and practice this skill. For example, one teacher in Irving's (1990) study successfully presented the concepts of the AND/OR/BUT NOT operators by having the class divide and regroup itself according to eye color and hair color. This makes particularly good sense in light of the research findings by Sein and Bostrom (1989) that concrete thinkers who may have low visualization skills find analogic models more effective as instructional aids than abstract visualizations.

For teachers and librarians, presearch activities provide time and opportunity to assess student knowledge of the topics, their general skill levels, and their mental models of the information search process. Instructors can also use the presearch "space" as a time for activities that alert students to the many pitfalls that may await them in accessing information online and to make students aware of the range and levels of assistance that school library professionals can provide. Using presearch activities to help students plan in advance may alert students to the realities of the information universe in addition to reducing the "cognitive load" (Marchionini 1987, 70) for novice searchers.

Loranger (1994) said that good thinkers "make plans for learning." However, research indicates that preplanning of sequential activities is not a part of the repertoire of novice searchers (Grover et al. 1996; Marchionini 1989), who often tend to rely instead on system feedback. For example, high school students in Fidel et al.'s (1999) study believed that "there was no need" for planning the search in advance, as they expected to follow whatever leads and links presented themselves as a result of inputting their original search terms.

Search Strategizing

Over time, researchers have created an impressive literature on the information-seeking behavior of adults. Among the most helpful have been studies that examined the ways in which end users go about seeking information in online environments. In an often-cited study by Bates (1989), it was found that in actual search situations, end users rarely followed a linear course but rather invoked an iterative, "berrypicking" process that evolved and changed as their searches unfolded. Research on information seeking and children (Borgman et al. 1995) suggests that searches conducted by children on their own also tend to follow nonlinear patterns. However, Kafai and Bates (1997) noted that student searchers need assistance and support with many aspects of their search process, including "scanning text and using hypertext links" (107). The problem for novice searchers in Neuman's (1995a) view is that they often lack either the domain knowledge or the cognitive flexibility to allow them to change their perspective, their focus, or their direction without some assistance. These problems can be complicated by the reluctance many children have to asking for help, particularly as they enter adolescence. For this reason, young searchers might welcome and benefit from the instruction that includes the "idea tactics" that Bates (1979) suggests.

While it would appear that children's difficulties with electronic resources result from cognitive and skill deficits, an equally cogent argument could be made that their problems in the past were created by the failure of database designers to create accessible, user-friendly information systems. Fortunately, this problem has been addressed by vendors who now provide safe, kid-friendly search engines such as Kidtopia (created by school librarians for elementary school students "indexing only educator approved web sites"), Kiddle (a vetted visual search engine), and Kid Rex ("a search engine for kids, by kids") (Educational Technology and Mobile Learning 2018).

Although many search strategies are generic and can be applied to information-seeking tasks in print as well as to online resources (Irving 1990), some aspects of electronic resource searching are unique. Assignments that are planned to capitalize on the specific challenges that the uses of such resources pose and the possibilities for learning that they engender should be encouraged. In fact, Mark and Jacobson (1995) suggest modifying student assignments to take advantage of learning opportunities offered by specific kinds of electronic resources—activities that, in the process, will reveal their advantages and their limitations. In some instances, there may be a tendency by some teachers to require that students use electronic resources exclusively without realizing that such resources are most valuable when they are "integrated" (Markless & Lincoln 1986, cited in Irving 1990, 14) with "books, magazines, newspapers, video and audio tape, slides, posters, museums, historic sites, [and] field trips" (7). Problems also occur when students are searching for very specific information. According to Mark and Jacobson, without asking students to think critically about the relevance, utility, and authority of the resources they consult, the requirement to use a particular number of sources is meaningless.

New strategies for organizing research and assisting students in collaborating on projects center around the abundance of electronic apps and tools available, such as those found in Google G Suite (free) and the packages that now come with purchased productivity software such as Microsoft and Adobe. A subscription tool that is specifically designed to assist students in collaboration, creating references, and organizing their research is NoodleTools. This application helps students organize their research by creating digital note cards, outlines, and lists of things to do. According to Buerkett (2011), "Noodletools includes great help menus, articles, and search tools. An online notecard tool assists student with paraphrasing, and both the bibliography and notecards can be shared with the classroom teacher and school librarian" (23).

Journaling

The use of teacher/librarian-monitored journals to chronicle student experience and to track projects and problems has been effective in helping all ages of students from primary school to college (Mark & Jacobson 1995). Kuhlthau (1991, 1993b), for example, found that journals provide a means for the recording of students' thoughts, problems, and concerns. In addition, a student's journal becomes a permanent artifact of the process and a resource that can be used by him or her as a springboard to the next project and consulted as a tutorial for review before the next project begins. Students can also use these notations as a basis for evaluating the research process and the final project or product.

By the same token, teachers and librarians can use journals as venues within which to pose questions that will stimulate student thinking. Hayes (1994, cited in Mark & Jacobson 1995, 29) found that relating questions to specific aspects of Kuhlthau's information search process was particularly useful. Appropriate questions might include the following: Does the focus relate to the reading and to the topic? Should the focus be narrowed further (or broadened)? Do terms and key words relate directly to the focus? As the work and instruction continue, teachers can pose other types of questions to check for student understanding.

Mark and Jacobson (1995) also recommend the use of student journals and class sessions devoted to presearch discussion of research topics. While journaling and discussion are time consuming, Hayes (1994, cited in Mark & Jacobson 1995) found that their use "improved [both the] focus of the student's first drafts" and the "quality of the final papers" (29), while Mark and Jacobson (1995) report that teachers' responses in student journals promote "a stronger focus and can prevent a disappointing final product" (28). In addition, student complaints recorded in journals can pinpoint weaknesses in the collection, in instruction, and in programming. A view of library resources and insights on instruction and intervention strategies from the perspective of students can be powerful tools for improving the quality of services in the school library.

CHANGES FOR SCHOOL LIBRARIANS: TEACHER AND INFORMATION SPECIALIST ROLES

The AASL National School Library Standards (2018) define the new roles of the school librarian to include that of a teacher and an information specialist:

As teachers the school librarian empowers learners to become critical thinkers, enthusiastic readers, skillful researchers, and ethical users of information. The school librarian supports students' access by guiding them to read for understanding, breadth, and pleasure; use information for defined and self-defined purpose; build on prior knowledge and construct new knowledge; embrace the world of information and all its formats; work with each other in successful collaborations for learning; constructively assess their own work and the work of their peers; [and] become their own best critics. (AASL 2009, 18)

As an information specialist, the school librarian uses technology tools to supplement school resources, assist in the creation of engaging learning tasks, connect the school with the global learning community, communicate with students and classroom teachers at any time, and provide [continuous] access to library services. The school librarian introduces and models emerging technologies as well as strategies for finding, assessing, and using information. (AASL 2009, 17)

The informational and technical needs of students involved in online searching should at last put to rest vestigial models of librarianship that claim that collecting and organizing informational materials, creating an information environment, and teaching library skills necessary for library use encompass all dimensions of the school librarian's job. Current research confirms the need for variety and dynamism in instructional strategizing and for introducing additional levels of assistance and service. In point of fact, roles for school librarians in supporting students in searching online will appropriately include instruction, facilitation, advising/counseling, and occasionally, information provision. Since research has shown that in online environments student access to resources is reduced where personal assistance is not provided (Edmonds et al. 1990, 31), there may even be ethical issues involved when school librarians fail to anticipate and supply the degree of assistance that novice searchers require for successful curricular outcomes.

Within the context of instruction for electronic and online searching, school librarians should count on teaching the mechanics of searching, presearch planning (such as identifying key words and creating search questions), selecting search strategies and databases, and managing search results. In addition, librarians can help students in reviewing lists of citations, interpreting output, assisting with the redesign of the search when necessary, and helping students make relevance judgments (e.g., using criteria such as depth of information, length, reading level, and up-to-dateness in addition to "aboutness") (Smith 1987). Finally, research indicates that students may need encouragement and assistance with "end-game" activities, which involve organizing and using the information obtained (Irving 1990, 1991). The value of support provided by knowledgeable school librarians—who not only understand search techniques but also possess an understanding of the possibilities and idiosyncrasies of online resources—should not be underestimated. And, because online searching of bibliographic records yields citations and abstracts for which the full texts may ultimately be desired, knowing how the documents can be obtained quickly and cheaply requires professionals who are capable and willing to acquire them through interlibrary loan. Neuman's (1997) research in particular illuminates a central issue in online and electronic environments: matching the database of resources to the information needs of the students. The truth is that school librarians must stay ahead of the learning curve in understanding both the technical aspects and the instructional implications of new electronic resources in order to keep pace with a rapidly accelerating technological context (Bruce 1994).

The problems that await student learners in seeking information in online environments argue for librarians to anticipate, diagnose, and remediate student skills. In turn, "this type of diagnostic learning requires information-searching experiences that are introduced, reinforced, and expanded upon across grade levels and content areas rather than presented as 'one-shot' instruction" (Nahl & Harada 1996, 206) sessions. It also argues for documenting instructional intervention as a part of a coordinated program of information literacy and the creation of carefully articulated lesson plans that provide for the assessment of student and class progress (Markuson 1986, 39).

NEW COMPETENCIES

Key to the use of technology in the workplace are the skills needed for the effective use of Web 2.0 technologies, hence the need for new instructional objectives and learning outcomes. A case in point relates to copyright and ethics issues for students (Dow 2008). Technological innovations that now help students create and share—as well as to consume—information "products" makes their understanding of intellectual property rights a matter of considerable importance and interest. For instance, with mashup applications (wherein two or more creative entities are merged into a new product or presentation), questions occur regarding actual copyright ownership for the newer versions. Because conventional copyright laws are based on the concept of original authorship, creative endeavors such as mashups are the cause of considerable copyright confusion (Kapitzke 2009). In today's online-based creative playgrounds, it is interesting to note trends toward tighter intellectual property and copyright controls, even while government policies recommend the use of collaborative creative problem solving. As Kapitzke notes, "[t]he trend towards privatizing information through strong copyright law is also at odds with the eruption of creative self-expression afforded by social networking tools" (99). In their role as technology and ethical information use experts, school librarians are poised on the front lines to teach students how to navigate knotty issues regarding copyright and intellectual property in the "global world of information" (Dow 2008, 49).

However, students will be ill served by fear of punishment for displaying creative license in mixing elements from a variety of sources found online. "Clearly, commercial piracy of cultural materials is wrong and should be prohibited, but regulatory environments that prosecute young people for tinkering with text (language, image, or sound) by sharing digital resources as part of their meaning-making universe are socially dangerous" (Kapitzke 2009, 103). For this reason, handling questions concerning intellectual property and copyright law in Web 2.0 environments requires finesse, creativity, and sensitivity. Suggestions offered by Kapitzke include an appreciation for and understanding of changes occurring to traditional producer-user relationships as well as knowledge and support of alternative copyright frameworks, such as open-source software and Creative Commons licensing. Creative Commons materials are easily located via the Internet (http://www.creativecommons.org), and the organizational mission makes clear its encouragement and promotion of using materials protected and guided by totally new legal parameters:

Creative Commons is a non-profit organization dedicated to making it easier for people to share and build upon the works of others, consistent with the rules of copyright. We provide free licenses and other tools to mark creative work with the freedom the creator wants it to carry, so others can share, remix, use commercially, or any combination thereof. (Creative Commons 2010)

Involved in Creative Commons rights are the following:

- Issues surrounding attribution, such as giving the original author credit after modifying and distributing materials;
- Noncommercial intent;
- No derivatives, meaning that words might be modified and provided to users but not for the purpose of creating derivative works;
- Share Alike, a concept wherein new producers modifying and creating derivative works must make the changed products available to users within the same licensing terms as outlined in the original work. (Kapitzke 2009, 204)

These suggestions are important and compelling in an environment where more than 300 million creations are labeled with Creative Commons licensing and are available for mass consumption via the Internet.

TEACHER-SCHOOL LIBRARIANS AS INSTRUCTIONAL PARTNERS

Collaboration between the classroom teacher and the school librarian is important to increasing students' academic achievement. The 2018 AASL standards describe this role as that of an instructional partner:

The school librarian collaborates with classroom teachers to develop assignments that are matches to academic standards and include key critical thinking skills, technology and information literacy skills, and core social skills and cultural competencies. The school librarian guides instructional design by working with the classroom teacher to establish learning objectives and goals. (AASL 2018, 14)

As noted in previous chapters, research has extended our understanding of the importance of collaboration between school librarians and teachers in helping students make meaningful and ethical use of information they find online and integrating electronic resources into curricular units (Heeks 1997; Irving 1991). Interestingly, Heeks (1989, cited in Irving 1990) reports that collaboration between teachers and school librarians on student assignments "helps to make [student] searches result in more relevant retrieval" (14). However, successful integration assumes that teachers themselves understand the process of information seeking, the range of electronic resources available, and the characteristics of these resources as well as the potential difficulties online searching poses for students. In fact, Irving (1990) found than many teachers lacked knowledge of the research process and of information skills generally. This may be the case even among more technologically adept educators. For example, Fidel et al. (1999) reported that, in their study, teacher-designed online searching tasks were fill-in-the-blanks activities that amounted to little more than electronic scavenger hunts. Where situations such as those Irving and Fidel et al. describe exist, school librarians may have to "educate" some teachers to the benefits of using a "model" for research and assist teachers in creating assignments that facilitate rather than finesse the important learning opportunities such projects can provide. Teachers unfamiliar with the vicissitudes often experienced in information seeking online may need assistance in designing assignments that take into account the additional time required when searching electronically (Neuman 1997).

In the mid-1990s, Barron (1994) noted the phenomenon of technophobia (48) among school staff. This problem has abated over time as younger and more technologically savvy teachers have entered the instructional arena. In fact, Means and Olson (1994) found that student access to electronic databases caused teachers in the study to create more complex assignments. It is probable that the greater a teacher's experience and effectiveness in searching for information online, the more likely it is that the use of electronic resources will be incorporated within research tasks in meaningful ways.

CONCLUSION

Moran (2010) redefined the digital divide in terms not of access to online resources but of adequate instruction that helps students successfully develop search acumen and judgment—skills that will in turn translate into benefits and knowledge that form the basis for future successes in school, jobs, and life. "While," as Moran notes, "not every school librarian is yet adapting to the new reality of what is demanded of the role, thousands of dedicated librarians . . . are turning school media centers into 'learning commons' where students seamlessly use state-of-the-art Web tools to consume and produce content."

The learning gap that Moran (2010) warns of is created when "elite" students in well-funded school districts and private schools are "learning critical

21st century skills" while in "budget-stressed school districts" youngsters without school librarians are being left to fend for themselves. The result, as Moran opines, is "[w]hat a University College of London study called a 'new divide,' with students who have access to librarians 'taking the prize of better grades' while those who don't have access to school librarians" show up "at college beyond hope, having 'already developed an ingrained coping behaviour: they learned to 'get by' with Google." Predicting that "this new divide is only going to widen and leave many students hopelessly lost in the past, while others fully embrace the future," Moran concludes that schools that rely exclusively on classroom teachers who are "stressed by assessment testing and ever-growing paperwork burdens" to "help students figure this all out" will not only fail their students but also fail in their mandate to educate students for a century's worth of new information challenges.

NOTES

1. The Department of Commerce asserts that the K–12 years are critical in generating student interest in "information technology and the career opportunities now possible for students with the requisite skills and access to computer technology" (Twist 2004).

2. Todd (1998) cites Burbules (1997) in describing "the Net as an indiscriminate mix of five types of information, where quality, importance and reliability of information is [sic] difficult to determine. These types are: Information: factual, clearly sourced; bears all the traditional hallmarks of reliability and quality. Misinformation: information judged to be false, out of date, or incomplete in a misleading way. Malinformation: potentially dangerous or damaging information, inappropriate information; information people feel uncomfortable with in openly accessible circulation. Messed Up Information: poorly organized and presented information; sloppy design; problematic navigation. Useless Information: (recognizing one person's trash is another person's treasure) Information that appears to serve little informing purpose."

7

Creating Effective Inquiry-Based Educational Tasks

> In the real world, information seeking takes a long time. It is character-
> ized by blind alleys and false scents, and answers often need to be con-
> structed following critical consideration of the available information.
> —Moore (1993)

This chapter examines inquiry-based learning and how that approach, when well conceived, can require students to think deeply and critically as they learn from information-seeking tasks. Learners' levels of searching expertise and prior content knowledge are essential starting points when planning inquiry-based assignments, while building in self-evaluation as a metacognitive component enhances insight into the inquiry process. Information-seeking activities that spark curiosity as well as those that give students opportunities to engage in real-world problem solving are also ways of increasing student enthusiasm and content knowledge. These issues and topics constitute the focus of this chapter.

INQUIRY-BASED LEARNING

Inquiry-based learning is grounded in a constructivist educational theory whereby learners construct meaning from their learning activities (McKinney 2014). Gordon (2010) asserts that inquiry-based teaching contexts create a "culture of inquiry" where students are not mere recipients, but rather active participants in learning (79). In such a learning environment, student-centered learning intersects with teacher-directed learning and is often supported with information technologies.

Inquiry-based learning is as much about the process as it is about the content (Center for Inspired Teaching 2008). Callison and Baker (2014) describe inquiry as composed of five elements. The first element is, of course, *questioning,* which they describe as a continuing cycle in which the answer to a question becomes the basis for the next question in an ongoing search for increasingly sophisticated knowledge. Their second element is *exploration* where the researcher seeks out information, as their search for information becomes incrementally more refined and more focused. *Assimilation,* the third element, calls for the learner to integrate new knowledge into what is already known or believed; assimilation requires the learner to make judgments about information, often discarding or altering what was thought to be and integrating new understandings with prior knowledge. *Inference* is the element that calls on the learner to draw conclusions or arrive at solutions based on information. Finally, *reflection* involves the learner in looking back at the inquiry process to assess what went well and what may have gone wrong. Callison and Baker (2014) assert that mastering such self-reflection leads to becoming a truly independent learner. Too often assignments simply ask learners to collect information and report it. However, this kind of "research," comprised only of fact-finding tasks (e.g., about animals or nations or battles or events), needs to be reframed as building baseline knowledge, which can serve as a starting— not ending—point of inquiry. For example, only once students have base knowledge about a third-world country are they then able to ponder and investigate *what if?* questions that allow them to explore, for instance, what would be necessary for that country to move up to second-world or even first-world status. Yet too often, we have been satisfied to end with the beginning—to accept fact-finding missions as inquiry. The expectations in inquiry-based learning go beyond facts—expecting students to arrive at insights, solutions, and further questions.

Inquiry-based learning is characterized by some or all of the following key components: "1) a driving question; 2) authentic, situated inquiry; 3) learner ownership of the problem; 4) teacher-support, not teacher-direction; and 5) artifact creation" (Buchanan, Harlan, Bruce, & Edwards 2016, 27). These components make learning experiences meaningful, challenging, and interesting. Such qualities also result in students' greater engagement and deeper learning.

CHARACTERISTICS OF EFFECTIVE, RESEARCH-BASED ASSIGNMENTS

Research paper assignments in secondary school curricular programs in history/social studies or English/language arts seek to provide students experience in the use of primary and secondary sources and the structures and mechanics of formal writing, as they also gain knowledge about the content of the discipline as a whole. Important in these assignments is the demand for high cognitive levels of questioning—beyond *what, where,* and *when.* Assignments that only require fact-gathering develop in students an inaccurate mental model of the meaning of research that lacks the notions of wonder and discovery. Assignments that do not reach this intellectual level actually "reinforce" fact-oriented learning—a practice that can be antithetical to critical thinking. True inquiry must take students further toward new insights and discoveries, that is, toward answers to questions of *how, why,* and/or *what if.* In short, their mental models need to expand to include such processes as analyzing, predicting, inferring, and synthesizing.

Critical thinking is not an option, Norris (1985) asserts; rather, it is "an indispensable part of education" (40). Research projects that do not push students to engage intellectually with course content have little value. For this reason, research assignments must be designed to require higher-order thinking (Honebein 1996; Jay 1986) in completing the research task rather than permitting students merely "to recite facts related to a topic" (Clarke, Martell, & Willey 1994, 70) obtained in a "search, print, and run" library activity (Jacobson & Mark 1995, 116). Perhaps the hardest lesson that students will learn "is that information is not the same as knowledge and that facts are not understanding" (Sauer 1995, 142). But it is an important lesson and one that teachers and librarians must learn as well.

A fact-finding view of investigation too often begins when younger students are asked to create reports—and these reports are simply transferring of facts from source to product. Indeed, it is not unusual to see information age kindergarten youngsters engaged in library activities requiring them to "research" sets of specific facts. Citing Marland (1978), Moore (1993) describes this instructional strategy as "the project method," in which

> students are typically given a topic to research, generally a person, place or event, and are told to use resources from the library, take notes, make an outline, and produce a report. [Sheingold] makes the point that the kind of topic assigned in this context is often a category (Switzerland, music, the 18th century, spiders . . .) and the task can be completed by reviewing a limited number of resources, writing about a few appropriate subcategories, and producing an attractive cover page. (2)

Kuhlthau (2013) defines the distinctions between these traditional assignments and inquiry by noting that "traditional" projects have a template approach, employ predetermined questions, have a report style, and are fact-oriented. On the other hand, inquiry-based research is process driven, with student-generated questions related to content-area curriculum, stress deep learning, and call for creating and sharing new knowledge (7).

In Moore's (1993) view, a major flaw in information-seeking activities predicated on fact-finding is that children develop an expectation that their hunt in the library will eventually uncover a source that provides "the exact answer to their questions in the exact format required" (17). However, even when students understand the synthesis aspects of the task (Gordon 1999), they expect to do little more than report what they find and create some concluding statements based on their reading. Moore (1993) believed students in her study created simple rules for the research task: "Think of a question, identify its keywords, look up the subject index for a Dewey number, go to the shelves and find the answer. . . . If any part of that sequence failed," Moore continued, her students "often seemed surprised and confused."

In a study comparing college students' understanding of a research paper with their instructor's view, Baer (2014) found differences that reveal the importance of changing students' mental models of the research process. In this study, interviewees' responses illustrated notable differences between instructors' and students' conceptions of their assignments. While instructors in her study perceived the research paper to be argumentative, analytical, and interpretive, students generally described it as informative and factual. Students identified central purposes of a research paper to be learning facts, demonstrating knowledge, or learning to use the library. In contrast, instructors saw the purpose of the research paper, for example, to be exploring a problem or pursuing "an elusive truth" (819).

It is important to note that habits and mental models developed in primary and secondary school may contribute to misunderstandings of the true meaning of research. Such findings suggest the importance of a librarian in teaching the inquiry process. For example, in a study focusing on 315 first-year college writing students, Enders (2001) found a relationship between the amount and kind of writing students had done in high school with their confidence and competence to complete college-level writing. He reported that many of his students described their high school writing as summarizing or reporting what they found in sources. One representative student described writing a research paper as "checking lots of books out from the library and rewording what they said" (64).

As noted, typical student "research" assignments constitute examples of the "imposed inquiry" approach described by Gross (1999). In her analysis of this type of inquiry, Gross concluded that teachers and librarians must build a sense of student ownership into assignments and design projects so that each child can respond at her or his developmental level, a point also made by Van Merriënboer and Kirschner (2012). When students are challenged to seek information in a concept-based inquiry, it becomes necessary for them to engage in analyzing the information they uncover as an intermediary stage between searching and reporting (Donham 2010). Consider, for example, the typical animal report wherein students gather information about a particular animal— its life expectancy, the number of young it bears, its enemies, etc. Now if that examination of animals is contextualized within a concept, such as migration, new and more challenging questions emerge to frame the inquiry: *Why? How do they know? What if?* For example, *Why does this animal migrate? How does it know when to go? How does it know where to go? How does it manage its young while migrating? What if the climate is changing?* Similarly, at the high school level, if instead of researching Japanese internment by the U.S. government during World War II as a singular event, students are asked to research it through the lens of a specific concept, such as national security, or the concept of racism, the focus of the research changes dramatically, and the analysis of the factual information proceeds on different and more challenging lines. Besides increasing the complexity of the task, and thereby making the task more interesting and profound, it is likely that the student may, as Gross (1999) hopes, assume a greater sense of ownership of the entire project. This conceptual approach can increase the relevance of the inquiry for students and certainly engage students in higher-order thinking.

Research studies in the field of librarianship point to a variety of factors as essential components to successful project completion. Stripling and Harada (2012) describe a curricular-based inquiry learning experience where both content and process learning objectives are central. Their example features the all-important collaboration between teacher and librarian that results in a project that offers meaningful and well-timed opportunities for enhancing not only content learning but also inquiry process understanding. Further, a study of complex tasks revealed—not surprisingly—that more complex tasks require more time; this is an important consideration in moving toward true inquiry-based assignments (Walhout et al. 2017). Research also indicates that when students lack prior content knowledge, their ability to conduct independent and meaningful inquiry based on that content is compromised (Willoughby et al. 2009). In addition, having students engage in front-end activities such as brainstorming and planning has been recommended by Kuhlthau (1985) and others as important preliminary scaffolding for information seeking. Significantly, Wesley's (1991) research indicates that student planning prior to searching helps to minimize student anxiety and frustration that can subvert or even derail research activities.

In many cases, the student's background readings on a given topic will be textbook based. To increase student interest and also acquaint students with other information resources, Callison (1994) suggests moving beyond "textbook generalities and teacher-led discussion" to include the sharing of "books, newspaper articles, films, guest lectures" (51), and the like to help build content knowledge as a preresearch activity. A broad Google search may also provide a useful starting point for building background on an unfamiliar topic, according to Watson (2014). But Watson suggests that this initial dive into a topic be considered as outside the student's actual investigation and is not considered a reference or formal source of information—it is for the student's own background-building only. As an aside, Watson goes on to emphasize the power of primacy: "The primacy of such an article exerts considerable influence over any other information that is subsequently read by a student" (1402). In other words, the first information found becomes a touchstone against which all future findings will be compared. Until students have a knowledge base, their research questions cannot advance beyond the knowledge level.

Developing a research question is a key driver for inquiry-based learning (Buchanan et al. 2016). A question taxonomy attributed to Dahlgren and Öberg (2001) offers one way to help students generate research questions that will likely to lead to intellectual exploration beyond fact-gathering. By sharing such a taxonomy of questions with students, librarians can discourage questions that can be called encyclopedic, like "What are the characteristics of the habitat of wombats?" Instead, we can encourage questions fitting one of Dahlgren and Öberg's categories:

- Meaning-oriented (understanding the essence of a concept): How do plants and animals interact in a short-grass prairie habitat?
- Relational (exploring the relationship): What are the long-term effects of natural hazards like flooding or wildfire on the landscape?

- Value-oriented (applying a value to the question): What methods can conservationists employ to educate citizens about the importance of preservation of public land?
- Solution-oriented (finding solutions to a problem): What steps can be taken to protect wetlands in our state?

Younger children can be encouraged to ask *how, why,* or *what if* questions after they have answered *who, where,* and *when* questions. In a study of life-long learning and workplace skills, Head (2017) discovered, "[W]e were struck to find that far fewer graduates—one in four of the sample (27%)—reported that their university years had enabled them to develop the ability to frame and ask questions of their own as independent thinkers" (85). Such a finding speaks to the importance of developing skills in question asking.

It is clear that students are more successful when the goals and outcomes of an assignment are clearly stated (Thomas 1993) and when they understand assessment criteria and the reasoning behind research tasks. Irving's (1985) research indicates that children need to know up front what is being required of them. Without this knowledge, Irving believes that youngsters will lack the framework for "self-evaluation, which is essential to the development of good learners" (35).

The importance of evaluation as a part of the process of learning is well established in the literature of school librarianship (Callison 1994; Eisenberg & Berkowitz 1990; Grover 1993; Kuhlthau 1994) and education (Thomas 1993). Its purpose, Kuhlthau (1993b) writes, "is to identify what learning has taken place and where further instruction and practice are needed" (59). As Irving (1985) notes above, the evaluation tasks for student researchers include not only a critical review of information sources relevant to their projects but also assessment of their own learning as demonstrated in the completed project. Other library and information science (LIS) researchers and scholars (Craver 1989; Eisenberg & Berkowitz 1990; Harada 2010; Pitts 1995) agree with the importance of evaluating both product and process. Without this feature, students lack the opportunity to learn from their mistakes (Irving 1985) or to gain awareness of themselves as learners. Indeed, they may focus their time and energy on activities that, in the end, have little educational impact. For example, students in studies conducted by McGregor (1994b) and Pitts (1995) were so focused on product generation that the value of the subject content and process skills they were meant to learn were ignored. Students saw the research task as "a job," McGregor asserts, "rather than as an opportunity for learning" (74). The focus on learning and the learning process has another payoff: according to Kuhlthau (1997), students who are aware of the importance of process skill development are not as likely to copy informational texts verbatim.

SELF-ASSESSMENT

Self-assessment by students is essential for personal growth and development. Alverno College in Milwaukee, Wisconsin, has been developing a strong self-assessment culture for decades. Their work is based on the belief that students must leave school able to assess their own work as independent learners. Without such ability, how will they know what they must next learn? At Alverno College, faculty have identified four components inherent in self-assessment; there students learn a self-assessment framework that guides them to observe and analyze their own work using specific criteria, use feedback of their own and others, analyze patterns in their work, judge the quality of their own work by comparing it to standards of performance, and plan for future learning and performance based on what they have observed (Mentkowski & Sharkey 2011).

In K–12 settings, often that final stage is overlooked; finding time for it is difficult. Yet, if that stage of self-assessment is skipped, the likelihood of students applying what they have learned to their next inquiry experience, particularly about their inquiry process, seems far less likely; even brief explicit conversation of what they would do differently next time is likely to serve to advance their inquiry learning process.

Kuhlthau (1993b) suggests that "evaluation should take place immediately following the completion of the research assignment" (59) and should consider students' abilities to create a focus for their papers, to make good use of their time in planning and carrying out the research activity, and to make use of available resources, including the expertise of the school librarian. To facilitate self-assessment, Kuhlthau recommends the use of time lines (to help students visualize the stages in the process), flowcharts (to help students track their progress), and conferencing with the school librarian and the creation of a summary statement (to assist students in evaluating their participation in the process and their creation of a final product).

Louis and Harada (2012) emphasize that the overarching question to be posed to students in self-assessment is how will they know whether they have done a good job. Such a question can then lead to the collaborative development of assessment criteria to be used by both the students, as they consider their processes, and the instructors as they consider the students' products. Harada (2010) has considered the importance of self-assessment, as habits essential to the development of lifelong learners. She proposes several techniques for creating a metacognitive culture through the lenses of metacognition and self-regulation. Examples of these techniques include reflection logs, where students regularly record their research progress, perhaps with prompts from the librarian like "What part of this topic really intrigues me?" (14) She also proposes that students engage in conversation with a peer, a teacher, or a librarian, who poses such questions as "If I could start this project over again, how would I change my approach?" (14)

Owen and Sarles (2012) recommend using exit tickets to shift emphasis toward the inquiry process and away from the end product. Simply put, they recommend giving students a prompt at the end of a library session and having them write brief responses as tickets to exit; for example, the librarian might ask students to write about what they still need to find out to answer their research questions, or, what is the first thing they need to do at their next library work session, or what search terms yielded good results. Responses to these prompts will provide students starting points for their next sessions. They will also serve to inform their librarian of each students' progress, their needs for instruction or assistance. Such self-assessment needs to be integrated into the assignment as part of the expectation for students engaging in inquiry.

THE AFFECTIVE DOMAIN

Jakobovits and Nahl-Jakobovits (1990) call attention to the salience of student affect (e.g., "how we feel about and value learning experiences") (Jacobson & Mark 1995, 108) as a concomitant to success in information-seeking tasks. Kuhlthau's (2004) work also emphasizes the affective nature of the search task, specifically the feelings of uncertainty, confusion, and anxiety as common experiences for novice information seekers. In planning student assignments, librarians should anticipate these feelings of insecurity and allow time and space for students to discuss them as the information-seeking task unfolds. Similarly, Branch (2003) found in studying junior high school students that it was important for librarians to support both the cognitive and affective demands of research to ensure student success. She particularly emphasized the need to support students at points of challenge, such as information overload. Likewise, the librarian can help students by "normalizing" feelings of uncertainty. In their case study of work with undergraduates, Donham, Heinrich, and Bostwick (2010) began their students' inquiry project by asserting to the class:

> "If you are confident or comfortable at this stage of your process, there is a problem!" What followed was our assurance that support would not end with the determination of the topic or the identification of sources but would continue to be available throughout the process from both the professor and the consulting librarian, for Pitts' (1995) exploratory study suggested that the research process is complex enough that students benefit from supportive expertise that represents both content and process. (10)

This kind of guidance, support, and feedback along the way is essential if students are to understand the value of the teacher and school librarian to the learning process—as well as to students themselves—over and above the project that comes at the end (Pitts 1995).

Kuhlthau's (2004) mapping of the affective domain across the information-seeking process offers significant guidance for maintaining awareness of not only the cognitive demands of inquiry but also the affective. By helping students know the normalcy of beginning with a high level of uncertainty, then briefly feeling some relief at the point of deciding on a topic, only to find oneself back to a higher level of concern in determining how to proceed to continue the inquiry, then arriving at a focus for the investigation and feeling some relief from the uncertainty, only to continue, ideally, with decreasing, but continuous uncertainty, the librarian helps assuage some of the anxiety so that students can proceed productively to pursue their inquiry.

Akin's (1998) research considers the issue of information overload as a problem for youngsters engaged in information-seeking activities. In this context, information overload may occur when too many topics are offered as research alternatives, too many resources are suggested as relevant, or too much information is retrieved as a result of information seeking. Akin's study sought to learn through survey data how fourth and eighth graders in two Texas public schools felt about information overload and what they did about it. It was Akin's view that "knowing how the child feels can help the librarian be more empathetic. But knowing what the child does allows the school media specialist to respond with instruction" (6). Particularly, Akin was looking for strategies that students used and the relationship of gender to the overload experience. Results indicated that 80 percent of students surveyed reported the experience of information overload, with girls and younger students "more likely than boys" and older students "to have felt overloaded" (4). Techniques reported by students in easing overload included selecting a few items from all those available, "filtering" and "chunking" the information, or linking "large amounts of information into some common shape" (e.g., "a teacher-supplied outline").

Feelings reported by fourth-grade students in Akin's (1998) study included confusion, frustration, depression, anger, and physical distress. As Akin notes, "These visceral responses speak to the degree of disillusionment or disappointment with the information at hand and the expectations of the child."(8) Eighth graders experienced similar reactions to overload, although the expression of their reactions tended to the vulgar in boys and to reflect stress, tension, and panic in girls. "The eighth graders reported additional feelings of being stuffed and bored" (9). Akin concluded that some kinds of inattention and acting out, swearing, or physical ailments necessitating trips to the school nurse might be the result of overload.

Although limited in terms of the number of students and the self-report method involved in survey research, Akin's (1998) study is interesting in that it indicates that overload does, indeed, affect children and that admitting and discussing the overload issue and possible strategies for coping with this syndrome are an important part of library and information skills sessions. Kuhlthau (1999) describes this feeling as "the dip" in confidence that searchers experience when encountering new and confusing information: "Advances in information systems that open access to a vast assortment of resources has . . . in many cases . . . intensified the sense of confusion and uncertainty." This is especially true when information retrieval systems overwhelm "the user with everything all at once, rather than an offering a few well-chosen introductory pieces for initial exploration."

Taking the availability of information into account in structuring lessons and information tasks also seems reasonable. According to Akin (1998), it may be useful to teach students to reduce the number of types of materials to be considered, change the topic, seek assistance, and take a break as ways to cope when the demands of the task overwhelm them. Brainstorming such coping techniques in advance would also assist learners to "identify the overload reduction strategies on their own, learn more about manipulating information products, and adopt a proactive response to information overload" (10).

Gordon (2000) has identified an effective presearch strategy that helps children cope with overload: concept mapping. In fact, Gordon's informants indicated experiencing less overload when concept maps were used. Gordon indicated that this technique is one way to provide an overview of both general and specific terms that describe the topic.

TABLE 7.1   Characteristics of Effective Student Inquiry Assignments

Effective assignments:

- Are developmentally appropriate for each student.
- Begin by accessing prior knowledge to arrive at an appropriate starting point.
- Present clear objectives/outcomes and evaluation criteria for process and product.
- Engage students in high-level questioning and thinking.
- Develop students' understandings of the inquiry process.
- Are meaningful to students and linked to student experience.
- Enhance learning in the content area.
- Involve students in critical thinking rather than recalling or reporting.
- Take the affective needs of students into account.
- Are broken down into manageable elements and supported by teachers and librarians.
- Provide opportunities for self-assessment of the inquiry process.
- Are structured to allow time for searching and task completion, taking into account task complexity.

Dispositions, or habits of mind, can be considered to fall within the affective domain. These are the attitudes that students themselves bring to the inquiry process. Ritchhart (2001) identifies key dispositions of learners as curious, open-minded, strategic, investigative, reasoning, metacognitive, using evidence. These dispositions are indeed the disposition of a student who successfully engages in inquiry as they lead to a holistic understanding of the inquiry process. For this reason, they should be a part of assignments and expectations.

Librarians can teach these dispositions by direct, explicit instruction, as well as by modeling them for students with "think-aloud" strategies. In addition, librarians can employ script theory (Rugg 1997) to teach dispositions by using consistent "scripts" across grade levels in talking about inquiry (Donham 2016). For example, consistently using the scripted phrase, "I wonder . . ." can help students develop the habit of curiosity. Alternatively, consistently using the scripted question, "What more do I need to know?" can help students develop the habit of being investigative. It is important that these dispositions are embedded into the assignment expectations set for students and that such habits of mind are seen to be as important as skills in inquiry-based learning. Table 7.1 summarizes characteristics of effective inquiry-based assignments.

EFFECTIVE ASSIGNMENTS FROM THE STUDENT'S POINT OF VIEW

Student motivation to engage in inquiry has been investigated by various scholars, and several key features of assignments have been noted in their findings. For example, ownership of the problem is identified as a central feature of inquiry-based learning, according to Buchanan et al. (2016). Similarly, Hirsh (1999) related student choice and student interest in a topic to her informants' ability to personalize their searches, their eagerness to undertake the research task, and their care in evaluating the search results. "Students were absorbed in the search process," Hirsh wrote, "and generally did not settle for the first piece of information they found" (1278).

Crow (2009) also found interest in a topic to be an important motivator for students. In her study of 10-year-olds in Colorado Springs who were identified to be intrinsically motivated to seek information, she requested that informants name their favorite two information-seeking episodes and then asked them to give the reasons why they named those specific experiences as their favorites. The most frequent reason given was their interest in or the personal relevance of the topic. Other reasons they listed were (in order of prevalence) "working in a group, the experiences of the information seeking itself, creating the final product, choice of aspect within topic, and no time limit" (101). In later studies, Crow (2015) and Crow and Kastello (2017) found that interest/personal relevance was also the most frequent reason for the child subjects from collectivist (Uganda) and collectivist/individualistic (India) cultures in choosing their favorite information-seeking episodes. It is interesting to note that none of the children gave "working individually" as a reason for preferring a research episode, pointing to the fact that relational needs outweighed the need for autonomy for these three diverse groups of students.

Garland's (1995) study of information seeking in school contexts sought to tap the information-seeking experience from the point of view of the students involved. Specifically, Garland was interested in finding out how 387 high school students in 18 classrooms studying a range of subjects from physiology to composition regarded the research task and those elements that related to student achievement and feelings of satisfaction. The tasks themselves were as "heterogeneous" as the students and subject matter and included formal papers and a variety of creative presentation formats. Garland identified several criteria as important to students: choice of topics, which gave students "a sense of control" (178); experience with the type of project assigned; background knowledge of the topic; access to assistance in choosing a topic and understanding the research process, particularly if the task "required a higher level of thinking" (176); an explicit connection between course content and the topic; explicit goals and processes for task completion; specific evaluation criteria; and opportunities for social interaction and group work.

In her study, Burdick (1997) raised the issue of gender as it relates to information seeking and the character of student research assignments. Citing the work of Gilligan (1982) and Pipher (1994) related to the socialization of adolescent girls in the United States, Burdick particularly noted the need for school librarians to support girls in creating and expressing their own personal perspectives in their research projects, to include women as well as men as researchable "topics," and to legitimate connectedness and syntheses, which often characterize a feminine approach to learning, in addition to the informational approach and logical argument formats, which tend to reflect a male perspective. These themes resonate with the work of Ford (1996), who has noted the need to expand curriculum to include all races and ethnic groups. Ford reminds us that "students learn through acts of omission and commission; they learn from what is present in and left out of the curriculum" (143). Where topic choices fail to acknowledge "the contributions [to history, literature, science, etc.] of various racial, cultural, and economic groups" (143), the "invisible veil" (193) of monoculturalism effectively masks the biases that such omissions portend.

TABLE 7.2 Strategies for Building Motivation in Information-Seeking Projects

- Stimulate interest in the activity at the outset in an engaging way based on student interests.
- Ensure relevance through sensitivity to student experience, gender, culture, and values.
- Increase student confidence by explaining what is expected, what students will be doing, and the availability of assistance, expertise, and emotional support provided by teachers, librarians, and peers.
- Ensure that expectations are achievable—challenging but not overwhelming—and that the achievement of goals lies within students' ability levels.
- Inspire intrinsic motivation by encouraging student enjoyment of the research experience and discussing the value of the activity to other school-related and life-related tasks.
- Provide time for students to explore topics of interest and build necessary background knowledge to allow for deep learning.

More recently, Heath (2015) undertook a qualitative study of high school students engaged in a history research assignment in Jamaica. A particularly noteworthy aspect of her work was to determine how to increase student engagement and interest in their research. She began the investigation by inviting students to work together to construct their own definition of meaningful research; the result was key to the students' commitment to the task and resonates with earlier findings regarding student interest:

> Meaningful research assignments are those which make sense to the learner; they allow learners to have a say in the topics to be researched, satisfying individual areas of interest. They allow for a wide scope of discovery which encourages personal and intellectual maturity. (373)

Similarly, Lewis, Simmons, and Maniotes (2018) report on a professional development program where teachers were taught strategies for giving agency to their students to generate their own research questions in an inquiry-based learning experience. They found that student engagement increased and that students were learning at deeper levels as they moved toward asking more complex questions. Likewise, Power (2012) found that allowing students greater say on the focus or topic of their inquiry promoted higher levels of engagement in science topics, along with deeper understandings, but that it was essential to provide adequate time for initial exploration of the topic. Table 7.2 summarizes factors that can increase student interest in information-seeking assignments.

AUTHENTIC RESEARCH: BUILDING COMPETENCIES THROUGH "REAL" TASKS

"Reporting has masqueraded as researching for so long that the terms are used interchangeably" Gordon wrote in 1999, with the result that the ever-popular research project has become a bromide, "analogous to 'Take two aspirins and call me in the morning.' . . . Educators adjust the dosage for older students; the length of the paper grows with the time allotted to the task but the prescription is the same." As Gordon notes, students have come to view the research task as a writing assignment in which factual accuracy, grammar, and writing style are emphasized over individual thoughtfulness or creativity in problem solving.

The use of authentic research assignments is consistent with trends in education that center on experiential learning. Examples of experiential learning include inquiry or discovery learning (Kuhlthau, Heinström, & Todd 2008), situated learning (Brown, Collins, & Duguid 1989), cognitive flexibility and cognitive apprenticeship (Collins, Brown, & Newman 1989), anchored learning, and problem-based learning. There is a growing number of examples of middle and high school students involved in researching real-world problems and issues like climate, homelessness, sustainability, food insecurity. For example, a 2011 report details a class project that engaged students in researching water runoff and infiltration into soils (Moebius-Clune et al. 2011). Student engagement and learning were assessed through testing, final projects, a student survey, and observations of student attitudes. Pretest to posttest gains showed significant science-content learning. Further, the report indicates that students expressed a high level of interest in a topic they found to be of authentic importance to their locale and reported an increased interest in science in general at the end of the experience.

Gordon's (1999) study involved a group of tenth graders in an action research project as part of "a performance-based assessment task, including rubrics, student journals, and peer editing" (1). In the process, it was hoped that students would learn the difference between report preparation and original research. Essentially, the researcher wanted to know the following:

> [C]an students successfully use primary research methods to collect their own data? What if teachers and librarians designed research assignments that distinguished between information and data—that is, between fact and ideas recorded in books and electronic sources—as evidence or data collected firsthand by the student researcher? What if teachers and librarians became reflective practitioners who saw the research assignments as an opportunity to . . . evaluate and revise the learning task? (1)

Before beginning their research projects, students in Gordon's (1999) study attended a 10-session advisory class to learn the fundamentals of action research: research design, proposal writing, research questions, research methods, and data collection and analysis. Results of Gordon's research indicated that students need time to write and reflect; they also require instruction in the correct form and use of citations and practice in Internet searching and key word use. The study also provided additional evidence that student research is an iterative, idiosyncratic, and messy process that involves students in rereading background information at various times and modifying research questions as the task unfolds.

Teachers created advanced organizers that focused students' attention on the inquiry process, beginning with brainstorming, then generating a testable question, collecting data, and graphing the data to make meaning. Such emphasis on the inquiry process provides the scaffolding students often need. Their teachers reported that students displayed a high sense of ownership in their work and pride in their discovery in this authentic investigation assignment. Importantly, Gordon asserts that presenting the research process as a simple and finite sequence of steps is not helpful for students or teachers. Gordon also advises that students build "prior knowledge of the topic" (17) as preparation for authentic research tasks.

Authenticity can emerge from students having the opportunity to formulate their own topic. Klipfel (2014), in discussing the importance of authenticity to student motivation, emphasizes the need of educators to engage students in conversations in order to discover their interests and then to support them in pursuing those personal interests. In this study, in the experimental group, the librarian modeled a narrative of identifying a topic of authentic interest, in contrast to the control group where the librarian used a generic topic to model search strategies. Klipfel found that the authentic, interest-based instruction correlated with students expressing greater interest in their research; these students showed greater enthusiasm for working on their research and continued engagement in the assignment. These findings suggest that assignments be designed as open-ended enough for students to fit their own curiosities to requirements.

COMPETENCIES FOR INDEPENDENT RESEARCH IN THE SCHOOL LIBRARY

It is worth noting that when students are sent to the library to look up "facts" and report them back to the classroom, when they are required to participate in a scavenger hunt, or when they are given skills worksheets that essentially require them to "fill in the blanks" (e.g., questions that ask students to list, name, define, or describe), they are seldom being asked to operate above the knowledge or recall levels of Bloom's Taxonomy. Although these levels of thinking may occasionally be appropriate for the very youngest information seekers, it does little to extend the thinking and learning capacities of older children and youth, nor does it prepare students to engage in "authentic" and independent information-seeking activities upon which, as Walter's (1994) research indicates, their educational success may well depend.

Cognitive Barriers to Inquiry

Humans demonstrate a surprisingly common set of cognitive biases that can interfere with the inquiry process. For example, confirmation bias leads information seekers to look for evidence that confirms their existing thoughts or views and to discount evidence that seems contrary (Miller 2016). Due to this natural tendency toward confirmation bias, a Rand Corporation report asserts that people will naturally decide how and where to search for information, based on the likelihood of confirming their existing beliefs (Kavanaugh & Rich

2018). Further the Rand report states that people will disparage sources of conflicting information or frame their positions in terms of religious or emotional beliefs. The report also describes the effect of echo chambers on our tendency to ignore information that suggests new perspectives; close networks of family and friends can establish points of view that limit one's ability to see alternative views. Framing of ideas is also described as a process that can interfere with understanding and acceptance of information; a simple example is whether a group is framed or labeled as terrorists or freedom fighters. Similarly, the bandwagon effect can be a particularly powerful bias among information seekers; while this bias is often associated with advertising, the rise of social media as a source of information embodies the power of the bandwagon as participants see groupthink develop and emerge in the form of likes and shares so that without critical thinking, one becomes a believer without adequate skepticism (Lee et al. 2018). These cognitive tendencies call for raising awareness of them among students and embedding in inquiry-based assignments expectations to intentionally work to counter inherent biases. Expectations for dispositions of open-mindedness and healthy skepticism need to be explicit to counter these inherent cognitive behaviors.

Critical Thinking and Information Literacy

In 1987, Michael Scriven and Richard Paul, presented at the 8th Annual International Conference on Critical Thinking and Education Reform a definition of critical thinking as:

> the intellectually disciplined process of actively and skillfully conceptualizing, applying, analyzing, synthesizing, and/or evaluating information gathered from, or generated by, observation, experience, reflection, reasoning, or communication (http://www.criticalthinking.org/pages/defining-critical-thinking/766)

Clearly, these intellectual processes intersect with the skills associated with information literacy, particularly the evaluation of information and information sources. The information skills identified by scholars and educators as dimensions of critical thinking include the ability to distinguish fact from opinion, to establish the authority of sources, to assess the accuracy and relevance of information, and to detect bias and underlying assumptions in data found in information sources. Often, when librarians collaborate with faculty in teaching students inquiry processes for assignments, librarians fall prey to the temptation to teach students only about sources of information and how to find them. As Paterson and Gamtso (2011) assert, no amount of retrieved material understands or interprets itself. Indeed, it is the understanding and interpreting of information that lies at the heart of inquiry assignments, and it is here where students need to apply critical thinking. Hence, instruction to support the inquiry process must include techniques not only for locating but also for evaluating, selecting, extracting, recording, organizing, and synthesizing information. Questions of relevance and authority need to be at the forefront.

Helping Students Develop Evaluation Skills

Evaluation of information and information sources has become increasingly important as the information landscape has widened and the editorial controls of the past have weakened in favor of a democratization of information dissemination (Ostenson 2014). In response, the need to teach critical evaluation confronts librarians in all settings. In this information environment, the responsibility for determining the credibility of found information has shifted from editors to the information consumer. Approaches to addressing the need for a critical stance have varied. One approach has been to provide students with a set of criteria or a checklist to be applied generically to all information. An example is the ABCD set of criteria—authority, bias, coverage, and date (Krueger 2013). While such an approach can offer young students an introduction to the idea that one cannot always accept at face value found information, this approach may, particularly for older students, oversimplify the critical process. Indeed, in a study of seventh graders evaluating Web-based information, the findings made clear students' inability to apply formulaic questions effectively to evaluate the authority of found information (Coiro et al. 2015). Ostenson (2014) critiques the idea of a checklist, and suggests that this approach may oversimplify the critical thinking needed to accurately evaluate information or may indeed lead a student away from a viable information source. Indeed, the *Framework for Information Literacy* developed by the Association of College and Research Libraries describes the authority of information as constructed and contextual (ACRL 2015). Such a designation raises a question of how the purpose for searching or the context of the inquiry should influence the evaluation criteria. Ostenson (2014) also raises the issue of whether such checklists lead students toward a belief that there is one right answer or whether it can cloud the fact that not all information is objectively right or wrong, useful or useless.

The International Baccalaureate Program applies a set of criteria that perhaps addresses the nuances of authority more intentionally (Knutson 2014). They engage students in analyzing sources of information through four lenses: origin, purpose, value, and limitations. Certainly, this model includes questions found in traditional evaluation checklists such as "When was it published?" However, it challenges students to think about some aspects of information evaluation in deeper ways. For example, besides asking students to look at who the author is, this model encourages them to look further at whether there is anything more to be known about the author to help us evaluate— for example, affiliations or credentials. A particularly challenging set of questions appears under the heading of *purpose*, asking students to consider such questions as why this document even exists or who is its intended audience. Under the heading *value*, students ponder such queries as the circumstances under which the document was written, for example, what was going on at the time it was written or what can we tell from the author's perspective. Finally, and perhaps of greatest importance, students are asked to express the limitations of the source. Here the student might ponder what has been left out or how to verify what the author has said. Expecting students to be explicit in their assessment of the sources of information they cite serves to increase their consciousness of being a critical information consumer.

Ostenson (2014) recommends that students be taught from the beginning that subscription databases are a highly appropriate starting point for information seeking, since they contain publications that have been subjected to editorial controls. By placing high value on these resources, rather than beginning on the Web, the likelihood of beginning with more trustworthy information increases.

Evaluation skills are at the highest of Bloom's thinking levels and are essential components of literacies of all kinds. Bloom (1956) describes evaluation as judging the value of ideas, works, solutions, or methods, using explicit criteria and/or standards. The process may be either quantitative or qualitative, and the criteria may be determined by the student or the teacher.

As important as evaluation is in so many instructional contexts, it is not an easy skill for many students to develop. According to Fitzgerald (1999), knowledge of the domain, knowledge of the processes of decision making, the context, the culture, the amount of time to devote, the nature of the problem, the willingness to expend effort, the level of support ("instruction, practice and cues"), developmental level, and educational (or reading comprehension) level all have a bearing on a student's ability to evaluate information.

Fitzgerald's (1999) study highlights the difficulty many students have in evaluating information. Particularly noteworthy is her discussion of the process of deliberation. Deliberation involves a process of thinking through the information in a logical way and then deciding as to its value or truth. Since children tend to trust adults as authority figures and often believe that "there is an absolute correspondence between what is seen or perceived and what is (pp. 47–48)" (King & Kitchener 1994, quoted in Fitzgerald 1999), evaluating information created by adults can be bewildering. For this reason, many, "elementary school-aged children are particularly unlikely" to question the information they find unless prompted to do so (Markman 1979, cited in Fitzgerald 1999). Having said that, studies by McGregor (1994b) and Pitts (1995) noted the failure in older students to consider the quality of the information they encountered. Carey (1985) ascribes this failure to a lack of domain knowledge rather than immature thinking.

Finally, Fitzgerald (1999) makes a case for teaching evaluation within the context of ongoing classroom activities. "Few topics could be more boring or incomprehensible to children than critical thinking or argumentation taught out of context," (20) she writes. "The best approach is to choose a subject area of current controversial interest to the student in a given class and integrate the suggested strategies into a unit about that topic" (20). Fitzgerald recommends the following teaching strategies: teaching evaluation strategies one or a few at a time and spread out over a number of sessions, providing specific examples, teaching subskills involved in the evaluation, providing practice with well-defined and ill-defined problems, clarifying the biases that might be involved in information texts, providing practice in arguing both sides of controversial questions, assigning a variety of research tasks on a regular basis, and involving children in the production of a variety of media.

Reading Skills

Research in reading suggests a number of activities that school librarians can use in helping youngsters increase reading performance and comprehension. Moreillon (2013) suggests several reading comprehension strategies that librarians can embed into instruction. One such strategy is accessing background knowledge; Moreillon suggests asking students to make connections with the text before reading by thinking of how the title connects to self, or to other texts, or to the world. Another strategy she suggests is making predictions or drawing inferences. She also encourages librarians to assist learners to focus on the main ideas in the passage and promote readers' awareness of their own comprehension by asking questions. In some instances, Moreillon recommends using sensory images to improve comprehension.

Reading in the online environment involves processes not always inherent in reading print media (Lee et al. 2018). For example, Internet users must learn to read for the purpose of locating information; the reader must read and infer which links within a text may be most useful in a set of search results; also, the reader must be able to efficiently scan for relevant information within websites. Similarly, unlike the reader of a printed text, the online reader must read to evaluate critically what appears on the page, distinguishing between marketing and substantive information. Another online reading task is to determine from a vast set of options what is worthy of including and what should be excluded in one's collection of information. Coiro (2011) recommends using think-aloud strategies to model for students the critical thinking necessary in reading online. She emphasizes the importance of metacognition, that is, self-awareness of the reader's critical stance.

Writing activities can also improve students' reading comprehension, especially when these activities help focus the students' attention and extend the time they spend on reading tasks. Among the most valuable writing exercises are summarizing, "abstract writing," "outlining, paraphrasing, note taking and writing paragraph headings" (Stosky 1983, cited in Craver 1989, 15). Although no one strategy has been proven consistently superior for all students, Nagel (1972, cited in Craver 1989) found that "students showed greater comprehension when they summarized paragraphs in a single sentence" than when they "wrote nothing" (15).

Although reading well is certainly an essential skill for information seeking, the ability to read critically is required if students are to make judgments about the relevance, point of view, authority, and bias of the sources they encounter. Reading is a foundational skill for learning, personal growth, and enjoyment. The degree to which students can read and understand text in all formats (e.g., picture, video, print) and all contexts is a key indicator of success in school and in life.

CONCLUSION

Inquiry-based learning fits naturally within a constructivist learning environment. Research indicates that since students frequently lack an understanding of the inquiry process (Kuhlthau 2004; Pitts 1995) as a whole, they both need and welcome assistance in understanding the processes required in seeing their projects through to completion. Carey (1998) claims that the differences inherent in the terms "library skills" and "information literacy" are philosophical and substantive, denoting two distinct wings of cognitive psychology: the objectivist wing and the constructivist wing. In Carey's view, the now defunct scope and sequence approach to instruction is objectivist, as is an approach that calls for the sorts of lesson planning frameworks that specify in advance the goals and outcomes of instruction, the skills required for the implementation of the activity, the ability levels and needs of student learners, and the tasks to be undertaken in implementing the lesson. On the contrary, constructivist approaches, including inquiry learning, focus on problem solving and call on the students to struggle through the complexities of the problem and themselves to come up with the "tactics and strategies" (7) they will need in resolving research questions for which no single answer exists.

In Kuhlthau's model of the search process, the exploratory stage represents the heart of inquiry as the student gains knowledge about a topic of interest in order to begin to focus an investigation that calls for higher-level questioning and deeper learning. It is the exploratory stage of inquiry that is most likely to be rushed, thus resulting in a lack of focus. This shortcut in the inquiry process can easily lead to the locate-collect-report model of inquiry that misses the entire point of curiosity-driven inquiry (Jones et al. 2015). A focus on exploration represents a paradigm shift from the traditional teacher-driven project to projects generated out of students' own curiosity and subsequently projects with high levels of student ownership and commitment.

Inquiry requires important skill sets related to locating information and evaluating it for both relevance to the information need and its authority. In addition to skills but equally important is the set of dispositions the student brings to the inquiry experience. Curiosity, open-mindedness, an investigative stance, and strategic planning are examples of habits of mind that aid the inquiring student. These dispositions may not be innate, and librarians can teach them directly and model them.

In instruction, the librarian cannot focus solely on resources, but must also consider the processes of inquiry—gathering background knowledge, generating sound research questions, continually wondering what more needs to be known, and planning and organizing for efficiency. Likewise, modeling the behaviors and dispositions of a researcher gives students a mental model of the work they are undertaking. Showing enthusiasm and encouragement to support the persistence needed to carry out an investigation is also a role for the librarian.

Inquiry-based assignments take students beyond fact-finding, although they may begin with fact-gathering as background knowledge is constructed. Fundamental to inquiry-based learning is the creation of an environment that cultivates curiosity (Jones et al. 2015). This may be the most crucial starting point for a library program.

8

Evaluating Students, Librarians, and Libraries

It may be that by shifting the paradigm of education reform and teaching from one modeled after the clocklike character of the assembly line into one that is closer to the studio or innovative science laboratory might provide us with a vision that better suits the capacities and the futures of the students we teach.

—Elliot Eisner (2004)

National concerns for evaluating every aspect of the educational enterprise have increased pressures on public school librarians to demonstrate their contributions to the creation of information literate students and links between an "information age" literacy skills curriculum and student achievement. Thus, librarians who were in earlier times preoccupied with creating collections of a certain size and programming that reached a certain number of students are today focusing their attention on ensuring that benchmarks are met, outcomes are achieved, and competencies are developed. Within such a context, evaluation has become a priority. This chapter considers contemporary approaches to educational assessment, in particular as they relate to standards-based educational initiatives and authenticity. It also describes the evolution of school library evaluation, the roles for librarians in assessment, the continuing role of standards for library media programs in publications of the American Association of School Librarians (AASL), and the research findings related to library and information skills instruction (see Table 8.1). A concluding section summarizes the implications of school library research for instructional programming, student achievement, and lifelong learning.

TABLE 8.1　The Benefits of Library Instruction: Summary of Major Research Findings

- School libraries have a positive effect on student achievement (Gaver 1963; Greve 1974; Hall-Ellis & Berry 1995; Lance, Rodney, & Hamilton-Pennell 2000a, 2000b; Lance, Welborn, & Hamilton-Pennell 1992).
- Student achievement is higher in schools where library services and instruction are provided by school library professionals (Achterman 2009; Dow, Lakin, & Court 2010; Willson 1965).
- Information literacy instruction has a positive effect on student achievement in reading comprehension (Didier 1982, 1985; Gaver 1963; Thorne 1967; Yarling 1968), language development (Didier 1982, 1985; Yarling 1968), and knowledge of library skills (Gaver 1963; Thorne 1967; Yarling 1968).
- Where school libraries are well funded and librarians participate in the instructional process, academic achievement is higher (Hall-Ellis & Berry 1995; Lance, Welborn, & Hamilton-Pennell 1992; Smith 2001).
- Integration of library skills and classroom curriculum resulted in an increase in library use (Nolan 1989) and higher achievement in information-gathering skills and chart and graph readings (Becker 1970).
- Instruction in library resources resulted in more independence and increased use of specific types of library resources (Brodie 1988; Didier 1982; Gifford & Gifford 1984).
- Library skills instruction resulted in more positive attitudes about the library and its usefulness (Nolan 1989) and higher test scores on locational skills (Gilliland 1986), research skills (Dewees 1987), and study skills (Didier 1982).
- An integrated approach to library and information skills instruction has a positive effect on student learning related to test scores, recall, concentration, focus on the task, and reflective thinking (Todd, Lamb, & McNicholas 1993).
- Library skills instruction using a six-step process model can have a positive impact on student learning of science content (Todd 1995).
- School libraries and school librarians help students become better learners by providing resources in a variety of media to support curricular tasks and leisure reading and providing instruction in the search process, problem solving, and technology; by engaging students with information and assisting with research projects; by promoting reading; and by individualizing and personalizing instruction (Todd & Kuhlthau 2003).

CONCERN FOR STUDENT ACHIEVEMENT

The claim that American public schools are no longer graduating students capable of competing in the global workplace has led to widespread demands for "school improvement" from worried parents, taxpayers, and politicians. Site-based management, charter schools, magnet schools, teacher accountability, and school choice are just a few contemporary approaches to restructuring public school systems; at the same time, educators have instituted instructional reforms related to basic skills, literature- or resource-based instruction, standards-based education, early childhood education, and national guidelines for curricular content and student achievement. Increasing teacher competence has also been a focus. Improving instructional expertise through the creation of certification benchmarks has been the goal of the National Board for Professional Teaching Standards, which rewards teachers and school librarians for excellence.

There is little consensus or research to support the educational efficacy of any of these remedies; indeed, many educators continue to be skeptical of those who seek a single model for public education designed to cure the nation's disparate educational ills or create "quick-fix" solutions to the complex problems involved in educating 21st-century children. Many educators believe that the nationalization of curriculum and curricular objectives as is exemplified in the National Common Core Standards (NCCS) is not the answer. At one point, 46 of the departments of education in the United States had adopted or at least partially adopted the NCCS, though numerous states revised the standards when public opinion turned against the NCCS (Hamlin & Peterson 2018). Educators claim that performance norms, as is typified in standardized tests, used as a sort of "national yardstick" of achievement for decades, have in fact not served well the needs of educational systems trying to cope with student diversity, emerging technologies, and public ambivalence. Their views clash with certain federal programs, such as the 2010 Race to the Top initiative, which provided funding for school districts that provide evidence of increased levels of student achievement in alignment with national standards. These initiatives fly in the face of views espoused by nationally known educators for decades. For example, as long ago as 1993, Stanford professor Elliot Eisner challenged educators to abandon the notion of national standards, which themselves imply a parity across school districts that does not exist, in order to "create schools that excite both teachers and students and provide the conditions that improve the quality of teaching" (23). And that same year, Harold Howe II (1993) opined that "tests have become the tail that wags the dog in the public discussion of educational change in the United States" (9).

Nonetheless, educators continue to invest time and effort in seeking national solutions for problems experienced at the local level. Of course, criticisms aimed at public education in the United States are hardly new; in fact, since the launching of *Sputnik* in 1957, every decade has witnessed similar demonstrations of what amounts to a sort of national educational angst (Madaus & Tan 1994). As Madaus and Tan have succinctly explained, the civil rights movement of the 1960s produced evidence of educational inequities; in the 1970s, national concern focused on an apparent decline in students' SAT scores; in the 1980s, they centered on concerns for quality in *A Nation at Risk*; while in the 1990s, educational pundits predicted the future failure of American students to compete in the global marketplace.

Additional alarm by U.S. educators can be seen in the results of the international testing of U.S. students. The Programme for International Student Assessment (PISA) rates elementary and secondary students from 60 countries in the areas of reading, math, and science. From the beginning of the PISA testing in 2000, the assessment results "generally show American students falling far behind their 'peers' in other developed industrial countries and barely keeping ahead of deprived students in the developing world" (O'Leary 2010, 34). According to PISA testing statistical analysis, the U.S. students performed below many of the countries' average scores; however, the United States also had students performing at both the highest and lowest levels (O'Leary 2010).

What makes the most recent round of educational criticisms so compelling is that it comes at a time when the schools are struggling to deal effectively with increasingly diverse school populations and amid concerns for educational equity in an economic climate that demands not only that schools educate students "better" but also that they do it for "less" (Craver 1995, 13). Given a situation that many consider a crisis of national confidence in public education, it is perhaps not surprising that the methods by which academic achievement and student progress are assessed have also come under scrutiny. In some places, new assessment methods have also been instituted as a way to push school reform agendas, with the idea that if assessment changes, so must instruction and ultimately school culture.

EDUCATIONAL ASSESSMENT: THE STANDARDIZED TESTING IMPERATIVE

For years, the public has relied on standardized achievement tests to take the educational pulse of virtually every school district in the country. The appeal of this type of testing, which has grown in popularity since its introduction in the early part of the 20th century, lies not only in its comparatively low cost and the ease of administration but also in the apparent capacity of such tests to quantify educational achievement across a playing field that encompasses all students, all subject area content, all grade levels, and all school districts. Indeed, Madaus and Tan (1994) and Killaghan (1992, cited in Madaus & Tan 1994, 4) assert that bureaucratic rather than educational motives frequently drive interest in standardized test scores. So complete has public confidence risen in the results of standardized tests over time that most states have implemented testing programs (O'Neil 1992), and results that were once employed in creating programs of remediation are now being used in making a spate of crucial educational decisions, from the placement of individual students in alternative programs to the renewal of teacher's contracts and the allocation of resources among school districts (Madaus & Tan 1994).

Why have American educators and parents put so much emphasis on standardized test results? One answer surely lies in their apparent reliability—that is, the consistency of test results across situations, time, and context. The fact that standardized tests produce numbers, which at least on their face seem so objective, straightforward, and unambiguous, partially explains their appeal as well. However, critics of this type of testing have become increasingly vocal, calling into question the practice of using single-measure "IQ" tests as predictors of ability and challenging, convincingly, the fairness of test items on the grounds that they reflect gender, culture, and socioeconomic biases. While in at least some cases test makers have made an effort to create instruments that are more culturally "fair," Neuman (1994) argues that such efforts do not ameliorate the deleterious effects of using assessment models that both encourage instructors to "teach to the test" (O'Neil 1992, 15) and skew instructional attention in the direction of basic skills rather than problem solving and critical thinking.

Importantly, Neuman (1994) goes on to assert that the short-answer format of most tests undermines instructional goals by reinforcing the notion that "knowledge consists simply of identifying the one and only correct answer to a question formulated by someone else" (68). In her view, defining learning in this way stands in direct opposition to constructivist theories, which hold that learning is a complex activity involving the creation of personal understandings. Herman (1992) agrees, suggesting further that the "narrowing" of the curriculum to basic skills, the recall of facts, and test preparation activities are particularly detrimental "in schools serving at-risk and disadvantaged students, where there is the most pressure to improve test scores" (74). For this reason, some critics believe that standardized testing may actually exacerbate inequities "for minorities and non-English speakers" (Madaus & Tan 1994, 5).

The emphasis on standardized testing peaked in the early years of the new millennium in the federal mandate for higher achievement and greater accountability embedded in the No Child Left Behind Act passed in 2001. In brief, this legislation called for states to create educational standards, implement annual progress testing, and impose penalties on schools whose students failed to meet required state minimums. The program emphasized literacy and reading, early childhood education, and staff development for K–3 teachers in reading instruction. The impact of the No Child Left Behind initiative's emphasis on standardized testing has led to changes in curriculum and instruction and has left library media specialists to find a niche in helping schools achieve goals outlined by the law.

In December 2015, the Elementary and Secondary Education Act (ESEA) was reauthorized. The ESEA was changed from No Child Left Behind to Every Student Succeeds Act (ESSA). This was the eighth time since the inception of ESEA in 1965 that it has been reauthorized; however, the goal of this legislation has always been to support the educational opportunities and outcomes for children from lower-income families (Roper & Rossi 2018). The significance of ESSA is that for the first time the language of "effective school library programs" is included in the legislation in conjunction with student learning outcomes.

OUTCOMES-BASED EDUCATION

A major initiative in schools across the country since the early 1990s has been the adoption of variations of a model for curricular reform based on the "outcomes" rather than "inputs" of instruction. According to Grover (1994), outcomes-based education focuses attention on the student as a learner and provides a "comprehensive approach to teaching and learning and to instructional management that has its origin in mastery learning and competency-based education" (Burns & Wood 1990, quoted in Grover 1994, 174). Outcomes differ from behavioral objectives, which created a focus for instruction in the 1970s and 1980s, in their concern for ensuring that students actually acquire the skills that are the focus of instruction; in addition, the "skills" that students are to "master" relate less to content than they do to critical thinking and problem-solving processes. Since outcomes-based educational strategies call for the assessment of "student progress toward the stated outcomes" (174), the evaluation techniques used to chart this project must be redesigned. In fact, a variety of new assessment models that build in opportunities for the remediation and enrichment deemed necessary for the achievement of skill mastery are clearly required. Grover also suggests "multi-dimensional" assessment strategies that "accommodate the various learning styles" (175) of students. Because outcomes-based education moves the emphasis from rote learning of traditional course content to critical thinking, it has proven to be very controversial in some school districts.

THE SCHOOL LIBRARIAN AND FORMATIVE ASSESSMENT

As schools become more data driven using summative assessment to show student academic achievement, there is also an opportunity to improve school library instruction with formative assessments. According to Stefl-Mabry (2018), "Formative assessment provides evidence of students' learning as well as the effectiveness of instructional practice" (52). School librarians should use formative assessment as a way of documenting learning and determining how well the student has met the objective. Formative assessments should be implemented often throughout the unit to show understanding with the possibility of reteaching a concept that students did not understand. This practice is a way for school librarians to improve their teaching skills.

An information literacy lesson with a learning objective designed to teach students how to determine the credibility of news sources can use formative assessment to ensure the objective has been met. Stefl-Mabry (2018) begins with a preassessment to determine the "students' prior knowledge, preconceptions, and misconceptions" (54). For this lesson the teacher librarian can use exit/entrance tickets to determine objective achievement or also to allow the students to anonymously "write down questions, concerns, or comments they have about what has been taught" (55). Through this assessment, the teacher librarian can get inside the minds of their students to determine their perceptions of the information literacy lesson. With this information, the lesson can be adjusted to focus on the perceived student concerns. Formative assessments are not designed for a grade, but rather to allow the teacher librarian to evaluate how the instruction itself can be improved. "The systematic use of formative assessment provides school librarians with vital information that can be used to document evidence of their practice, and evaluate and increase the value of their school library programs" (Stefl-Mabry 2018, 56).

ALTERNATIVE MODELS FOR STUDENT ASSESSMENT

Attempts to answer the challenges posed by new instructional initiatives such as outcomes-based education have sparked a number of innovative "alternatives," which will undoubtedly continue to shape school efforts to assess student achievement for years to come. A major difference between alternative assessment and traditional paper-and-pencil assessment procedures is that the former allows students to show what they have learned in a variety of different ways. As noted above, these include portfolios of a student's written and graphic work; student projects of various kinds including those produced electronically; student journals and "learning logs" that record their responses, thinking, and activities; and oral and dramatic presentations of their work. An important element in this form of assessment is the active involvement of students in planning and designing rubrics, as well as self-evaluation and peer evaluation as part of the learning process. As Maeroff (1991) suggests, with alternative assessment, "students, under the tutelage of their teachers, are trained to provide evidence of their own learning" (274).

Although the creation of alternative models for evaluating students are many and varied, all share an intent to substitute for the indirect means represented by the usual types of test questions some form of direct measurement of learning through the "performance" of what has been learned (Grover et al. 1996). One of the advantages of alternative assessment models that are supported in school districts across the country (Maeroff 1991) and often cited in the literature is that such methods are not add-ons, "busy work," or "gotcha games" (274) that interrupt the flow of ongoing classroom instruction; instead, they are classroom activities that, because they are actually "embedded in instruction" (276), grow directly out of the curriculum rather than appearing as a single, stressful, end-of-unit or end-of-term event. For this reason, they can be used formatively to serve as a basis for improving instruction as the activities proceed.

Moreover, a number of assessment alternatives also propose to provide "in-progress" ongoing measures of student learning as it continues over time. In fact, these kinds of "test" activities themselves are motivating and can have a positive impact on student performance (Chatman 1996; Quellmaltz & Burry, cited in Herman 1992) when conducted within the framework of ongoing classroom activity because they provide students an additional opportunity "to practice the knowledge and skills learned" (Grover et al. 1996, 2). When implemented properly, "the line between curriculum and assessment" (Krechevsky 1991, 45) practically disappears.

Alternative assessment techniques also provide an additional dimension to many traditional types of assessments in that they aim specifically to measure critical thinking and process skills as well as student acquisition of subject "content." According to Neuman (1994), "[T]his focus on the student's direct and purposeful involvement is consistent with current cognitive theory, which holds that deep understanding occurs only when learners actively construct their own knowledge rather than passively absorbing facts and ideas presented by others" (69–70). Grover et al. (1996) agree, asserting that the types of alternative assessment models that require the performance of the learning tasks are more likely than traditional kinds of testing methods to tap into critical thinking and the other complex processes that are inevitably involved in information seeking. Finally, Frazier and Paulson (1992) argue that the opportunities that assessment alternatives provide allow students to gain practice in self-evaluation and encourage "ownership, pride, and high self-esteem" (64), all of which are related to school success and achievement.

In addition to focusing attention on critical thinking and active participation on the part of the student learner, alternative assessment models return the professional responsibility for student learning to the educators in the classroom (Neuman 1994) in ways that allow differentiated approaches to instruction. Many leaders in education have advocated the importance of this approach to instructional design. For instance, Eisner (1993) has argued that assessment must take into account "where [a] student started, the amount of practice and effort expended, the student's age and developmental level, and the extent to which his or her current work displays progress" (23).

AUTHENTIC ASSESSMENT

What is authentic assessment, and how does it differ from alternative and performance assessment strategies? The goals and strategies of alternative and authentic assessment are very similar in that they both aim to allow the presentation of "a reliable picture of a student's understandings" (Stripling 1994a, 79). That is, they measure how well instructional objectives have been mastered by allowing students to demonstrate what they know. The difference between the alternative and authentic forms of assessment is that in the latter, students are asked to enact the specific skills in question instead of answering questions related to that skill or performing specific behaviors in contrived contexts (Meyer 1994).

To a great extent, the success of authentic assessment lies with teachers who have the ability to make the connections between an academic subject and real-world applications at levels appropriate and consistent with a student's developmental level and background knowledge. In addition, authentic assessments of student performance necessarily presuppose and demand an "authentic" curriculum—one that allows students access to the same sorts of information and resources that would be "available in real-life, problem-solving situations" (Stripling 1994a, 80). Other conditions that support authentic curriculum are frameworks for collaboration among students, teachers, and community members; student discretion in what work will be used in assessing learning; and flexibility in terms of time limits for completion of products and processes.

AUTHENTIC ASSESSMENT MODELS

Data collection for authentic assessment requires teachers to evaluate student learning on authentic tests, "questionnaires, interviews, ratings, observations, performance samples, and work products (Crittenden, 1991)" (Stripling 1994a, 79). Assessment models can include a variety of evaluative instruments and approaches, including one or a combination of locally produced and standardized tests, student-created portfolios, student performances and exhibitions, and personal contacts between the students and their instructors.

Authentic Tests

To be authentic, tests must provoke or stimulate problem solving, critical thinking, and writing. In addition, they must (1) allow students to demonstrate their strengths through the employment of multiple measures, including the student's self-assessment; (2) apply reasonable real-world standards in the assignation of grades; and (3) allow for different approaches to learning. According to Stripling (1994a), authentic tests should also be enjoyable activities in themselves. Reliability for "authentic tests" needs to be established through a pretesting of the test items and through the creation of scoring rubrics so that the outcomes of the testing can be used to inform future instruction.

Authentic Portfolios

Valencia (1991) notes that portfolios not only allow teachers to track student cognitive, affective, social, and motivational progress but also make teachers more "sensitive to processes of learning" in ways that allow them to "select and create measures of students' talents and weaknesses so that appropriate instructional opportunities can be provided" (680). At the same time, authentic portfolios may actually increase the time students spend in reading and writing and provide the vehicles for monitoring more closely and accurately their progress in developing these literacy skills.

Two types of portfolios have been described in the literature. The first represents a compilation of student work carried out over time, with specific items selected by students to meet goals they themselves establish in collaboration with the teacher. Students are usually asked to write an introduction to the portfolio that reflects their own evaluation as well as evaluation by the instructor. A second portfolio model, suggested by Gardner (1991, cited in Stripling 1994b), documents the thinking and activity involved in the creation of major projects and may contain records of original brainstorming sessions, early and current drafts, written critiques by instructors and peers, "works by others that particularly inspired or influenced the project," and student self-assessments, instructor evaluation, and student thoughts on future projects (106). The arrangement of portfolio documents (e.g., finished pieces, drafts, revisions, and journals) is usually an individual matter chosen by the student, who may opt to present items by topic, by format, by achievement level, or chronologically (Stripling 1994a).

Authentic Performances

Authentic performances and exhibitions, defined as "prepared demonstration[s] of student learning" (Stripling 1994b, 106) as options to more traditional models of assessment, are suitable for activities and learning that do not easily lend themselves to paper-and-pencil assessments or to portfolios. These might include musical activities, speech and debate exercises, and physical expression in athletics, dance, or drama (especially the re-creation or reenactment of historical events).

Student Profiles

Project Spectrum, a joint educational initiative created by educators from Harvard University and Tufts University in 1984, uses the creation of student profiles to assess the strengths and weaknesses of student skills. Based on Gardner's (1983) multiple intelligences theory and the theory of development in nonuniversal domains of Feldman (1994), a program of activities is created for individual students that capitalizes on their strengths and develops areas where skills need to be improved (Krechevsky 1991). Student profiles log the linguistic and mathematical aspects of student progress as well as the "mechanical, spatial, bodily, musical, social and scientific abilities" (44) in "a short description of the child's participation in the project's activities" (46).

Personal Contacts

Personal contacts, observations, conferencing, and diagnostic interviews allow students and teachers to explore student achievement interactively and can provide an index of student strengths and weaknesses, an opportunity for support for student thinking, and a forum for the discussion of student ideas. Observation is a particularly valuable way of assessing interactions between and among individuals and between groups and to monitor the activity and operation of student participation in multistudent projects (Stripling 1994a). Interviews can be formal or informal and may involve students and teachers or peers.

ALTERNATIVE/AUTHENTIC ASSESSMENT: DIFFICULTIES AND DISADVANTAGES

A number of difficulties often accompany efforts to implement alternative and authentic assessment models. Staff development and support are almost always necessary since new ways to measure achievement usually necessitate changes in instructional strategies and lesson plans (Herman 1992, 77). Maeroff (1991) has addressed these issues, identifying preparation and training time, expense, complexity, and imprecision as some of the costs of implementing alternative assessment formats. She also voices a concern that lies at the heart of many of the arguments against attempts to adopt alternative assessment models; because they lack a comparative aspect, they do not allow parents and teachers to chart a child's progress against the levels achieved by his or her peers. Indeed, "psychometricians have raised serious questions about establishing the validity, reliability, generalizability, and comparability of assessments conducted according to methods that are individualized and dependent on human judgment (Koretz et al. 1992; Linn, Baker, & Dunbar 1991; Moss 1992)" (Neuman 1994, 71).

In point of fact, alternative assessment strategies may not be suitable for all assessment needs, and critics have also noted that non–norm-referenced assessments are open to inequities and misrepresentations. In addition, while creative efforts at assessment abound, research on the resulting evaluation is minimal at the present time. For these reasons, Maeroff (1991) hopes "that alternative assessment is not rushed onto the battlefield of testing so hastily as to produce in its unperfected form friendly fire that harms the very children who are supposed to be the beneficiaries" (276).

THE SCHOOL LIBRARIAN AND ALTERNATIVE ASSESSMENT

Stripling (1994a, 1994b, 2006) clearly considers alternative assessment as the model for the future and sees a central role for school librarians in helping to anticipate the changes that the implementation of new assessment models will require. "If the primary goal of education is to cultivate thoughtfulness and understanding, and if the school library media center is at the core of that effort, then the school library media specialist must lead in changing assessment techniques" (Stripling 1994b, 106). In fact, Neuman (1994) suggests that school librarians have roles to play in the creation of an "assessment culture" (Wolfe et al. 1991, quoted in Neuman 1994, 73) that relies on "new understandings of learning and intelligence, new standards of evidence" and "sensitivity and rigor in the application of [assessment] alternatives" (73). And "since learning theory shows that students learn far more by 'doing' than by any other method," librarians can "provide the logical information laboratory for practice within an educational setting" (Markuson 1986, 39).

Stripling (1994b) posits a three-level taxonomy of involvement for library media specialists in the initiation and progress of authentic assessment (see Figure 8.1). At the initial level, the school librarian does not play a role in instructional design of projects but can provide information on the use of assessment alternatives, perhaps developing a professional collection of materials and resources on which school staff can draw. In addition, the media specialist can facilitate discussion on assessment alternatives and create collections that support students involved in the creation of "alternative" projects.

At the moderate level, school librarians collaborate in planning instruction and assessment and otherwise provide professional assistance by teaching production techniques (e.g., word processing; video production), and by monitoring student performance practices. At the highest, or in-depth, level, Striping (1994a) suggests that school librarians are intimately involved in designing "authentic assessment strategies" (92) with teachers, in helping students select their work for inclusion in their portfolios, in providing assistance with evaluating student products, and in conducting in-service instruction to staff on alternative assessment techniques and strategies. In creating evaluative measures for alternative projects, Stripling suggests that rubrics be developed that

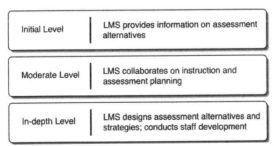

Initial Level	LMS provides information on assessment alternatives
Moderate Level	LMS collaborates on instruction and assessment planning
In-depth Level	LMS designs assessment alternatives and strategies; conducts staff development

FIGURE 8.1   Stripling's (1994b) Taxonomy of Library Media Specialist (LMS) Assessment Involvement

allow comments on the overall framework of the project (clarity and achievement of goals and the organization of information), reflection (student assessments and depth of comments), content, style (originality, creativity, and personal connection or "voice"), and presentation (fluency and form).

Neuman (1994) notes the basic compatibility of the move to create alternatives to traditional methods of assessment with contemporary library information skills curricula in that "library media center programs are grounded in many of the same assumptions that undergird alternative assessment" (72). This affinity should not be surprising, as both initiatives draw on constructivism as a theory base and focus on the processes of learning. Nor has this new approach to information skills instruction, with its emphasis on collaboration and instructional intervention, gone unnoticed in the education community. Theodore Sizer (1990, quoted in Stripling 1994b), the creator of the Coalition of Essential Schools, has observed, "One good way to start designing an Essential School is to plan a library and let its shadow shape the rest" (105).

It is interesting to note that the techniques for data collection (e.g., observation, interviewing, and analyzing student projects) as suggested by Kuhlthau (1993b) and others are fundamentally the same as those used in alternative assessment approaches. Moreover, these techniques mirror approaches to "qualitative inquiry," which is achieving greater acceptance in the fields of education and school librarianship (Neuman 1994).

EVALUATING THE SCHOOL LIBRARY

Three major approaches to library evaluation characterize the research literature in school librarianship: library standards, library use measures, and library skills achievement measures. As has typically been true with innovations in educational assessment, evaluation methods employed by researchers and librarians reflect passions and preoccupations in educational vogue at various times and over time. During the 1940s and 1950s, which in many respects constituted the formative years of school librarianship, the primary concerns lay in establishing a well-stocked central facility staffed by certified library personnel. For this reason, assessment attention turned to comparisons between individual schools or school districts and national or state library standards as measures of a quality library "presence" (Gallivan 1974). Once most schools had installed centralized facilities for school resources and libraries opened their doors to students and school staff, librarians tended to follow the public library model, often employing circulation and library visits as measures of a library's value. Since the 1960s, however, there have been a number of research efforts to show the impact of library programming on the acquisition of library skills, library use, and student attitudes. Assessments since the 1980s have focused on student learning as measured on the library skills portion of standardized tests. This shift in evaluation focus reflected *Information Power*'s (AASL & AECT 1988) emphasis on the teaching role of the school librarian.

Most recently, Keller (2018) suggests school librarians use the *2018 National School Library Standards for Learners, School Librarians, and School Libraries* as an assessment tool when evaluating their library:

- AASL Standards Framework for School Libraries (58–64);
- Evaluating School Libraries (169–174);
- School Library Evaluation Checklist (174–180).

A checklist for School Library Evaluation of the School Library at the Building and District Level is provided in the AASL (2018) standards publication that can be completed by the school librarian and the school library advisory committee working together to assess the current state of the school library. Elements incorporated in the checklist represent the school library alignments from the National School Library Standards Integrated Framework that are evident in an effective school library (AASL 2018). "The framework and the checklist do overlap in some ways but not exactly. Therefore, both tools should be used as is or adapted for evaluating the school library" (Keller 2018, 20).

According to Keller (2018) evaluating a school library program is ongoing and should assess how the library is meeting the mission, vision, and philosophy of the school district. The focus of these recent assessments is on the importance of the learning community, and evaluation as a collaborative process, including input from all library stakeholders. "The stakeholders will review the goals and objectives, help gather and analyze data, determine if goals and objectives are being met according to the standards, and assist in planning for continuous program improvement" (Keller 2018, 18).

Library Standards

As originally conceived, library standards for collection size, library staff, and library facilities were at one time thought to be the essentials of quality and value in public libraries (Joeckel 1943). Over time, a number of researchers have sought to relate library collection size to exemplary library programs (Greve 1974; Loertscher, Ho, & Bowie 1987) and the presence of certified staff to both programming excellence (Loertscher et al. 1987) and higher levels of service (Loertscher & Land 1975). Although useful, at least initially, in supporting budgetary requests, employing standards as evaluation measures has been problematic in that a causal linkage between such standards and the improvement of library services has never been definitely established (Baker & Lancaster 1991). For one thing, the findings of "standards" studies are often ambiguous, having meant different things to different people at different times. To some, evaluation standards represent the "ideal" in terms of collections and services; to others, they represent the "minimum" required to open a library's doors. Another problem is that standards tend to become obsolete quickly. This is particularly true in and across school settings, where communities change, enrollments fluctuate, curricula shift, and instructional approaches and innovations wax and wane. Furthermore, library standards represent types of "input" measures, which focus on materials but do not assess the value of these materials for student learning. In some cases, the invocation of standards has even created problems, especially in situations where a desire to maintain numerical minimums discourages librarians from discarding outdated or inappropriate resources and equipment.

Library Use: Circulation and Library Visits

From time to time, counting the circulation and library contacts in the aggregate and per student has been advanced as an appropriate assessment measure in some school libraries. Although such data are relatively easy to gather and document, they do not necessarily indicate use of information nor indicate why some resources are chosen over others. Indeed, they reveal next to nothing about the value of a collection for the curricular needs of a particular school nor the ability of the resources to match the developmental levels of particular students. In schools where library policies, library hours, or other situational factors constrain visits, library use as a measure is also problematic. Additionally, library contacts do not always reflect a positive attitude toward the library and library materials (or their utility for that matter), especially where children are compelled to come to the library as part of regularly scheduled "library skills" classes. Finally, when teachers require students to check out a prescribed book or a number of books for classroom or recreational use, circulation statistics can often be misleading or useless as measures of student performance or interest.

The first edition of *Information Power* (ALA 1988) suggested that libraries attempt to document library use and utility in a different way—through patterns of planning and teaching. Quantitative measures, such as the number of students and teachers served, the number and frequency of group activities in the library, the number of collaborative projects, the extent of collaborative planning, and student use of library resources to meet classroom objectives, were all advanced as alternatives to tracking the circulation of library materials. More recently, librarians are able to track the use of their virtual resources by the number of "hits" or "clicks." However, professionals and researchers have argued that these approaches are themselves too indirect to support persuasive arguments of program value. As Berkowitz (1994) has argued, such measures do not reveal anything about what students learn as a result of library "lessons" nor document the impact of that instruction on students' success as learners (36).

Standardized Tests

According to Jackson (1994), the content of standardized measures used to assess library skills is usually based on curricular guides and textbooks in general use across the United States, and a multiple-choice structure for test items is the form most often employed. The fact that "the cognitive skill most [easily and therefore] frequently" (25) tested through multiple-choice questions is recall has made problematic their use in assessing student thinking in terms of analysis, synthesis, and evaluation skills. In a review of the major standardized basic skills assessments used at the time, Jackson found that, although test items aim to address process skills (e.g., identification of information problems, evaluation of sources, note taking, analysis of information, synthesis of ideas, and information use), the limited number of short-answer test items did not address the complexities of information seeking as it has been described in the work of Irving (1985), Kuhlthau (1993b), and other LIS theorists. In particular, Jackson noted the failure of these tests to assess information retrieval, search strategies, the "process of narrowing or broadening a topic" (30), selecting a research thesis, or creating researchable research questions.

FOCUSING ON THE EDUCATIONAL VALUE OF SCHOOL LIBRARY PROGRAMS

According to Berkowitz (1994), school librarians can establish the educational value of the library only if they undertake a more broad-based assessment plan that demonstrates how the use of "library resources help[s] to advance the district and school goals" and the "achievement, attitudes, and behaviors" of students (37). Indeed, in Berkowitz's view it is only outcomes in terms of student learning that will ensure that libraries continue to receive administrative support and adequate funding. In short, intuitive understandings that library programs and collections contribute to student learning are not enough. Ultimately, as Berkowitz points out, school librarians and researchers alike must find ways to make the effectiveness of information skills instruction both "describable and visible" (33).

In 2015 the Washington Library Media Association published a book with research on the importance of a school library program. This study involved 1,487 K–12 schools in Washington state. Results from this study revealed the quality of the school library program increased student academic achievement. The Coker (2015) study showed that students who attend schools with credentialed school librarians with a quality library performed better on standardized tests and were more likely to graduate from high school. Astute librarians can present information in research findings, such as those suggested in the impact studies of the Washington Library Media Association (Coker 2015), to substantiate claims they make of the value of a school library in furthering the schools' educational missions, goals, and programs.

Determining the Value of the School Library Program

The library impact studies in the past 25 years with research conducted by Gretes (2013) and Lance (Scholastic 2016) indicate "positive correlations between high-quality library programs and student achievement" (Lance & Kachel 2018, 16). In addition, students in a school with a credentialed full-time school librarian scored higher on language arts assessments. In this same study there were fewer students who scored below the proficiency level on state assessments. "Graduation rates and test scores in reading and math were significantly higher in schools with high-quality libraries and certified librarians" (Lance & Kachel 2018, 16).

Many international studies show a correlation between a school library with extensive up-to-date library resources and increased student academic achievement. In addition, teaching information literacy in the contest of a research paper with inquiry-based instruction fosters a comprehensive understanding of the subject. "It is believed that inquiry learning promotes a deeper understanding of the subject matter through the process of questioning, seeking evidence, developing explanations, evaluating explanations, and communicating conclusions" (Chen, Huang, & Chen 2017, 257). A six-year study showed inquiry-based instruction "can help elementary students memorize and comprehend subject content in spite of their prior academic achievement levels" (Chen et al. 2017, 265). The study also showed that inquiry was an effective teaching strategy for all levels of learners from the low-achieving students to the high achievers.

It is also thought that a high-functioning school library and certified library staff can even the playing field academically for the poor students and their wealthier counterparts. A study by Adkins (2014) examined this phenomenon and determined that school librarians, "especially those working with disadvantaged populations, should know that the resources they provide are essential to helping students increase achievement" (18).

Research in library and information skills instruction has generally shown that a positive relationship exists between library programming and student achievement; and, at least in a general way, the types of measures used can tell us which teaching strategies are or are not effective. Less frequently, however, do such measures offer insights into how learning can be enhanced or how programs might be improved. In addition, the types of skills often tested are not those that contemporary librarians regard as the most important. For example, despite the fact that for many years educators have known that "being able to locate information was of little intellectual benefit to students" (Henne 1966, cited in Jackson 1994, 26), assessment questions that ask students to identify specific reference sources or demonstrate the acquisition of location and access skills are still being used as measures of students' information competence. In addition, changes in the structure of library and information skills instruction, particularly the redefinition of literacy to include information-seeking and technology skills, a process approach to information skills instruction (Kuhlthau 1993b), and an inquiry-based (Kuhlthau, Maniotes, & Caspari 2007) "critical thinking curriculum" (Callison 1994, 43), argue for the development of new approaches to information skills assessment.

When applied within the context of the school library, Grover (1993, 1994) sees assessment as part of the overall program requiring school librarians to diagnose the student's information needs in ways that help achieve curricular goals, design customized learning opportunities, and assess the outcomes of instructional interventions. "The library media specialist," according to Grover, "must be able to diagnose or analyze the information skills level of individuals or groups, prescribe or recommend appropriate learning activities, teach or assist with the implementation of work for teaching information skills . . . and [develop] a framework for assessing instruction" (187). Given the challenges of assessing a multidimensional program of instruction and an information skills curriculum focused on developing critical thinkers and problem solvers, librarians are faced with a question: What kinds of measures can be devised that will provide such information?

The truth is that the processes underlying contemporary models of information seeking and teaching a process approach to library skills instruction are difficult to measure using paper-and-pencil tests conducted at the local level. One solution to this assessment conundrum clearly lies with alternative testing initiatives that are now a part of contemporary educational reform efforts in many states (Grover 1994; Maeroff 1991). These include a multimodal menu of strategies for gathering data on student progress: observations, interviews, journals, projects, formal tests, self-evaluation and peer evaluation, and portfolios. Information obtained through these means can be used to plan "additional learning activities" (187), class groupings, and peer tutoring pairs.

As will be seen, a major strength of these assessment models, which assume the expertise of a master teacher, is the opportunity they provide for students to reflect on their own work, skills, or progress as well as on the work of their peers. Indeed, contemporary assessment models must be inclusive of the various talents that students may have. The valuing of alternative intellectual, artistic, and social "gifts" has been duly noted in *Empowering Learners: Guidelines for School Library Programs* (AASL 2009), which suggests that "[w]hile school curricula often test analytical, mathematical, or linguistic skills, many learners excel in areas outside of these traditional fields. Instructional design must address a variety of learning styles, giving every student a chance to find his or her own strengths." In the *National School Library Standards* (2018) this sentiment is expressed in the Framework for Learners, Standard V. B. "Learners construct new knowledge by persisting through self-directed pursuits by tinkering and making" (38).

Measuring Student Achievement

Although research efforts in library and information science continue to grow in number and sophistication, studies designed to establish a relationship between information skills instruction and student learning are only just beginning to yield results to which librarians can point as justification for their programs (for an overview of early studies, see Didier 1985). One problem has been the fragmentary nature of the research (Aaron 1982; Eisenberg & Brown 1992; Kuhlthau 1987). With the exception of studies by Lance and his colleagues and research based on Kuhlthau's (1993a) information search process, few studies have been either theory-based or replicable, while the use of natural settings where variables are hard to control have yielded results that are not generalizable beyond a specific context. In the early 1990s, Haycock (1992) also complained that studies too often addressed issues of peripheral interest. And while scholars and practitioners concede that student achievement is the appropriate yardstick for assessing value, particularly as the teaching role has become the standard for school librarianship, until recently few studies were able to show that such links actually exist (Eisenberg & Brown 1992; Vandergrift & Hannigan 1986).

SHIFTING THE EVALUATION PARADIGM

Among the earliest of the research efforts "to evaluate the effectiveness of elementary school libraries" were studies by Mary Gaver (1963), who found a positive relationship between the presence of school libraries and student achievement. In her studies, Gaver attempted to determine the impact of centralized library facilities on student reading and library skills by surveying 271 schools in 13 states. Findings of the study revealed that students experienced "higher educational gain in schools with school libraries" (Gallivan 1974). In another study, Willson (1965) used survey instruments developed by Gaver to compare reading achievement and library skills proficiency of sixth graders in 12 schools to assess the impact of a library program administered by a professional librarian. Willson's study found that students with access to a central library and organized instruction achieved higher scores on skills and reading as measured on the Iowa Test of Basic Skills than those who lacked such programs.

Since these early studies, library practitioners and scholars have launched a spate of studies across many states. The first major study that sought to link the presence of an active library professional, the presence of library materials, and student learning was conducted by educators in Colorado schools in 1992. Results of this research verified "the importance of the library media specialist's instructional role" and the expenditure of funds to maintain school library collections and staff in "promoting academic achievement" (Lance, Welborn, & Hamilton-Pennell 1992). In a second Colorado study, Lance, Rodney, and Hamilton-Pennell (2000a) sought to remedy the methodological shortcomings critics noted in the first study while replicating their research in Alaska (Lance et al. 2000), Pennsylvania (Lance, Rodney, & Hamilton-Pennell 2000b), New Mexico (Lance et al. 2003), Oregon (Lance et al. 2001), Texas (Smith 2001), and Iowa (Rodney, Lance, & Hamilton-Pennell 2002). These studies confirm that student competency test scores improve in schools where school library programs are clearly developed, where students have access to information technology, where libraries are run by qualified professionals, where librarians and teachers collaborate to integrate technology into the curriculum, where librarians provide in-service training in technology integration, and where independent use of the library is encouraged and supported.

A study of New York school librarians and library programs extended the Lance studies by exploring not only the impact of school libraries and librarians on student achievement but also "(1) the influence of the SLMS on technology use, (2) the relationship between principals and their SLMSs and (3) the level of service to students with disabilities" (Small, Shanahan, & Stasak 2010; Small and Snyder 2009; Small, Snyder, & Parker 2009). The primary research included more than 1,600 schools, while a qualitative component was conducted in 10 selected schools to gather information on motivation and learning. Findings indicate that (1) all groups perceive greater emphasis on skills for finding information than on skills for using or evaluating information; (2) elementary students perceive the SLMS as more autonomy supportive than do middle or high school students; (3) students are largely unaware of librarian-teacher collaboration; (4) 69 percent of students visit their school library at least once a week, and most come to do research; (5) students perceive "maintaining a neat and orderly collection" and "maintaining a quiet study environment" as the two most important services provided by the LMS; and (6) there is a lack of library services to students with disabilities (Small & Snyder 2009, 1). Additionally, the study supports the notion that school libraries and librarians positively influence students' motivation for research and inquiry, their reading development, and their development of reading interests (Small et al. 2010).

Another important study was undertaken in selected schools in Ohio during the 2002–2003 academic year (Kuhlthau & Todd 2005a, 2005b). Kuhlthau and Todd, two major researchers in the field of school librarianship, directed the research, which was funded through a grant from the Library Services and Technology Act/Institute of Museum and Library Services. In essence, the study aimed "to provide comprehensive and detailed empirical evidence of how libraries help students learn, and to provide recommendations for further research, educational policy development, and tools for the school librarian to chart how their school library impacts learning" (Todd 2002). Of particular interest as well was the study's effort to ascertain the value of libraries to student learning from the student point of view and as such is the "first comprehensive study based on students' evaluation of their media centers" (Whelan 2004). According to Todd (2002), *Student Learning through Ohio School Libraries* provided significant findings that demonstrate "the multidimensional relationship between an effective school library instructional program and student learning outcomes." For their part, students reported that the information skills instruction they received in the library "helped them with using and accessing information for their research assignments" (Todd, quoted in Whelan 2004) and helped them do better on class work and tests. African American youngsters in the study also reported getting help for their reading in the school library. Overall, students reported that access to and instruction in technology was especially valued (Todd & Kuhlthau 2003).

A study to link school library services to student achievement is reported in a dissertation by Achterman (2009), who looked at different levels of professional practice across public schools in California and noted that where staffing levels and library services were robust, students at all grade levels scored higher on "California criterion-referenced state-wide tests." Indeed, "the strength of the correlations between both certified and total staffing tend to increase with grade level; at the high school level, correlations were among the strongest reported in any statewide study to date." The key in this study, as with Lance's early work, is the presence of qualified library staff. "At every level," Achterman asserts, "certified and total staffing levels were associated with the strength of library program elements."

A similar theme can be found in Dow, Lakin, and Court's (2010) longitudinal study, which aimed to determine how Kansas school libraries contribute to student achievement. These researchers analyzed quantitative and qualitative data in an effort to examine linkages between an aligned state curriculum and established library media and technology standards. Recently reported findings established links between the presence of licensed school librarians and student gains in achievement across the curriculum. This point is also illustrated in the results of a study by Lance, Schwarz, and Rodney (2014). The quantitative study examined students' English Language Arts (ELA) writing assessments on different standards on the Palmetto Assessment of State Standards (PASS) when the school library was staffed with a full-time credentialed library. The data supported the idea that schools with a library, fully staffed with qualified personnel, scored higher on the PASS ELA standards writing assessments in content, organization, literary text, informational text, and research. This is one study of many that shows how school librarians transform the school's culture by contributing to students' academic success.

READING ACHIEVEMENT AND SCHOOL LIBRARIES

The most powerful case made in American public education is embedded in the work of Stephen Krashen, whose extensive research has provided evidence that school libraries promote reading behavior in students at all levels. Simply stated, Krashen believes that the availability of reading resources in the school library results in an increase in student reading. As evidence, Krashen (1993) reported the results of a meta-analysis of reading research in *The Power of Reading,* published in 1993. On the basis of his research, Krashen concluded that higher reading gains were made by children with access to high-quality collections of books in the school library. He also found the library superior to classroom collections because of children's comparative ease of access to these materials and their ability to "provide a comfortable and relaxing reading environment" and "qualified school librarians." Two other studies reported by Krashen also linked reading achievement and the presence of a certified school librarian in the library. In 1995, Krashen found a correlation between reading comprehension scores and high-quality collections, while an international study of more than 200,000 children in 32 countries in 1992 found that the size of school libraries had a positive impact on reading achievement scores (Elley 1992, cited in Krashen 1993). A later study using data obtained in the earlier research (Novlijan 1998, cited in Krashen 1993) found that students with access to a library professional within the school library scored higher on reading tests than did those students whose libraries were staffed by a teacher. This led Novlijan to conclude "that the presence of a professional school librarian in the school library was a positive factor in the development of reading literacy."

Although these studies do not address the teaching of library and information skills as having an impact on reading achievement, there is limited evidence for this connection in longitudinal studies in school libraries conducted by both Thorne (1967) and Yarling (1968). Thorne used a purposive sample of two schools, randomly selecting 640 students for a two-year study. Pretest and posttest reading comprehension instruments were used to determine the effects of augmented library services on reading comprehension. Thorne found that augmented services resulted in significant gains in reading comprehension and knowledge of library skills. Thorne also noted gender differences in terms of achievement. Girls improved their library skills to a greater degree than did boys, while the boys' reading comprehension scores advanced more than did those of the girls.

Yarling's (1968) study, on the other hand, compared groups of children within and between two elementary schools over three years. One school had a library, and one did not. As a result of exposure to a program that ostensibly provided practice in library location skills, index use, and a variety of study techniques, students in the school with a library performed significantly better on tests in library skills and language competence than groups in the same school tested previously and as compared with groups in the control school. During the same period, the control groups did not show a significant increase in their achievement on the same instruments.

Some studies have considered both reading achievement and study skills. For example, Didier (1982) looked at the relationship between students' reading achievement (measured by standardized test scores) and study skills and library skills instruction. The seventh graders in Didier's study demonstrated higher levels of achievement in reading and study skills and use of newspapers than did students in the control group, who had limited exposure to media centers or professional library staff. In a study two years later, Gifford and Gifford (1984) randomly selected and assigned 26 students in selected classes in one school to control and experimental groups. These researchers used a post-test design to determine the effect of a two-week program of bibliographical instruction on library use and ease of use by students. Dependent measures in this study were the use of specific library resources (e.g., card catalog, newspapers, magazines, vertical file, dictionaries, fiction, and nonfiction) and the number of times students requested assistance in the library. Findings revealed that the experimental group asked for less help and used some specific types of resources significantly more often than did students in the control group.

Gilliland's (1986) informal study of groups of California high school seniors found that test scores on the "study-locational portion of a state-wide mandated test rose appreciably after students had completed an exercise in which they reviewed basic library skills" (67). The exercise, the Senior Library Review, was a worksheet activity that "require[d] students to participate actively, to act and think independently," to use reading and writing skills, and "to use some higher order thinking skills such as analysis, and problem solving skills that would result in a product that they could use to write a paper or speech" (67).

Dewees (1987) employed an experimental research design to compare groups of randomly assigned students in fifth-grade classes in a single elementary school. The experimental group received six weeks of process-oriented instruction, which culminated in the production of a research paper. Student learning was assessed on a standardized achievement test. Results indicated that the experimental group scored significantly higher on the research skills portion of the test. Finally, Brodie (1988) also employed standardized test scores as measures in a study that compared student knowledge of library skills and the amount of library use by two groups of youngsters involved in special programs for gifted fourth- and fifth-grade students. In this study, Brodie found that "students in the experimental group" increased their "use of the media center . . . and [the] use of six types of library materials: fiction, nonfiction, reference, encyclopedias, periodicals, and audiovisual materials" (Bracy 1990, 128).

Curriculum Integration

It is widely assumed that teaching information literacy skills within the context of ongoing classroom activities increases student learning. A number of researchers have investigated the relationship of instructional intervention, library use, and achievement. In a study in the late 1980s, Nolan (1989) looked at the effects of type of instructional design on patterns of student use of the media center. This researcher found that students for whom research skills instruction was delivered within the context of curricular tasks tended to use the library more, had better attitudes about the library, and had higher expectations as to its accessibility and utility than did students taught library skills in stand-alone lessons.

At the end of the 20th century, Todd, Lamb, and McNicholas (1993, cited in Todd 1995) reported research that concludes that an integrated information skills approach to teaching and learning can have a positive effect on a variety of learning outcomes, including improvement of student test scores, recall, concentration, focus on the task, and reflective thinking. In a second study, Todd (1995) compared the effectiveness of a "conventional approach" to information skills instruction and an "integrated approach" on student achievement, attitudes, and motivation. The study itself was undertaken in a culturally diverse girls' Catholic secondary school in Australia. Study participants were divided into treatment groups and control groups, with the former receiving instruction in a six-step process model for information seeking "explicitly aimed at the development of information skills as a basis for the meaningful learning of science" (134). The lessons were planned and taught collaboratively by the science teachers and the school librarian. Students in the control group learned the same science content but without an integrated program of library skills intervention. Science concepts were measured on annual science tests given at midyear and on end-of-year exams. Information literacy skills were assessed through the use of a problem-solving technique Todd devised to show student use of the information process model. Results of Todd's study indicate that students in the treatment group achieved significantly higher scores on both science content and information skills than those in the control groups. Thus, Todd concluded that, within this specific research context and for the specific students involved, integrated information skills instruction appeared to have a significant positive impact on students' mastery of prescribed science content and on their ability to use a range of information skills (37). While Todd calls for additional studies to test his conclusions, his study is particularly significant in that it ties information skills instruction and an integrated, process-oriented instructional program to student achievement within the context of the regular school curriculum.

EMPHASIS ON EVIDENCE-BASED PRACTICE

School librarianship has not been immune from nor outside the scope of pressures to prove quality, as noted in writings by Todd (2008a), beginning with his *Evidence-Based Manifesto for School Librarians*, which reported on discussions at the School Library Leadership Summit held in Phoenix, Arizona, in 2007. Todd's focus on evidence-based practice within the context of school libraries calls attention to the many deficits in the school library literature that scholars have noted over time (Callison 2006). Callison in particular characterizes most research in school librarianship as falling well below the "gold standard" in terms of "rigorous evidence of randomly assigned students" (Todd 2009, 91), the use of control groups, and scientific and experimental methods. In the main, small samples, qualitative methods, uneven quality, focus on inputs rather than outcomes related to student learning, and failure to replicate studies certainly compromise the issuing of definitive statements about what works across student groups and schools. Whether a single, uniform, standardized model for library skills instruction is a desirable goal, to the contrary notwithstanding, Todd's (2008a) message and model for evidence-based practice is a formidable challenge for school library scholars in addressing research deficits.

Of course, a number of barriers exist to the conduct of research that will yield generalizable findings. Many of the small-scale studies are the work of solitary researchers with limited funding. However, it is Todd's (2009) view that one remedy is the creation of a "sustained research culture" (92). Such a community would be able to take a more coordinated approach to the planning of research and provide for systematic data. In this way, research scholars would be in a position to demonstrate more definitely how instructional interventions increase students' knowledge and produce young learners with "competences and skills for thinking, living and working" (88). Such a community would necessarily involve individual schools and districts as well as professionals across regions, states, and the nation. Unfortunately, mechanisms for the collection of such rich data are not yet in place. Todd's (2009) agenda is an ambitious one, and its success means a rethinking of how research in school librarianship is planned and funded and building the research capacity of school library professionals so that practitioners themselves can use the data they collect locally within the larger frameworks of nationwide studies. Todd also believed that the AASL's *Standards for 21st Century Learner* (2007) would focus the attention of library professionals on student outcomes and "provide a framework for identifying evidence of the professional work of school librarians" (86).

Todd has created a three-phase model of evidence-based practice that categorizes research evidence as it relates to the basis, practice, and evaluation of instruction. Within this model, *evidence for practice* is comprised of theories and models that create frameworks for instruction. *Evidence in practice* is the use of research findings in shaping the content and direction of instruction. Research data that mark learning and knowledge outcomes of instruction make up *evidence of practice*.

The importance that Todd places in the anchoring of school library practice in evidence provided by research probably cannot be overstated. As Todd (2008a) asserts:

> A profession without reflective practitioners who are willing to learn about relevant research is a blinkered profession—one that's disconnected from best practices and best thinking, and one which, by default, often resorts to advocacy rather than evidence to survive. (43)

As noted, Todd is not alone in calling for added rigor in research and systematicity in data collection. As long ago as the mid-1990s Berkowitz urged librarians to find and use "measures of effectiveness" (Berkowitz 1994) such as those tested by Todd (1995), which can show that information skills instruction results in student achievement and an improvement in test results in content areas. Berkowitz also urges librarians to share the results with others in the school and the community.

More recently school librarians were asking for evidence of the best practices for teaching information literacy and inquiry-based learning that makes a difference in student achievement. In 2014, AASL organized a national forum to "articulate a research agenda and investigate causal phenomena in school library instruction, resources and services" (Soulen 2016, 45). The forum was called the Causality: School Libraries and Student Success (AASL 2014). This forum was followed by another AASL-sponsored causality summit in 2016 to further define the best practices for school librarians to teach motivated, engaged, and successful students. It is the goal of these studies to measure the impact of library teaching practices on student learning. "Ideally, future research related to school libraries will incorporate strong causal research designs while integrating best practices with theory and policy" (Soulen 2016, 45). Knowing school librarians and libraries impact learning has been established. Now the profession is looking for evidence that identifies the best library practices that increase student academic achievement.

Research in Practice

An assessment model, the Tool for Real-Time Assessment for Information Literacy Skills (TRAILS), was developed by Schloman and Gedeon (2010), through a grant funded by the Institute for Library and Information Literacy Education, the Institute of Museum and Library Services, and the U.S. Department of Education. Their assessment tool, launched in 2004, ties specific library and information assessment questions to the Ohio state academic standards and also aligns with standards outlined in *Information Power* (AASL & AECT 1998) and *Standards for the 21st-Century Learner* (AASL 2007).

Students in grades 6 and 9 could take an online assessment designed to provide teachers and school librarians with baseline data indicating areas of strengths and weaknesses. "TRAILS is designed as a classroom tool that enables a library media specialist easily to obtain a snapshot of skills levels in order to better tailor instructional efforts" (Schloman & Gedeon 2007, 45). TRAILS was notable in that assessments were co-created with practitioners in the field within the context of state curricular standards. The assessment tool was created for students in Ohio public schools but has also been used nationwide to help school librarians determine how to proceed with integrated instruction. The program, which was made free to all educators (http:// www.trails-9.org), instantly provided individual, class, and school data. Unfortunately, this valuable tool's last year of use as an interactive tool was 2018–2019 due to budget and staffing concerns. Over its lifetime, TRAILS registered nearly 30,000 users, and was delivered to over 2.3 million students (http://www.trails-9.org). It is hoped that funding and personnel will be found, or that someone else will take up the mantel left by TRAILS.

ASSESSING THE SCHOOL LIBRARIAN

Within the realm of assessment, school librarians also need to be concerned about their own performances and ways they might ascertain whether or not they are providing expert services for their clientele. Inherent in this self-assessment are the uses of evidence-based practice, strategic planning, environmental scans, data analysis, and continuing evaluation (AASL 2009). Evidence gathered from practice informs the development of a strategic plan. In order to develop and revisit the plan, however, school librarians must first perform an environmental scan by examining community analysis data that describe the school's surrounding community, stakeholders, and culture.

The next step is conducting a needs assessment, which takes into account budgeting, information access, staffing, collection, and instructional practices. "The [school library media specialist] analyzes data from the needs evaluation, identifies strengths and weaknesses of the program, and writes a plan of action that includes long-term goals and short-term (annual) objectives, and the monies needed to finance specific components of the program" (AASL 2009, 31).

The South Carolina Association of School Librarians commissioned a study on the impact of school libraries and librarians in South Carolina. The qualitative study under the leadership of Gavigan and Lance surveyed 273 school administrators and 917 classroom teachers on their "perceptions of the school librarians' role in collaborative teaching and leadership activities" (Gavigan & Lance 2015, 8). Results of this research showed that school librarians are important for their coteaching and collaboration roles. The study also revealed that educators surveyed were united in their belief that librarians and library programs contribute to student success" (Gavigan & Lance 2015, 11).

Keeling (2015) theorized the best way to measure a school librarian's impact on student achievement is through carefully developed rubrics to assess skills in "using text feature to find information in grades 3–5, note-making and creating citations in grade 6, and website evaluation in grade 9" (14). Each of the student assessment rubrics are then evaluated to assist school librarians in revising and fine-tuning future instruction. Woolls (2008) explains that the most effective form of evaluation may be direct observation, even though it may cause discomfort for both practitioner and evaluator. "However," as she notes, "media professionals must be evaluated as they interact with students and teachers" (118).

CONCLUSION

Clearly, there is a need for more research not only in terms of the effectiveness of library skills instruction but also in terms of the impact that library programs can have on the contexts for learning. Information skills instruction based on a process approach to information seeking and inquiry learning certainly addresses the need for improving critical thinking and problem-solving skills that have purchase in real-world contexts. However, Herman (1992) notes that changes in assessment are only part of the answer to improved instruction and learning. Schools need support to implement new instructional strategies and to institute other changes to ensure that all students can achieve the complex skills that these new assessments strive to represent (77). Most particularly, school librarians and teachers must take into account the outcomes that the AASL set forth in the *2018 National School Library Standards for Learners, School Librarians, and School Libraries* and together provide assignments and activities that demand inquiry, critical thinking, and problem-solving skills.

9

Attending to the Social Needs of Today's Learners

[S]tudents value professional, respectful, and courteous interactions and appear to engage more readily with library services when their needs are met in a supportive, constructive, and pleasant manner.
—Todd and Kuhlthau (2003)

One sign, observed on the desk of a middle school librarian, sums up concerns that make manifest the social nature of library activities: "Our students," the sign reads, "may not remember whether or not you found the information they were seeking in the library, but they will never forget how you treated them." The simplicity of this idea and the common-sense aspect of such a message tend to obscure its importance, and perhaps it is for that reason that the relational aspects of library-student interactions have so seldom been addressed in the scholarly literature on school librarianship. Indeed, it is fair to say that most of the research interest in the area of school library instruction takes as a focus the cognitive aspects of information seeking and learning.

ACKNOWLEDGING THE SOCIAL DIMENSION OF SCHOOL LIBRARY WORK

The contemporary emphases on the development of mental models and on information seeking as a cognitive task have proved extremely valuable in providing direction for school librarians in creating meaningful programs of instruction. It seems likely that the excitement generated by the advances in our understanding of the information search process and concomitant pressures related to information literacy issues have made inquiries into the relational nature of teaching and the service aspects of the school library programs appear peripheral, at best. However, Frohmann (1992) and others have cautioned against reducing to "a narrative of mental events" the "complexities of real practices, conduct, accomplishments and actions of information seeking, information use, and 'information processing'" (375).

In fact, Crow (2009) suggests that school librarians necessarily invoke an interactional model whenever they use the relational aspects of play, humor, and group-related project assignments to foster intrinsic motivation for information seeking. Interest in the social and psychological aspects of library service have also surfaced in the work of Agosto and Hughes-Hassell (2006a, 2006b), whose study of information seeking in everyday life found that social, affective, and psychological needs form the focus of adolescent information seeking; to ignore these elements in our research is to present a far too narrow view of information issues, particularly as they relate to children and youth. It is true that over time a number of scholars have attempted to incorporate a concern for the affective experience of information users into their research and models. For example, Nahl-Jakobovits and Jakobovits (1993) noted the "serious affective information needs" that students have related to their own abilities in accessing library resources. Specifically, these researchers found that students "fear making mistakes," are often "intimidated by the complexity of search tools," and lack "confidence in their ability to find information" (83). Kuhlthau's (1993b, 2004) research also focused attention on the anxieties experienced by many students at the initial stages of the information search process and stresses the importance of providing support for students experiencing the dip in confidence during the initiation and exploration phases of the research activity. However, in other respects, Kuhlthau's emphasis is squarely on those uncertainties that are directly related to information and information tasks rather than those arising from or in librarian-student interactions or from aspects of the social context. Even those studies that have included "attitudes" toward the library as measures of its value (e.g., Todd 1995) have as their primary concern the relationship between student attitudes and the library's resources or a particular instructional approach; only secondarily is attention paid to the social experiences that may contribute to the creation of those attitudes.

Chelton (1999) has noted that pressures to promote the independence of students as information seekers have sometimes led to a reluctance on the part of library professionals to provide the kinds of service support to students that are frequently available to adult users in public libraries (see Chapter 1 for a discussion of service models in academic and public libraries). In fact, Chelton asserts that the school librarian often "defines her role as helping people find information on their own." Yet given the increasing complexities of the information universe, one questions, with Liesener (1985), the efficacy of predicating all services related to information seeking in school libraries on a "self-sufficiency" (17) model. This is particularly the case where, as in Chelton's study, there is "little follow up by library staff to see if users" (283) actually find the information being sought. Indeed, this attitude is illustrated by *Empowering Learners: Guidelines for School Library Programs* (American Association of School Librarians 2009), which seldom directly addresses the need for compassion and sensitivity in dealing day to day with the students who are not only the primary clientele of the school library but its raison d'etre as well.

The *National School Library Standards* (American Association of School Librarians 2018) provides guidance to a more user-centric approach to school library services, primarily through the shared foundation of "Include." School librarians are described as "differentiating instruction to support learners' understanding of cultural relevancy and placement within the global learning community" (76), and are admonished to "devise learning activities that require learners to evaluate a variety of perspectives" (80). School librarians show growth when they "explicitly lead learners to demonstrate empathy and equity in knowledge building" (80), the assumption being that they themselves also show empathy and equity in their services to the learning community.

INFORMATION SEEKING AS A SOCIAL ACTIVITY

As we have seen, contemporary trends in teaching emphasize inquiry and the "active" and "constructed" nature of learning as well as the importance of interaction among students and between students and teachers (Bruner 1975, 1977; Kuhlthau, Maniotes, & Caspari 2007; Vygotsky 1978). And there is an increasing awareness and valuing of group processes and social engagement as essential parts of the instructional context, thanks to input from many education researchers. This seems logical when one considers that the very act of teaching is itself inherently social and interactive. For example, the importance of "affective bonds" between adults and students has been recognized by Winograd and Gaskins (1992, 232), who assert that "the need for a supportive, trusting advocate is particularly important for students experiencing academic difficulties." Suggesting that schools need to become as concerned about being "high touch" as they are about being "hi-tech" (232), Mann (1986, cited in Winograd & Gaskins 1992) argues that reaching out to less successful students and providing personal contact constitute essential parts of all successful intervention programs. Delpit and Kohl (2006) and others note that this may be especially true for some minority students. However, "even advocates of systemic change . . . often leave off of their agenda any recognition of the importance of having schools see students as people" (Howe 1993, 130). And unhappily, even in the few studies where the social aspects of library service and instruction are reflected in the data, as, for example, in Nahl-Jakobovits and Jakobovits's (1993) finding "that students fear talking to librarians," they are often ignored by practitioners and seldom pursued further by researchers.

Having said that, there are some exceptions. For example, the interactive nature of the school librarian's role has been marked in a study of achievement effects by Ryan (1991, cited in Bialo & Sivin-Kachala 1996), who identified social interaction among students and between students and teachers and/or librarians as one of the three characteristics essential for the creation and maintenance "of the most effective learning environments" (54). Kulleseid (1986) also noted the contribution of the librarian's interpersonal skills to the successful modeling and facilitation of student-student and teacher-student interactions. Gehlken's (1994) examination of library programs in three exemplary schools in South Carolina called attention to the importance of "proactivity and commitment in meeting student needs." Indeed, Gehlken observed that "in every case, student samples overwhelmingly identified the single most important service provided by the library media program as help from the media specialist." Students surveyed by Todd and Kuhlthau (2003) felt the same way. "It wasn't really the library," reported one student, "it was the librarians that helped" (22). Finally, esteem needs appear to be implicated in Todd and Kuhlthau's conclusion that "students value professional, respectful, and courteous interactions and appear to engage more readily with library services when their needs are met in a supportive, constructive, and pleasant manner" (15).

Kuhlthau's (1996) intervention model, which describes tutoring and counseling activities for librarians in supporting students in seeking information, clearly assumes high-level communication and interactional skills. This model is based on Vygotsky's (1978) assertion that the most effective teaching activities are structuring interactions that enable students to function at a higher level than could be managed if they were left to struggle along on their own. Swain's (1996) extension of Kuhlthau's (1993a) research provides further insights into the role of social interaction in information seeking. In particular, Swain noted the importance of the social relationships that developed between students and library staff members who provided assistance in helping relieve the stresses and anxieties that the students experienced in selecting their topics, using library tools, and conducting their searching activities.

SOCIAL IDENTITY ISSUES IN THE SCHOOL LIBRARY

Issues of identity construction, which are usually considered of paramount interest and importance in other contexts, have seldom been the objects of interest in school library research. Recently, however, a number of scholars, including Radford (2006), Connaway et al. (2008), Radford and Connaway (2007), and Crow (2009), have expressed a concern for this important aspect of librarianship, and their explorations of service interactions provide evidence that there is often more at stake in library encounters than simply the transfer of information. If, as Haycock (1992) suggests, interactional skills are essential elements in the librarian's professional tool kit, and if librarians wish to implement programs that are truly learner centered, then the social experiences that students have in school libraries should be studied and the findings used, where necessary, to rethink and reshape professional attitudes and behavior. The rest of this chapter reviews some of the salient studies related to interactional aspects of the library experience in the hope that the insights they provide will raise sensitivity and spark discussion among both researchers and practitioners.

INTERPERSONAL INTERACTIONS IN THE SCHOOL LIBRARY CONTEXT

Writing in the *School Library Media Quarterly*, in 1982, Martin was one of the first to recognize the relational nature of teaching and learning in the library. Specifically, she considered the value of interpersonal relationships with students, school administrators, faculty, parents, and community members in creating trust, communicating clearly, building influence, and solving problems essential to the creation of exemplary library programs. According to Martin, self-acceptance, self-confidence, the ability to exhibit warmth, a sense of caring, and sensitivity to the feelings of others are all characteristics fundamental for establishing a context of support for information-seeking activities. In providing assistance, Martin admonished readers to attend "to the affective domain, valuing each person as unique, then showing individuals that you know their worth, and accepting them, recognizing their accomplishments, and helping them to develop self esteem" (54). Strategies that Martin suggested for librarians to use in making library visitors feel welcome included responding positively to their interests, respecting their rights and needs in terms of acceptance and valuing, and taking care to "avoid interrupting, shaming, name calling, commanding, moralizing, lecturing, arguing, or criticizing" (56).

Martin (1982) also called attention to the variety of paralinguistic (e.g., voice tone, rate of speech, and modulation) and nonverbal behaviors (e.g., gestures, expressions, posture, personal distance, and style of dress) that have a bearing on the ways in which librarians relate to their users. In fact, she asserted that "non-verbal messages may be more powerful in communicating feelings than verbal ones" (54). But Nahl-Jakobovits and Jakobovits (1990) and Thomas (1996, 2002) have also urged librarians to attend to textual "messages" librarians direct at users in the form of signage, notes, list of rules, and directions. In a study of the signage in three school libraries (one elementary, one middle, and one high school), Johnston and Mandel (2014) found that the most noted issues were with signs that were unclear because of text that was too small, signs poorly placed, text that did not make sense, and poor use of color. Researchers also warn against library jargon, such as using the term "serials" instead of "magazines" (Connaway & Randall 2013, 50) or using the term "source" when referring to a database (Koshik & Okazawa 2012, 2011). Stating "rules" or prohibitions in positive rather than negative ways, personalizing library messages, and minimizing the punitive aspects of library postings are suggested as techniques that contribute to the creation of welcoming and confirming library environments.

LIBRARY ENCOUNTERS AS COMMUNICATIVE ACTION

Research studies by Mokros, Mullins, and Saracevic (1995), Radford (1996, 1998, 1999, 2006), Radford and Connaway (2007), and Chelton (1997) address issues identified by Martin (1982) and others as barriers to "exemplary library program[s]" (56). These studies draw on communication theory as explained in the work of Goffman (1967) and Watzlawick, Beavin, and Jackson (1967) to investigate interactions in a variety of library contexts. Within this framework, an act of communication includes not only the expression of the report, or informational content, within a given utterance but also the "relational content," the feelings participants have about themselves, each other, and the interactive situation in which they find themselves. For this reason, the manner in which words are spoken (e.g., whether deferential and respectful or condescending and demeaning) are at least as powerful as the meanings of the words themselves. In addition, these researchers understand that language in use is, itself, value laden rather than merely representational, "even though such 'valuing' proceeds out of awareness and is seldom explored" (Thomas 2002, 80).

According to interactionists, *social identity*, the sense of who one is in relation to social others, arises in knowing how we regard ourselves and how we are ourselves regarded in social situations (Goffman 1967). There is a possibility in every social interaction that an individual will be accepted, respected, and honored or, conversely, rejected, shamed, or ignored and that there will be consequences in terms of personal identity formation depending on which treatment an individual perceives him- or herself to have received. For this reason, the "selves" of all interactants are potentially "at risk" in every social engagement. Mokros et al.'s (1995) and Radford's (1996, 1998, 2006) studies are significant for what each contributes to our understandings of the instructional context and to the relational aspects embedded within each informational encounter. As noted above, these scholars would argue that the "self" needs of library users are at least as important as their information needs (Thomas 2000b).

Acknowledging the role of communication in creating meaning, context, and the self, Mokros et al. (1995) studied interactions between librarians and students involved in an online searching activity in an academic library. In the view of these researchers, library activities that are undertaken with such frequency that they are enacted routinely and "unconsciously" are nonetheless charged with relational messages about who is in control and the nature of the relationship between the interactants (e.g., parity or asymmetry) within the context of the activity. Through an analysis of videotaped reference encounters, researchers concluded that the opening moments of service interactions are particularly significant in setting the stage for all the activities that follow. Their study revealed that in some cases the librarians' own self-identity and control needs took precedence, resulting in personally disaffirming experiences for the library users who had come to them for research assistance. Considered as personally affirming for both librarians and users in the study were those interactions that demonstrated, through words and gestures, a sense of parity in terms of status between the interactants and marked them as coparticipants in the shared research activity.

Approachability: A Key Aspect of Library Service

Radford (1998) explored the dimensions of approachability in a study among high school and college students, all of whom were engaged in a reference activity that required the use of library resources. Citing the uncertainty and anxiety that Kuhlthau (1993b) identified as common experiences for users in the initial and exploratory phases of a research task, and the important role that librarians can play in mediating these experiences for users as they contemplated the complexities of the contemporary library, Radford sought to determine what barriers might exist for users in seeking reference assistance. Her results indicated that the librarians in her study exhibited nonverbal "gestures," such as eye contact, manner, and deference, to which library users were extremely sensitive. In addition, the students Radford interviewed revealed that they used these nonverbal cues in assessing the "approachability" of the librarians and planned their information-seeking strategies accordingly. In short, they avoided some reference librarians and sought assistance from others on the basis of whether or not they thought a particular librarian seemed open and friendly. Significantly, the students in Radford's study considered that obtaining the desired information in a reference interaction, while important, was not as important as having their relational needs met. This led Radford (1996) to conclude that library users "may still leave the interaction with a negative impression of the librarian and of the library experience in general" (125) regardless of the informational outcome of a library visit.

Agosto, Magee, Dickard, and Forte (2016) found in their study of high-tech urban teens' use and nonuse of libraries that about a quarter of the nonusers perceived libraries as being uninviting, both in atmosphere and staff. Interestingly, the most frequent reason given for using libraries was for social interaction, including "hanging out, socializing, and eating in library spaces" (258).

Self-Esteem Needs of Library Users

The "negative attitudes" identified by Radford's (1996) informants included "(a) having no time, (b) unhelpful, (c) uncaring, (d) sour, (e) abrupt, and (f) impatient" (130). These kinds of behaviors seem to reflect those described in a study by Mellon (1990, cited in Chelton 1997) in which high school students reported that librarians tended to respond only to direct questions, made disparaging remarks about the kinds of questions that students posed, and made them feel stupid. Similarly, research conducted by the Pew Research Center (Simon, Graziano, & Lenhart 2001) indicated that the "bad attitude" of librarians led many students to abandon libraries altogether in favor of information seeking on the Internet. However, on a positive note, in a similar survey conducted by the Pew Research Center (Horrigan 2016), 87 percent of Millennials (those ages 18–35 in 2016) indicated that the public library helps them "find information that is trustworthy and reliable," and 85 percent say that public libraries help them "learn new things."

Building Self-Esteem through Library Interactions

The psychological dimension of library-student interaction created a focus for the dissertation work of Diane McAfee Hopkins (1989). In particular, Hopkins's work considered the contributions that library programming and services could make to the development of feelings of self-worth in student users and the importance of establishing a positive atmosphere in the school library. Hopkins's research identified the provision of appropriate library materials, maintaining the accessibility to a variety of resources, and the creation of a welcoming physical setting as contributing to students' feelings of being valued in the library. In addition, Hopkins's research found that students also experienced a sense of affirmation and acceptance through participation in library activities that fostered cooperation and independence (McAfee 1981, cited in Haycock 1992). Irving (1990) also noted the importance of this kind of library activity in her observation that learning to obtain "information personally" created a "tremendous sense of independence" (86) and was an important by-product of information skills instruction; while students in Nahl-Jakobovits and Jakobovits's (1990) study found "deeply rewarding" those "required course-integrated library research" tasks that led them to "an enlarged conception of their capacity to learn and succeed" (80).

Fourie and Kruger (1995) identified a number of psychosocial, cognitive, and affective needs behind the information-seeking behavior of secondary school students. They theorized that the fulfillment of these needs is the basis of teens' motivation to choose particular books and media. Todd and Dadlani (2013) describe the use of collaborative inquiry groups in digital environments to support a network of social justice in the high school classroom.

Respecting Students in the School Library

In her dissertation research, Chelton (1997) confirmed the multidimensional nature of the school librarian's job and the many kinds of interactions that take place in high school libraries. Drawing on the works of Kuhlthau (1993a), Radford (1996), and Mokros et al. (1995), Chelton used communication frameworks to explore these interactions, particularly as they involved issues of identity construction of the adolescents she observed. In her study, Chelton (1997, 1999) noted in particular many library interactions she observed in which the adults assumed "authority" positions in enforcing school and library rules. She then considered the ways in which these manifestations of authority might interfere with a librarian's ability to support information seeking predicated on a participatory, interactional model.

Chelton's (1997) adolescent informants expressed, sometimes poignantly, sometimes angrily, their sensitivity to deference issues and the disrespect many had themselves encountered in all kinds of service settings. The specific behaviors of which the youngsters complained included being ignored, being watched, and being stereotyped. These same students identified listening skills, courteous behavior, niceness, helpfulness, and promptness as important elements in positive service encounters.

It is especially important to note here that although the students themselves identified "respect" as their primary information need in library interactions, the adults Chelton (1997) interviewed failed to recognize this as an aspect of their encounters with students. Thus, while the adolescents appeared to want "an identity-confirming, emotional connection to adult service providers" (179) in the library as elsewhere, the librarians tended to view student needs as primarily informational in nature and isomorphic with the questions that the students asked! This is a significant disconnect and may well explain the differences in how library interactions are perceived by students and librarians.

Echoing Mokros et al. (1995), Chelton (1997) argued that the opening "moves" of a library interaction, when the participants greeted or failed to greet each other, established the nature of the relationship (e.g., who is in control of the interaction), signaled the deference with which students would be treated, and defined the "situation" or interactional context as potentially productive or adversarial. Chelton concluded that where expectations created in these interactional openings are negative, the chances for productivity later in the encounters are severely compromised.

An important aspect of Chelton's (1997) research is the concern it expresses with regard to the impact of "everyday" types of library interactions and routine activities on the selves of the youngsters involved. Thus, Chelton concludes,

> Helping an adolescent to use the photocopy machine, or checking out a book or asking to see a pass may seem mundane and tedious to someone who does it constantly. The young person receiving the service, however, is neither mundane nor tedious, but rather, another person who wants an emotional connection (Scheff 1990). Providing library service without it is otherwise a very empty and possibly meaningless activity. (208)

The Cultural Dimensions of Relational Work

The fact that in some cultures the relational "work" to establish a basis for further interaction must precede information tasks (Bialo & Sivin-Kachala 1996; Delpit & Kohl 2006; Salvatore 2000) appears to suggest that the social aspects of service are especially important for school librarians serving multicultural/multiethnic school communities. In light of the research findings of Bialo and Sivin-Kachala and Salvatore, direct inquiries by the librarian, which constitute the warp and woof of the traditional reference interview, and which frequently characterize the opening moves in other kinds of school library interactions, may be seen by some minority students as overly inquisitive, inappropriate, and even rude. Studies have revealed that the cultural group of LGBTQ+ teens have found traditional library services to be insufficient, even presenting barriers for these teens to find answers about coming out and gay identity (Hamer 2003; Kitzie 2017; Kitzie & Radford 2017; Moorefield-Lang & Kitzie 2018). Using neutral questions as a reference technique in such instances, as explained in the work of Dervin and Dewdney (1986), might well be a useful way to interact with students for whom a more direct line of questions would be construed as disrespectful or even intrusive (for a discussion of Dervin and Dewdney's neutral questioning model, see Chapter 5). Providing safe places, including students of diverse cultures in library decision making, and implementing antibullying policies (Moorefield-Land & Kitzie 2018) also build a foundation on which connections between school librarians and a diverse student body will evolve.

REFERENCE INTERACTIONS ONLINE: TEENAGE EXPERIENCES AND PREFERENCES

Some interesting and potentially disturbing research findings can be found in the work of Radford (2006) and Radford and Connaway (2007), who took as their research focus the experience of online information-seeking encounters between young adults and reference librarians. Radford and Connaway's research centered on library users' experiences with chat reference. Data in these studies came from focus group interviews as well as from transcripts of chats recorded in virtual reference service settings in public libraries. Citing her own work as well as studies by Dewdney and Ross (1994), and Walter and Mediavilla (2005), Radford asserts that "interpersonal aspects have been shown to be critical to client's perceptions of success in both face-to-face reference interactions and virtual environments."

Unfortunately, comments by the informants in her study led Radford et al. (Radford, Radford, Connaway, & DeAngelis 2011) to conclude that in many cases the Millennials in the study not only make "limited use of libraries" but also tend to "view librarians in negative terms." Even where students reported preferring face-to-face interactions with school and public librarians as a general rule, they continued to be concerned for "face" (Goffman 1967) issues in interacting with library professionals. Fears of ridicule or humiliation at the hands of insensitive service providers made youngsters reluctant to ask for additional assistance even when they felt the need to do so. However, such feelings were lessened for students who had developed a relationship with specific reference librarians.

Millennials in Radford's study preferred the independence of online searching to asking for help from a librarian and were mixed in their perceptions of librarians' information-seeking expertise and knowledge; thus, while some appreciated the quality of the information that librarians could help them find, others preferred to trust information they found online on their own. Data from the recorded chat sessions also indicated problems between cyberlibrarians and Millennials. A number of negative interactions led Radford (2006) to conclude that when librarians reacted negatively and reproached youthful information seekers online for chat behaviors of which they disapproved, these reprimands actually exacerbated rude behavior.

The fact that many students in Radford's (2006) study reported a reluctance to engage via e-mail or other online chat strategy when adolescents today are often so comfortable in other kinds of online environments was surprising. Radford's informants tended to explain this behavior in terms of the more impersonal dimension of mediated communication with librarians and expressed concerns for privacy in dealing online with strangers.

More recent studies have highlighted the improvement of virtual reference service as technology has improved, pointing to the fact that the problem may not all be on the shoulders of poor communication by the librarian. "Since their inception, virtual reference services have evolved considerably and are now a significant component of library services in many types of library environments" (Cote, Kochkina, & Mawhinney 2016). Academic libraries in particular have taken the virtual reference environment seriously, conducting action research with students and faculty alike and discovering new ways to make virtual reference work. Adhering to the principle of "service at the point of need," the use of strategically placed pop-up chat boxes that can be programed to "pop up" based on criteria set by the library (such as when a user is on a page more than 30 seconds) is an innovation that has increased client-librarian interactions from 300 to 600 percent in some libraries (Epstein 2018; Fan, Fought, & Gahn 2017; Kemp, Ellis, & Maloney 2015). Still, there are communication problems in virtual reference interactions to overcome, such as mistyping, typing in the wrong window, using ambiguous terminology, and dealing with varying levels of expertise (Koshik & Okazawa 2012), all communication issues that cycle back to the importance of the finely honed communication skills of the librarian, especially those that are needed to write succinct text (Zemel 2017).

HOW WE DESCRIBE LIBRARY USERS' MATTERS

Chelton (conversation with author, August 24, 1997) has argued that the ways in which adolescents are discussed in the media and popular culture create stereotypes and expectations, frequently negative, which are then reflected in treatment adolescents receive at the hands of service providers. This theme appears in an article by Marcus (2002). This author identifies titles such as *Unglued and Tattooed: How to Save Your Teen from Raves, Ritalin, Goth, Body Carving, GHB, Sex and 12 Other Emerging Threats, Parenting Your Out-of-Control Teenager, Yes, Your Teen Is Crazy*, and *Now I Know Why Tigers Eat Their Young: Surviving a New Generation of Teenagers* as not only pejorative, in the sense that they condition service providers to view all adolescents with suspicion, but also grossly insensitive to youngsters who are striving, often successfully, to navigate the often turbulent waters of adolescence.

The idea that the choice of words we use in describing library clients often has unintended consequences for library service delivery has been the subject of an interesting study by Tuominen (1997). Drawing on communication theory, Tuominen applied a discourse-analytic lens to the vocabulary that Kuhlthau (1993b) and others have employed in studies related to information seeking in libraries. Discourse analysis acknowledges the constitutive and value-laden character of language and argues that the terms we employ in describing our experience actually create and constitute one version of reality: our own. Tuominen suggests that characterizing the library user as "uncertain," "anxious," "confused," and "unfocused," while at the same time identifying the librarian as an "expert," "rational," problem solver," and "teacher," creates a context for relational asymmetry that may actually stymie our ability to delivery effective library services. This asymmetry is especially problematic where successful service interventions are predicated on a model of shared responsibility and cooperation between users and librarians. Tuominen also argues that when anxiety is considered as a personal characteristic of the library user rather than as an outcome of the interaction between the library user and the more complex and arcane aspects of an information system or environment, librarians are released from the responsibility of examining the very practices that make libraries and information seeking intimidating for many people.

CONCLUSION

Table 9.1 summarizes the research findings related to social interaction in the library context. Taken together, this research underscores the importance of students' experiences in library settings. Considering the interactional issues related to instruction and service encounters serves to confirm not only the complexities of the librarians' tasks but also the significant roles that librarians can play in creating opportunities for positive encounters between their students and the school. Librarians must be intentional in their building of connections with students. They can do this in many ways, but a few are by implementing library student aides, library clubs, involving students in library decision making, and by becoming part of the educational team with classroom teachers (Moreillon 2014a). Librarians devoted to helping students achieve educational and life goals must pay serious attention to this very important aspect of school librarianship. As Haycock (1991) reminds us, in the final analysis we are in the business of teaching kids, not content (15).

TABLE 9.1 Research Insights Related to Social Interaction in the Library Context

- Information seeking is affective and social as well as cognitive and informational.
- The relational aspects of a library encounter are at least as important as the informational aspects.
- Students have self-needs and want to feel respected in all kinds of service encounters.
- The opening moments of a library interaction establish the relational nature (adversarial, participatory; expert, novice; superior, inferior) of the encounter.
- Approachability and negativity are expressed in verbal and nonverbal actions and are "read" by students and considered when they plan their information-seeking strategies.
- The portrayal of library users in the research literature can promote asymmetry in librarian-user interactions.
- The pejorative characterizations of teenagers in and by media create narratives that, if unchallenged by library professionals, can condition attitudes that jeopardize service provision to teens in school libraries.
- Librarians must be intentional in their building of connections with students and not just expect them to "happen."
- Service providers need to be as sensitive to the deference needs of adolescents in online interactions as they are in face-to-face encounters.
- The use of relational facilitators online is an especially important aspect of mediated communication in libraries.
- Face-to-face interactions between librarians and youth within the framework of a physical library space remain a vital part of service in school libraries.
- Librarians show empathy and equity by implementing user-centered approaches to their instruction and interactions with youth.

Epilogue

As school leaders, it is critical that we advocate articulately and passionately for our programs and, more importantly, for the youngsters we meet in the library on a daily basis. To do the job well demands that we set for ourselves service as well as instructional goals as we strive to make our libraries supportive and caring places for all children.
— Thomas, Crow, & Franklin (2011)

From its inception some 21 years ago, *Information Skills and Information Literacy Instruction* has represented a bridge between researchers in library and information studies and school library practitioners through the sharing of theories and models for creating effective information literacy curricula and insights based on observations of students and practices in professional and academic literatures. Reviewing research relating to instruction and learning in the contemporary school library reminds us that in addition to helping students build essential skills we are educating youngsters for the long haul. However, we must also be concerned about the short term, that is, helping students meet their immediate goals, only some of which will involve their school assignments. For these reasons, additional studies focused on motivation and on the independent information-seeking activities of students outside the confines of school-related information needs are of special value.

As we have seen, an inquiry approach to teaching and learning relies on cooperative and collaborative instructional teams, of which the creation and implementation require initiative and investment of time and energy. Making changes that will result in higher levels of achievement for students often— and sometimes inevitably—demands that we take the lead in instructional team building. As librarians, we rely on teachers to provide the curricular context for the integration of information skills, while they can count on our technological expertise and knowledge of information-seeking processes and resources. Thinking strategically, acting collaboratively, and communicating effectively will aid school librarians in this important endeavor. Assessing and capitalizing on our own strengths and developing new skill sets when necessary is a professional responsibility and one that will lead to increased levels of professional competence and self-confidence.

As school leaders, it is critical that we advocate articulately and passionately for our programs and, more importantly, for the youngsters we meet in the library on a daily basis. To do the job well demands that we set for ourselves well-defined, thoughtful, and compassionate service goals that make our libraries supportive and safe places for all children. To ensure such outcomes, our library volunteers and aides must embrace our dedication to service and equity as enthusiastically as we do ourselves. It is our responsibility to see that this is so. Never has this been more critical than it is today.

Because we have access to all the students in our schools, school librarians are in a position to make real differences in the lives of every one of these children every day. Vandergrift and Hannigan (1986) have acknowledged this aspect of school librarianship and the role librarians can take in helping students "develop the kind of educated imagination that empowers them to consider alternatives and to construct possible models of a better and more humane world" (171). The challenges of such an opportunity are striking and should surely shift our focus from the mundane aspects of "the job" to much loftier and more meaningful goals.

As a career path, school librarianship should not be undertaken casually: our commitments to children and their educational success must be total. Indeed, our tasks are complex—requiring wisdom, intelligence, and empathy as well as patience, in addition to advanced communication skills, creativity, stamina, humor, sensitivity, and a loving heart—and yet it is this very complexity that makes our professional lives both exciting and fulfilling.

On a final note, we offer one caveat: as important an activity as establishing unequivocally the educational value of school libraries is in ensuring support for the profession at large, and as critical as it is to help prepare our students for the jobs of tomorrow, we should also take time to savor the joy of engaging with them. We have much to learn from them, just as they have much to learn from us. Of the latter, one of the most important is introducing youngsters to literary works—that inspire as well as instruct—as they embark on their personal intellectual journeys. It is in this way that we can advance the common good and secure for future generations the values that may have drawn us into the field of school librarianship in the first place. Finally, we must not overlook or fail to appreciate fully the satisfactions inherent in positive interpersonal interactions with the children we meet in our libraries, for it is these that will enrich both their lives and our own.

References

Aaron, S. L. (1982). Review of Selected Doctoral Dissertations about School Library Media Programs and Resources January 1972–December 1980. *School Library Media Quarterly, 10,* 210–240.

Abrahamson, R. F. (1979, March). *The Ultimate Developmental Task in Adolescent Literature* (p. 3) (ERIC Document No. 161 075).

Abrizah, A., Inuwa, S., & Afiqah-Izzati, N. (2016). Systematic Literature Review Informing LIS Professionals on Embedding Librarianship Roles. *Journal of Academic Librarianship, 42,* no. 6, 636–643.

Achterman, D. L. (2009). *Haves, Halves, and Have-Nots: School Libraries and Student Achievement in California.* PhD diss., University of North Texas.

Adeoye, B. F. (2011). Culturally Different Learning Styles in Online Learning Environments: A Case of Nigerian University Students. *International Journal of Information and Communication Technology Education, 7,* no. 2, 1–12.

Adkins, D. (2014). U.S. Students, Poverty, and School Libraries: What Results of the 2009 Programme for International Student Assessment Tell Us. *School Library Research, 17,* 1–26.

Agosto, D. E. (2001). Propelling Young Women in the Cyber Age: Gender Considerations in the Evaluation of Web-Based Information. *School Library Media Research, 4.* Available: http://www.ala.org/ala/mgrps/divs/aasl/aaslpub sandjournals/slmrb/slmrcontents/volume42001/agosto.cfm (accessed May 26, 2010).

Agosto, D. E. (2002). Bounded Rationality and Satisficing in Young People's Web-Based Decision Making. *Journal of the American Society for Information Science and Technology, 53,* no. 1, 16–27.

Agosto, D. E., & Hughes-Hassell, S. (2006a). Toward a Model of the Everyday Life Information Needs of Urban Teenagers, Part 1: Theoretical Model. *Journal of the American Society for Information Science and Technology, 57,* no. 10, 1394–1403.

Agosto, D. E., & Hughes-Hassell, S. (2006b). Toward a Model of the Everyday Life Information Needs of Urban Teenagers, Part 2: Empirical Model. *Journal of the American Society for Information Science and Technology, 57,* no. 11, 1418–1426.

Agosto, D. E., Magee, R. M., Dickard, M., & Forte, A. (2016). Teens, Technology, and Libraries: An Uncertain Relationship. *Library Quarterly, 86,* no. 3, 248–269.

Aho, M. K., Beschnett, A. M., & Reimer, E. Y. (2011). Who Is Sitting at the Reference Desk? *Collaborative Librarianship, 3,* no. 1, 46–49.

Akin, L. (1998). Information Overload and Children: A Survey of Texas Elementary School Students. *School Library Media Quarterly, 1.* Available: http://www.ala.org/ala/mgrps/divs/aasl/aaslpubsandjournals/slmrb/slmrcontents/volume11998slmqo/akin.cfm (accessed May 26, 2010).

Allen, K., & Hughes-Hassell. (2010). Meeting the Needs of Students with Disabilities. *School Library Monthly, 27,* no. 1, 52–54.

Alverno College. *Assessment and Outreach Center.* Available: https://www.alverno.edu/assessment/index.php (accessed December 10, 2018).

American Association of School Librarians. (1960). *Standards for School Library Media Programs.* Chicago: American Library Association.

American Association of School Librarians. (2007). *Standards for the 21st-Century Learner.* Chicago: American Library Association.

American Association of School Librarians. (2009). *Empowering Learners: Guidelines for School Library Media Programs.* Chicago: American Library Association.

American Association of School Librarians. (2014). *Causality: School Libraries and Student Success (CLASS)—A White Paper.* Available: http://www.ala.org/aasl/advocacy/research (accessed May 24, 2019).

American Association of School Librarians. (2018). *National School Library Standards for Learners, School Librarians, and School Libraries.* Chicago: ALA Editions.

American Association of School Librarians & Association for Education Communications and Technology. (1975). *Media Programs: District and School.* Chicago: American Library Association.

American Association of School Librarians & Association for Educational Communications and Technology. (1988). *Information Power: Guidelines for School Library Media Programs.* Chicago: American Library Association.

American Association of School Librarians & Association for Educational Communications and Technology. (1998). *Information Power: Building Partnerships for Learning.* Chicago: American Library Association.

American Library Association. (1945). *School Libraries for Today and Tomorrow: Functions and Standards.* Chicago: Author.

Anderson, J. A. (1988). Cognitive Styles and Multicultural Populations. *Journal of Teacher Education, 39,* no. 1, 2–9.

Anderson, L. W., & Krathwohl, D. R. (Eds.). (2001). *A Taxonomy for Learning, Teaching, and Assessing: A Revision of Bloom's Taxonomy of Educational Objectives.* Boston: Allyn & Bacon.

Anderson, M. (2018, September 10). About a Quarter of Rural Americans Say Access to High-Speed Internet Is a Major Problem. *Pew Research Center.* Available: https://www.pewresearch.org/fact-tank/2018/09/10/about-a-quarter-of-rural-americans-say-access-to-high-speed-internet-is-a-major-problem.

Anderson, M., & Jiang, J. (2018a). Teens, Social Media and Technology 2018. *Pew Research Center: Internet & Technology.* Available: https://www.pewinternet.org/2018/05/31/teens-social-media-technology-2018.

Anderson, M., & Jiang, J. (2018b). Teens' Social Media Habits and Experiences. *Pew Research Center: Internet & Technology.* Available: https://www.pewinternet.org/2018/11/28/teens-social-media-habits-and-experiences.

Angell, K. (2018). An Exploration of Academic Librarian Positions Dedicated to Serving First Year College Students. *Collaborative Librarianship, 10,* no. 1, 18–29.

Armstrong, M., & Costa, B. (1983). Computer Cat at Mountain View Elementary School. *Library Hi Tech, 1,* no. 3, 47–52.

Arnone, M. P., & Reynolds, R. (2009). Empirical Support for the Integration of Dispositions in Action and Multiple Literacies into AASL's *Standards for the 21st-Century Learner. School Library Media Research, 12,* 1–8. Available: http://www.aasl.org/ala/mgrps/divs/aasl/aaslpubsandjournals/slmrb/slmrcontents/volume12/arnone_reynolds.cfm (accessed March 31, 2010).

Arnone, M. P., Reynolds, R., & Marshall, T. (2009). The Effect of Early Adolescents' Psychological Needs Satisfaction upon Their Perceived Competence in Information Skills and Intrinsic Motivation for Research. *School Libraries Worldwide, 15,* no. 2, 115–134.

Asselin, M., & Doiron, R. (2008). Towards a Transformative Pedagogy for School Libraries 2.0. *School Libraries Worldwide, 14,* no. 2, 1–18.

Association of College and Research Libraries. (2015). *Framework for Information Literacy in Higher Education.* Available: www.ala.org/acrl/standards/ilframework (accessed May 24, 2019).

Badke, W. (2016). Stressing Out about the Framework. *Online Searcher, 40,* no. 1, 71–73.

Badke, W. E. (2019). Ten Considerations for Inquiry-Based Learning. *Online Searcher, 43,* no. 1, 55–57. Available: https://unk.idm.oclc.org/login?url=https://search.proquest.com/docview/2167242213?accountid=8115.

Baer, A. (2014). Why Do I Have to Write That? Compositionists Identify Disconnects between Student and Instructor Conceptions of Research Writing That Can Inform Teaching. *Evidence Based Library & Information Practice, 9,* no. 2, 37–44.

Baker, S. L., & Lancaster, F. W. (1991). *The Measurement and Evaluation of Library Services.* Arlington, VA: Information Resources Press.

Bandura, A. (1989). Human Agency in Social Cognitive Theory. *American Psychologist 44,* no. 9, 1175–1184.

Baro, E. K., & Keboh, T. R. (2012). Teaching and Fostering Information Literacy Programmes: A Survey of Five University Libraries in Africa. *Journal of Academic Librarianship, 38,* no. 5, 311–315.

Baron, N. S., Calixte, R. M., & Havewala, M. (2017). The Persistence of Print among University Students: An Exploratory Study. *Telematics and Informatics, 34,* no. 5, 590.

Barron, D. D. (1994). School Library Media Specialists and the Internet: Road Kill or Road Warriors? *School Library Media Activities Monthly, 10,* no. 9, 48–50.

Bash, C. (2015). One-on-One versus One-Shot. *Catholic Library World, 85,* no. 3, 167–171.

Bates, M. J. (1979). Idea Tactics. *Journal of the American Society for Information Science, 30,* no. 5, 280–289.

Bates, M. J. (1989). Design of Browsing and Berrypicking: Techniques for the Online Search Interface. *Online Review, 13,* no. 4, 407–423.

Baumbach, D. T. (1986). Information Skills for the Information Age: The State of Our States. In S. L. Aaron & P. R. Scales (Eds.), *School Library Media Annual* (Vol. 4, pp. 278–285). Littleton, CO: Libraries Unlimited.

Becker, D. E. (1970). *Social Studies Achievement of Pupils in Schools with Libraries and Schools without Libraries.* PhD diss., University of Pennsylvania.

Belkin, N. J. (1980). Anomalous State of Knowledge for Information Retrieval. *Canadian Journal of Information Science, 5,* no. 13, 133–143.

Belkin, N. J., Oddy, R. N., & Brooks, H. M. (1982a). Ask for Information Retrieval: Part II. *Journal of Documentation, 38,* no. 3, 145–164.

Belkin, N. J., Oddy, R. N., & Brooks, H. M. (1982b). Information Retrieval: Part I. Background and Theory. *Journal of Documentation, 38,* no. 2, 61–71.

Belmont, J. M. (1989). Cognitive Strategies and Strategic Learning: The Socio-Instructional Approach. *American Psychologist, 44,* no. 2, 142–148.

Berg, C. (2017). Teaching Website Evaluation. *Internet@Schools, 24,* no. 2, 8–10.

Berkowitz, R. E. (1994). From Indicators of Quantity to Measures of Effectiveness: Ensuring Information Power's Mission. In C. C. Kuhlthau, M. E. Goodin, & M. J. McNally (Eds.), *Assessment in the School Library Media Center* (pp. 33–42). Englewood, CO: Libraries Unlimited.

Berkowitz, R. E., & Serim, F. (2002). *Moving Every Child Ahead: The Big6 Success Strategy.* Available: http://www.infotoday.com/MMSchools/may02/berkowitz.htm (accessed May, 26, 2010).

Berlyne, D. E. (1960). *Conflict, Arousal and Curiosity.* New York: McGraw-Hill.

Bernier, A. (2007). Introduction: "Not Broke by Someone Else's Schedule": On Joy and Young Adult Information Seeking. In M. K. Chelton and C. Cool (Eds.), *Youth Information-Seeking Behavior II: Context, Theories, Models, and Issues* (pp. xiii–xxviii). Lanham, MD: Scarecrow Press.

Bialo, E. R., & Sivin-Kachala, J. (1996). The Effectiveness of Technology in Schools: A Summary of Recent Research. *School Library Media Quarterly, 25,* no. 1, 51–57.

Biggers, D. (2001). The Argument against Accelerated Reader. *Journal of Adolescent & Adult Literacy, 45,* no. 1, 72–75.

Bilal, D. (2005). Children's Information Seeking and the Design of Digital Interfaces in the Affective Paradigm. *Library Trends, 54,* no. 2, 197–208.

Bilal, D., & Watson, J. S. (1998). Children's Paperless Projects: Inspiring Research via the Web. In *Proceedings of the 64th IFLA General Conference, August 16–21, 1998, Amsterdam, The Netherlands* (101–107, Booklet 3). Amsterdam: Xerox. Available: http://archive.ifla.org/IV/ifla64/009-131e.htm (accessed November 10, 2010).

Bishop, W. W. (1986). Training in the Use of Books. In L. L. Hardesty, J. P. Schmitt, & J. M. Tucker (Eds.), *User Instruction in Academic Libraries: A Century of Selected Readings* (pp. 69–85). Metuchen, NJ: Scarecrow Press.

Black, S., & Allen, J. D. (2018). Part 5: Learning Is a Social Act. *The Reference Librarian, 59,* no. 2, 76–91.

Bloom, B. (1956). *Taxonomy of Educational Objectives.* New York: David McKay.

Blue, E. V., & Pace, D. (2011). UD and UDL: Paving the Way toward Inclusion and Independence in the School Library. *Knowledge Quest, 39,* no. 3, 48–54.

Bobotis, N. C. (1978). *Relationship of Modes of Instruction and Bilingualism to Achievement in Library Skills.* PhD diss., University of New Mexico.

Bodi, S. (1992). Collaborating with Faculty in Teaching Critical Thinking: The Role of Librarians. *Research Strategies, 10,* no. 2, 69–76.

Bogel, G. (2012). Public Library Summer Reading Programs Contribute to Reading Progress and Proficiency. *Evidence Based Library & Information Practice, 7,* no. 1, 102–104.

Bogen, J. E. (1969). Some Educational Aspects of Hemispheric Specialization. *UCLA Educator, 17,* 24–32.

Boggiano, A. K., Flink, C., Shields, A., Seelbach, A., & Barrett, M. (1993). Use of Techniques Promoting Students' Self-Determination: Effects on Students' Analytic Problem-Solving Skills. *Motivation and Emotion, 17,* no. 4, 319–336.

Bondy, E. (1984). Thinking about Thinking: Encouraging Children's Use of Metacognitive Processes. *Childhood Education, 60,* no. 4, 234–238.

Borgman, C. L., Hirsh, S. G., Walter, V. A., & Gallagher, A. L. (1995). Children's Searching Behavior on Browsing and Keyword Online Catalogs: The Science Library Catalog Project. *Journal of the American Society for Information Science, 46,* no. 9, 663–684.

Bowie, M. M. (Comp.). (1986). *Historic Documents of School Libraries.* Fayetteville, AR: Hi Willow Research Publishing.

Bowler, L., Julien, H., & Haddon, L. (2018). Exploring youth information-seeking behaviour and mobile technologies through a secondary analysis of qualitative data. *Journal of Librarianship and Information Science, 50,* no. 3, 322–331. Available: doi:http://dx.doi.org.unk.idm.oclc.org/10.1177/0961000 618769967.

Bowles-Terry, M., & Donovan, C. (2016). Serving Notice on the One-Shot; Changing Roles for Instruction Librarians. *International Information & Library Review, 48,* no. 2, 137–142.

Bracy, P. (1990). Completed Research Pertinent to School Library Media Programs. In J. B. Smith (Ed.), *School Library Media Annual* (Vol. 8, pp. 126–134). Littleton, CO: Libraries Unlimited.

Branch, J. L. (2003). Instructional Intervention Is Key: Supporting Adolescent Information Seeking. *School Libraries Worldwide, 9,* no. 2, 47–61.

Branscomb, H. (1940). *Teaching with Books: A Study of College Libraries.* Chicago: American Library Association.

Bransford, J. D., Brown, A. L., & Cocking, R. R. (2000). *How People Learn: Brain, Mind, Experience, and School.* Washington, DC: National Academy Press.

Breivik, P. S., & Senn, J. A. (1994). *Information Literacy: Educating Children for the 21st Century.* New York: Scholastic.

Brien, D. P. (1995). *The Teaching and Learning Processes Involved in Primary School Children's Research Projects.* EdD diss., University of New South Wales.

Broch, E. (2000). Children's Search Engines from an Information Search Process Perspective. *School Library Media Research, 3.* Available: http://www.ala.org /ala/mgrps/divs/aasl/aaslpubsandjournals/slmrb/slmrcontents/volume 32000/childrens.cfm (accessed May 26, 2010).

Brodie, C. S. (1988). *Library Programs for the Gifted and Talented: Differentiated versus Traditional.* PhD diss., Texas Women's University.

Brown, J. S., Collins, A., & Duguid, P. (1989). Situated Cognition and the Culture of Learning. *Educational Researcher, 18,* no. 1, 32–42.

Bruce, H. (1994). Media Center Automation: A Watershed for the School Library Media Specials. *School Library Media Quarterly, 22,* no. 4, 206–212.

Bruner, J. (1975). *Toward a Theory of Instruction.* Cambridge, MA: Harvard University Press.

Bruner, J. (1977). *The Process of Education.* Cambridge, MA: Harvard University Press.

Bruner, J. (1980). *Beyond the Information Given.* New York: Norton.

Bruner, J. (1986). *Actual Minds, Possible Worlds.* Cambridge, MA: Harvard University Press.

Buchanan, S., Harlan, M. A., Bruce, C., & Edwards, S. (2016). Inquiry Based Learning Models, Information Literacy, and Student Engagement: A Literature Review. *School Libraries Worldwide, 22,* no. 2, 23–39.

Buerkett, R. (2011). Inquiry and Assessment Using Web 2.0 Tools. *School Library Monthly, 28,* no. 1, 21–24.

Burdick, T. A. (1996). Success and Diversity in Information Seeking: Gender and the Information Search Styles Model. *School Library Media Quarterly, 25,* no. 1, 19–26.

Burdick, T. A. (1997). Snakes and Snails and Puppy Dog Tails: Girls and Boys Expressing Voice in Information Research Projects. *Journal of Youth Services in Libraries, 11,* no. 1, 28–36.

Butler, P. (1933). *An Introduction to Library Science.* Chicago: University of Chicago Press.

Buzan, T. (1991). *Use Both Sides of Your Brain.* New York: Dutton.

Cai, Z., Fan, X., & Du, J. (2017). Gender and Attitudes toward Technology Use: A Meta-Analysis. *Computers & Education, 105,* 1–13.

Callison, D. (1986). School Library Media Programs and Free Inquiry Learning. *School Library Media Quarterly, 15,* no. 6, 20–24.

Callison, D. (1990). A Review of the Research Related to School Library Media Collections: Part I. *School Library Media Quarterly, 19,* no. 1, 57–62.

Callison, D. (1994). Expanding the Evaluation Role in the Critical-Thinking Curriculum. In C. C. Kuhlthau, M. E. Goodin, & M. J. McNally (Eds.), *Assessment in the School Library Media Center* (pp. 43–57). Englewood, CO: Libraries Unlimited.

Callison, D. (2006). Editor's Choice: Enough Already? Blazing New Trails for School Library Research: An Interview with Keith Curry Lance, Director, Library Research Service, Colorado State Library & University of Denver. *School Library Media Research,* 1–12. Available: http://www.ala.org/ala/mgrps/divs /aasl/aaslpubsandjournals/slmrb/editorschoiceb/lance/interviewlance .cfm (accessed January 23, 2010).

Callison, D., & Baker, K. (2014). Elements of Information Inquiry, Evolution of Models and Measured Reflection. *Knowledge Quest, 43,* no. 2, 18–24.

Canada, K., & Brusca, F. (1991). The Technological Gender Gap: Evidence and Recommendations for Educators and Computer-Based Instruction Designers. *Educational Technology Research and Development, 39,* no. 2, 43–51.

Carey, J. O. (1997, April). *From Library Skills to Information Literacy: Implications for Teaching and Learning.* Presentation at Treasure Mountain Research Retreat, Portland, OR.

Carey, J. O. (1998). Library Skills, Information Skills, and Information Literacy: Implications for Teaching and Learning. *School Library Media Quarterly Online,* 1. Available: http://www.ala.org/aasl/pubs/slr/vol1 (accessed December 12, 2018).

Carey, S. (1985). Are Children Fundamentally Different Kinds of Thinkers and Learners Than Adults? In S. F. Chipman & J. W. Segal (Eds.), *Thinking and Learning Skills* (pp. 485–517). Hillsdale, NJ: Lawrence Erlbaum.

Carroll, F. L. (1981). *Recent Advances in School Librarianship.* Oxford: Pergamon Press.

Carson, C. H., & Curtis, R. V. (1991). Applying Instructional Design Theory to Bibliographic Instruction: Microtheory. *Research Strategies, 9,* no. 2, 20–76.

Carvin, A. (2000a). *Beyond Access: Understanding the Digital Divide.* Keynote Address, New York University Third Act Conference, May 19, 2000.

Carvin, A. (2000b). *Mending the Breach: Overcoming the Digital Divide.* Available: http://www.edutopia.org/mending-breach-overcoming-digital-divide (accessed May 26, 2010).

Casstevens, S. W. (2017). *Joint Use Library Standards for Texas School/Public Libraries: A Delphi Study.* EdD treatise, Dallas Baptist University.

Cecil, H. L., & Heaps, W. A. (1940). School Library Service in the United States: An Interpretive Survey. In M. M. Bowie (Comp.), *Historic Documents of School Libraries.* Fayetteville, AR: Hi Willow Research Publishing, 1986.

Center for Applied Special Technology. (2019). *About Universal Design for Learning.* Available: http://www.cast.org/our-work/about-udl.html#.XjNSSRNKi3c.

Center for Inspired Teaching. (2008). *Issue Brief: Inquiry-Based Teaching.* Available: https://inspiredteaching.org/wp-content/uploads/impact-research-briefs-inquiry-based-teaching.pdf (accessed May 24, 2019).

Chatman, E. A. (1996). The Impoverished Life-World of Outsiders. *Journal of the American Society for Information Science and Technology, 47,* no. 3, 193–206.

Chelton, M. K. (1997). *Adult-Adolescent Service Encounters: The Library Context.* PhD diss., Rutgers University.

Chelton, M. K. (1999). Structural and Theoretical Constraints on Reference Service in a High School Library Media Center. *Reference & User Services Quarterly,* 38, no. 3, 275–287.

Chen, J. Q. (2004). Theory of Multiple Intelligences: Is it a Scientific Theory? *Teachers College Record, 106,* 17–23.

Chen, L. C., Huang, T. W., & Chen, Y. H. (2017). The Effects of Inquiry-Based Information Literacy Instruction on Memory and Comprehension: A Longitudinal Study. *Library & Information Science Research, 39,* no. 4, 256–266.

Chen, S.-H. (1993). A Study of High School Students' Online Catalog Searching Behavior. *School Library Media Quarterly, 22,* no. 1, 33–40.

Childress, S., & Benson, S. (2014). Personalized Learning for Every Student Every Day. *Phi Delta Kappan, 95,* no. 8, 33–38.

Chirkov, V. I., & Ryan, R. M. (2001). Parent and Teacher Autonomy Support in Russian and U.S. Adolescents. *Journal of Cross-Cultural Psychology, 32,* 618–635.

Chirkov, V. I., Ryan, R. M., Kim, Y., & Kaplan, U. (2003). Differentiating Autonomy from Individualism and Independence: A Self-Determination Theory Perspective on Internalization of Cultural Orientations and Well-Being. *Journal of Personality and Social Psychology, 84,* no. 1, 97–110. Available: http://dx.doi.org/10.1037/0022-3514.84.1.97.

Chooi, W., Long, H. E., & Thompson, L. A. (2014). The Sternberg Triarchic Abilities Test (Level-H) Is a Measure of g. *Journal of Intelligence, 2,* no. 3, 56–67.

Chow, A. S., & Croxton, R. A. (2014). A Usability Evaluation of Academic Virtual Reference Services. *College & Research Libraries, 75,* no. 3, 309–361.

Cianciolo, A. T., & Sternberg, R. J. (2008). *Intelligence: A Brief History.* Blackwell Brief Histories of Psychology. Malden, MA: Blackwell.

Clark, L. A., & Halford, G. S. (1983). Does Cognitive Style Account for Cultural Differences in Scholastic Achievement? *Journal of Cross-Cultural Psychology, 14,* no. 3, 279–296.

Clarke, J., Martell, K., & Willey, C. (1994). Sequencing Graphic Organizers to Guide Historical Research. *The Social Studies, 85,* no. 5, 70–78.

Claxton, C. S. (1990). Learning Styles, Minority Students, and Effective Education. *Journal of Developmental Education, 14,* no. 1, 6–8, 35.

Coffman, S. (2002). What's Wrong with Collaborative Digital Reference? *American Libraries, 33,* no. 11, 56–58.

Cohen, N., Holdsworth, L., Prechtel, J. P., Newby, J., Mery, Y., Pfander, J., & Eagleson, L. E. (2016). A Survey of Information Literacy Credit Courses in US Academic Libraries. *Reference Services Review, 44,* no. 4, 564–582.

Coiro, J. (2011). Talking about Reading as Thinking: Modeling the Hidden Complexities of Online Reading Comprehension. *Theory into Practice, 50,* no. 2, 107–115.

Coiro, J., Coscarelli, C., Maykel, C., & Forzani, E. (2015). Investigating Criteria That Seventh Graders Use to Evaluate the Quality of Online Information. *Journal of Adolescent & Adult Literacy, 59,* no. 3, 287–297.

Coker, E. (2015). *Certified Teacher-Librarians, Library Quality and Student Achievement in Washington State Public Schools.* Edmonds, WA: Washington Library Media Association.

Coleman, J., Mallon, M. N., & Lo, L. (2016). Recent Changes to Reference Services in Academic Libraries and Their Relationship to Perceived Quality: Results of a National Survey. *Journal of Library Administration, 56,* no. 6, 673–696.

Coleman, J. G. (1989). Library Media Personnel: The Essential Ingredient. In J. B. Smith (Ed.), *School Library Media Annual* (Vol. 7, pp. 46–56). Englewood, CO: Libraries Unlimited.

Collins, A., Brown, J. S., & Newman, S. E. (1989). Cognitive Apprenticeship: Teaching the Crafts of Reading, Writing, and Mathematics. In L. B. Resnick (Ed.), *Knowing, Learning, and Instruction: Essays in Honor of Robert Glaser* (pp. 453–494). Hillsdale, NJ: Lawrence Erlbaum.

Colon-Aguirre, M., & Fleming-May, R. (2012). You Just Type in What You Are Looking For: Undergraduates' Use of Library Resources vs. Wikipedia. *The Journal of Academic Librarianship, 38,* no. 6, 391–399.

Comer, J. P. (2001, April 22). Schools That Develop Children. *The American Prospect Online, 12,* no. 7. Available: http://www.prospect.org/cs/articles?article =schools_that_develop_children (accessed May 26, 2010).

Common Core State Standards. (2012). Available: http://www.corestandards.org /read-the-standards (accessed May 24, 2019).

Common Core State Standards Initiative (CCSS). (2019). *Common Core State Standards for English Language Arts & Literacy in History/Social Studies, Science and Technical Subjects.* Available: http://www.corestandards.org.

Condliffe, B., Visher, M. G., Bangser, M. R., Drohojowska, S., & Saco, L. (2017). *Project-Based Learning: A Literature Review.* Available: https://s3-us-west-1 .amazonaws.com/ler/MDRC+PBL+Literature+Review.pdf.

Connaway, L. S., Radford, M. L., Dickey, T. J., Williams, J. D., & Confer, P. C. (2008). Sense-Making and Synchronicity: Information-Seeking Behaviors of Millennials and Baby Boomers. *Libri, 58,* 123–135.

Connaway, L. S., & Randall, K. M. (2013). Why the Internet Is More Attractive Than the Library. *The Serials Librarian, 64,* 41–56.

Cooper, L. Z. (2002). A Case Study of Information-Seeking Behavior in 7-Year-Old Children in a Semi-Structured Situation. *Journal of the American Society for Information Science and Technology, 53,* no. 11, 904–922.

Cote, M., Kochkina, S., & Mawhinney, T. (2016). Do You Want to Chat? Reevaluating Organization of Virtual Reference Service at an Academic Library. *Reference & User Services Quarterly, 56,* no. 1, 36–46.

Cottrell, J. R., & Eisenberg, M. B. (2001). Applying an Information Problem-Solving Model to Academic Reference Work: Findings and Implications. *College & Research Libraries, 62,* no. 4, 334–347.

Cox, J. E. (2004). *Accessibility of Rural Missouri Library Media Centers.* Master's thesis, Central Missouri State University. UMI No. 1421608.

Craver, K. W. (1989). Critical Thinking: Implications from Research. *School Library Media Quarterly, 18,* no. 1, 13–18.

Craver, K. W. (1995). Shaping Our Future: The Role of School Library Media Centers. *School Library Media Quarterly, 24,* no. 1, 13–18.

Creanor, L., Durndell, H., Henderson, F. P., Primrose, C., Brown, M. I., Draper, S. W., & McAteer, E. (1995). *A Hypertext Approach to Information Skills: Development and Evaluation.* Glasgow, Scotland: University of Glasgow Series, TLT Publications.

Creative Commons. (2010). *About.* Available: http://creativecommons.org/about (accessed November 10, 2010).

Crow, S. R. (2004). The Colorado Children's Book Award Program: Why All the Shouting? *Colorado Libraries,* Spring, 17–20.

Crow, S. R. (2009). Relationships That Foster Intrinsic Motivation for Information Seeking. *School Libraries Worldwide, 15,* no. 2, 91–112.

Crow, S. R. (2010). Children's Choice Book Award Programs: Effective Weapons in the Battle to Get and Keep Kids Reading. *School Library Monthly, 26,* no. 9, 12–13.

Crow, S. R. (2011). Exploring the Experiences of Upper Elementary School Children Who Are Intrinsically Motivated to Seek Information. *School Library Research, 14.* Available: http://www.ala.org/aasl/slr/volume14/crow.

Crow, S. R. (2015). The Information-Seeking Behavior of Intrinsically Motivated Elementary School Children of a Collectivist Culture. *School Library Research, 18.* Available: http://www.ala.org/aasl/sites/ala.org.aasl/files/content/aaslpubsandjournals/slr/vol18/SLR_InformationSeeking Behavior_V18.pdf.

Crow, S. R., & Kastello, L. (2016). The Dispositions of Elementary School Children of Individualistic and Collectivist Cultures Who Are Intrinsically Motivated to Seek Information. *School Library Research, 19.* Available: http://www.ala.org/aasl/slr/volume19/crow-kastello.

Crow, S. R., & Kastello, L. (2017). A Tale of Three Cities: Fostering Intrinsic Motivation for Information Seeking in Children of Diverse Cultures. *International Education Studies, 10,* no. 5, 157–166.

Csikszentmihalyi, M. (1975). *Beyond Boredom and Anxiety.* San Francisco: Jossey-Bass.

Csikszentmihalyi, M. (1990). *Flow: The Psychology of Optimal Experience.* New York: Harper & Row.

Csikszentmihalyi, M., & Hermanson, K. (1999). Intrinsic Motivation in Museums: Why Does One Want to Learn? In E. Hooper-Greenhill (Ed.), *The Educational Role of the Museum* (2nd ed., pp. 147–160). New York: Routledge.

Dahlgren, M. A., and Öberg, G. (2001). Questioning to Learn and Learning to Question: Structure and Function of Problem-Based Learning Scenarios in Environmental Science Education. *Higher Education, 44,* no. 3, 263–282.

Dauterive, S., Bourgeois, J., & Simms, S. (2017). How Little Is Too Little? An Examination of Information Literacy Instruction Duration for Freshmen. *Journal of Information Literacy, 11,* no. 1, 204–219.

Davies, R. A. (1974). Educating Library Users in the Senior High School. In J. Lubans (Ed.), *Educating the Library User* (pp. 39–52). New York: Bowker.

Davies, R. A. (1979). *The School Library Media Program: Instructional Force for Excellence* (3rd ed.). New York: Bowker.

Deci, E. L. (1975). *Intrinsic Motivation.* New York: Plenum Press.

Deci, E. L., Nezlek, J., & Scheinman, L. (1981). Characteristics of the Rewarder and Intrinsic Motivation of the Rewardee. *Journal of Personality and Social Psychology, 40,* 1–10.

Deci, E. L., Schwartz, A. J., Sheinman, L., & Ryan, R. M. (1981). An Instrument to Assess Adults' Orientations toward Control versus Autonomy with Children: Reflections on Intrinsic Motivation and Perceived Competence. *Journal of Educational Psychology, 73,* 642–650.

Delpit, L. D. (1995). *Other People's Children: Cultural Conflict in the Classroom.* New York: The New Press.

Delpit, L. D., & Kohl, H. (2006). *Other People's Children: Cultural Conflict in the Classroom* (Updated ed.). New York: The New Press.

Denison, D. R., & Montgomery, D. (2012). Annoyance or Delight? College Students' Perspectives on Looking for Information. *Journal of Academic Librarianship, 38,* no. 6, 380–390.

Dervin, B. (1983). *An Overview of Sense-Making Research: Concepts, Methods, and Results to Date.* Seattle: School of Communication, University of Washington.

Dervin, B. (1989). Users as Research Inventions: How Research Categories Perpetuate Inequities. *Journal of Communication, 39,* no. 3, 216–232.

Dervin, B. (1999). The Implications of Connecting Metatheory to Method. *Information Processing & Management, 35,* no. 6, 727–750.

Dervin, B., & Dewdney, P. (1986). Neutral Questioning: A New Approach to the Reference Interview. *Research Quarterly, 35,* no. 4, 506–513.

Dervin, B., & Nilan, M. (1986). Information Needs and Uses. In M. E. Williams (Ed.), *Annual Review of Information Science and Technology* (ARIST) (Vol. 21, pp. 3–33). White Plains, NY: Knowledge Industry Publications.

DeVillar, R. A., & Faltis, C. J. (1991). *Computers and Cultural Diversity: Restructuring for School Success.* Albany, NY: SUNY Press.

Dewdney, P., & Ross, C. S. (1994). Flying a Light Aircraft: Reference Service Evaluation from the User's Viewpoint. *Reference Quarterly, 34,* no. 2, 217–230.

Dewees, K. B. (1987). *The Effect of Teaching Library Skills Using "The Pooh Step-by-Step Guide for Writing the Research Paper" at Lieder Elementary School in the Cypress Fairbanks Independent School District. A Research Report.* Houston: Prairie View A&M University. (ERIC ED 284 577)

Dewey, J. (1915). *The School and Society.* Chicago: University of Chicago Press.

Dewey, J. (1916). *Democracy and Education: An Introduction to the Philosophy of Education.* New York: Macmillan.

Dewey, J. (1933). *How We Think.* Lexington, MA: Heath.

Dickinson, D. W. (1981). Library Literacy: Who? When? Where? *Library Journal, 106,* no. 8, 853–855.

Dickinson, G., Kimmel, S., & Doll, C. (2015). Common Core and Common Good: Educational Standards and the Future of Libraries. *Library Quarterly, 85,* no. 3, 225–243.

Didier, E. K. (1982). *Relationships between Student Achievement in Reading and Library Media Programs and Personnel.* PhD diss., University of Michigan.

Didier, E. K. (1985). An Overview of Research on the Impact of School Library Media Programs on Student Achievement. *School Library Media Quarterly, 14,* no. 1, 33–36.

Diem, R. A. (1985). Computers in a School Environment: Preliminary Report of the Social Consequences. *Theory and Research in Social Education, 14,* no. 2, 163–170.

Dike, V. W. (1993). School Libraries/Media Centers. In R. Wedgeworth (Ed.), *World Encyclopedia of Library and Information Services* (3rd ed., pp. 743–753). Chicago: American Library Association.

Dolan, Jennifer E. (2016). Splicing the Divide: A Review of Research on the Evolving Digital Divide among K–12 Students. *Journal of Research on Technology in Education, 48,* no. 1, 16–37.

Donham, J. (2010). Deep Learning through Concept-Based Inquiry. *School Library Monthly, 27,* no. 1, 8–11.

Donham, J. (2016). Mental Scripts for Nurturing Student Dispositions of Inquiry. *Teacher Librarian, 43,* no. 4, 24–27.

Donham, J., Bishop, K., Kuhlthau, C. C., & Oberg, D. (2001). *Inquiry-Based Learning: Lessons from Library Power.* Worthington, OH: Linworth.

Donham, J., & Green, C. W. (2004). Developing a Culture of Collaboration: Librarian as Consultant. *Journal of Academic Librarianship, 30,* no. 4, 314–321.

Donham, J., Heinrich, J., & Bostwick, K. (2009). Mental Models of Research: Generating Authentic Questions. *College Teaching, 58,* no. 1, 8–14.

Donham, J., & Steele, M. (2008). Instructional Interventions across the Inquiry Process. *College and Undergraduate Libraries, 14,* no. 4, 3–18.

Dow, M. J. (2008). Teaching Ethical Behavior in the Global World of Information and the New AASL Standards. *School Library Media Activities Monthly, 25,* no. 4, 49–52.

Dow, M. J. I., Lakin, J. M., & Court, S. (2010). *Kansas School Library Media Statewide Study.* Presentation at KSDE Annual Conference, October 26–27, Wichita, KS.

Doyle, C. S. (1994). Information-Literate Use of Telecommunications. *CMLEA Journal, 17,* no. 2, 17–20.

Driver, R., Asoko, H., Leach, J., Mortimer, E., & Scott, P. (1994). Constructing Scientific Knowledge in the Classroom. *Educational Researcher, 23,* no. 1, 8–14.

Dubicki, E. (2013). Faculty Perceptions of Students' Information Literacy Skills Competencies. *Journal of Information Literacy, 7,* no. 2, 97–115.

Duby, H. R. (2018). What a Load of CRAAP: Evaluating Information in an Era of "Fake News." *Tennessee Libraries, 68,* no. 4, 4.

Duckworth, E. R. (2006). *"The Having of Wonderful Ideas" and Other Essays on Teaching and Learning* (3rd ed.). New York: Teachers College Press.

Duckworth, E. R. (2008). Teaching as Research. In A. Miletta & M. Miletta (Eds.), *Classroom Conversations: A Collection of Classics for Parents and Teachers* (pp. 119–144). New York: The New Press.

Dunn, R., Beasley, M., & Buchanan, K. (1994). What Do You Believe about How Culturally Diverse Students Learn? *Emergency Librarian, 22,* no. 1, 8–14.

Dunn, R., & Dunn, K. (1993). *Teaching Secondary Students through Their Individual Learning Styles: Practical Approaches for Grades 7–12.* Boston: Allyn & Bacon.

Dunn, R., & Dunn, K. (1999). *The Complete Guide to the Learning Styles Inservice System.* Boston: Allyn & Bacon.

Dunn, R., & Smith, J. B. (1990). Learning Styles and Library Media Programs. In J. B. Smith (Ed.), *School Library Media Annual* (Vol. 8, pp. 32–49). Englewood, CO: Libraries Unlimited.

Edmonds, L., Moore, P., & Balcom, K. M. (1990). The Effectiveness of an Online Catalog. *School Library Journal, 36,* no. 10, 28–32.

Educational Technology and Mobile Learning. (2018). *11 Great Kids Safe Search Engines.* Available: https://www.educatorstechnology.com/2018/01/11-great-kids-safe-search-engines.html.

Eisenberg, M. B., & Berkowitz, R. B. (1990). *Information Problem-Solving: The Big Six Skills Approach to Library and Information Skills Instruction.* Norwood, NJ: Ablex.

Eisenberg, M. B., & Berkowitz, R. B. (1996). *Helping with Homework: A Parent's Guide to Information Problem-Solving.* Syracuse, NY: ERIC Clearinghouse in Information and Technology.

Eisenberg, M. B., & Brown, M. K. (1992). Current Themes Regarding Library and Information Skills Instruction: Research Supporting and Research Lacking. *School Library Media Quarterly, 20,* no. 2, 103–109.

Eisenberg, M. B., Johnson, D., & Berkowitz, R. (2010). Information, Communication, and Technology (ICT) Skills Curriculum Based on the Big6Skills Approach to Information Problem-Solving. *Library Media Connection, 28,* 24–27.

Eisenberg, M. B., & Spitzer, K. L. (1991). Information Technology and Service in Schools. In M. E. Williams (Ed.), *Annual Review of Information Science and Technology* (ARIST) (Vol. 26, pp. 243–285). Medford, NJ: Learned Education.

Eisner, E. W. (1993). Why Standards May Not Improve Schools. *Educational Leadership, 50,* no. 5, 22–23.

Eisner, E. W. (2004). "Artistry in Teaching," *Cultural Commons.* In M. K. Smith, Elliot W. Eisner, Connoisseurship, Criticism and the Art of Education: The Encyclopedia of Informal Education. Available: www.infed.org/mobi/elliot-w-eisner-connoisseurship-criticism-and-the-art-of-education/.

Elmborg, J. (2016). Tending the Garden of Learning: Lifelong Learning as Corel Library Value. *Library Trends, 64,* no. 3, 533–555.

Ely, D. P. (1992). Response 1 to Ann Irving. In J. B. Smith (Ed.), *School Library Media Annual* (Vol. 10, pp. 46–47). Englewood, CO: Libraries Unlimited.

Enders, D. (2001). Crossing the Divide: A Survey of the High School Activities That Best Prepared Students to Write in College. *Clearing House, 75,* no. 2, 62–67.

Engledinger, E. A. (1988). Bibliographic Instruction and Critical Thinking: The Contribution of the Annotated Bibliography. *Research Quarterly, 28,* no. 2, 195–202.

Engledinger, E. A., & Stevens, B. R. (1984). Library Instruction within the Curriculum. *College & Research Libraries, 45,* no. 11, 593–598.

Ennis-Cole, D. & Smith, D. (2011). Assistive Technology and Autism: Expanding the Technology Leadership Role of the School Librarian. *School Libraries Worldwide, 17,* no. 2, 86–98.

Entwistle, N. (1981). *Styles of Learning and Teaching: An Integrative Outline of Educational Psychology.* Chichester, UK: Wiley.

Epps, A., & Nelson, M. S. (2013). One-Shot or Embedded? Assessing Different Delivery Timing for Information Resources Relevant to Assignments. *Evidence-Based Library & Information Practice, 8,* no. 1, 4–18.

Epstein, M. (2018). That Thing Is So Annoying: How Proactive Chat Helps Us Reach More Users. *College & Research Libraries News,* September 2018, 436–437.

Eriksen, E. H. (1968). *Identity, Youth, and Crisis.* New York: Norton.

Everhart, N. (2005). A Cross-Cultural Inquiry into the Levels of Implementation of Accelerated Reader and Its Effect on Motivation and Extent of Reading: Perspectives from Scotland and England. *School Library Media Research, 8,* 1–15. Available: http://www.ala.org/ala/aasl/aaslpubsandjournals/slmrb/slmr contents/volume82005/reader.htm (accessed September 10, 2010).

Fabbi, J. L. (2015). Fortifying the Pipeline: A Quantitative Exploration of High School Factors Impacting the Information Literacy of First-Year College Students. *College & Research Libraries, 76,* no. 1, 31–42.

Fan, S. C., Fought, R. L., & Gahn, P. C. (2017). Adding a Feature: Can a Pop-Up Chat Box Enhance Virtual Reference Services? *Medical Reference Services Quarterly, 36,* no. 3, 220–228.

Farber, E. I. (1995). Bibliographic Instruction, Briefly. In Fifteenth Anniversary Task Force, Library Instruction Round Table, American Library Association (Comp.), *Information for a New Age: Redefining the Librarian* (pp. 153–169). Englewood, CO: Libraries Unlimited.

Farkas, M. (2018). Beyond Fake News: Determining What Sources to Trust. *American Libraries, 49,* no. 6, 78.

Farrell, R., & Badke, W. (2015). Situating Information Literacy in the Disciplines. *Reference Services Review, 43,* no. 2, 319–340.

Feldman, D. H. (Ed.). (1994). *Beyond Universals in Cognitive Development* (2nd ed.). Westport, CT: Ablex.

Ferer, E. (2012). Working Together: Library and Writing Center Collaboration. *Reference Services Review, 40,* no. 4, 543–547.

Fidel, R., Davies, R. K., Douglass, M. H., Holder, J. K., Hopkins, C. J., Kushner, E. J., Miyagishima, B. K., & Toney, C. D. (1999). A Visit to the Information Mall: Web Searching Behavior of High School Students. *Journal of the American Society for Information Science, 50,* no. 1, 24–37.

Fitzgerald, M. A. (1999). Evaluating Information: An Information Literacy Challenge. *School Library Media Research, 2.* Available: http://www.ala.org/aasl/pubs /slr/vol2 (accessed December 12, 2018).

Fjällbrant, N., & Sjöstrand, B. (1983). Bridging the Gap: Library User Education to New User Categories. *Tidskrift för Dokumentation: The Nordic Journal of Documentation, 39,* no. 4, 106–110.

Flink, C., Boggiano, A. K., & Barrett, M. (1990). Controlling Teaching Strategies: Undermining Children's Self-Determination and Performance. *Journal of Personality and Social Psychology, 59,* 916–924.

Folk, A. L. (2016). Information Literacy in Postsecondary Education in the United Kingdom, the United States, Australia, and New Zealand. *Portal: Libraries & the Academy, 16,* no. 1, 11–31.

Ford, D. Y. (1996). *Reversing Underachievement among Gifted Black Students.* New York: Teachers College Press.

Forehand, G. A., Regosta, M., & Rock, D. A. (1976). *Conditions and Processes of Effective School Desegregation: Final Report.* Princeton, NJ: Educational Testing Service.

Fourie, J. A., & Kruger, J. A. (1995). Basic and Developmental Information Needs of Secondary School Pupils. *Mousaion, 13,* nos. 1/2, 225–249.

Francke, H., Sundin, O., & Limberg, L. (2011). Debating Credibility: The Shaping of Information Literacies in Upper Secondary School. *Journal of Documentation, 67,* no. 4, 675–694.

Frazier, D. U., & Paulson, F. L. (1992). How Portfolios Motivate Reluctant Writers. *Educational Leadership, 49,* no. 8, 62–65.

Freedman, K. (1989). Microcomputers and the Dynamics of Image Making and Social Life in Three Art Classrooms. *Journal of Research on Computing in Education, 21,* no. 3, 290–298.

Freedman, K., & Liu, M. (1996). The Importance of Computer Experience, Learning Processes, and Communication Patterns in Multicultural Networking. *Educational Technology Research and Development, 44,* no. 1, 43–59.

Freud, S. (1925). Instincts and Their Vicissitudes. In *Collected Papers* (Vol. 4). London: Hogarth.

Freud, S. (1957). On Narcissism. In *The Standard Edition of the Complete Works of Sigmund Freud* (Vol. 14). London: Hogarth Press.

Frohmann, B. (1992). The Power of Image: A Discourse Analysis of the Cognitive Viewpoint. *Journal of Documentation, 48,* no. 4, 365–386.

Gallivan, M. F. (1974). Research on Children's Services in Libraries: An Annotated Bibliography. *Top of the News, 30,* no. 3, 275–293.

Gardner, H. (1983). *Frames of Mind: The Theory of Multiple Intelligences.* New York: Basic Books.

Gardner, H. (1996). Probing More Deeply into the Theory of Multiple Intelligences. *NASSP Bulletin, 80,* no. 583, 1–7.

Gardner, H. (1999). *Intelligence Reframed: Multiple Intelligences for the 21st Century*. New York: Basic Books.

Gardner, H. (2003, April 21). *Multiple Intelligences after Twenty Years*. Paper presented at the annual meeting of the American Educational Research Association, Chicago. Available: http://www.pz.harvard.edu/PIs/HG_MI_after_20_years.pdf (accessed November 8, 2010).

Garland, K. (1995). The Information Search Process: A Study of Elements Associated with Meaningful Research Tasks. In B. J. Morris, J. L. McQuiston, & C. L. Saretsky (Eds.), *School Library Media Annual* (Vol. 13, pp. 171–183). Englewood, CO: Libraries Unlimited.

Garrison, K. L., FitzGerald, L., & Sheerman, A. (2018). Just Let Me Go at It: Exploring Students' Use and Perceptions of Guided Inquiry. *School Library Research, 21*, 1–37.

Gaver, M. V. (1963). *Effectiveness of Centralized Library Service in Elementary Schools*. New Brunswick, NJ: Rutgers University Press.

Gavigan, K., & Lance, K. C. (2015). Everybody's Teacher. *Teacher Librarian, 43*, no. 1, 8–11.

Gedeon, R. (2000). Accessing the Right Brain with Bibliographic Instruction. *Research Strategies, 16*, no. 4, 259–269.

Gehlken, V. S. (1994). *The Role of the High School Library Media Program in Three Nationally Recognized South Carolina Blue Ribbon Secondary Schools*. PhD diss., University of South Carolina.

German, E. (2017). LibGuides for Instruction. *Reference & User Services Quarterly, 56*, no. 3, 162–167.

Gerrity, C. (2018). The New National School Library Standards: Implications for Information Literacy Instruction in Higher Education. *Journal of Academic Librarianship, 44*, no. 4, 455–458.

Gersten, R., Compton, D., Connor, C. M., Dimino, J., Santoro, L., Linan-Thompson, S., & Tilly, W. D. (2009). *Assisting Students Struggling with Reading: Response to Intervention (RtI) and Multi-Tier Intervention for Reading in the Primary Grades* (NCEE 2009–4045). Washington, DE: Institute of Education Sciences.

Ghikas, M. W. (1989). Collection Management for the 21st Century. In P. Woodrom (Ed.), *Managing Public Libraries in the 21st Century* (pp. 119–135). New York: Haworth Press.

Gifford, V., & Gifford, J. (1984). *Effects of Teaching a Library Usage Unit to Seventh Graders*. Paper presented at the annual conference of the Mid-South Educational Research Association, New Orleans. (ERIC ED 254 230)

Gillespie, J. T., & Spirt, D. L. (1973). *Creating a School Media Program*. New York: Bowker.

Gilligan, C. (1982). *In a Different Voice*. Cambridge, MA: Harvard University Press.

Gilliland, M. J. (1986). Can Libraries Make a Difference? Test Scores Say "Yes"! *School Library Media Quarterly, 15*, no. 2, 67–70.

Goffman, E. (1967). *Interaction Ritual: Essays in Face-to-Face Behavior*. New York: Pantheon.

Goodin, M. E. (1987). *The Transferability of Library Skills from High School to College*. PhD diss., Rutgers University.

Goodin, M. E. (1991). The Transferability of Library Research Skills from High School to College. *School Library Media Quarterly, 20*, no. 1, 33–41.

Gordon, C. (1999). Students as Authentic Researchers: A New Perspective for the High School Research Assignment. *School Library Media Research, 2*. Available: http://www.ala.org/aasl/pubs/slr/vol2 (accessed May 22, 2019).

Gordon, C. (2000). The Effects of Concept Mapping on the Searching Behavior of Tenth-Grade Students. *School Library Media Research, 3.* Available: http://www.ala.org/aasl/pubs/slr/vol3 (accessed May 22, 2019).

Gordon, C. (2010). The Culture of Inquiry in School Libraries. *School Libraries Worldwide, 16,* no. 1, 73–88.

Gordon, C., & Lu, Y. (2008). "I Hate to Read—or Do I?": Low Achievers and Their Reading. *School Library Media Research, 11,* 1–13. Available: http://www.aasl.org/ala/mgrps/divs/aasl/aaslpubsandjournals/slmrb/slmrcontents/volume11/gordon_lu.cfm (accessed March 31, 2010).

Gordon, H. (1996). Hemisphericity. In J. G. Beaumont, P. M. Kenealy, & M. K. Rogers (Eds.), *The Blackwell Dictionary of Neuropsychology* (pp. 388–395). Cambridge, MA: Blackwell.

Gretes, F. (2013). *School Library Impact Studies: A Review of Findings and Guide to Sources.* Prepared for the Harry & Jeanette Weinberg Foundation. Available: https://www.baltimorelibraryproject.org/wp-content/uploads/downloads/2013/09/Library-Impact-Studies.pdf.

Greve, C. L. (1974). *The Relationship of the Availability of Libraries to the Academic Achievement of Iowa High School Seniors.* PhD diss., University of Denver.

Gross, M. (1995). The Imposed Query. *Research Quarterly, 35,* no. 2, 236–243.

Gross, M. (1997). Pilot Study on the Prevalence of Imposed Queries in a School Library Media Center. *School Library Media Quarterly, 25,* no. 3, 157–166.

Gross, M. (1999). Imposed Queries in the School Library Media Center: A Descriptive Study. *Library and Information Science Research, 21,* no. 4, 501–521.

Grouzet, F. M. E., Otis, N., & Pelletier, L. G. (2006). Longitudinal Cross-Gender Factorial Invariance of the Academic Motivation Scale. *Structural Equation Modeling, 13,* no. 1, 73–98. Available: http://dx.doi.org/10.1207/s15328007sem1301_4.

Grover, R. (1993). A Proposed Model for Diagnosing Information Needs. *School Library Media Quarterly, 21,* no. 2, 95–100.

Grover, R. (1994). Assessing Information Skills Instruction. *The Reference Librarian, 20,* no. 44, 173–189.

Grover, R., Blume, S., Dickerson, J., Lakin, J., & Schumacher, M. (1996). *An Interdisciplinary Model for Assessing Learning.* Paper presented at the Library Research Seminar I, Tallahassee, FL.

Hale-Benson, J. E. (1982). *Black Children: Their Roots, Culture, and Learning Styles.* Provo, UT: Brigham Young University Press.

Hall-Ellis, S. D., & Berry, M. A. (1995). School Library Media Centers and Academic Achievement in South Texas: Summary of a Survey of 79 Public Schools during the 1991–1992 School Year. *Texas Library Journal, 71,* 94–97.

Hamer, J. S. (2003). Coming-Out: Gay Males' Information Seeking. *School Libraries Worldwide, 9,* no. 2, 73–89.

Hamlin, D., & Peterson, P. E. (2018). Have States Maintained High Expectations for Student Performance? An Analysis of 2017 State Proficiency Standards. *Education Next, 18,* no. 4, 42–48.

Hanchett, T. W. (1988). The Rosenwald Schools and Black Education in North Carolina. *North Carolina Historical Review, 64,* 4.

Harada, V. H. (2002). Personalizing the Information Search Process: A Case Study of Journal Writing with Elementary-Age Students. *School Library Media Research, 5.* Available: http://www.ala.org/ala/mgrps/divs/aasl/aaslpubsandjournals/slmrb/slmrcontents/volume52002/harada.cfm (accessed November 7, 2010).

Harada, V. H. (2010). Self-Assessment: Challenging Students to Take Charge of Learning. *School Library Monthly, 26,* no. 10, 13–15.

Hardesty, L. L., Schmitt, J. P., & Tucker, J. M. (Comps.). (1986). *User Instruction in Academic Libraries: A Century of Selected Readings.* Metuchen, NJ: Scarecrow Press.

Harmon, C. T., & Bradburn, F. B. (1988). Realizing the Reading and Information Needs of Youth. *Library Trends, 37,* no. 1, 19–27.

Harris, P., & McKenzie, P. J. (2004). What It Means to Be "In-Between": A Focus Group Analysis of Barriers Faced by Children Aged 7 to 11 Using Public Libraries. *The Canadian Journal of Information and Library Science, 28,* no. 4, 3–24.

Harter, S. (1980). *A Scale of Intrinsic versus Extrinsic Orientation in the Classroom.* Available from Susan Harter, Department of Psychology, University of Denver, Denver, CO 80208.

Harter, S. (1981). A New Self-Report Scale of Intrinsic versus Extrinsic Orientation in the Classroom: Motivational and Informational Components. *Developmental Psychology, 17,* no. 3, 300–312.

Hartzell, G. N. (1994). *Building Influence for the School Librarian.* Worthington, OH: Linworth Publishing.

Hasler, L., Ruthven, I., & Buchanan, S. (2014). Using Internet Groups in Situations of Information Poverty: Topics and Information Needs. *Journal of the Association for Information Science and Technology, 65,* no. 1, 25–36.

Havighurst, R. I. (1953). *Human Development and Education.* New York: McKay.

Haycock, C. A. (1991). Resource-Based Learning: A Shift in the Roles of Teacher, Learner. *NASSP Bulletin, 75,* no. 535, 15–22.

Haycock, K. (1992). *What Works: Research about Teaching and Learning through the School's Library Resource Center.* Vancouver, BC: Rockland Press.

Head, A. (2013). Project Information Literacy: What Can Be Learned about the Information-Seeking Behavior of Today's College Students? *College & Research Libraries, 62,* no. 3, 275–278.

Head, A. (2017). Posing the Million-Dollar Question: What Happens after Graduation? *Journal of Information Literacy 11,* no. 1, 80–90.

Heath, R. A. (2015). Toward Learner-Centered High School Curriculum-Based Research: A Case Study. *Journal of Librarianship & Information Science, 47,* no. 4, 368–379.

Heeks, P. (1997). School Libraries. In J. Feather & P. Sturges (Eds.), *International Encyclopedia of Information and Library Science* (pp. 410–412). London: Routledge.

Heine, S. J., Lehman, D. R., Markus, H. R., & Kitayama, S. (1999). Is There a Universal Need for Positive Self-Regard? *Psychological Review, 106,* 766–794. Available: http://dx.doi.org/10.1037/0033-295X.106.4.766.

Heinström, J. (2006a). Fast Surfing for Availability or Deep Diving into Quality: Motivation and Information Seeking among Middle and High School Students. *Information Research, 11,* no. 4, 1–12. Available: http://information.net/ir//11-4/paper265.htm (accessed April 1, 2011).

Heinström, J. (2006b). Broad Exploration of Precise Specificity: Two Basic Information Seeking Patterns among Students. *Journal of the American Society for Information Science and Technology, 57,* no. 11, 1440–1450.

Hensley, R. (1991). Learning Style Theory and Learning Transfer Principles during Reference Interview Instruction. *Library Trends, 39,* no. 3, 203–209.

Herman, J. L. (1992). What Research Tells Us about Good Assessment. *Educational Leadership, 48,* no. 5, 74–78.

Herold, B. (2018, April 4). Students Home Internet, Computer Access: 10 Numbers to Know. *Digital Education: Tech Topic and Trends in K–12.* Available:

https://blogs.edweek.org/edweek/DigitalEducation/2018/04/gap_home
_internet_computer_access_study.html.

Hidi, S., & Ainley, M. (2008). Interest and Self-regulation: Relationships between Two Variables That Influence Learning. In D. Schunk & B. J. Zimmerman (Eds.), *Motivation and Self-Regulated Learning: Theory, Research, and Applications* (pp. 77–109). New York: Taylor & Francis.

Hidi, S., & Baird, W. (1986). Interestingness—A Neglected Variable in Discourse Processing. *Cognitive Science, 10,* no. 2, 179–194.

Hinchliffe, L. J., Rand, A., & Collier, J. (2018). Predictable Information Literacy Misconceptions of First-Year College Students. *Communications in Information Literacy, 12,* no. 1, 4–18.

Hirsh, S. G. (1997). How Do Children Find Information in Different Tasks? Children's Use of the Science Catalog. *Library Trends, 45,* no. 4, 725–745.

Hirsh, S. G. (1998). Relevance Determinations in Children's Use of Electronic Resources: A Case Study. *Proceedings of the ASIS Annual Meeting* (Vol. 35, pp. 63–72). Medford, NJ: Learned Information.

Hirsh, S. G. (1999). Children's Relevance Criteria and Information Seeking on Electronic Resources. *Journal of the American Society for Information Science, 50,* no. 14, 1265–1283.

Hofstede, G., & Bond, M. (1988). The Confucian Connection: From Cultural Roots to Economic Growth. *Organizational Dynamics, 16,* no. 4, 5–12.

Hofstede, G., Hofstede, G. J., & Minkov, M. (2010). *Cultures and Organizations: Software of the Mind* (3rd ed.). New York: McGraw-Hill.

Hofstede Insights. (2019). *About Gert Hofstede.* Available: https://www.hofstede-insights.com/about-us/about-geert-hofstede.

Holliday, W., & Li, Q. (2004). Understanding the Millennials: Updating Our Knowledge about Students. *Reference Services Review, 32,* no. 4, 356–366.

Honebein, P. (1996). Seven Goals for the Design of Constructivist Learning Environments. In B. G. Wilson (Ed.), *Constructivist Learning Environments: Case Studies in Instructional Design* (pp. 11–24). Englewood Cliffs, NJ: Educational Technology Publications.

Hooten, P. A. (1989). Online Catalogs: Will They Improve Children's Access? *Journal of Youth Services in Libraries, 2,* no. 3, 267–272.

Hopkins, D. M. (1989). Elementary School Library Media Programs and the Promotion of Positive Self-Concept: A Report of an Exploratory Study. *Library Quarterly, 59,* no. 2, 131–147.

Horrigan, J. B. (2016). *Libraries 2016.* Pew Research Center. Available: http://www.pewinternet.org/2016/09/09/2016/Libraries-2016.

Howe, H., II. (1993). *Thinking about Our Kids.* New York: Free Press.

Huang, S. (2012). A Mixed Method Study on the Effectiveness of the Accelerated Reader Program on Middle School Students' Reading Achievement and Motivation. *Reading Horizons, 51,* no. 3, 229–246.

Hull, C. L. (1943). *Principles of Behavior: An Introduction to Behavior Theory.* New York: Appleton-Century-Crofts.

Huston, M. M. (1989). Search Theory and Instruction of End Users of Online Bibliographic Information Retrieval Systems: A Literature Review. *Research Strategies, 7,* no. 1, 14–32.

Hyland, A. H. (1978). Recent Directions in Educating the Library Use: Elementary Schools. In J. Lubans Jr. (Ed.), *Progress in Educating the Library User* (pp. 29–44). New York: Bowker.

Hyldegärd, J. (2009). Beyond the Search Process: Exploring Group Members' Behavior in Context. *Information Processing & Management: An International Journal, 45,* no. 1, 142–158.

Inhelder, B., & Piaget, J. (1958). *The Growth of Logical Thinking: From Childhood to Adolescence*. New York: Basic Books.

International Society for Technology in Education. (2016). *ISTE Standards for Students*. Available: https://www.iste.org/standards/for-students (accessed May 20, 2019).

International Society for Technology in Education (ISTE). (2017). *The ISTE Standards*. Available: http://www.iste.org/standards (accessed December 14, 2018).

Ireland, S. (2018). Fake News Alerts: Teaching News Literacy Skills in a Meme World. *Reference Librarian, 59,* no. 3, 122–128.

Irvine, J. J., & Irvine, R. W. (1995). Black Youth in School: Individual Achievement and Instructional/Cultural Perspectives. In R. L. Taylor (Ed.), *African-American Youth: Their Social and Economic Status in the United States* (pp. 129–142). Westport, CT: Praeger.

Irving, A. (1983). Educating Information Users in Schools. In *British Library Research Reviews* (Vol. 4). London: British Library.

Irving, A. (1985). *Study and Information Skills across the Curriculum*. London: Heinemann.

Irving, A. (1990). Wider Horizons: Online Information Services in Schools. *Library and Information Research Report,* 80. London: British Library.

Irving, A. (1991). The Educational Value and Use of Online Information Services in Schools. *Computers and Education, 17,* no. 3, 213–225.

Jackson, M. M. (1994). Library Information Skills and Standardized Achievement Tests. In C. C. Kuhlthau, M. E. Goodin, & M. J. McNally (Eds.), *Assessment in the School Library Media Center* (pp. 25–32). Englewood, CO: Libraries Unlimited.

Jacobson, F. F. (1997). Introduction. *Library Trends, 45,* no. 4, 575–581.

Jacobson, F. F., & Ignacio, E. N. (1997). Teaching Reflection: Information Seeking and Evaluation in a Digital Library Environment. *Library Trends, 45,* no. 4, 771–802.

Jacobson, F. F., & Jacobson, M. J. (1993). Representative Cognitive Learning Theories and BI: A Case Study of End User Searching. *Research Strategies, 11,* no. 3, 124–137.

Jacobson, T. E., & Mark, B. L. (1995). Teaching in the Information Age: Active Learning Techniques to Empower Students. *The Reference Librarian,* nos. 51–52, 105–120.

Jakobovits, L. A., & Nahl-Jakobovits, D. (1990). Measuring Information Searching Competence. *Research Libraries, 51,* no. 5, 448–462.

Jang, H., Reeve, J., Ryan, R. M., & Kim, A. (2009). Can Self-Determination Theory Explain What Underlies the Productive, Satisfying Learning Experiences of Collectivistically Oriented Korean Students? *Journal of Educational Psychology, 101,* no. 3, 644–661. Available: http://dx.doi.org/10.1037/a0014241.

Jay, M. E. (1986). The Elementary School Library Media Teacher's Role in Educating Students to Think. *School Library Media Quarterly, 15,* no. 1, 28–32.

Joeckel, C. B. (1943). *Post-War Standards for Public Libraries*. Chicago: American Library Association.

Johnson, P. R. & Daumer, C. R. (1993). Intuitive Development: Communication in the Nineties. *Public Personnel Management, 22,* 263.

Johnston, M. P., & Green, L. S. (2018). Still Polishing the Diamond: School Library Research over the Last Decade. *School Library Research, 21.* Available: http://www.ala.org/aasl/slr/volume21/johnston-green.

Johnston, M. P., & Mandel, L. H. (2014). Are We Leaving Them Lost in the Woods with No Breadcrumbs to Follow? Assessing Signage Systems in School Libraries. *School Libraries Worldwide, 20,* no. 2, 38–53.

Jonassen, D. H., Myers, J. M., & McKillop, A. M. (1996). From Constructivism to Constructionism: Learning with Hypermedia/Multimedia Rather Than from It. In B. Wilson (Ed.), *Constructivist Learning Environments: Case Studies in Instructional Design* (pp. 93–106). Englewood Cliffs, NJ: Educational Technology Publications.

Jones, J., Martin, M., & Flohr, B. R. (2015). Theories Holding Promise for Supporting the Constructivist Behaviors of Inquiry. *School Libraries Worldwide, 21,* no. 2, 115–126.

Joyce, M. Z., & Tallman, J. I. (1997). *Making the Writing and Research Connection with the I-Search Process.* New York: Neal-Schuman.

Joyce, M. Z., & Tallman, J. I. (2006). *Making the Writing and Research Connection with the I-Search Process* (2nd ed.). New York: Neal-Schuman.

Julien, H. E. (1999). Barriers to Adolescents' Information Seeking for Career Decision-Making. *Journal of the American Society for Information Science, 50,* no. 1, 38–48.

Kafai, Y., & Bates, M. J. (1997). Internet Web-Searching Instruction in the Elementary Classroom: Building a Foundation for Information Literacy. *School Library Media Quarterly, 25,* no. 2, 103–111.

Kaiser Family Foundation. (2002). *See No Evil: How Internet Filters Affect the Search for Online Health Information: A Kaiser Family Foundation Study.* Available: http://www.kff.org/entmedia/upload/See-No-Evil-How-Internet-Filters-Affect-the-Search-for-Online-Health-Information-Executive-Summary.pdf (accessed May 26, 2010).

Kapitzke, C. (2009). Rethinking Copyrights for the Library through Creative Commons Licensing. *Library Trends, 58,* no. 1, 95–108.

Karasic, V. M. (2016). From Commons to Classroom: The Evolution of Learning Spaces in Academic Libraries. *Journal of Learning Spaces, 5,* no. 2, 53–60.

Kasasa (2019, April 22). *Boomers, Gen X, Gen Y, and Gen Z Explained.* Available: https://www.kasasa.com/articles/generations/gen-x-gen-y-gen-z.

Kavanaugh, J., and Rich, M. (2018). *Truth Decay: An Initial Exploration into the Diminishing Role of Facts and Analysis in American Public Life.* Santa Monica, CA: RAND Corporation.

Keeling, M. (2015). Building a performance evaluation system for school librarians. *School Library Monthly, 31,* no. 7, 12.

Keller, C. (2018). AASL Standards for Supporting Library Evaluation: Linking to Building, District, and State Levels. *Teacher Librarian, 45,* 17–21.

Keller, J. M. (1987). The Systematic Process of Motivational Design. *Performance and Instruction, 26,* no. 8, 1–8.

Kelly, G. A. (1963). *A Theory of Personality: The Psychology of Personal Constructs.* New York: Norton.

Kemp, J. H., Ellis, C. L., & Maloney, K. (2015). Standing by to Help: Transforming Online Reference with a Proactive Chat System. *Journal of Academic Librarianship, 41,* 764–770.

Kennedy, J. R., Jr. (1986). Integrated Library Instruction. In L. L. Hardesty, J. P. Schmitt, & J. M. Tucker (Comps.), *User Instruction in Academic Libraries: A Century of Selected Readings* (pp. 231–242). Metuchen, NJ: Scarecrow Press.

Kester, D. D. (1994). Secondary School Library and Information Skills: Are They Transferred from High School to College? *The Reference Librarian,* no. 44, 9–17.

Kirk, J., Poston-Anderson, B., & Yerbury, H. (1990). *Into the 21st Century: Library & Information Services in Schools.* Canberra: Australian Library and Information Association for the Commonwealth of Australia.

Kitzie, V. L. (2017). Affordances and Constraints in the Online Identity Work of LGBTQ+ Individuals. *Proceedings from the 80th Annual Meeting of the Association for Information Science & Technology*, Washington, DC, October 27–November 1, 2017, 222–231.

Kitzie, V. L., & Radford, M. L. (2017). Engaging at the Margins: Theoretical and Philosophical Approaches to Social Justice. *Proceedings from the 80th Annual Meeting of the Association for Information Science & Technology*, Washington, DC, October 27–November 1, 2017, 574–577.

Kleen, H., & Glock, S. (2018). A Further Look into Ethnicity: The Impact of Stereotypical Expectations on Teachers' Judgments of Female Ethnic Minority Students. *Social Psychology of Education, 21,* no. 4, 759–773.

Klipfel, K. M. (2014). Authentic Engagement: Assessing the Effects of Authenticity on Student Engagement and Information Literacy in Academic Library Instruction. *Reference Services Review, 42,* no. 2, 229–245.

Kluever, J., & Finley, W. (2012). Making Connections: Challenges and Benefits of Joint Use Libraries as Seen in One Community. *School Libraries Worldwide, 18,* no. 1, 48–55.

Knapp, P. B. (1966). *The Monteith College Library Experiment.* New York: Scarecrow Press.

Knapp, P. B. (1986). A Suggested Program of College Instruction in the Use of the Library. In L. L. Hardesty, J. P. Schmitt, & J. M. Tucker (Comps.), *User Instruction in Academic Libraries: A Century of Selected Readings* (pp. 151–166). Metuchen, NJ: Scarecrow Press.

Knutson, J. (2014). *Nurturing Critical Thinking in the Classroom with OPVL.* Available: https://www.kidsdiscover.com/teacherresources/critical-thinking-in -the-classroom/ (accessed October 25, 2018).

Koch, S. (1956). Behavior as "Intrinsically" Regulated: Work Notes toward a Pre-Theory of Phenomena Called "Motivational." In M. R. Jones (Ed.), *Nebraska Symposium on Motivation* (Vol. 4). Lincoln: University of Nebraska Press.

Koch, S. (1961). Psychological Science vs. the Science-Humanism Antinomy: Intimations of a Significant Science of Man. *American Psychologist, 16,* 629–639.

Koestner, R., Ryan, R. M., Bernieri, F., & Holt, K. (1984). Setting Limits on Children's Behavior: The Differential Effects of Controlling versus Informational Styles on Intrinsic Motivation and Creativity. *Journal of Personality, 52,* no. 3, 233–248.

Kohlberg, L. (1969). *Development of Moral Thought and Action.* New York: Holt, Rinehart & Winston.

Kolb, D. A. (1983). *Experiential Learning.* Englewood Cliffs, NJ: Prentice Hall.

Kolb, D. A., & Fry, R. E. (1975). Toward an Applied Theory of Experiential Learning. In C. Cooper (Ed.), *Theories of Group Process* (pp. 33–57). London: Wiley.

Koshik, I., & Okazawa, H. (2012). A Conversation Analytic Study of Actual and Potential Problems in Communication in Library Chat Reference Interactions. *Journal of the American Society for Information Science and Technology, 63,* no. 10, 2006–2019.

Kozol, J. (1994). *Savage Inequities: Children in America's Schools.* New York: Harper.

Kozol, J. (1996). *Amazing Grace: The Lives of Children and the Conscience of the Nation.* New York: Harper.

Kozol, J. (2000). An Unequal Education. *School Library Journal.* Available: http://www.schoollibraryjournal.com/article/CA153042.html (accessed May 27, 2010).

Kozol, J. (2006). *The Shame of the Nation: The Restoration of Apartheid in America.* New York: Three Rivers Press.

Krapp, A., & Fink, B. (1992). The Development and Function of Interests during the Critical Transition from Home to Preschool. In K. A. Renninger, S. Hidi, & A. Krapp (Eds.), *The Role of Interest in Learning and Development* (pp. 397–429). Hillsdale, NY: Lawrence Erlbaum.

Krashen, S. (1993). *The Power of Reading: Insights from Research.* Littleton, CO: Libraries Unlimited.

Krashen, S. (2003). The (Lack of) Experimental Evidence Supporting the Use of Accelerated Reader. *Journal of Children's Literature, 29,* no. 2, 9–30.

Krechevsky, M. (1991). Project Spectrum: An Innovative Assessment Alternative. *Educational Leadership, 48,* no. 5, 43–48.

Krueger, K. S. (2013). Evaluating Information with ABCD (Authority, Bias, Coverage, and Date). *School Library Monthly, 30,* no. 1, 36–38.

Kuhlthau, C. C. (1985). *Teaching the Library Research Process: A Step-by-Step Program for Secondary School Students.* West Nyack, NY: Center for Applied Research in Education.

Kuhlthau, C. C. (1987). An Emerging Theory of Library Instruction. *School Library Media Quarterly, 16,* no. 1, 23–27.

Kuhlthau, C. C. (1988a). Longitudinal Case Studies of the Information Search Process of Users in Libraries. *Library and Information Science Research, 10,* no. 3, 257–304.

Kuhlthau, C. C. (1988b). Perceptions of the Information Search Process in Libraries: A Study in Changes from High School through College. *Information Processing & Management, 24,* no. 4, 419–427.

Kuhlthau, C. C. (1991). Inside the Search Process: Information Seeking from the User's Perspective. *Journal of the American Society for Information Science, 42,* no. 5, 361–371.

Kuhlthau, C. C. (1993a). Implementing a Process Approach to Information Skills: A Study Identifying Indicators of Success in Library Media Programs. *School Library Media Quarterly, 22,* no. 1, 11–18.

Kuhlthau, C. C. (1993b). *Seeking Meaning.* Norwood, NJ: Ablex.

Kuhlthau, C. C. (1994). Assessing the Library Research Process. In C. C. Kuhlthau, M. E. Goodin, & M. J. McNally (Eds.), *Assessment and the School Library Media Center* (pp. 59–65). Englewood, CO: Libraries Unlimited.

Kuhlthau, C. C. (1995). The Process of Learning from Information. *School Libraries World Wide, 1,* no. 1, 1–13.

Kuhlthau, C. C. (1996). The Concept of a Zone of Intervention for Identifying the Role of Intermediaries in the Information Search Process. *Proceedings of the ASIS Annual Meeting.* Available: http://www.asis.org/annual-96/Electronic Proceedings/kuhlthau.html (accessed May 27, 2010).

Kuhlthau, C. C. (1997). Learning in Digital Libraries: An Information Search Process Approach. *Library Trends, 45,* no. 4, 708–724.

Kuhlthau, C. C. (1999). Accommodating the User's Information Search Process: Challenges for Information Retrieval Systems Designers. *Bulletin of the American Society for Information Science, 25,* no. 3. Available: http://www.asis.org/Bulletin/Feb-99/kuhlthau.html (accessed May 27, 2010).

Kuhlthau, C. C. (2001). *Rethinking Libraries for the Information Age School: Vital Roles in Inquiry Learning.* Keynote Address, International Association of School Librarians: Conference and International Research Forum on Research in School Librarianship, Auckland, New Zealand, July 9. Available: http://www.iasl-online.org/events/conf/keynote-kuhlthau2001.html (accessed May 27, 2010).

Kuhlthau, C. C. (2004). *Seeking Meaning: A Process Approach to Library and Information Services* (2nd ed.). Westport, CT: Libraries Unlimited.

Kuhlthau, C. C. (2005). Information Search Process. In K. E. Fisher, S. Erdelez, & L. McKechnie (Eds.), *Theories of Human Information Behavior.* Medford, NJ: Information Today.

Kuhlthau, C. C. (2013). Inquiry Inspires Original Research. *School Library Monthly, 30,* no. 2, 5–8.

Kuhlthau, C. C., Goodin, M. E., & McNally, M. J. (Eds.). (1996). *Assessment and the School Library Media Center.* Englewood, CO: Libraries Unlimited.

Kuhlthau, C. C., Heinström, J., & Todd, R. (2008). The "Information Search Process Revisited": Is the Model Still Useful? *Information Research, 13,* no. 4. Available: http://informationr.net/ir/13-4/paper355.html (accessed June 2, 2010).

Kuhlthau, C. C., & Maniotes, L. K. (2010). Building Guided Inquiry Teams for 21st-Century Learners. *School Library Monthly, 26,* no. 5, 18–21.

Kuhlthau, C. C., Maniotes, L. K., & Caspari, A. K. (2007). *Guided Inquiry: Learning in the 21st Century.* Westport, CT: Libraries Unlimited.

Kuhlthau, C. C., Maniotes, L. K., & Caspari, A. K. (2015). *Guided Inquiry: Learning in the 21st Century* (2nd ed.). Westport, CT: Libraries Unlimited.

Kuhlthau, C. C., & Todd, R. J. (2005a). Student Learning through Ohio School Libraries. Part 1: How Effective School Libraries Help Students. *School Libraries Worldwide, 11,* no. 1, 63–68.

Kuhlthau, C. C., & Todd, R. J. (2005b). Student Learning through Ohio School Libraries. Part 2: Faculty Perceptions of Effective School Libraries. *School Libraries Worldwide, 11,* no. 1, 89–110.

Kulleseid, E. R. (1986). Extending the Research Base: Schema Theory, Cognitive Styles, and Types of Intelligence. *School Library Media Quarterly, 15,* no. 1, 41–48.

Kuykendall, C. (2001). *Improving Black Student Achievement by Enhancing Student's Self Image.* Available: http://www.maec.org/achieve/achieve.html (accessed May 27, 2010).

Lance, K., Schwarz, B., & Rodney, M. J. (2014). *How Libraries Transform Schools by Contributing to Student Success: Evidence Linking South Carolina School Libraries and PASS & HSAP Results.* Columbia: South Carolina Association of School Libraries.

Lance, K. C., Hamilton-Pennell, C., Rodney, M. J., Peterson, L., & Sitter, C. (2000). *Information Empowered: The School Librarian as an Agent of Academic Achievement in Alaska Schools.* Available: http://www.library.state.ak.us/dev/infoemp.html (accessed May 27, 2010).

Lance, K. C., & Hofschire, L. (2012). *Change in School Librarian Staffing Linked with Changes in CSAP Reading Performance, 2005 to 2011.* Denver, CO: Library Research Service.

Lance, K. C., & Kachel, D. (2018). Why School Librarians Matter: What Years of Research Tell Us. *Phi Delta Kappan, 99,* no. 7, 15–20.

Lance, K. C., Rodney, M. J., & Hamilton-Pennell, C. (2000a). *How School Libraries Help Kids Achieve Standards. The Second Colorado Study.* Denver: Colorado Department of Education. Available: http://www.lrs.org/documents/lmcstudies/CO/execsumm.pdf (accessed May 27, 2010).

Lance, K. C., Rodney, M. J., & Hamilton-Pennell, C. (2000b). *Measuring Up to Standards: The Impact of School Library Programs and Information Literacy in Pennsylvania Schools.* Pennsylvania Department of Education Office of

Commonwealth Libraries. Gainsburg: Pennsylvania Citizens for Better Libraries. Available: http://www.lrs.org/impact.php (accessed May 27, 2010).

Lance, K. C., Rodney, M. J., & Hamilton-Pennell, C. (2001). *Good Schools Have
School Librarians: Oregon School Libraries Collaborate to Improve Academic
Achievement.* Salem: Oregon Educational Media Association. Available: http://
www.lrs.org/impact.php (accessed May 27, 2010).

Lance, K. C., Rodney, M. J., & Hamilton-Pennell, C. (2003). *How School Librarians
Improve Outcomes for Children: The New Mexico Study.* Santa Fe: New Mexico
State Library.

Lance, K. C., Welborn, L., & Hamilton-Pennell, C. (1992). *The Impact of School
Library Media Centers on Academic Achievement.* Denver: State Library and
Adult Education Office, Colorado Department of Education.

Lanning, S., & Mallek, J. (2017). Factors Influencing Information Literacy Competency of College Students. *Journal of Academic Librarianship, 43,* no. 5,
443–450.

Large, A., & Beheshti, J. (2000). The Web as a Classroom Resource: Reactions from
the Users. *Journal of the American Society for Information Science, 51,* no. 12,
1069–1080.

Latrobe, K., & Havener, W. M. (1997). The Information-Seeking Behavior of High
School Honors Students: An Exploratory Study. *Youth Services in Libraries,
10,* no. 2, 188–200.

Lau, J. (2006). *Guidelines on Information Literacy for Lifelong Learners.* The Hague,
Netherlands: International Federation of Library Associations. Available:
https://www.ifla.org/publications/guidelines-on-information-literacy-for
-lifelong-learning (accessed May 21, 2019).

Lazarus, W., & Mora, F. (2000). Online Content for Low-Income and Underserved
Americans: *The Digital Divide's New Frontier.* Available: http://www
.childrenspartnership.org (accessed May 27, 2010).

Lazear, D. (1991). *Seven Ways of Knowing: Teaching for Multiple Intelligences.* Palatine, IL: Skylight Publishing.

Lazear, D. (1999). *Multiple Intelligence Approaches to Assessment: Solving the
Assessment Conundrum.* Chicago: Zephyr Press.

Lee, E., & Hannafin, M. J. (2016). A Design Framework for Enhancing Engagement
in Student-Centered Learning: Own It, Learn It, and Share It. *Educational
Technology Research and Development, 64,* no. 4.

Lee, S., Ha, T., Lee, D., & Kim, J. H. (2018). Understanding the Majority Opinion
Formation Process in Online Environments: An Exploratory Approach to Facebook. *Information Processing & Management, 54,* no. 6, 1115–1128.

Lepper, M. R., Corpus, J. H., & Lyengar, S. S. (2005). Intrinsic and Extrinsic Motivational Orientations in the Classroom: Age Differences and Academic Cor-
relates. *Journal of Educational Psychology, 97,* no. 2, 184–196.

Levitov, D. (2014). School Librarians and the CCS: Knowing, Claiming, and Acting
on Their Expertise. In V. Harada & S. Coatney (Eds.), *Inquiry and the Common Core.* Santa Barbara, CA: Libraries Unlimited.

Lewis, K. R., Simmons, S., & Maniotes, L. (2018). Building a Culture for Learner
Voice and Choice through Inquiry. *Teacher Librarian, 45,* no. 4, 24–27.

Liebscher, P., & Marchionini, G. (1988). Browse and Analytical Search Strategies
in a Full-Text CD-ROM Encyclopedia. *School Library Media Quarterly, 16,*
no. 4, 223–233.

Liesener, J. W. (1985). Learning at Risk: School Library Media Programs in an Information World. *School Library Media Quarterly, 14,* no. 1, 11–20.

Lighthart, M., & Spreder, C. (2014). Partners in Lifelong Learning. *Knowledge Quest, 42,* no. 4, 32–37.

Limberg, L., Alexandersson, M., Lantz-Andersson, A., & Folkesson, L. (2008). What Matters? Shaping Meaningful Learning through Teaching Information Literacy. *Libri: International Journal of Libraries & Information Services, 58,* no. 2, 82–91.

Lin, P. (1994). Library Instruction for Culturally Diverse Populations: A Comparative Approach. *Research Strategies, 12,* no. 3, 168–173.

Lindlof, T. R. (1995). *Qualitative Communication Research Models.* Thousand Oaks, CA: Sage.

Linnenbrink, E. A., & Pintrich, P. R. (2002). Motivation as an Enabler for Academic Success. *School Psychology Review, 31,* no. 3, 313.

Little, G. (2012). Thinking about Discovery Layers. *The Journal of Academic Librarianship, 38,* no. 6, 346–347.

Loerke, K. (1994). Teaching the Library Research Process in Junior High. *School Libraries in Canada, 14,* no. 2, 23–26.

Loertscher, D. V. (1985). Collection Mapping: An Evaluation Strategy for Collection Development. *Drexel Library Quarterly, 21,* no. 2, 9–21.

Loertscher, D. V. (1996). A Farewell Challenge. *School Library Media Quarterly, 24,* no. 4, 192, 194.

Loertscher, D. V., Ho, M. L., & Bowie, M. M. (1987). "Exemplary Elementary Schools" and Their Library Media Center: A Research Report. *School Library Media Quarterly, 16,* no. 3, 147–153.

Loertscher, D. V., & Land, P. (1975). An Empirical Study of Media Services in Indiana Elementary Schools. *School Library Media Quarterly, 4,* no. 1, 8–18.

Loranger, A. L. (1994). The Study Strategies of Successful and Unsuccessful High School Students. *Journal of Reading Behavior, 26,* no. 2, 347–360.

Louis, P., & Harada, V. (2012). Did Students Get It? Self-Assessment as Key to Learning. *School Library Monthly, 29,* no. 3, 13–16.

Lovelace, M. K. (2005). Meta-Analysis of Experimental Research Based on the Dunn and Dunn Model. *Journal of Educational Research, 98,* no. 3, 176–183.

Lu, Y.-L. (2010). Children's Information Seeking in Coping with Daily-Life Problems: An Investigation of Fifth- and Sixth-Grade Students. *Library and Information Science Research, 32,* 77–88.

Lu, Y.-L., & Gordon, C. (2007). Reading Takes You Places: A Study of a Web-Based Summer Reading Program. *School Library Media Research, 10,* 1–14. Available: http://www.aasl.org/ala/mgrps/divs/aasl/aaslpubsandjournals/slmrb/slmrcontents/volume10/lu_reading.cfm.

Lubans, J. (Ed.). (1974). *Educating the Library User.* New York: Bowker.

Madaus, G. F., & Tan, A. G. A. (1994). The Growth of Assessment. In C. C. Kuhlthau, M. E. Goodin, & M. J. McNally (Eds.), *Assessment in the School Library Media Center* (pp. 1–24). Englewood, CO: Libraries Unlimited.

Maeroff, G. I. (1991). Assessing Alternative Assessment. *Phi Delta Kappan, 73,* no. 4, 273–281.

Maliszewski, D. P., & Soleas, E. K. (2018). *School Libraries Worldwide, 24,* no. 2, 46–61.

Mallette, M., Henk, W., & Melnick, S. (2004). The Influence of Accelerated Reader on the Affective Literacy Orientations of Intermediate Grade Students. *Journal of Literacy Research, 36,* no. 1, 73–84.

Mancall, J. C., Aaron, S. L., & Walker, S. A. (1986). Educating Students to Think: The Role of the School Library Media Program. *School Library Media Quarterly, 15,* no. 1, 18–27.

Mancall, J. C., Lodish, E. K., & Springer, J. (1992). Searching across the Curriculum. *Phi Delta Kappan, 73,* no. 7, 526–528.

Maniotes, L. (2005). *The Transformative Power of Literary Third Space.* PhD diss., University of Colorado.

Marchionini, G. (1987). An Invitation to Browse: Digital Text Systems for Novice Users. *Canadian Journal of Information Science, 12,* nos. 3–4, 69–79.

Marchionini, G. (1989). Information-Seeking Strategies of Novices Using a Full-Text Electronic Encyclopedia. *Journal of the American Society for Information Science, 40,* no. 1, 54–66.

Marchionini, G., & Teague, J. (1987). Elementary Students' Use of Electronic Information Service: An Exploratory Study. *Journal of Research in Computing in Education, 20,* no. 2, 139–155.

Marcus, D. L. (2002). Her Parents Look at Her as a Problem. *Knowledge Quest, 30,* no. 5, 19–21.

Marino, J., & Eisenberg, M. (2018). Beyond the Research Project: Inquiry Every Day and Every Way. *Knowledge Quest, 47,* no. 2, 56–60.

Mark, B. L., & Jacobson, T. E. (1995). Teaching Anxious Students Skills for the Electronic Library. *College Teaching, 42,* no. 1, 28–31.

Markless, S., & Streatfield, D. R. (2007). Three Decades of Information Literacy: Redefining the Parameters. In S. Andretta (Ed.), *Change and Challenge: Information Literacy for the 21st Century* (pp. 15–36). Blackwood, South Australia: Auslib Press. Available: http://www.informat.org/pdfs/streatfield-markless.pdf (accessed June 2, 2010).

Markuson, C. (1986). Making It Happen: Taking Charge of the Information Curriculum. *School Library Media Quarterly, 15,* no. 1, 37–40.

Martin, B. (1982). Interpersonal Relations and the School Library Media Specialist. *School Library Media Quarterly, 11,* no. 1, 43–44, 53–57.

Martinez, M. E. (1994). Access to Information Technologies among School-Age Children: Implications for a Democratic Society. *Journal of the Association for Information Science, 45,* no. 6, 393–400.

Marzano, R. J. (1992). *A Different Kind of Classroom: Teaching with Dimensions of Learning.* Alexandria, VA: Association for Supervision and Curriculum Development.

Marzano, R. J. (2000). *Designing a New Taxonomy of Educational Objectives.* Thousand Oaks, CA: Corwin Press.

Maslow, A. H. (1970). *Motivation and Personality.* New York: Harper & Row.

Maughan, S. (2016). Schools, Libraries, and Publishers Tackle the Summer Slide. *Publishers Weekly, 263,* no. 24, 44–50.

Maughan, S. (2017). School Librarians Are Teaching Digital Citizenship. *Publishers Weekly,* August 18, 2017. Available: https://www.publishersweekly.com/pw/by-topic/industry-news/libraries/article/74535-school-librarians-are-teaching-digital-citizenship.html.

Mayer, J., & Bowles-Terry, M. (2013). Engagement and Assessment in a Credit-Bearing Information Literacy Course. *Reference Services Review, 41,* no. 1, 62–79.

McCarthy, B. (1996). *About Learning.* Barrington, IL: Excel.

McDonald, F. B. (1988). Information Access for Youth: Issues and Concerns. *Library Trends, 37*(1), 28–42.

McGregor, J. H. (1994a). Cognitive Processes and the Use of Information: A Qualitative Study of Higher Order Thinking Skills Used in the Research Process by Students in a Gifted Program. *School Library Media Annual, 12,* 124–133.

McGregor, J. H. (1994b). Information Seeking and Use: Students' Thinking and Their Mental Models. *Youth Services in Libraries, 8,* no. 1, 69–76.

McGregor, J. H. (2002). Flexible Scheduling: How Does a Principal Facilitate Implementation? *School Libraries Worldwide, 8,* no. 1, 71–84.

McKinney, P. (2014). Information Literacy and Inquiry-Based Learning: Evaluation of a Five-Year Programme of Curriculum Development. *Journal of Librarianship and Information Science, 46,* no. 2, 148–166.

McNally, M. J. (2004). *Analysis of Students' Mental Models: Using the Internet in an Authentic Learning Situation.* PhD diss., Rutgers University.

McNally, M. J., & Kuhlthau, C. C. (1994). Information Search Process in Science Education. *The Reference Librarian, 20,* no. 44, 53–60.

Means, B., & Olson, K. (1994). The Link between Technology and Authentic Learning. *Educational Leadership, 51,* no. 7, 15–18.

Mediavilla, C. (2018). Staffing Your Homework-Help Center: Pairing the Right Minds with Student Learners. *American Libraries, 49,* nos. 7/8, 34–37.

Mendrinos, R. (1994). *Building Information Literacy Using High Technology: A Guide for Schools and Libraries.* Englewood, CO: Libraries Unlimited.

Menell, P. S. (2016). Adapting Copyright for the Mashup Generation. *University of Pennsylvania Law Review, 164,* 441–512.

Mery, Y., Newby, J., & Peng, K. (2012). Why One-Shot Information Literacy Sessions Are Not the Future of Instruction: A Case Study for Online Credit Courses. *College & Research Libraries, 73,* no. 4, 366–377.

Meyer, A., Rose, D. H., & Gordon, D. (2014). *Universal Design for Learning: Theory and Practice.* Wakefield, MA: CAST.

Meyer, C. A. (1994). What's the Difference between "Authentic" and "Performance" Assessment. In C. C. Kuhlthau, M. E. Goodin, & M. J. McNally (Eds.), *Assessment in the School Library Media Center* (pp. 99–101). Englewood, CO: Libraries Unlimited.

Miller, A. C. (2016). Confronting Confirmation Bias: Giving Truth a Fighting Chance in the Information Age. *Social Education, 80,* no. 5, 276–279.

Mitchell, M. S., Comer, C. H., Starkey, J. M., & Francis, E. A. (2011). Paradigm Shift in Reference Services at the Oberlin College Library: A Case Study. *Journal of Library Administration, 51,* no. 4, 359–374.

Moebius-Clune, B., Elsevier, I., Crawford, B., Trautmann, N., Schindelbeck, R., & van Es, H. (2011). Moving Authentic Soil Research into High School Classrooms: Student Engagement and Learning. *Journal of Natural Resources & Life Sciences Education, 40,* no. 1, 102–113.

Mokia, R., & Rolen, R. (2012). LibGuides: Improving Student and Faculty Access to Information Literacy. *Codex, 1,* no. 4, 37–45.

Mokros, H. B., Mullins, L. S., & Saracevic, T. (1995). Practice and Personhood in Professional Interaction: Exploring Social Identities in the Addressing of Information Needs. *LISR, 17,* no. 3, 237–257.

Momani R. T. H., & Gharaibeh, S. A. (2017). Investigating the Construct Validity of Sternberg's Triarchic Abilities Test Level-H (Arabic Version). *International Journal of Advanced and Applied Sciences, 4,* no. 11, 28.

Montgomery, P. (1997). Use of Information: The Information Literacy Phenomenon. In A. E Tepe & J. Calarco (Eds.), *A Handbook for Pathways to Knowledge* (pp. 8–10). McHenry, IL: Follett Software.

Moore, P. (1993). Information Problem Solving: A Wider View of Library Skills. *Contemporary Educational Psychology, 20,* no. 1, 1–31.

Moore, P. A., & St. George, A. (1991). Children as Information Seekers: The Cognitive Demands of Books and Library Systems. *School Library Media Quarterly, 19,* no. 3, 161–168.

Moorefield-Lang, H., & Kitzie, V. (2018). Makerspaces for All: Serving LGBTQ Makers in School Libraries. *Knowledge Quest, 47,* no. 1, 47–49.

Moran, M. (2010). *Young Learners Need Librarians, Not Just Google.* Available: http://forbes.com/2010/03/22/moran-librarian-skills-intelligent-investing -google.html (accessed June 2, 2010).

Moreillon, J. (2013). *Coteaching Reading Comprehension in Elementary School Libraries: Maximizing Your Impact.* Chicago: American Library Association Editions.

Moreillon, J. (2014a). Building Collaborative Relationships with Students. *School Library Monthly, 31,* no. 5, 27–28.

Moreillon, J. (2014b). Leadership: Fixed, Flexible, and Mixed Library Scheduling. *School Library Monthly, 30,* no. 7, 25–26.

Morton, C. (1996). The Modern Land of Laputa: Where Computers Are Used in Education. *Phi Delta Kappan, 77,* no. 6, 416–419.

Murray, J. (2001). Teaching Information Skills to Students with Disabilities: What Works? *School Libraries Worldwide, 7,* no. 2, 1–16.

Nahl, D., & Harada, V. H. (1996). Composing Boolean Search Statements: Self Confidence, Concept Analysis, Search Logic, and Errors. *School Library Media Quarterly, 24,* no. 4, 199–207.

Nahl-Jakobovits, D., & Jakobovits, L. A. (1990). Learning Principles and the Library Environment. *Research Strategies, 8,* no. 2, 74–81.

Nahl-Jakobovits, D., & Jakobovits, L. A. (1993). Bibliographic Instructional Design for Information Literacy: Integrating Affective and Cognitive Objectives. *Research Strategies, 11,* no. 2, 73–88.

Napier, T., Parrott, J., Presley, E., & Valley, L. (2018). A Collaborative, Trilateral Approach to Bridging the Information Literacy Gap in Student Writing. *College & Research Libraries, 79,* no. 1, 120–145.

National Center for Educational Statistics. (2018, April). *Children and Youth with Disabilities.* Available: https://nces.ed.gov/programs/coe/indicator _cgg.asp.

National Disability Authority. (2014). *What Is Universal Design?* Available: http:// universaldesign.ie/What-is-Universal-Design.

National Education Association & North Central Association of Colleges and Secondary Schools. (1920). *Standard Library Organization and Equipment for Secondary Schools of Different Sizes.* (C. C. Certain, Chair) Chicago: American Library Association.

Naylor, A. P., Emdad, K., & Ward, M. W. (1994). What Are the Reference Needs of Whole Language Teachers? and/or What Is a Whole Language Librarian? *Reference Librarian, 20,* no. 44, 29–40.

Neuman, D. (1994). Alternative Assessment, Promises and Pitfalls. In C. C. Kuhlthau, M. E. Goodin, & M. J. McNally (Eds.), *Assessment in the School Library Media Center* (pp. 67–75). Englewood, CO: Libraries Unlimited.

Neuman, D. (1995a, October). *High School Students' Use of Databases: Competing Conceptual Structures.* Paper presented at the annual meeting of the American Society for Information Science, Chicago.

Neuman, D. (1997). Learning and the Digital Library. *Library Trends, 45,* no. 4, 687–707.

Neuman, S. B., & Celano, D. (2001). Access to Print in Low-Income and Middle-Income Communities: An Ecological Study of Four Neighborhoods. *Reading Research Quarterly, 36,* no. 1, 8–26.

Newell, T. S. (2010). Examining Information Problem-Solving Instruction: Dynamic Relationship Patterns Mediated by Distinct Instructional Methodologies. *School Libraries Worldwide, 15,* no. 2, 49–76.

Nolan, J. P. (1989). *A Comparison of Two Methods of Instruction in Library Research Skills for Elementary School Students.* PhD diss., Temple University.

Norris, S. P. (1985). Synthesis of Research on Critical Thinking. *Educational Leadership, 2,* no. 8, 40–45.

Nowicki, S. (2003). Student vs. Search Engine: Undergraduates Rank Results for Relevance. *Libraries and the Academy, 3,* no. 3, 503–515.

Oberman, C. (1995). Avoiding the Cereal Syndrome; Or, Critical Thinking in the Electronic Environment. In Fifteenth Anniversary Task Force, Library Instruction Round Table, American Library Association (Comp.), *Information for a New Age: Redefining the Librarian* (pp. 107–119). Englewood, CO: Libraries Unlimited.

O'Leary, M. (2010). Educational Score Cards Give U.S. Bad Grades. *Information Today, 27,* 34–34, 40. Available: https://unk.idm.oclc.org/login?url=https://search.proquest.com/docview/214825036?accountid=8115.

Oliver, R., & Oliver, H. (1997). Using Context to Promote Learning from Information-Seeking Tasks. *Journal of the American Society for Information Science, 48,* no. 6, 519–526.

O'Neil, J. (1992). Putting Performance Assessment to the Test. *Educational Leadership, 49,* no. 8, 14–19.

Ostenson, J. (2014). Reconsidering the Checklist in Teaching Internet Source Evaluation. *Portal: Libraries & the Academy, 14,* no. 1, 33–50.

Owen, D., & Sarles, P. (2012). Exit Tickets: The Reflective Ticket to Understanding. *Library Media Connection, 31,* no. 3, 20–22.

Pane, D. M. (2009). Third Space: Blended Teaching and Learning. *Journal for the Research Center for Educational Technology, 5,* no. 1, 64–92.

Pappas, M. L., & Tepe, A. E. (1997). *Pathways to Knowledge: Follett's Information Skills Model* (3rd ed.). McHenry, IL: Follett Software.

Pappas, M. L., & Tepe, A. E. (2002). *Pathways to Knowledge® and Inquiry Learning.* Englewood, CO: Libraries Unlimited.

Pask, G. (1972). A Fresh Look at Cognition and the Individual. *International Journal of Man-Machine Studies, 4,* 211–216.

Pask, G. (1975). *Conversations, Cognition, and Learning.* Amsterdam: Elsevier.

Pask, G., & Scott, B. C. E. (1972). Learning Strategies and Individual Competence. *International Journal of Mathematics and Mathematical Sciences, 4,* 217–253.

Paterson, S. F., & Gamtso, C. W. (2011). Guiding Students from Consuming Information to Creating Knowledge. *Communications in Information Literacy, 5,* no. 2, 117–126.

Patrick, B. C., Skinner, E. A., & Connell, J. P. (1993). What Motivates Children's Behavior and Emotion? Joint Effects of Perceived Control and Autonomy in the Academic Domain. *Journal of Personality and Social Psychology, 65,* no. 4, 781–791.

Peck, K. L., & Dorricott, D. (1994). Why Use Technology? *Educational Leadership, 51,* no. 7, 11–14.

Perrault, A. M. (2011). Reaching all Learners: Understanding and Leveraging Points of Intersection for School Librarians and Special Education Teachers. *School Library Media Research, 14.* Available: http://www.ala.org/aasl/sites/ala.org.aasl/files/content/aaslpubsandjournals/slr/vol14/SLR_ReachingAllLearners_V14.pdf.

Pipher, M. (1994). *Reviving Ophelia: Saving the Selves of Adolescent Girls.* New York: Putnam.

Pitts, J. M. (1995). Mental Models of Information: The 1993–94 AASL/Highsmith Research Award Study. *School Library Media Quarterly, 23,* no. 3, 177–184.

Available: http://www.ala.org/ala/mgrps/divs/aasl/aaslpubsandjournals /slmrb/editorschoiceb/infopower/selctpittshtml.cfm (accessed February 24, 2020).

Power, B. (2012). Enriching Students' Intellectual Diet through Inquiry Based Learning. *Libri, 62,* 305–325.

Pringle, B. E., Lyons, J. E., & Booker, K. C. (2010). Perceptions of Teacher Expectations by African American High School Students. *Journal of Negro Education, 79,* no. 1, 33–40.

Public Library Association. (2013). *Digital Learn.* Available: https://www.digitallearn .org (accessed May 21, 2019).

Purcell, K., Rainie, L., Buchanan, J., Friedrich, L., Jacklin, A., Chen, C., & Zickuhr, K. (2012). How Teens Do Research in the Digital Work. *Pew Research Center: Internet & Technology.* Available: https://www.pewresearch.org /internet/2012/11/01/how-teens-do-research-in-the-digital-world.

Radford, M. L. (1996). Communication Theory Applied to the Reference Encounter: An Analysis of Critical Incidents. *Library Quarterly, 66,* no. 2, 123–137.

Radford, M. L. (1998). Approach or Avoidance? The Role of Nonverbal Communication in the Academic Library User's Decision to Initiate a Reference Encounter. *Library Trends, 46,* no. 4, 699–717.

Radford, M. L. (1999). The Reference Encounter: Interpersonal Communication in the Academic Library. *Publications in Librarianship,* no. 52. Chicago: American Library Association and Association of College and Research Libraries.

Radford, M. L. (2006). Encountering Virtual Users: A Qualitative Investigation of Interpersonal Communication in Chat Reference. *Journal of the American Society for Information Science and Technology, 57,* no. 8, 1046–1059.

Radford, M. L., & Connaway, L. S. (2007). "Screenagers" and Live Chat Reference: Living Up to the Promise. *Scan, 26,* no. 1, 31–39.

Radford, M. L., Radford, G. P., Connaway, L. S., & DeAngelis, J. A. (2011). On Virtual Face-Work: An Ethnography of Communication approach to a Live Chat Reference Interaction. *Library Quarterly, 81,* no. 4, 431–453.

Ray, J. T. (1994). Resource-Based Teaching: Media Specialists and Teachers as Partners in Curriculum Development and the Teaching of Library and Information Skills. *The Reference Librarian, 44,* 19–27.

Renninger, K. A., Hidi, S., & Krapp, A. (Eds.). (1992). *The Role of Interest in Learning and Development.* Hillsdale, NY: Lawrence Erlbaum.

Ritchhart, R. (2001). From IQ to IC: A Dispositional View of Intelligence. *Roeper Review, 23,* no. 3, 143–150.

Robbins, E., & Thompson, L. (1991). *A Study of the Indianapolis-Marion County Public Library's Summer Reading Program for Children.* East Lansing, MI: National Center for Research on Teacher Learning. (ERIC Document Reproduction Service No. ED355647)

Robins, J., & Antrim, P. (2012). School Librarians and Response to Intervention. *School Library Research, 15.* Available: http://www.ala.org/aasl/sites/ala.org .aasl/files/content/aaslpubsandjournals/slr/vol15/SLR_School_Librarians _and_Response_V15.pdf.

Rodney, M. J., Lance, K. C., & Hamilton-Pennell, C. (2002). *Make the Connection: Quality School Library Programs Impact Academic Achievement in Iowa.* A Research Project by Iowa Area Education Agencies. Bettendorf, IA: Mississippi Bend Area Education Agency.

Roper, T., & Rossi, M. (2018). ESSA Opens Windows of Opportunity for School Library Programs. *Texas Library Journal, 94,* no. 1, 8–9.

Rosenblatt, L. M. (1978). *The Reader, the Text, the Poem: The Transactional Theory of the Literary Work.* Carbondale, IL: Southern Illinois University Press.

Roth, G., Asor, A., Kanat-Maymon, Y., & Kaplan, H. (2006). Assessing the Experience of Autonomy in New Cultures and Contexts. *Motivation and Emotion 30,* no. 4, 365–376. Available: http://dx.doi.org/10.1007/s11031-006-9052-7.

Rothstein, S. (1955). *The Development of Reference Services through Academic Traditions, Public Library Practice, and Special Librarianship.* Chicago: Association of College and Research Libraries.

Rothstein, S. (1994). Reference Services. In W. A. Wiegand & D. G. Davis Jr. (Eds.), *Encyclopedia of Library History* (pp. 541–546). New York: Garland.

Rowlands, I., & Nicholas, D. (2008). Understanding Information Behaviour: How Do Students and Faculty Find Books? *Journal of Academic Librarianship, 34*(1), 3–15. Available: https://doi-org.unk.idm.oclc.org/10.1016/j.acalib.2007.11.005.

Rugg, M. D. (1997). *Cognitive Neuroscience.* East Sussex, UK: Psychology Press.

Ryan, R. M., & Deci, E. L. (2000). Self-Determination Theory and the Facilitation of Intrinsic Motivation, Social Development, and Well-Being. *American Psychologist, 55,* no. 1, 68–78.

Ryan, R. M., & Deci, E. L. (2017). *Self-determination Theory: Basic Psychological Needs in Motivation, Development, and Wellness.* New York: The Guilford Press.

Salmon, L. M. (1986). Instruction in the Use of a College Library. In L. L. Hardesty, J. P. Schmitt, & J. M. Tucker (Comps.), *User Instruction in Academic Libraries: A Century of Selected Readings* (pp. 86–101). Metuchen, NJ: Scarecrow Press.

Salvatore, C. L. (2000). *Community, Institutions, and Identity in the Chamorro Speech Community: An Ethnographic Study of How They Shape Information-Seeking Discourses in the Library.* PhD diss., University of Texas.

Sauer, J. A. (1995). Conversation 101: Process, Development, and Collaboration. In Fifteenth Anniversary Task Force, Library Instruction Round Table, American Library Association (Comp.), *Information for a New Age: Redefining the Librarian* (pp. 135–151). Englewood, CO: Libraries Unlimited.

Saunders, L., Severyn, J., & Caon, J. (2017). Don't They Teach That in High School? Examining the High School to College Information Literacy Gap. *Library and Information Science Research, 39,* no. 4, 276–283.

Saunders-Stewart, K., Gyles, P., Shore, B., & Bracewell, R. (2015). Student Outcomes in Inquiry: Students' Perspectives. *Learning Environments Research, 18,* no. 2, 289–311.

Savolainen, R. (2003). Book Review: Looking for Information: A Survey of Research in Information Seeking, Deeds, and Behavior. By D. O. Case. *Journal of the American Society for Information Science and Technology, 54,* no. 7, 695–697.

Schacter, J., Chung, K. W. K., & Dorr, A. (1998). Children's Internet Searching on Complex Problems: Performance and Process Analyses. *Journal of the American Society for Information Science, 44,* no. 9, 840–849.

Schenck, J., & Cruickshank, J. (2015). Evolving Kolb: Experiential Education in the Age of Neuroscience. *Journal of Experiential Education, 38,* no. 1, 73–95.

Schiefele, U., & Csikszentmihalyi, M. (1995). Motivation and Ability as Factors in Mathematics Experience and Achievement. *Journal of Research in Mathematics Education, 26,* no. 2, 163–181.

Schiller, A. (1986). Reference Service: Instruction or Information. In L. L. Hardesty, J. P. Schmitt, & J. M. Tucker (Comps.), *User Instruction in Academic Libraries: A Century of Selected Readings* (pp. 189–203). Metuchen, NJ: Scarecrow Press.

Schloman, B. F., & Gedeon, J. A. (2007). Creating TRAILS: Tool for Real-Time Assessment of Information Literacy Skills. *Knowledge Quest, 35,* no. 5, pp. 44–47.

Schloman, B. F., & Gedeon, J. A. (2010). *TRAILS—Tool for Real-Time Assessment of Information Literacy Skills.* Available: http://www.trails-9.org (accessed June 10, 2010).

Schmidt, R. (2008). Really Reading: What Does Accelerated Reader Teach Adults and Children? *Language Arts, 85,* no. 3, 202–211.

Schmidt, R. K., Kowalski, V., & Nevins, L. (2010). Guiding the Inquiry Using the Modified Scientific Literature Review. *School Libraries Worldwide, 16,* no. 1, 13–32.

Scholastic. (2016). *School Libraries Work! A Compendium of Research Supporting the Effectiveness of School Libraries.* Available: http://www.scholastic.com /SLW2016.

Schön, D. A. (1983). *The Reflective Practitioner: How Professionals Think in Action.* New York: Basic Books.

School Libraries Work! 2016 Edition. (2016). New York: Scholastic Publishing. Available: http://www.scholastic.com/slw2016 (accessed May 21, 2019).

Schulte, S. J. (2012). Embedded Academic Librarianship: A Review of the Literature. *Evidence Based Library and Information Practice, 7,* no. 4, 122–138.

Scott, M., & VanNoord, G. (1996). Conducting Original Research at the High School Level—The Student's Perspective. *The American Biology Teacher, 58,* no. 4, 217–219.

Secreast, D. (2013). Three Problems That Make Literacy Education So Difficult: Using Grown Up Digital to Discuss Students' Attitudes toward Reading and Writing. *Virginia English Journal, 63,* no. 2, 18–33.

Sein, M. K., & Bostrom, R. P. (1989). Individual Differences and Conceptual Models in Training Novice Users. *Human-Computer Interaction, 4,* no. 3, 197–229.

Sheingold, K. (1986). Keeping Children's Knowledge Alive through Inquiry. *School Library Media Quarterly, 15,* no. 1, 80–85.

Shenton, A. K., & Dixon, P. (2003). A Comparison of Youngster's Use of CD-ROM and the Internet as Information Resources. *Journal of the American Society for Information Science and Technology, 54,* no. 11, 1029–1049.

Shores, L. (1986). The Liberal Arts College: A Possibility in 1954? In L. L. Hardesty, J. P. Schmitt, & J. M. Tucker (Comps.), *User Instruction in Academic Libraries: A Century of Selected Readings* (pp. 121–129). Metuchen, NJ: Scarecrow Press.

Sillars, M. O. (1991). *Messages, Meanings, and Culture: Approaches to Communication Criticism.* New York: HarperCollins.

Silverstein, J. (2005). Just Curious: Children's Use of Digital Reference for Unimposed Queries and Its Importance in Informal Education. *Library Trends, 54,* no. 2, 228–244.

Simon, M., Graziano, M., & Lenhart, A. (2001). *The Internet and Education: Main Report.* Available: https://www.pewresearch.org/internet/2001/09/01/main -report-21.

Sirota, E., & Bailey, L. (2009). The Impact of Teachers' Expectations on Diverse Learners' Academic Outcomes. *Childhood Education, 85*(4), 253–256.

Slavin, R. V. (1990). *Cooperative Learning: Theory, Research, and Practice.* Needham, MA: Allyn & Bacon.

Small, R. V. (1998). Designing Motivation into Library and Information Skills Instruction. *School Library Media Quarterly, 1.* Available: http://www.ala.org /ala/mgrps/divs/aasl/aaslpubsandjournals/slmrb/slmrcontents/volume 11998slmqo/small.cfm (accessed May 28, 2010).

Small, R. V. (1999). An Exploration of Motivational Strategies Used by Library Media Specialists during Library and Information Skills Instruction. *School Library Media Research, 2,* 1–23. Available: http://www.ala.org/ala/aasl /aaslpubsandjournals/slmrb/slmrcontents/volume21999/vol2small.htm (accessed June 2, 2010).

Small, R. V., Arnone, M. P., Stripling, B. K., Berger, P. (2012). *Teaching for Inquiry: Engaging the Learner Within.* New York: Neal-Schuman.

Small, R. V., Shanahan, K. A., & Stasak, M. (2010). The Impact of New York's School Libraries on Student Achievement and Motivation: Phase III. *School Library Media Research, 13,* 1–27. Available: http://www.ala.org/ala/mgrps/divs /aasl/aaslpubsandjournals/slmrb/slmrcontents/volume13/small_phase3 .cfm (accessed September 11, 2010).

Small, R. V., & Snyder, J. (2009). The Impact of New York's School Libraries on Student Achievement and Motivation: Phase II—In-Depth Study. *School Library Media Research, 12,* 1–17. Available: http://www.nyla.org/content /user_4/Impact%20Phase%202.pdf (accessed June 2, 2010).

Small, R. V., Snyder, J., & Parker, K. (2009). The Impact of New York's School Libraries: Phase I. *School Library Media Research, 12.* Available: http://www.aasl .org/ala/mgrps/divs/aasl/aaslpubsandjournals/slmrb/slmrcontents /volume12/small.cfm (accessed June 2, 2010).

Small, R. V., & Stewart, J. (2013). Meeting Needs: Effective Programs for Students with Disabilities. *School Library Monthly, 29,* no. 8, 11–13.

Smalley, T. N. (2004). College Success: High School Librarians Make the Difference. *Journal of Academic Librarianship, 30,* no. 3, 193–198.

Smith, E. G. (2001). *Texas School Libraries: Standards, Resources, and Students' Performance.* Austin: Texas State Library and Archives Commission. Available: http://www.tsl.state.tx.us/ld/pubs/schlibsurvey/survey.pdf (accessed May 28, 2010).

Smith, J. B. (1987). Higher Order Thinking Skills and Nonprint Media. *School Library Media Quarterly, 16,* no. 1, 38–42.

Smith, J. K., Given, L. M., Julien, H., Oulette, D., & DeLong, K. (2013). Information Literacy Proficiency: Assessing the Gap in High School Students' Readiness for Undergraduate Academic Work. *Library and Information Science Research, 35,* no. 2, 88–96.

Solomon, P. (1993). Children's Information Retrieval Behavior: A Case Analysis of an OPAC. *Journal of the American Society for Information Science, 44,* no. 5, 245–264.

Solomon, P. (1994). Children, Technology, and Instruction: A Case Study of Elementary School Children Using an Online Public Access Catalog (OPAC). *School Library Media Quarterly, 23,* no. 1, 43–51.

Soulen, R. R. (2016). From Mary Virginia Gaver to the CLASS Research Summit. *Knowledge Quest, 45,* no. 2, 42–47.

Springer, S. P., & Deutsch, G. (1993). *Left Brain, Right Brain.* New York: Freeman.

State Library of Iowa. (2006). *Is a Combined School/Public Library Right for Your Community? A Guide for Decision-Makers.* Available: http://publications.iowa .gov/3759 (accessed May 22, 2019).

Stead, T. (2005). *Reality Checks: Teaching Reading Comprehension with Nonfiction K–5.* Portland, ME: Stenhouse Publishers.

Stefl-Mabry, J. (2018). Documenting Evidence of Practice: The Power of Formative Assessment. *Knowledge Quest, 46,* no. 3, 50–57.

Sternberg, R. J. (1985). *Beyond IQ: A Triarchic Theory of Intelligence.* Cambridge: Cambridge University Press.

Sternberg, R. J. (1992). *Sternberg Triarchic Abilities Test.* Unpublished test.

Sternberg, R. J. (1997). *Successful Intelligence.* New York: Plume.

Sternberg, R. J. (1999). The Theory of Successful Intelligence. *Review of General Psychology, 3,* 292–316.

Sternberg, R. J. (2002). Cultural Explorations of Human Intelligence around the World. *Online Readings in Psychology and Culture, 4,* no. 3. Available: https://doi.org/10.9707/2307-0919.1035.

Sternberg, R. J., Castejón, J. L., Prieto, M. D., Hautamäki, J., & Grigorenko, E. L. (2001). Confirmatory Factor Analysis of the Sternberg Triarchic Abilities Test in Three International Samples: An Empirical Test of the Triarchic Theory of Intelligence. *European Journal of Psychological Assessment, 17,* no. 1, 1–16.

Stoan, S. K. (1984). Research and Library Skills: An Analysis and Interpretation. *College and Research Libraries, 45,* no. 2, 99–108.

Stone, S. S. (2014). Breaking the Ice. *Reference & User Services Quarterly, 54,* no. 1, 44–49.

Stripling, B. (2010). Teaching Students to Think in the Digital Environment: Digital Literacy and Digital Inquiry. *School Library Monthly, 26,* no. 8, 16–19.

Stripling, B., & Harada, V. (2012). Designing Learning Experiences for Deeper Understanding. *School Library Monthly, 29,* no. 3, 5–12.

Stripling, B. K. (1994a). Assessment of Student Performance: The Fourth Step in the Instructional Design Process. In C. C. Kuhlthau, M. E. Goodin, & M. J. McNally (Eds.), *Assessment in the School Library Media Center* (pp. 77–97). Englewood, CO: Libraries Unlimited.

Stripling, B. K. (1994b). Practicing Authentic Assessment in the School Library. In C. C. Kuhlthau, M. E. Goodin, & M. J. McNally (Eds.), *Assessment in the School Library Media Center* (pp. 103–118). Englewood, CO: Libraries Unlimited.

Stripling, B. K. (1995). Learning-Centered Libraries: Implications from Research. *School Library Media Quarterly, 23,* no. 3, 163–170.

Stripling, B. K. (2006). Formative Assessment for Learning. AASL Fall Forum, Warwick, RI: October 13–15.

Stripling, B. K., & Pitts, J. M. (1988). *Brainstorms and Blueprints: Teaching Library Research as a Thinking Process.* Englewood, CO: Libraries Unlimited.

Subramaniam, M., Oxley, R., & Kodama, C. (2013). School Librarians as Ambassadors of Inclusive Information Access for Students with Disabilities. *School Library Research, 16.* Available: http://www.ala.org/aasl/sites/ala.org.aasl/files/content/aaslpubsandjournals/slr/vol16/SLR_SchoolLibrariansasAmbassadorsofInclusiveInformationAccess_V16.pdf.

Swain, D. E. (1996). Information Search Process Model: How Freshmen Begin Research. In *Proceedings of the ASIS Annual Meeting.* Available: http://www.asis.org/annual-96/ElectronicProceedings/swain.html (accessed May 28, 2010).

Tallman, J., & Henderson, L. (1999). *Constructing Mental Model Paradigms for Teaching Electronic Resources.* Chicago: American Association of School Librarians. Available: http://www.ala.org/ala/mgrps/divs/aasl/aaslpubsandjournals/slmrb/slmrcontents/volume21999/vol2tallman.cfm (accessed May 28, 2010).

Tapscott, D. (1998). *Growing Up Digital: The Rise of the Net Generation.* New York: McGraw-Hill.

Tapscott, D. (2009). *Grown Up Digital: How the Net Generation Is Changing Your World.* New York: McGraw-Hill.

Taylor, R. S. (1968). Question-Negotiation and Information Seeking in Libraries. *College and Research Libraries, 29,* no. 3, 178–194.

Teele, S. (1996). Redesigning the Educational System to Enable All Students to Succeed. *NASSP Bulletin, 80,* no. 583, 65–75.

Tenenbaum, H. R., & Ruck, M. D. (2007). Are Teachers' Expectations Different for Racial Minority Than for European American Students? A Meta-Analysis. *Journal of Educational Psychology, 99,* no. 2, 253–273.

Tewell, E., Mullins, K., Tomlin, N., & Dent, V. (2017). Learning about Student Research Practices through an Ethnographic Investigation: Insights into Contact with Librarians and Use of Library Space. *Evidence Based Library & Information Practice, 12,* no. 4, 78–101.

Thomas, J. W. (1993). Promoting Independent Learning in the Middle Grades: The Role of Instructional Support Practices. *The Elementary School Journal, 93,* no. 5, 575–591.

Thomas, N. P. (1996). *Reading Libraries: An Interpretive Study of Discursive Practices in Library Architecture and the Interactional Construction of Personal Identity.* PhD diss., Rutgers, the State University of New Jersey.

Thomas, N. P. (2000a). A Multiplicity of (Research) Models: Alternative Strategies for Diverse Learners. *School Library Media Activities Monthly, 17,* no. 1, 25.

Thomas, N. P. (2000b). Teaching "Kids" Not Content: Recreating the School Library Media Center as a Caring Context for Student Learning. *School Library Media Activities Monthly, 1,* no. 2, 23.

Thomas, N. P. (2002). Design Matters: Relational Projections in Library Environments. In H. B. Mokros (Ed.), *Identity Matters: Communication-Based Explorations and Explanations* (pp. 77–108). Creskill, NJ: Hampton Press.

Thomas, N. P., Crow, S. R., & Franklin, L. L. (2011). *Information Literacy and Information Skills Instruction: Applying Research to Practice in the 21st Century School Library* (3rd ed.). Santa Barbara, CA: Libraries Unlimited.

Thomas, N. P., Vroegindewey, D., & Wellins, C. (1997, April 4). *4MATing the Big Six©: Tailoring Research Assignments to Student Learning Styles.* Paper presented at the annual conference of the American Association of School Librarians, Portland, OR.

Thorne, L. M. (1967). *The Influence of the Knapp School Libraries Project on the Reading Comprehension and the Knowledge of Library Skills of the Pupils at the Farrar Junior High School, Provo, Utah.* PhD diss., Brigham Young University.

Tilke, A. (2011). International Baccalaureate Diploma Programme: What It Means to a School Library and Librarian. *School Library Monthly, 27,* no. 5, 8–10.

Tobisch, A., & Dresel, M. (2017). Negatively or Positively Biased? Dependencies of Teachers' Judgments and Expectations Based on Students' Ethnic and Social Backgrounds. *Social Psychology of Education, 20,* no. 4, 731–752.

Todd, R. J. (1995). Integrated Information Skills Instruction: Does It Make a Difference? *School Library Media Quarterly, 23,* no. 2, 133–139.

Todd, R. J. (1998). WWW, Critical Literacies and Learning Outcomes. *Teacher Librarian, 26,* no. 2, 16–21.

Todd, R. J. (2002). Press release. Available: http://www.oelma.org/OhioResearch Study.htm (accessed May 29, 2010).

Todd, R. J. (2008a). The Evidence-Based Manifesto for School Librarians. *School Library Journal, 4,* no. 1. Available: http://www.schoollibraryjournal.com /article/CA6545434.html (accessed November 3, 2010).

Todd, R. J. (2008b). Youth and Their Virtual Networked Worlds: Research Findings and Implications for School Libraries. *School Libraries Worldwide, 14,* no. 2, 19–34.

Todd, R. J. (2009). School Librarianship and Evidence Based Practice: Progress, Perspectives, and Challenges. *Evidence Based Library and Information Practice, 4,* no. 2, 78–96.

Todd, R. J., & Dadlani, P. (2013). Collaborative Inquiry in Digital Information Environments: Cognitive, Personal and Interpersonal Dynamics. *Proceedings of the 42nd International Conference Incorporating the 17th International Forum on Research in School Librarianship.* Sanur, Bail, Indonesia, August 26–30, 2013.

Todd, R. J., & Kuhlthau, C. C. (2003). *Student Learning through Ohio School Libraries: Background, Methodology, and Report of Findings.* Columbus: Ohio Educational Library Media Association.

Todd, R. J., Lamb, E., & McNicholas, C. (1993). Information Skills and Learning: Some Research Findings. *Access, 7,* no. 1, 14–16.

Todorinova, L. (2015). Wikipedia and Undergraduate Research Trajectories. *New Library World, 116,* no. 3, 201–212.

Tuck, K., & Holmes, D. (2016). *Library/Media Centers in U.S. Public Schools: Growth, Staffing, and Resources; Executive Summary.* Washington, DC: National Education Association.

Tucker, J. M. (1994). Library Instruction. In W. A. Wiegand & D. G. Davis Jr. (Eds.), *Encyclopedia of Library History* (pp. 364–366). New York: Garland.

Tuckett, H. W., & Stoffle, C. J. (1984). Learning Theory and the Self-Reliant Library User. *RQ, 24,* no. 1, 58–66.

Tuominen, K. (1997). User-Centered Discourse: An Analysis of the Subject Positions of the User and the Librarian. *Library Quarterly, 67,* no. 4, 352–371.

Turner, P. M. (1990). Research Reviews from the Treasure Mountain Research Retreat. In J. B. Smith (Ed.), *School Library Media Annual* (Vol. 8, pp. 139–153). Englewood, CO: Libraries Unlimited.

Turovsky, B. (2016). *Found in Translation: More Accurate, Fluent Sentences in Google Translate.* Available: https://www.blog.google/products/translate/found-translation-more-accurate-fluent-sentences-google-translate.

Twist, K. L. (2004). *Disparities along the Information Age Career Path.* Digital Divide Network. http://www.digitaldividenetwork.org.

Tyler, K. M., & Boelter, C. M. (2008). Linking Black Middle School Students' Perceptions of Teachers' Expectations to Academic Engagement and Efficacy. *The Negro Educational Review, 59,* nos. 1–2, 27–44.

Valencia, M. (2019). How to Safeguard Children against Cyberbullying. *The New York Times,* September 5, 2019. Available: https://www.nytimes.com/2019/09/05/well/family/how-to-safeguard-children-against-cyberbullying.html.

Valencia, S. W. (1991). Portfolio Assessment for Young Readers. *The Reading Teacher, 44,* no. 9, 680–682.

van Deusen, J., & Tallman, J. (1994). The Impact of Scheduling on Curriculum Consultation and Information Skills Instruction. *School Library Media Quarterly, 23,* no. 1, 17–25.

Van Merriënboer, J. J., & Kirschner, P. A. (2012). *Ten Steps to Complex Learning: A Systematic Approach to Four-Component Instructional Design.* New York: Routledge.

Vandergrift, K. E., & Hannigan, J. A. (1986). Elementary School Library Media Centers as Essential Components in the Schooling Process. *School Library Media Quarterly, 14,* no. 2, 171–173.

Vansteenkiste, M., Zhou, M., Lens, W., & Soenens, B. (2005). Experiences of Autonomy and Control among Chinese Learners: Vitalizing or Immobilizing? *Journal of Educational Psychology, 97,* no. 3, 468–483. Available: http://dx.doi.org/10.1037/0022-0663.97.3.468.

Vercelletto, C. (2019). The A to Z of Gen Z. *Library Journal, 144,* no. 7, 26–28.

Visser, B. A., Ashton, M. C., & Vernon, P. A. (2006). G and the Measurement of Multiple Intelligences: A Response to Gardner. *Intelligence, 34,* no. 5, 507–510.

Von Glasersfeld, E. (1995). *Radical Constructivism: A Way of Knowing and Learning*. London: Falmer.

Vroom, V. H. (1964). *Work and Motivation*. New York: Wiley.

Vygotsky, L. (1978). *Mind in Society: The Development of Higher Psychological Processes*. Cambridge, MA: Harvard University Press.

Walhout, J., Oomen, P., Jarodzka, H., & Brand-Gruwel, S. (2017). Effects of Task Complexity on Online Search Behavior of Adolescents. *Journal of the Association for Information Science & Technology, 68,* no. 6, 1449–1461.

Walker, K., & Pearce, M. (2014). Student Engagement in One-Shot Library Instruction. *The Journal of Academic Librarianship, 40,* nos. 3–4, 281–290.

Walter, V. A. (1994). The Information Needs of Children. In I. P. Godden (Ed.), *Advances in Librarianship* (pp. 111–129). San Diego: Academic Press.

Walter, V. A., Borgman, C. L., & Hirsh, S. G. (1996). The Science Library Catalog: A Springboard for Information Literacy. *School Library Media Quarterly, 24,* no. 2, 105–110.

Walter, V. A., & Mediavilla, C. (2005). Teens Are from Neptune, Librarians Are from Pluto: An Analysis of Online Reference Transactions. *Library Trends, 54,* no. 2, 209–227.

Waterhouse, L. (2006). Multiple Intelligences, the Mozart Effect, and Emotional Intelligence: A Critical Review. *Educational Psychologist, 41,* no. 4, 207–225.

Watson, C. (2014). An Exploratory Study of Secondary Students' Judgments of the Relevance and Reliability of Information. *Journal of the Association for Information Science & Technology, 65,* no. 7, 1385–1408.

Watson, J. S. (1998). "If You Don't Have It, You Can't Find It": A Close Look at Students' Perceptions of Using Technology. *Journal of the American Society for Information Science, 49,* no. 11, 1024–1036.

Watson, J. S. (2003). Examining Perceptions of the Science Fair Project: Content or Process? *School Library Media Research, 6.* Available: http://www.ala.org/ala/mgrps/divs/aasl/aaslpubsandjournals/slmrb/slmrcontents/volume62003/sciencefair.cfm (accessed September 11, 2010).

Watzlawick, P., Beavin, J. H., & Jackson, D. D. (1967). *Pragmatics of Human Communication: A Study of Patterns, Pathologies, and Paradoxes*. New York: Norton.

Weiner, B. (1992). *Human Motivation: Metaphors, Theories, and Research*. Newbury Park, CA: Sage.

Wells, J., & Lewis, L. (2006). *Internet Access in U.S. Public Schools and Classrooms: 1994–2005* (NCES 2007–020). U.S. Department of Education. Washington, DC: National Center for Educational Statistics.

Wert, A., & Pell, R. E. (1965). An Experiment in Flexible Scheduling. *School Libraries, 14,* 41–43.

Wesley, T. (1991). Teaching Library Research: Are We Preparing Students for Effective Information Use? *Emergency Librarian, 18,* no. 3, 23–30.

Whelan, D. L. (2004). 13,000 Kids Can't Be Wrong: A New Ohio Study Shows How School Librarians Help Students Learn. *School Library Journal, 50,* no. 2, 46–50.

White, R. W. (1959). Motivation Reconsidered: The Concept of Competence. *Psychological Review, 6,* no. 5, 297–323.

Wiggins, G., & McTighe, J. (1998). *Understanding by Design*. Arlington, VA: Association for Supervision and Curriculum Development.

Wiggins, G., & McTighe, J. (2005). *Understanding by Design* (Expanded 2nd ed.). Arlington, VA: Association for Supervision and Curriculum Development.

Wilhelm, T., Carmen, D., & Reynolds, M. (2002). *Annie E. Casey Foundation and Benton Foundation Connecting Kids and Technology: Challenges and*

Opportunities. Baltimore: Kids Count Snapshot. Available: http://www.eric
.ed.gov/ERICDocs/data/ericdocs2sql/content_storage_01/0000019b/80
/1a/42/a5.pdf (accessed May 30, 2010).

Willoughby, T., Anderson, S. A., Wood, E., Mueller, J., & Ross, C. (2009). Fast
Searching for Information on the Internet to Use in a Learning Context: The
Impact of Domain Knowledge. *Computers & Education, 52,* no. 3, 640–648.

Willson, E. J. (1965). *Evaluating Urban Centralized Elementary School Libraries*. PhD
diss., Wayne State University.

Wilson, L. R. (1933). The Development of Research in Relation to Library Schools.
Library Journal, 58, no. 22, 817–821.

Winograd, P., & Gaskins, R. W. (1992). Metacognition: Matters of the Mind, Matters
of the Heart. In A. L. Costa, J. A. Bellanca, & R. Fogarty (Eds.), *If Minds Matter:
A Foreword to the Future* (Vol. 1, pp. 225–238). Palatine, IL: IRI/Skylight
Publishing.

Winsor, J. (1986). The College Library. In L. L. Hardesty, J. P. Schmitt, & J. M.
Tucker (Comps.), *User Instruction in Academic Libraries: A Century of Selected
Readings* (pp. 5–16). Metuchen, NJ: Scarecrow Press.

Wittebols, J. H. (2016). Empowering Students to Make Senses of an Information-
Saturated World: The Evolution of Information Searching and Analysis. *Communications in Information Literacy, 10,* no. 1, 1–13. Available: doi:http://dx
.doi.org/10.15760/comminfolit.2016.10.1.18.

Woolls, B. (2008). *The School Library Media Manager* (4th ed.). Westport, CT: Libraries Unlimited.

Woronov, T. (1994). Machine Dreams: Six Myths (and Five Promising Truths) about
the Uses of Educational Technology. *Harvard Education Letter, 10,* no. 5, 1–3.

W3Techs. (2019). *Usage of Content Languages for Websites*. Available: https://
w3techs.com/technologies/overview/content_language/all.

Wyer, J. (1930). *Reference Work: A Textbook for Students of Library Work and Libraries*. Chicago: American Library Association.

Yang, S., & Dalal, H. A. (2015). Delivering Virtual Reference Services on the Web:
An Investigation into the Current Practice by Academic Libraries. *Journal of
Academic Librarianship, 41,* no. 1, 68–86.

Yarling, J. R. (1968). *Children's Understandings and Use of Selected Library-Related
Skills in Two Elementary Schools, One with and One without a Centralized
Library*. PhD diss., Ball State University.

Zemel, A. (2017). Texts as Actions: Requests in Online Chats between Reference
Librarians and Library Patrons. *Journal of the Association for Information Science and Technology, 68,* no. 7, 1687–1697.

Zurkowski, P. (1974). *The Information Service Environment Relationships and Priorities*. Related Paper No. 5. Available: https://eric.ed.gov/?id=ED100391.

Index

Note: Page numbers followed by *t* indicate tables and *f* indicate figures.

About the Authors

NANCY PICKERING THOMAS received her PhD in communication, information and library studies from Rutgers, the State University of New Jersey and is professor emeritus in the School of Library and Information Management at Emporia State University. Thomas has taught graduate courses in research foundations, theoretical foundations of library service, children's literature and programming, managing the school library, and services for special populations. In addition to a number of scholarly articles and book chapters, she is the author of *Information Literacy and Information Skills Instruction: Applying Research to Practice in the School Library Media Center* (1999), a second edition published in 2004, and served as first author for *Information Literacy and Information Skills Instruction: Applying Research to Practice in the 21st Century School Library* published in 2011. Since retiring in 2009, Dr. Thomas has volunteered as editor-in-chief of the Estes Park Museum Friends & Foundation, Inc. Press in Estes Park, Colorado.

SHERRY R. CROW received her PhD in library and information science from Emporia State University. She is currently professor and administrator of the school library science program at the University of Nebraska Kearney. Dr. Crow, author of *Information Literacy: A Guide for the Library Media Specialist* (2005), was named Colorado Librarian of the Year in 2004, and was awarded UNK's Outstanding Scholar of the College of Education in 2010, Outstanding Teacher of the College of Education in 2011, was a featured researcher in *New Frontiers Magazine* in 2014, and received the Pratt-Heins Award for Excellence in Teaching in 2015. In 2017 she received the Nebraska School Librarians Association's Meritorious Service Award and the Nebraska Library Association's Mad Hatter Award. Her research interest is in the area of children's intrinsic motivation for information seeking.

JUDY A. HENNING received her EdD in Educational Leadership with an emphasis in effective schools from Grand Canyon University, Phoenix, Arizona. Her undergraduate and master's degrees were from the University of Nebraska Kearney, where she is currently assistant professor in the school library science graduate program. She has over 35 years of teaching experience as a language arts educator and school librarian. Dr. Henning has been president of the Nebraska Educational Media Association and received the association's President's Award in 2010. During her NEMA presidency, she organized the efforts for state school library leaders to update and publish the seventh edition to the *Guide for Developing and Evaluating School Library Programs* (2010). Dr. Henning also served as the American Association of School Librarians Learning for Life state liaison. She has received the Kearney Public Schools Outstanding Educator Award (1998) and also the Nebraska Library Association's Mad Hatter Award for library service to youth in 2010. Dr. Henning's research interest is project-based learning.

JEAN DONHAM received her PhD in educational administration from the University of Iowa and her MLS from the University of Maryland. She is a retired professor of school library studies, a position she held at the University of Northern Iowa. Previously, she directed the library at Cornell College, a selective liberal arts college. Earlier, she was associate professor in library and information science at the University of Iowa and coordinated the library and technology program for Iowa City Community Schools for 13 years. She has published widely on information literacy and library leadership at both the K–12 and college levels.